RESOLVING COMMUNITY CONFLICTS AND PROBLEMS

RESOLVING COMMUNITY CONFLICTS AND PROBLEMS

PUBLIC DELIBERATION AND SUSTAINED DIALOGUE

Edited by Roger A. Lohmann and Jon Van Til

COLUMBIA UNIVERSITY PRESS   NEW YORK

COLUMBIA UNIVERSITY PRESS
Publishers Since 1893
New York Chichester, West Sussex

Chapter 7, "Diving In: A Handbook for Improving Race Relations on College Campuses Through the Process of Sustained Dialogue," by Teddy Nemeroff and David Tukey, is reproduced here by permission of the International Institute for Sustained Dialogue, Washington, D.C.

Library of Congress Cataloging-in-Publication Data

   Resolving community conflicts and problems : public deliberation and sustained dialogue / edited by Roger A. Lohmann and Jon Van Til.
      p. cm.
   Includes bibliographical references and index.
      ISBN 978-0-231-15168-9 (cloth : alk. paper) — ISBN 978-0-231-52528-2 (e-book)
   1. Conflict management.   2. Forums (Discussion and debate)   3. Intergroup relations.
4. Interpersonal communication.   5. Civil society.   I. Lohmann, Roger A., 1942–
II. Van Til, Jon.
   HM1126.R46 2011
   303.6'9—dc22

                                                                                    2011005378

Columbia University Press books are printed on permanent and durable acid-free paper.
This book is printed on paper with recycled content.
Printed in the United States of America

c 10 9 8 7 6 5 4 3 2 1

References to Internet Web sites (URLs) were accurate at the time of writing. Neither the author nor Columbia University Press is responsible for URLs that may have expired or changed since the manuscript was prepared.

CONTENTS

PREFACE

AT LEAST SINCE THE "war on poverty" in the 1960s, with its famous strategy of "maximum feasible participation of the poor," community organizers and social administrators in social work and colleagues in related disciplines have been concerned with questions of the place of citizen involvement in postindustrial democracy. The dawn of the Obama administration in January, 2009 had every appearance of a major departure from the public practices of recent decades in a number of different respects. Obama's 2008 campaign had appeared to suggest the possible beginning of a dramatic and entirely new approach to national government in the United States, with greater involvement from individual citizens and the general public in the business of government. Burdened in the short run by economic and international concerns and the polarities that the health care debate exposed, participatory politics has taken something of a backseat, and advanced forms of "e-government" still appear a ways off. But there is little doubt that there was greater emphasis on social networking and grassroots involvement in the Obama presidential campaign than at any time in the recent past. It also appears that the new administration is seeking to take fuller advantage of approaches to citizen participation and involvement that have developed as a community-level field of practice and have been discussed by small groups of community practitioners and political theorists for the past four decades.

By necessity, such activities have largely been conducted outside of mainstream public talk about public affairs for at least two reasons: Most important, within the media-generated public sphere, public talk has been increasingly held captive by the banal, barren, cliché-ridden pronouncements of political factions largely bereft of ideas and, it appears at times, thought itself. Meanwhile, within the academy, assorted older models of representative democracy have largely held sway, with few notable exceptions, and the role of citizen has been seen as limited largely to casting periodic votes for elected officials, who are still viewed as the main actors in public life. Theoretically, the debate between representative and participatory forms of democracy is a legitimate and ongoing one in political philosophy, with a rich literature by contributors such as John Rawls, Jürgen Habermas, Michael Sandel, Benjamin Barber, Charles Taylor, Robert Nozick, and many others. While much of this discussion has been highly theoretical and abstruse, it has also served to legitimize a climate for practical experimentation and involvement in many communities.

Over against a national climate of deliberately cultivated divisiveness, many independent, community-level efforts have sought to promote serious citizen-to-citizen conversations across racial, gender, ethnic, religious, and other political frontiers. International efforts have included those of CIVICUS, one of whose board members is a contributor to this volume. These diverse efforts have produced a bewildering variety of models and approaches, as well as some efforts at coalition building among the advocates and convenors of public talk, such as members of the National Coalition for Deliberation and Dialogue. Much of this practical effort has involved more advocacy than critical reflection within the academy or in the community. A body of critical reflection on the multitude of practice models, to stand alongside the growing body of theoretical reflection, is long overdue. Two models with wide applicability to social work and community practice—public deliberation and sustained dialogue—are the central focus of this volume.

Within a social work context, public deliberation and sustained dialogue can be juxtaposed against all forms of therapy and counseling as different but allied forms of strategic talk. This obtains in more than a shared sense of presumed wellness, for the point appears to hold for approaches based on the strengths perspective as well. The adjectives in the titles of the two approaches are where the main difference is to be found: "Public" generally refers to issues of public or general interest as opposed to the private, intimate, personal, and confidential interests of therapy and counseling. Likewise, "sustained" refers to ongoing as opposed to short-term, one-time or quick-fix conversations, whether private or public. Deliberation and dialogue may be differentiated from therapy and counseling further in terms of the assumed equality of discussion leaders and participants as opposed to the implicit inequalities—of knowledge, skill, and values—implied by professional models of therapist and client. Deliberation among fellow citizens over social problems and issues can be clearly and carefully differentiated from conversations between therapist and client on this basis. Such assumptions have long set community organizers, social administrators, and social policy analysts apart from "clinical-" and "direct-" practice perspectives in social work. Even so, as the entry on family therapy in this volume shows, such divisions are by no means absolute or unbridgeable.

Another underlying assumption of nearly all approaches to deliberation and dialogue is that a candid, open, and frank exchange of views is preferable to most alternative approaches to dealing with conflict. Illustrative of this phenomenon was a public deliberation held on a university campus recently: Upon reading an announcement of an upcoming deliberation called "Alternatives to War," a loose network of roughly two dozen Vietnam-era veterans attended the event as a group. Apparently assuming from the title that the event was to promote a distinct ideological antiwar or pacifist focus, they came ready for a fight (in a few cases, literally). Instead, under the skilled leadership of the moderator (who is one of the contributors to this volume) they were invited to participate in discussions of all sides of the question and did so alongside Marxists, pacifists, and all shades of opponents, skeptics, and supporters of the Iraq War. Every experienced moderator has similar stories to relate, most often with similar results: Discussions on controversial issues have been held in many settings between faculty and students; between black and white students; among Muslim, Christian, Hindu, Buddhist, and other students; between Jewish and Islamic congregations; and across many other lines of disagreement and difference. Sometimes those dialogues result in actual changes in behavior or circumstances; sometimes they are just prelude to more talk. In either case, the result is preferable to most alternatives.

For a brief time in 2008, numerous political commentators suggested that the "wedge politics" of division, discontent, fear, and suspicion of others that originated four decades ago had been defeated. The presidential campaign of 2008 appeared to many to reveal huge untapped reserves of pent-up citizenship. (For details on the strategic nature of wedge politics, see Perlstein 2008.) It was anticipated that in the wake of the 2008 election, many new approaches to democratic governance might enter mainstream American political society. Only gradually did it become clear, however, that defeat in a single campaign does not equal disappearance. Underlying tensions and differences, aggravated by the wedge politics of recent decades, remain, and they emerged again in the Tea Party movement of 2009. The great insight upon which almost all approaches to citizen involvement are based is that of civil comity—the belief that, all other things being equal, it is better for those who differ to honestly and openly confront, discuss, explore, and examine their differences than to simply attempt to overwhelm, defeat, or destroy one another.

Many people in the hyperpartisan environment in the United States today have made very public note of their contempt for civil comity and bipartisan discourse of any type in both domestic and international arenas. This was particularly evident in the congressional health care debate in 2009. Previously, the obvious public rejection of wedge politics meant that both presidential candidates in 2008 ran on platforms promising greater "bipartisanship," and it is likely that the immediate future will also see dramatically increased interest in methods of deliberation and dialogue. The obvious failure of bipartisanship in Washington since the 2008 election, however, raises an important question: If community leadership for honest, open discussion of difference cannot be expected from national political leaders and the media, where is it to come from? Higher education, even in the most engaged universities, is still notably ill prepared in this particular area, but disciplines like social work could become more and better prepared relatively quickly.

ORPHAN TOPICS

Public deliberation and sustained dialogue, along with most other forms of deliberation and dialogue, are among a shrinking group of serious intellectual topics and issues that have yet to find secure academic homes. At the higher reaches of theory, public talk falls safely within the domain of political philosophy, which is itself something of a vagabond discipline, long forced to roam between political science and philosophy departments, not entirely comfortable in either. Methodologically, a home might be found in interdisciplinary conflict-resolution programs, which are scattered widely throughout modern universities in assorted social science, management, labor relations, and communications departments and a bewildering additional variety of other locales (including English departments, communication studies, and elsewhere). Social work, with its policy and community-problem-solving foci, is one of several places in the modern university where a logical home for deliberation and dialogue efforts might be found.

At the same time, from predominantly grassroots origins a large and rapidly growing international practice community in peace and reconciliation centers, mediation and conflict-resolution programs, and an astounding array of community programs devoted to purposive communications to enhance understanding has emerged. Many of these efforts across perceived ethnic, religious, racial, gender, generational, identity, and other boundaries have arisen as part of the general expansion of national nonprofit, nongovernmental, or third sectors.

One of the longer-term issues, only touched on briefly in this volume, will be to separate out the genuinely unique and distinctive practice wisdom from the bewildering variety of unique labels and entrepreneurial claims of proponents of various approaches. First, however, some preliminary conceptions and models of practice that transcend the interests of particular organizations and approaches are needed. Indeed, the continuing need for such a critical perspective on practice is one of the strongest arguments for the approaches laid out in this volume.

Social work is well suited to providing a base for institution-building and practice-oriented academic programs in this area. For social work, such programs fit with the historic origins of the field in the settlement house movement, with its Americanization, citizenship, and multiethnic dialogues and deliberations, as well as with more recent efforts. Thus, it is appropriate that a broad interdisciplinary attempt to frame the practice of public deliberation and sustained dialogue like the present volume be included as part of the Columbia University Press social work program.

THE PRESENT VOLUME

The work presented here was organized and developed under the auspices of the Nova Institute within the Division of Social Work at West Virginia University. It has been produced by faculty within the School of Applied Social Sciences and other units of West Virginia University, along with invited faculty and alumni affiliated with other institutions, including Princeton University, the University of Virginia, Rutgers University, Portland State University, University of Nevada–Reno, Bucknell University, and Ulster University in Northern Ireland, as well as practitioners in Vermont, New Zealand, and South Africa.

The principal focus in the present work is on two general approaches to deliberation and dialogue, chosen from among many possibilities: Public deliberation, the encouragement of open, public discussion by groups and assemblies of citizens, is one of the oldest and most widespread practices in this area. Sustained dialogue, extensive, binary focused discussions between two parties with a history of animosity, misunderstanding, or conflict, is one of the newest.

ACKNOWLEDGMENTS

As with any project of this sort, there are a large number of people to thank for this effort. We would also like to acknowledge the ex-officio contributions of former West Virginia University provost Jerry Lang, former West Virginia University president David Hardesty, former dean of the Eberly College of Arts and Sciences (and now president of the University of Idaho) Duane Nellis, and interim dean of the Eberly College of Arts and Sciences Rudy Almasy for their various expressions of support for this effort.

Others who made important contributions to this project include Professor Ginny Majewski, former chair of the Division of Social Work, without whose support the deliberation and dialogue efforts of the Nova Institute would not have been possible, and Chris Plein, assistant dean of the Eberly College and chair of the School of Applied Social Sciences, whose own interest in community-design teams is an important related form of deliberation and dialogue.

Most of all, we would like to acknowledge the vital role of Dolly Ford in the initiation and early development of this project. As a graduate assistant and then as a key staff member of the evolving Nova Institute deliberation and dialogue effort, Dolly was instrumental in the success of this effort. Early on, she was actually a coeditor on this book, until the demands of her own social work career took her in other directions.

Also making important contributions were Noelle Lee, who organized, emceed, and wrote the grant for one of our first community public deliberations; Kelly Reimenschneider, who did a field placement with the Nova Institute; Jacki Englehardt, coordinator of professional continuing education at the Division of Social Work; and numerous staff members at the International Institute for Sustained Dialogue, who included us in their programs over several years.

RESOLVING COMMUNITY CONFLICTS AND PROBLEMS

Introduction

SUSTAINED DIALOGUE AND PUBLIC DELIBERATION: THE ROLE OF PUBLIC CONVERSATION IN A GROWING CIVIL SOCIETY AND COMMONS

Roger A. Lohmann, Jon Van Til, and Dolly Ford

OVER THE PAST THREE DECADES, at least two important modes of public conversation have been developed with the aim of strengthening civil society and the fabric of the social commons. Serving as assistant secretary of state in the 1970s, Harold Saunders was involved in crafting the process of "shuttle diplomacy" with Secretary of State Henry Kissinger, bringing into eventual dialogue the disparate leaders of Israel and Egypt. Saunders's work continued through the 1980s and 1990s with the Dartmouth Seminar, developing public conversation between Soviet and American citizen leaders, and has since spread to many other nations under the rubric of "sustained dialogue." During the same period, the Kettering Foundation in Dayton, Ohio, developed a variety of programs aimed at building public deliberation in communities in America and abroad. These two threads converged when Saunders went to work for Kettering and diverged again with the International Institute for Sustained Dialogue.

With the launch of IISD in Washington, D.C., Saunders and his collaborators (many of whom were students at or recent graduates from Princeton University and the University of Virginia) sought to start a social movement, particularly in dealing with race relations on university campuses. The organization's interest has since expanded into Anglo-Maori relations in New Zealand, Catholic and Protestant community organizations in Northern Ireland, and identity-bridging efforts in South Africa and India. Public deliberation remains a priority at Kettering, which has become something of a national lending library for ideas on the subject while remaining largely aloof from the academy, with certain highly selective exceptions.

Despite their obvious importance, models of sustained dialogue and public deliberation have registered only minimal recognition among third-sector researchers and scholars and in social work. This research community has generally been more focused upon large-scale structural and definitional matters than the process and face-to-face concerns addressed in sustained dialogue and public deliberation. We propose to begin to examine aspects of this work through the approaches of social work and social science research.

This volume assembles a diverse collection of authors who critically assess the emerging literature on sustained dialogue, which includes a book-length study of the Dartmouth Conference by James Voorhees (2002), a number of pamphlets on public deliberation (for example, "Creating Citizens Through Public Deliberation," Kettering Foundation, 1997), several papers and speeches by Saunders (especially Saunders 2005), and a handbook for improving race relations on colleges campuses through the process of sustained dialogue ("Diving In," by Teddy Nemeroff and David Tukey [2001], included in this volume).

Several of the key terms around which this project is organized require some brief clarification. First and foremost are "public deliberation," "sustained dialogue," and the accompanying ideas of pracademic and the engaged campus. Before proceeding further, let us look at each of these terms briefly and then concentrate on their implications

PUBLIC DELIBERATION

In conventional use, the term "deliberation" can be contrasted with the idea of dialogue largely in terms of its emphasis on certain key mental tasks, including consideration and cognition, with perhaps an emphasis on the plural nature of such considerations. In conventional use, in legal trials, for example, the jury deliberates to reach a verdict; the judge decides. Both, of course, are faced with similar rational and cognitive challenges, albeit at different levels of knowledge, training, and experience with the process of reaching legal decisions. And, of course, the plurality of the jury, like any other group, implies that any thinking that goes on must be communicated interpersonally in some manner, most typically in face-to-face encounters. Those elements combining rational thought and interpersonal communication in a group context define a beginning-level understanding of deliberation. Adding the term "public" raises several additional dimensions. It typically suggests that the thinking and communicating going on in a group may be in a setting open to all or on an issue of general interest or universal concern or a matter of governmental policy or action. All of the authors in this volume begin with this common, elementary conception of public deliberation and then take it in a variety of directions.

SUSTAINED DIALOGUE

When paired with deliberation, the idea of dialogue suggests both similarities and important differences. The usual meanings of "dialogue" are similarly focused on interpersonal communication in small group settings. The origins of the term alert us to the importance of language or speech and also the additional element of duality. The connotations of deliberate consideration and rationality of deliberation may or may not be implied in various references to dialogue. In any event, dialogue is not merely conversation in group settings. There is also the added element of stratification or division into two or more subgroups or "sides" and typically an additional note of conflict as well. Frequently, the element of dialogue that looms largest is some chasm of differences between the sides. Divisions and chasms associated with dialogue may be as large and public as opposing nations in the Middle East (as in the work of Saunders) or as small and intimate as conflict in a marriage between husband and wife or parents and children (as in the contribution here of Newfield and Newfield). Into dialogical situations characterized by group conversations among sides and over difference, the modifier "sustained" introduces an element of prolonging or duration. This may refer to either to the duration of the differences at the time talk begins or to expectations that these particular dialogical conversations will go on for a long time.

THEORETICAL PERSPECTIVES

There has been a genuine renaissance of interest in democratic political theory in recent decades,[1] and within that upsurge, a growing number of writers have focused not just on democracy but on the role of deliberation in particular.[2] Even a partial list of the major contributions in political philosophy would include John Rawls (1993, 2001; Rawls and Freeman 2007), Jean Cohen and Anthony Arato (1992), Will Kymlika (1995), and numerous others, including many cited in the reference list at the end of this volume. In political science, one might also note Barber (1984, 1998a), Fishkin (1997), and Warren (2001); in public administration, Crosby, Kelly, and Schaefer (1986); Roberts (1997); Schachter (1997); and King, Feltey, and Susel (1998).

Among works by deliberative theorists, an essay by Gutmann and Thompson (2002) is one of the most widely cited.[3] It concludes:

> Deliberative democratic theory is better prepared to deal with the range of moral and political challenges of a robust democratic politics if it includes both substantive and procedural principles. It is well equipped to cope with the conflict between substantive and procedural principles because its principles are to varying degrees morally and politically provisional.
>
> (174)

By reading the phrase "substantive and procedural principles" as referring to theory and practice, one can interpret this powerful statement as arriving from a theoretical direction at what we are calling the "pracademic" perspective on deliberative democracy. There is, Gutmann and Thompson say, an important role for theory in arriving at principles such as reciprocity, but political theory cannot remain authentically democratic if it limits or abridges the legitimate decision-making powers of autonomous citizens. But how are we to ensure this does not happen? Their answer is clear: "Deliberative democratic theory can avoid usurping the moral or political authority of democratic citizens and yet still make substantive judgments about the laws they enact because it claims neither more, nor less, than provisional status for the principles it defends" (176). In the key phrase "provisional status," the reader is reminded of Benjamin Barber's separation of an autonomous realm of political knowledge independent of theory or philosophy:

> The historical aim of political theory has been dialectical or dialogical: The creation of a genuine praxis in which theory and practice are . . . reconciled, and the criteria yielded by common action are permitted to inform and circumscribe philosophy no less than philosophical criteria are permitted to constrain the understanding of politics and informed political action. Yet in much of what passes for political philosophy in the age of liberalism, reductionism and what William James called 'vicious abstractionism' has too often displaced dialectics and dialogue. The outcome has been neither

political philosophy nor political understanding but the conquest of politics by philosophy.

(BARBER 1988, 4)

All practitioners of deliberation and dialogue, regardless of their degree of theoretical sophistication, must, at some point, struggle with the implications of Barber's assertion. Barber alludes to the nearly forgotten efforts by Dewey to "recover" philosophy and reminds us of an essential paradox in the writings of Jane Addams, not to mention in all of progressive thought from Herbert Croly ([1909] 2005) on: authentically democratic practice must be guided by theory but cannot be controlled or directed by the views of political philosophers, government experts, or professionals without becoming a mere puppet show. Perhaps no one in the history of social work was more aware of this than Jane Addams.

Recent critics continue to raise concerns about the viability of participatory democracy. (Berger 2009; Bohte 2007; Fiorina 1999; Irvin and Stansbury 2004, 56; and Smith and Huntsman 1997). Bohte questions whether most citizens have sufficiently detailed policy knowledge to make viable contributions to modern governance. Irvin and Stansbury seek to shift the question from "how to" encourage greater citizen participation to "whether to" at all. Fiorina and Smith and Huntsman are skeptical of the likelihood that large numbers of citizens have much interest in extensive participation in governance. Verba et al. (1993) call attention to the skewed nature of participation, with wealthier and better educated citizens disproportionately more engaged. Burtt's (1993) critique of Barber's (1988) model of strong democracy notes that people raised in a society that has active citizenship might enjoy participating; the challenge is in how to get people started, how to achieve such an activist society from our present condition.

PRACADEMICS

Growing out of this literature is the convergence of certain practical and theoretical concerns. We indicate this mixture of practice and academic with the term "pracademic." The term will be unfamiliar for many readers. It is a portmanteau term, combining "academic," in senses both of person and of subject matter, and "practice" or "practitioner." The implications of the approach we signal by the use of this term are explored more fully

throughout, but particularly in chapter 8. Suffice it to say here that the interests of faculty members, students, and alumni of social work programs and
such related disciplines as public administration, criminology, journalism,
public affairs, and nursing are consistently pracademic ones. In marked contrast to much of the academic literature on public deliberation in political
philosophy, for example, the pracademic concerns reflected here represent
a mixture of conceptual and theoretical concerns and a powerful applied
question: So what do we *do now?* Habermas's revival of the ancient Greek
distinctions among theory, practice, and technique comes to mind here,
with pracademics as a group all guided ultimately by theory but divided
between those most interested in the broader implications of practice and
those interested in specific techniques. Some of our authors, for example,
believe firmly that there is no one right way for citizens in a democracy to
engage one another in deliberation or dialogue, that the choice of how to
do so is properly theirs alone, while others spend considerable amounts of
time and energy spelling out a diversity of such ways.

THE ENGAGED CAMPUS

Closely associated with the theory and practice of deliberation and dialogue
is the notion of the engaged campus. The modern university is many different things to its multiple constituencies. For pracademics, the image of
the university as an ivory tower offering refuge from the distractions of the
outside world rings largely false. The contemporary university offers an opportunity to educate future practitioners in the arts and sciences but also
typically offers a base from which to continue and extend one's practice
interests. The ivory-tower image is a strong one in the popular imagination
(and often a frustrating one for scientists and humanists who know how
the many competing demands of university life distract from their other
interests). For pracademic faculty and students, however, the university can
offer a base of operations to carry out a lifetime of projects and attempt to
bring about changes in the world. As a result, wherever you have pracademics you are likely also to see movement in the direction of what we like to
think of as the engaged campus.

One of the themes that figures importantly in this volume is the concept
of the engaged campus as a starting point for a broader proliferation of
deliberation and dialogue into community life. At West Virginia University,

as at other institutions, deliberation and dialogue have touched the lives of hundreds who have participated in public forums, efforts to organize a campus network, and other community discussions. These dialogues have intersected with the interests of a wide variety of campus organizations and actors to put us well on the way to becoming a truly "engaged campus."

The "Engaged Campus," as described by Saltmarsh (2004), evinces such characteristics as:

1. *Mission and purpose* that explicitly articulate a commitment to the public purposes of higher education
2. *Administrative and academic leadership* (president, trustees, provost) that is at the forefront of institutional transformation in support of civic engagement
3. *External resource allocation* made available for community partners to create richer learning environments for students and for community-building efforts in local neighborhoods
4. *Disciplines, departments, and interdisciplinary work* that incorporate community-based education, allowing it to penetrate all disciplines and reach the institution's academic core
5. *Faculty roles and rewards* that embrace a scholarship of engagement, reflected by incorporation into promotion and tenure guidelines and review
6. *Internal resource allocation* adequate for establishing, enhancing, and deepening community-based work on campus for faculty, students, and programs that involve community partners
7. *Community voice* that deepens the role of community partners in contributing to community-based education and shaping outcomes that benefit the community
8. *Enabling mechanisms* in the form of visible and easily accessible structures on campus to assist faculty with community-based teaching and to broker community partnerships
9. *Faculty development* opportunities available for faculty to retool their teaching and redesign their curricula to incorporate community-based activities as well as reflection on those activities within the context of a course
10. *Integrated and complementary community-service activities* that weave together student service, service learning, and other community-engagement activities on campus

11. *Forums for fostering public dialogue* that include multiple stakeholders in public-problem solving

12. *Pedagogy and epistemology* that incorporate a community-based, public-problem-solving approach to teaching and learning

ENGAGED THROUGH DELIBERATION AND DIALOGUE

This book both considers and illustrates ways in which members of a social work (or any other) faculty and students on any campus can act upon Saltmarsh's "twelve-step program," demonstrate leadership in issue or problem discussion, and become active instigators of processes of deliberation and dialogue in the larger communities where the campus is located. This may be a city, a state or region, or even an entire country. Through certain pedagogical devices—class assignments, individual projects, marketing devices, organizing efforts (like a "Deliberation Day" event), the sponsorship of community forums on topics of interest and concern—undergraduate, graduate, and doctoral students and faculty can find ways to engage with communities through public talk.

This volume has been positioned as an interdisciplinary text in a social work publishing program for good reason. Several of the authors have no formal connection with social work, and some of them undoubtedly have other projects in mind and may even be uncomfortable with suggestions of the historical importance of social work to the deliberative tradition. In such cases, the characteristic social work response is a familiar one: Okay, let's talk about it. The legitimacy of differing points of view has long been one of the strengths of the social work tradition and one that has direct deliberative origins.

Notes

1. As already noted, this is a somewhat peculiar renaissance in that many writers appear so genuinely unaware that the topic under study is a reopened one rather than a subject of original inquiry.

2. In the view of some, this renaissance has purely theoretical origins. In particular, John Rawls's *Theory of Justice* (1971) is often cited as the fountainhead. This alone might account for the lack of historical perspective noted in later chapters since Rawls's approach was a Kantian one, working in the realm of "pure"

ideas and aspiring to universal generality. For others, the inspiration for the renewed interest is to be found in real-world events: the collapse of the Soviet empire and the accompanying failure of communism as a theoretical domain, along with the rise of democratic regimes in Latin American and Africa. In this literature, the decades-long experimentation of community practitioners with democratic organizations and greater citizen involvement in the consideration of social problems and policy issues garners little attention among the philosophers.

3. The practical and pracademic contributions of Amy Gutmann before, during, and after her term as president of Princeton University are also subjects for future consideration. Here the focus is purely on her theorizing.

SECTION I

BASIC STATEMENTS

Introduction

SUSTAINED DIALOGUE AND PUBLIC DELIBERATION are two of the most important attempts to take the next steps toward more deliberative democracy in government and society. In this section, five sets of authors offer their perspectives on the basic role and position of public conversation in modern life.

In the first "basic statement" in this section, coeditor Jon Van Til expands upon the theme stated in his opening sentence: "Sustained dialogue and public deliberation are forms of structured human interaction that address, name, and frame issues of mutual concern." Harold Saunders and Priya Parker lay out the fundamentals of the sustained dialogue perspective as it has developed through the work of the International Institute for Sustained Dialogue. In a second, related chapter, Saunders and Parker discuss a wide variety of local, campus, and international applications of sustained dialogue undertaken by groups associated with IISD. David Robinson ties thoughts on the deliberation and dialogue frame into another, contemporary framework of social capital from the perspective of his practice in Wellington, New Zealand. While there are numerous published studies of social capital, Robinson reports here on what is likely the first study to examine intergroup efforts at sustained dialogue in that context. In a paper originally written for another context and first published here, Lisa Bedinger expands upon the connection between sustained dialogue and higher education. In the last statement in this section, coeditor Roger A. Lohmann and Nancy Lohmann explore the long record of social work involvement with fundamental ideas of deliberative democracy in organizations and communities.

1

THE STRUCTURE OF SUSTAINED DIALOGUE AND PUBLIC DELIBERATION

Jon Van Til

SUSTAINED DIALOGUE and public deliberation are forms of structured human interaction that address, name, and frame issues of mutual concern. These approaches involve processes of deliberative democracy, or public talk, wherein citizen participants engage in designed and moderated discussions with the goal of increasing understanding and reducing conflict among themselves and the solidary groups to which they may belong.

Two major forms of such interaction are specifically identified as "sustained dialogue," as developed by Harold Saunders and colleagues at the Kettering Foundation and the International Institute for Sustained Dialogue, and "public deliberation," as developed by David Mathews and colleagues at the Kettering Foundation and the National Issues Forums. Other forms of sustained dialogue and public deliberation are as old as human society itself and have been practiced within traditional communities, town meetings, community workshops, and countless other locales within the commons or third spaces of society.

Dialogue requires a belief that it may succeed. Paolo Freire makes this point when he writes: "Dialogue cannot exist . . . in the absence of a profound love for the world and for people. The naming of the world, which is an act of creation and re-creation, is not possible if it is not infused with love" ([1970] 1973, 77–78). Harold Saunders, who named the process of sustained dialogue following on his experience as a U.S. State Department official participating in "shuttle diplomacy" between the leaders of Israel and Egypt, writes: "It is in th(e) human process, not in the official negotiating room, that conflictual relationships change" (1999, 5).

SUSTAINED DIALOGUE: BRIDGING DEEPER CONFLICTS

Communication among human beings enmeshed in deep and longstanding conflicts rooted in ethnicity, culture, and historical violence is often Hobbesian in nature: nasty, brutish, and short. It often takes a third party to convince individuals caught in the net of noise and hatred that entering into dialogue can be in both their interests.

Thus it was in 1974 that Secretary of State Henry Kissinger led a team of American diplomats in the task of creating an understanding between the leaders of Israel and its Arab neighbors. For three years, Kissinger and his associates, including an assistant secretary of state named Harold Saunders, shuttled between Tel Aviv, Cairo, and other Arab capitals in an emerging "peace process" that culminated in 1977 in a historic speech by the Egyptian president to the Israeli parliament. Capped by President Jimmy Carter's Camp David accords in 1978 and the Egyptian-Israeli Peace Treaty in 1979,

---

BOX 1.1

Stage One: Deciding to Engage
- Find willing and appropriate participants
- Agree to meet
- Reach an understanding of the nature, purpose, and rules of the dialogue

Stage 2: Mapping and Naming
- Set the tone and habits of the dialogue
- Set out the main problems that affect relationships among the participants
- Identify all significant relationships responsible for problems

Stage 3: Probing Problems and Relationships
- Probe specific problems in depth
- Frame choices among approaches
- Weigh choices to set a general direction for action

Stage 4: Scenario Building
- List obstacles to change
- Design steps to address these obstacles
- Identify people who can take these steps

Stage 5: Acting Together
- Decide whether the situation in the community can be solved by steps designated in stage 4
- Identify what resources and capacities can be used to take them
- Take steps

this was the official peace process—a diplomatic and mediation activity of governments.

When he left government, Saunders began more than two decades of work in nonofficial dialogue—what he later called "the public peace process," a continuing dialogue among citizens in the policy-influencing community outside of the government. As he cochaired a task force of the Dartmouth Conference in the 1980s, an ongoing dialogue between nongovernmental leaders in the United States and the Soviet Union, he came to the recognition that "citizens talking in depth together can become a microcosm of their communities, experiencing a change in relationships and then learning to design political actions and interactions that can change their larger bodies politic" (1999, 6). In the 1990s, Saunders named the processes he had participated in "sustained dialogue," identifying a process of five stages by which enmity and suspicion become transformed into understanding and accommodation (see chapters 2 and 3 of this volume). Box 1.1 shows Saunders's stages of sustained dialogue.

PUBLIC DELIBERATION: THE WORK OF ISSUE FORUMS

Saunders developed his writings on sustained dialogue during his service as director of international affairs with the Kettering Foundation, a research organization devoted to social innovation. During that same period, Kettering staffers, under the leadership of foundation president David Mathews, formerly president of the University of Alabama and secretary of the U.S. Department of Health, Education, and Welfare, played a central role in the development of National Issues Forums.

Issues forums build on concepts of deliberative democracy, seeking to create a basis for shared discussion and increased understanding among citizens on specific issues of public concern. Critical to this process is the careful naming and framing of public issues by the participants in the issues forums. In the naming process, an issue is selected for exploration, and its definition is crafted to reflect the concerns of involved citizens and to assure a full and fair consideration of the issue and its ramifications. In the framing process, the most central aspect of public deliberation, three or four principal options for responding to the issue are developed, assuring that the forum will address the issue in a full and fair manner. Each approach reflects something that people value. The tension within and between approaches

---

BOX 1.2

THE NATURE OF THE ISSUE FORUM

Deliberation is different. It is neither a partisan argument where opposing sides try to win nor a casual conversation conducted with polite civility. Public deliberation is a means by which citizens make tough choices about basic purposes and directions for their communities and their country. It is a way of reasoning and talking together.

National Issues Forum deliberations are framed in terms of three or four options for dealing with an issue—never just two polar alternatives. Framing an issue in this way discourages the diatribes in which people lash out at one another with simplistic arguments.

To deliberate is to weigh the benefits and costs of various options based on what is truly valuable to us. Think of the way people used to weigh gold on an old-fashioned scale. How much will each consequence tip the scale? What are the costs and benefits of doing what we want to do? Answering these questions requires a setting in which we can explore and test ideas about how to act.

Deliberation also involves weighing the views of others. Careful listening increases the chances that our choices will be sound because a wide range of people have pooled their experiences and insights. No one person or small group of people has all the experience and insight needed to decide what is best. That is why it is essential for an inclusive group of citizens to combine their perspectives.

While we can't know for certain that we have made the right decision until we have acted, deliberation forces us to anticipate consequences and ask ourselves whether we would be willing to accept the worst possible case.

Deliberation is looking before we leap.

(MATTHEWS AND MCAFEE 2003, 10)

---

fuels the deliberation and enriches the weighing of pros and cons for each approach.

WHY DIALOGUE AND DELIBERATION?

The achievement of true dialogue is an ancient goal of human beings. The sacred texts of world religions speak of the beauty of ongoing understanding and communication among brothers and sisters, lovers, children and parents, neighbors, communities, and nations, and between humans and the deity. The excerpt in box 1.3, developed by a group of Californians of Jewish and Palestinian background who meet in one another's living rooms,

BOX 1.3

WHY DIALOGUE?

Beginning with compassionate listening, dialogue can dissolve boundaries between people, heal relationships, and release unprecedented creativity. Dialogue can result in a wellspring of new social intelligence previously unimagined. Dialogue moves us out of our isolated existence and beyond our restricted views.

We begin to understand diversity in perception, in meaning, in expression—in people. With this authentic speaking and authentic listening to each other, to Earth, to Life, together we can invent a way of living that works for the benefit of all.

Dialogue Is Not Debate

- Dialogue causes introspection on one's own position. Debate causes critique of the other position.
- Dialogue opens the possibility of reaching a better solution than any of the original solutions. Debate defends one's own positions as the best solution and excludes other solutions.
- Dialogue creates an open-minded attitude: an openness to being wrong and an openness to change. Debate creates a closed-minded attitude, a determination to be right.
- In dialogue, one submits one's best thinking, knowing that other people's reflections will help improve it rather than destroy it. In debate, one submits one's best thinking and defends it against challenge to show that it is right.
- Dialogue calls for temporarily suspending one's beliefs. Debate calls for investing whole-heartedly in one's beliefs.
- In dialogue, one searches for basic agreements. In debate, one searches for glaring differences.
- In dialogue, one searches for strengths in the other positions. In debate, one searches for flaws and weaknesses in the other positions.
- Dialogue involves a real concern for the other person and seeks to not alienate or offend. Debate involves a countering of the other position without focusing on feelings or relationship and often belittles or deprecates the other person.
- Dialogue assumes that many people have pieces of the answer and that together they can put them into a workable solution. Debate assumes that there is a right answer and that someone has it.
- Dialogue remains open-ended. Debate implies a conclusion.

(JEWISH-PALESTINIAN LIVING ROOM DIALOGUE GROUP, SAN MATEO, CALIF., HTTP://
TRAUBMAN.IGC.ORG/DIALOGUE2.HTM [ACCESSED 6/4/2004; CONFIRMED 4/4/2010])

expresses the aspirations of those who seek dialogue as a way of increasing social understanding and achieving peace and reconciliation.

THE EMERGING ACADEMIC LITERATURE

Specific literature on sustained dialogue and public deliberation is mainly to be found in publications that have emerged from or been sponsored by the Kettering Foundation and the International Institute for Sustained Dialogue. This "in-house" literature reports the founding work in these fields, often in the words of those who have developed and supported these methods of structured social change. Particularly significant here are the books by Saunders (2005) and Voorhees (2002); the many Kettering issue books, papers, and pamphlets regarding the structuring of issues forums and other means of public deliberation; and *Politics for People* by David Mathews (1999).

Important as these testimonies and guidebooks to organization are, and their value is indisputable, no movement can sustain and reproduce itself unless it is subjected to an independent and critical examination by researchers drawn from a wider range of theoretical, methodological, and ideological backgrounds. Such a literature is beginning to emerge regarding sustained dialogue and public deliberation, but it remains partial and largely undeveloped.

Perhaps the most developed academic literature on these subjects focuses on theories of deliberative democracy (Cooke 2000; Fishkin and Laslett 2003; Gates and O'Connor 2000; Gutmann and Thompson 2002; Mouffe 1999; and Rodin and Steinberg 2003). A more empirical focus on experiences of public deliberation is found in the studies of David Ryfe (2002), John Gastil (Burkhalter, Gastil, and Kelshaw 2002; Gastil and Dillard 1999), Christian Hunold (2001), Christopher Plein (cf. Plein, Green, and Williams 1998), Carmen Sirianni and Lewis Friedland (2001), and David Williams (1992).

A much wider net is cast by a range of writers who consider the broader societal context underlying sustained dialogue and public deliberation (Cf. Brooks 2000; Florida 2002; Lohmann 1992b; Putnam 2000; Van Til 2000; and Wheen 2004). And a specific literature may be found regarding the role of sustained dialogue in Northern Ireland (Mitchell 1999; E. Porter 2000; N. Porter 2003; and Van Til 2008).

Beyond the two major approaches of sustained dialogue and public deliberation, each developed and nurtured at Kettering by Saunders, Matthews, and their colleagues, there exist many related forms of guided social inter-action that closely relate in goal and process. These range from on-campus forms of sustained dialogue to conversational structures to literally dozens of related efforts to mount and develop dialogue and deliberation throughout society. A few of these approaches are introduced in the following subsec-tions of this chapter.

SUSTAINED DIALOGUE ON CAMPUS

Sustained dialogue on campus emerged from conversations in the late 1990s between Saunders, then a member of the board of governors of Princeton University, and several undergraduates at that university. Following on this conversation, while they were Princeton students Teddy Nemeroff and David Tukey focused on the application of the principles of sustained dia-logue to the issue of relations between white and black students on the cam-pus. That same theme was subsequently taken up by Priya Parker and other students at the University of Virginia and then at other campuses through the efforts of IISD.

BOX 1.4

DIVING IN, BY TEDDY NEMEROFF AND DAVID TUKEY

Where does one dive in? The problem of race relations in any community seems too complex to tackle from any starting point. This is certainly true on college campuses where a microcosm of society at large exists and the issues that we face are as serious and real as those facing the rest of the world.

Racism is a profound human problem rooted in the complex sphere of human rela-tionships. When one realizes this, it becomes apparent that no government can solve racism with laws, nor can any one race do it without the cooperation of others. . . .

One purpose of Sustained Dialogue is to give you a place to dive in. Sustained Dialogue separates itself from other projects that seek to ameliorate ethnic and racial conflict in a very simple regard: it is sustained. The process engrosses all who become involved and carries them toward possible methods for combating the issue of racial tension on campus. As the process progresses, one realizes that it can be self-prolifer-ating. As such, simply getting the process started is taking the right direction toward improving race relations.

(CF. THIS VOLUME, PAGE 131)

While relations between the two races on campus cannot be said to exist in the state of hatred and hostility that characterized the earlier situations Saunders faced in dealing with the Arab-Israeli, U.S.-Soviet, or Tajik Muslim–elite conflict, relations between the groups were characterized by distance, uncertainty, and misunderstanding. The Princeton process, implemented in the form of twice-monthly meetings over dinner by groups of a dozen or so, was extended in the following years to a number of other elite colleges such as the University of Virginia, Notre Dame, Dickinson College, and Colorado College, as well as to several high schools. By 2004, several public universities, such as West Virginia and Rutgers, moved to extend the range of sustained dialogue on campus to issues of class, status, and gender relations.

DIALOGUE IN THE PRACTICE OF RELIGION

This is often central in both the processes of religious communities and their interreligious activities. The Quaker scholar and administrator Thomas Jeavons (1994, 144) observes that in effective Christian service organizations, "participants believe that serving and caring for one another are as important as serving and caring for others." Dialogue and deliberation are hallmarks of such organizations, Jeavons finds: "Where people are sharing their work because they share a common faith and sense of mission, and they have a genuine respect and affection for one another, their communication will generally have this quality about it" (145).

On his website, the Columban priest Sean Dwan (see box 1.5) drew directly on dialogue and deliberation in his prescriptions for interreligious dialogue. He presents two aphorisms that he identifies as essential for engaging in dialogue with other religions: "'Nothing human is foreign to me' (attributed to Lucretius) means that if a particular action is performed by a human being I, as a human being, ought to be able to make some sense of it. The second maxim comes from Spinoza who said 'I have always labored carefully when faced with human actions, not to mock, not to lament, not to condemn, but to understand.'" Dwan also presented a set of ten commandments for dialogue and deliberation, as developed by Leonard Swidler.

SIMPLE CONVERSATION

This approach is aimed at advancing dialogue and is presented by the organizational consultant Margaret Wheatley in her book *Turning to One*

BOX 1.5

LEONARD SWIDLER, "DIALOGUE DECALOGUE"

1st Commandment: The primary purpose of dialogue is to change and grow in the perception and understanding of reality and then to act accordingly.

2nd Commandment: Dialogue must be a two-sided project—within each religious community and between religious communities.

3rd Commandment: Each participant must come to the dialogue with complete honesty and sincerity.

4th Commandment: Each participant must assume a similar complete honesty and sincerity in the other partners.

5th Commandment: Each participant must define what it means to be a member of his own tradition; conversely, the one defined must be able to recognize him/herself in the interpretation.

6th Commandment: Each participant must come to the dialogue with no hard-and-fast assumptions as to where the points of disagreement are.

7th Commandment: Dialogue can take place only between equals (not between a skilled scholar and a "person in the pew" type).

8th Commandment: Dialogue can take place only on the basis of mutual trust.

9th Commandment: Participants must be at least minimally self-critical of both themselves and their own religious traditions.

10th Commandment: Each participant must eventually attempt to experience the partner's religion from within.

(HTTP://WWW.COLUMBAN.PH/SEANDWAN_INTERRELIGIOUS_DIALOGUE.HTM

[ACCESSED 13 MARCH 2005]

Another (2002). Wheatley explains: "I believe we can change the world if we start listening to one another again. Simple, honest, human conversation. Not mediation, negotiation, problem-solving, debate, or public meetings. Simple, truthful conversation where we each have a chance to speak, we each feel heard, and we each listen well" (3).

Wheatley describes such dialogue as sustained ("we need time to sit together, to listen, to worry and dream together") and capable of bridging differences ("we need to be able to talk with those we have named 'enemy'"). She uses poetic imagery to develop her point that much that is of value in this world begins when "a few friends" come together to talk.

Wheatley's approach is deeply personal, rooted in a secular humanism that draws on the power of individual and group passions. It is her vision that

BOX 1.6

SIMPLE CONVERSATION

We acknowledge one another as equals.
We try to stay curious about each other.
We recognize that we need each other's help to become better listeners.
We slow down so we have time to think and reflect.
We remember that conversation in the natural way humans think together.
We expect it to be messy at times.

(WHEATLEY 2002, 29)

dialogue blends the public and private, and should not be over-designed and programmed. Box 1.6 explains the principles on which simple conversation is founded.

COALITION BUILDING

This is yet another approach to dialogue and deliberation. Focusing on the appreciation of diversity, this approach has been formalized by the National Coalition Building Institute with the support of such major philanthropic organizations as the W. K. Kellogg Foundation. Typically referred to as NCBI, the institute's roots lie in reevaluation counseling, a staple of the human-potential movement as it emerged in the 1960s and 1970s.

In reevaluation counseling, two individuals meet in an intense sharing of past hurtful experiences, seeking an "emotional discharge" that frees them "from the rigid pattern of behavior and feeling left by the hurt" (www.rc.org). The NCBI approach seeks to transform the healing process into action by means of a group airing of the pain of segregation, discrimination, and oppression on the bases of race, class, sexual orientation, and the like. NCBI workshops are often presented on campus and focus on such issues as "building environments to welcome diversity," "healing ourselves to change the world," "becoming effective allies," and "empowering leaders to lead" (Brown and Mazza 1997).

BOX 1.7

BASIC NCBI PRINCIPLES

Building Environments to Welcome Diversity

Guilt is the glue that holds prejudice in place.

Welcoming diversity means that every person counts and every issue counts.

Treating everyone the same may be unintentionally oppressive.

Meetings go better when everyone is included.

Recognize and work with the diversity already present in what appear to be homogeneous groups.

People can take on tough issues more readily when the issues are presented in a spirit of hope.

Building a team around us is the most powerful way to bring about institutional change.

Healing Ourselves to Change the World

We all carry records about other groups that prevent us from building effective alliances.

Effective anti-racism leadership in the present means healing scars from the past.

When we respond top a present situation with intense emotion, we are usually acting out of a past unhealed difficulty.

Underneath every oppressive comment lies some form of injury.

People who feel good about themselves do not mistreat others.

When witnessing oppressive behavior, having a chance to vent leads to clearer thinking about what is useful to do next.

Diversity leadership requires reclaiming courage.

Being an ally to another group requires us to heal the negative messages we have internalized about our own group.

Healing discouragement leads to more effective activism.

(BROWN AND MAZZA 1997, VIII)

OTHER FORMS OF SUSTAINED DIALOGUE AND PUBLIC DELIBERATION

Various other forms manifest themselves on both the national and global levels. In the present volume, the reader will be introduced to variations on the theme as developed in a number of locations.

A review of the homepage on democratic dialogue of the U.N. Development Programme identifies fifty-five individual programs whose work centrally involves democratic dialogue. A selection from that list includes the organizations whose approaches to sustained dialogue and public deliberation are found in box 1.8.

BOX 1.8

DEMOCRATIC DIALOGUE HOMEPAGE, UNITED NATIONS
DEVELOPMENT PROGRAMME

1. AmericaSpeaks—Engaging Citizens in Governance. AmericaSpeaks is a national non-profit neutral convener of large-scale public participation forums, committed to the task of engaging citizen voices in local, regional and national governance.

2. Carter Center, The—The web page includes information on all of the organization's Peace Programs: the Americas Program, the Conflict Resolution Program, the Democracy Program and the Global Development Initiative.

3. Conflict Transformation—The Alliance for Conflict Transformation (ACT) is a non-profit organization dedicated to expanding the knowledge and practice of conflict transformation and peace building within U.S. and international communities.

4. EU Platform for Conflict Prevention and Transformation—The European Centre for Conflict Prevention acts as the secretariat for the EU Platform for Conflict Prevention and Transformation, an open network consisting of some 150 European organizations working in the field of conflict prevention and resolution in the international arena.

5. Future Search—The Future Search Network is a cross-cultural, multilingual network of volunteers worldwide providing Future Search planning meetings, employing the methodology of dialogue and mutual learning among diverse stakeholders as a catalyst for discovering common ground and concrete action.

6. Hewlett Foundation—The William and Flora Hewlett Foundation played a major role in developing and supporting the conflict resolution field for nearly two decades; the Conflict Resolution Program supported organizations that anticipated and responded to domestic and international strife.

7. International Conflict Research (INCORE)—The International Conflict Research Centre, set-up by the United Nations University and the University of Ulster in Northern Ireland, undertakes research and policy work that is useful to the resolution of ethnic, political and religious conflicts.

8. International Institute for Sustained Dialogue—The International Institute for Sustained Dialogue is an independent organization formed in collaboration with the Kettering Foundation. The Institute's purpose is to promote the process of sustained dialogue for transforming racial and ethnic conflicts around the world.

9. National Coalition for Dialogue and Deliberation—Thataway.org is the host for the National Coalition for Dialogue and Deliberation (NCDD), a coalition of organizations and individuals committed to strengthening and uniting the dialogue community.

10. National Issues Forum—The National Issues Forums (NIF) is a non-partisan network of organizations, in the USA, who bring people of diverse views together to discuss critical issues and to find common ground for action on such issues. Reports on the forums are shared with local, state and national stakeholders to give them insight into what the public is thinking.

11. Public Conversations Project—The Public Conversations Project (PCP) is an organization that seeks to foster a more inclusive, empathetic and collaborative society by promoting constructive conversations and relationships among those who have differing values, world views, and positions on divisive public issues.

12. Public Dialogue Consortium—The Public Dialogue Consortium (PDC) is comprised of a diverse group of educators, consultants and practitioners, based in the United States, who promote high quality communication on public issues.

13. The Centre for Humanitarian Dialogue—The Centre for Humanitarian Dialogue is an independent and impartial organization based in Geneva, Switzerland that is dedicated to the promotion of humanitarian principles, the prevention of conflict, and the alleviation of its effects through dialogue.

14. United Nations Development Programme—UNDP, the UN's global development network with a presence in 166 countries, is focused on assisting communities worldwide to build and share solutions to the challenges of democratic government, poverty reduction, crisis prevention and recovery, energy and environment, information and communications technology, and HIV/AIDS.

15. World Café—The World Café is a methodology and metaphor for understanding and working with the complex process by which we collectively construct our world, which has been introduced in a variety of group settings. World Café conversations are an intentional process for leading collaborative dialogue, sharing knowledge, and creating ever-widening possibilities for action and circles of conversation around questions that matter.

16. World Dialogue—The Centre for World Dialogue is a Cyprus-based independent NGO that provides a forum for the discussion of global issues through conferences, meetings, seminars and a quarterly journal "Global Dialogue". It is committed to engaging people in a free and open discussion of ideas, and to promoting greater understanding and cooperation at all levels.

17. WSP-International—WSP-International assists societies torn by war to overcome conflict and to build lasting peace. It does this by promoting processes of consultation, research and analysis with all sectors of society, including international assistance agencies and donors.

(HTTP://WWW.DEMOCRATICDIALOGUENETWORK.ORG)

DIMENSIONS OF DIALOGUE AND DELIBERATION

Review of the many forms of sustained dialogue and public deliberation that have been developed by creative individuals and groups across the globe, reveals a number of differences in form and substance.

1. In some cases, groups meet over a long period of time; in others, a single meeting is held. Thus, dialogue and deliberation may be a "sustained" or a "one-time" activity or anything in between.

2. In some cases, the form and process of the dialogue is deeply engrained in the culture of participants; in others, participants learn processes of dialogue as a new skill. Thus, dialogue and deliberation may be an "organic" or a "designed" activity.

3. In some cases, a single issue (or small set of issues) is identified and becomes the central focus of dialogue; in others, issues arise from the group discussion itself. Thus, dialogue and deliberation may be "problem focused" or "spontaneously generated."

4. In some cases, meetings of groups engaged in dialogue and deliberation are closed to observers and not recorded in any way; in others, meeting are open to observers and comments are recorded for public consideration. Thus, dialogue and deliberation may be "confidential" or "open" in its process.

5. In some cases, individuals meet on a basis of full equality within the group, regardless of their status in other walks of life; in other cases, different statuses are recognized within the group process. Thus, dialogue and deliberation may be "egalitarian" or "stratified."

6. In some cases, issues of diversity (on dimensions such as race, class, gender, etc.) underlie group structure and process; in other cases, diversity is not central to the structure and process. Thus, dialogue and deliberation may be "diverse" or "homogeneous" in design.

7. In some cases, the group process focuses on finding common ground among participants by working through issues; in other cases, groups consider issues by means of advocacy, expert presentation, and formal discussion. Thus, dialogue and deliberation may be "deliberative" or "debate-based" in structure and process.

8. In some cases, discussions take place under the guidance of a trained moderator who guides and focuses the discussion; in others, they are conducted without the use of a moderator. Thus, dialogue and deliberation may be "moderated" or "unmoderated" in structure and process.

9. In some cases, unmoderated discussions may take place under the guidance of a facilitator, who does not actively enter into the discussion, but merely guides the process. Thus, unmoderated discussions may still be facilitated.

10. In some cases, a group is convened in an effort to reconcile members of groups with long histories of antagonism toward each other; in others, groups are convened whose members do not have histories of antagonism toward each other. Thus, dialogue and deliberation may be "conflict based" or "conflict neutral" in its form and content.

11. In some cases, group process is aimed toward the presentation and consideration of options on selected public issues; in other, the group addresses issues as they arise among members. Thus, dialogue and deliberation may be "issue framed" or "issue open."

12. In some cases, group process focuses on the resolution of public issues within a pulic forum; in other cases, group process focuses on individual concerns within the context of an essentially private meeting. Thus, dialogue and deliberation may involve "public talk" or "private talk."

13. In some cases, the goal of the process involves achieving consensus on a problematic public issue; in other cases, the goal of the process involves understanding personal differences within and among participants. Thus, dialogue and deliberation may be "action aimed" or "discussion aimed."

MAPPING SUSTAINED DIALOGUE AND PUBLIC DELIBERATION

The five major forms of sustained dialogue and public deliberation identified and discussed above show important differences on the thirteen dimensions just identified. "Classical" sustained dialogue, as developed in the Dartmouth conference differs from "campus-based" sustained dialogue in that it is strongly conflict based, recognizes stratification among its participants, and often convenes over a period of years, although both use the same five-stage process.

Public deliberation, as embodied in National Issues Forums, differs from classical sustained dialogue in that the forums tend to meet only once, are reported, and are not conflict based. Other forms of dialogue and deliberation, such as the conversations reported by Wheatley and NCBI sessions also differ considerably on the dimensions from the classical pattern.

TABLE 1.1 Characteristics of Major Forms of Dialogue and Deliberation

	CLASSIC SD	CAMPUS SD	ISSUE FORUM	CONVERSATION	NCBI
Sustained	X	X		X	
Problem-focused			X		
Relationship-focused	X	X		X	X
Confidential	X	X		X	X
Diverse	X	X	X		X
Deliberative	X	X	X	X	X
Moderated	X	X	X		
Facilitated			X	X	
Conflict-based	X	X			X
Issue-framed	X		X		
Action-aimed	X	X			
Designed	X	X			X
Public talk	X		X		
Stratified	X		X		

NAMING AND FRAMING: HOW LEVEL IS THE PLAYING FIELD?

Dialogue and deliberation, involving as they do thinking and talking, are sometimes viewed as pallid cousins of "doing", or acting. But action without thought and deliberative dialogue can often misfire, and the modern world has taught that s/he who names and frames issues cleverly and well often wins the day.

Dystopian novelists like George Orwell (1984) and Ray Bradbury (*Fahrenheit 451*) have shown the power of the political slogan, a lesson not lost on contemporary political strategists. From the "Contract with America" through carefully named legislation such as "No Child Left Behind" or the proposal of "personal accounts," the Republican Party has proven particularly adept at guiding public opinion toward the support of its policy agenda in recent years.

The political scientists E. E. Schattschneider and Peter Bachrach have probed the dynamics of "nondecision-making" in political life, identifying ways in which organization as a "mobilization of bias" keeps some issues and options "off the table." Bachrach and Morton Baratz (1962: 950) wrote:

> The distinction between important and unimportant issues, we believe, cannot be made intelligently in the absence of an analysis of the 'mobilization of bias' in the community; of the dominant values and the political myths, rituals, and institutions which tend to favor the vested interests of one or more groups, relative to others. Armed with this knowledge, one could conclude that any challenge to the predominant values or to the established "rules of the game" would constitute an "important" issue; all else, unimportant.

If sustained dialogue and public deliberation are to address issues in society fairly, the processes they engender will need to be open to major ideological orientations and points of view.

SUSTAINED DIALOGUE, PUBLIC DELIBERATION, AND THE FUTURE

The many forms of sustained dialogue and public deliberation considered in this chapter and in those that follow are not merely designed to bring people together to share ideas; they are also intended to change the world and to bring better futures into view.

Those who study the future develop images what is possible, probable, and preferable. They often create scenarios depicting what may come to pass in the form of "histories of the future". Four such images of the future are typically presented:

1. Continuity, in which the future most nearly resembles the recent past
2. Hard luck, in which the future deteriorates from the present
3. Good luck, in which existing systems work more effectively to provide an improved future

4. Transformational, in which a significant idea or material change gives rise to new and improved societal arrangements

A criterion important to apply to processes of sustained dialogue and public deliberation is their ability to comprehend the wide range of possible and probable futures that may emerge around specific problems and issues. It is always prudent, after all, to plan for the worst and hope for the best. But an even older statement reminds us that without a vision, the people perish. In any case, a basic test to apply to experiences of sustained dialogue and public deliberation may involve the degree to which the process ignites at least some sparks of change.

2

THE SUSTAINED DIALOGUE MODEL:
TRANSFORMING RELATIONSHIPS, DESIGNING CHANGE

Harold H. Saunders and Priya Narayan Parker

SUSTAINED DIALOGUE is a *process* for transforming dysfunctional and conflictual relationships. That process of transformation can generate the capacity to change society more broadly. Sustained dialogue can become a change process.

Dialogue itself is a particular way of talking and relating. It "is a process of genuine interaction through which human beings listen to each other deeply enough to be changed by what they learn. Each makes a serious effort to take other's concerns into her or his own picture, even when disagreement persists. No participant gives up her or his identity, but each recognizes enough of the other's valid human claims that he or she will act differently toward the other" (Saunders 1999, 82). When sustained with a core group of participants coming together time after time, dialogue can become the carefully designed and rigorously implemented change process that we call sustained dialogue. To understand and to use this process to its fullest capacity requires a shifting of mental gears. Underlying sustained dialogue is a new paradigm for the study and practice of politics. We call it the relational paradigm.

Why should we as practitioners spend time talking about abstractions such as paradigm, worldview, and concept? There are two reasons: First, when experience causes citizens to take personal responsibility for changing a situation that hurts their interests, it is critical that their subconscious worldview includes the possibility that their action can make a difference. Soviet citizens, for instance, normally felt it impossible for anyone but government to solve society's problems. While the American worldview has traditionally encouraged citizen initiative, Americans over the last three generations have relied increasingly on government to solve problems and have steadily withdrawn from political life because they have felt their views made no difference.[1] Second, experience shows that the lenses we use to bring the world into focus and to give meaning to events around us—our worldview and concepts—determine how we act. The lenses we have used to interpret social, political, and economic life are more and more out of focus.

Change begins with new conceptual lenses—a new mindset. So we begin our discussion of sustained dialogue as an instrument for transforming relationships and designing change by presenting a political paradigm for the twenty-first century, which in a leap of faith we call "the citizens' century."

THE RELATIONAL PARADIGM

The relational paradigm: *Politics is a cumulative, multilevel, open-ended process of continuous interaction over time engaging significant clusters of citizens in and out of government and the relationships they form to solve public problems in whole bodies politic across permeable borders, either within or between communities or countries.*

That is a mouthful. What is important to understand are two ways in which this paradigm differs from the paradigm that has dominated U.S. political science for the past three generations. First, it broadens the focus of study from government and related political institutions—political parties, interest groups, lobbyists, and public opinion—to include *citizens outside government*. We speak of "whole bodies politic" to include citizens both inside and outside government. We see the energies and capacities of citizens outside government as the greatest untapped resources for meeting the challenges of the twenty-first century. Any paradigm that excludes them by focusing primarily on political institutions is ineffective because it fails to take advantage of those resources and is immoral because it marginalizes most of the world's people.

It is important to recognize that there are some things only governments can do, but it is critical to recognize that there are some things only citizens outside government can do—transform conflictual relationships, modify human behavior, and change political culture. Only governments can negotiate peace treaties; only people can make peace.

Second, the relational paradigm moves beyond a simple view of politics as a linear series of actions and reactions to an understanding of social, political, and economic life as a cumulative, multilevel, open-ended *process* of continuous interaction. Such a process may be impossible to study using the quantitative analytical techniques of recent social science. But that is where people live—and how the world really works. People need spaces in which they can experience that process of continuous interaction and discover the capacity to influence the course of events that can be generated through such interaction. Sustained dialogue provides one such space.

Focusing as it does on the citizen as a potential political actor, this paradigm contributes to a worldview that holds out the possibility that a citizen outside government can influence the course of change. Indeed, changing a citizen's mindset—a citizen's view of her/his needs and capacities and of the surrounding social, economic, and political context—may be the first element of a change process. Whether citizens come to see themselves as responsible for solving their problems—instead of leaving solutions to government—is a critical ingredient of change.

People may not usually see themselves explicitly as political actors or change agents. Their mindset may be the product of the surrounding worldview. It sometimes takes an acute catalytic event or a personal tragedy to cause a citizen to begin acting, but perhaps more often there is a gradual awakening of a feeling that things have gone too far and that something needs to be done. When experience or pain causes them to think about acting, it is important that their subconscious worldview includes the possibility of their being change agents. The relational paradigm is designed to open that door.

In this context, it is important to recognize that individual citizens do not have to act alone in developing a mindset and a capacity for change. Citizens' organizations may act as catalysts in a process of change—as articulators of a paradigm that encourages citizens to see themselves as actors.

Once citizens begin to think of themselves as political actors, they can proceed in a variety of ways with different combinations of other actors. At one end of the spectrum, some citizens together may have the capacity to initiate and organize change on their own. Other citizens on their own timetable and in differing degrees of involvement may seek out the experience an organization formed around a particular instrument for generating change. At the other end of the spectrum, those citizens' catalyst organizations may initiate change themselves by introducing processes of change, training citizens in their use, and helping those citizens connect with others sharing their objective. The catalyst organization's role is to help create spaces for citizens to discover and affirm their capacities to influence change. It is always seeking a balance between a role as teacher in response to citizens' approaches and as an active promoter of citizen engagement.

SUSTAINED DIALOGUE: TRANSFORMING RELATIONSHIPS

Sustained dialogue as a change process differs from most other instruments for change in its focus on the relationships that cause problems and generate conflict. These are the relationships that must be transformed if people are to overcome the obstacles to collaborative problem solving, whatever its form.

Given that focus on transforming relationships, sustained dialogue practitioners work within a concept of relationship carefully defined in terms of five arenas of interaction in constantly changing combinations within and among the parties in dialogue: (1) *identity*, defined in human as well as in physical characteristics—the life experience that has brought a person or group to the present moment; (2) *interests*, both concrete and psychological—what people care about—that bring them into the same space and into a sense of their dependence on one another, their *interdependence*, to achieve their goals; (3) *power*, defined not only as control over superior resources and the actions of others but as the capacity of citizens acting together to influence the course of events with or especially without great material resources; (4) *perceptions, misperceptions, and stereotypes*; and (5) *the patterns of interaction*—distant and close—among those involved, including respect for certain *limits on behavior* in dealing with others. In some ways, interaction is the essence of relationship.

The concept of relationship can be both a diagnostic and an operational tool. One can analyze observable interactions through this prism and can actually get inside any of these components to enhance understanding or to change a relationship. In dialogue, one's own sense of identity can grow. Another's identity can be understood, and a person can be humanized as misperceptions and stereotypes give way to realistic pictures. Common interests can be discovered. Patterns of interaction can change from confrontational to cooperative. As respect for another's identity grows, individuals impose limits on their behavior to reflect that respect; their understanding of their own identities may even grow when they see themselves through others' eyes. As one understands this dynamic process of continuous interaction, one learns that power in part may emerge from careful and sensitive conduct of the process, rather than only from wielding material resources. The experiences in many countries at the end of the 1980s indeed saw parties with no raw power succeeding authorities who controlled the tanks and guns, the security apparatus, and government structures.

In short, if sustained dialogue is an instrument for societal change, then we need to begin with two essential factors: one is the citizen who is ready to become an agent of change; the other is a citizens' organization that can help create a space in which citizens can discover how to make change happen by using an instrument of change, such as sustained dialogue.

THE FIVE STAGES OF SUSTAINED DIALOGUE

Knowing that relationships cannot be changed in a single meeting, sustained dialogue is a process that continues through repeated meetings. As such meetings in the 1980s unfolded, we began to recognize that participants move through a discernible pattern of changing interactions. Ultimately, we conceptualized sustained dialogue as a five-stage process.

STAGE 1: DECIDING AND PREPARING TO ENGAGE Community members identify a problem, determine stakeholders, identify moderators and participants, and create terms of engagement and ground rules for the group. This is a period of exploratory dialogue. A process of change begins when individuals start talking with likeminded others about a problem they see as hurting their interests, when they try to create a sense of urgency about the problem, and when they awaken in others a sense that as individuals or as a group they can do something about it. We call this period of informally coming together to talk about a problem and what to do about it "dialogue about dialogue." This experience can produce four products:

First is a judgment that action is needed. They talk together about the problem and particularly how it affects each of them—how it hurts their interests. They begin to get their minds around—to name—the dimensions of the problem in human terms. They come to a sense that something must be done.

Second, a citizen decides that he or she must act. Citizens are spurred to engage in public life when they see a connection between a problem and their interests. The tipping point from recognizing that something must be done to an individual's decision to act seems to lie in citizens' discovery of something he or she personally can do that could make a difference and the belief that others are likely to join them in such action. Two major obstacles to collective action are lack of skills for collective work and belief in the inability or unwillingness of others to join in collective action. This exploratory space provides an experimental face-saving venue to begin acquiring skills of collective work and testing others' willingness and capacity for such work.

Third, citizens select an instrument for change. Together—either from their own initiative or after agreeing to work with a catalyst organization—they decide to use a particular instrument for change. There are many instruments for organizing a group's work together. We focus here on sustained dialogue, but we recognize that citizens must diagnose their own situation—name the problem that they must deal with—and choose an instrument suited to their purposes. For instance, in a relatively coherent community where people are able to talk, they may choose a collaborative problem-solving process. In conflictual situations, they may choose a process, such as sustained dialogue, that focuses on transforming the dysfunctional relationships that block open communication and collaboration.

Once these citizens have chosen an instrument, they must prepare to put the instrument they have chosen into practice: (1) They may form a team and divide the labor of getting started among them as an informal steering group. They need organizers, funding, perhaps governmental acquiescence, and trained moderators. (2) They select others they feel need to be involved and draw them in or prepare to invite them to join at the appropriate moment. (3) They seek intensive training in use of the instrument. (4) They set a time and place to begin and invite participants.

Fourth, citizens—perhaps working with the catalyst organization—create a formal space specifically designed for the change instrument they have chosen. In the case of sustained dialogue, now having completed stage 1, they will create a space in which they can systematically work through stages 2, 3, and 4 and from which they can move back into the community in stage 5.

STAGE 2: DOWNLOADING/MAPPING AND NAMING PROBLEMS AND RELATIONSHIPS Participants share their experiences related to the issue at hand, and together, with the guidance of two trained moderators, attempt to expand their own picture of the dynamics of their community. Their purposes are:

- to get out on the table the array of problems and relationships among them and to examine how those problems affect real interests;
- to share participants' personal experiences with the relationships that would need to be changed to resolve those problems; and
- to identify and choose the two or three problems on which participants will focus in-depth attention one at a time.

It may be difficult to share personal experiences involving racial or ethnic tensions, but this is key. Probing the dynamics of the relationships that cause problems is essential to changing those relationships.

STAGE 3: EXPLORING PROBLEMS/SETTING A DIRECTION FOR CHANGE

Participants identify two or three specific problems in the community, select one to analyze more deeply, and begin assessing whether there is a commitment and willingness for action. There is always a dual agenda:

First, they will probe one problem at a time to expose the relationship dynamics that create the problems, focusing on such questions as:

- What are the main elements of the problem? What is the problem behind the problem?
- Describe the main people or groups involved in this problem.
- How does this problem affect what you or your group value most? Can you explain this is in a personal story?

Second, participants suggest possible directions to take in tackling the problem. The purpose is not to detail a course of action but to frame broad choices.

Third, they will weigh those choices and try to come to a sense of direction they feel should guide next steps.

Fourth, after full discussion of each problem, participants should step back and take stock of where they are headed by asking:

- Where is the situation going? What future would we prefer?
- Would we like to change course? What are the costs?

- What changes in relationships would be needed to move to the kind of community that would deal effectively with this problem?
- Where could we find common ground for changing relationships?

The key question is whether participants are ready to work together to design a series of interactive steps that could change relationships. If that seems like too big a step to take right now, it is worth talking about why it is difficult.

STAGE 4: FORMING SOLUTIONS/SCENARIO BUILDING In a sense, the group is a microcosm of a larger community, and, by this stage, relationships within the group have changed. Figuratively, participants are no longer sitting across the table talking at one another; they are sitting side-by-side, thinking *together* about how to generate changes they all agree should occur. Their task is now to develop a series of interactive steps—a scenario— that can gradually change how groups feel about each other. To do this, they should:

- List the resources the larger community can draw on
- List the main obstacles to change; these can be feelings as well as practical factors
- List the steps to overcome each obstacle
- List who can take those steps. What steps could you persuade your group to take? What steps would you be personally responsible for?
- Now list those steps in an order to show both their sequence and how steps by different groups can interact

STAGE 5: ACTING TOGETHER The purpose here is to decide whether to take their scenario into the larger community and, if so, to develop practical ways the scenarios developed in stage 4 might be put into action.

- Do conditions in the community permit implementing the scenario?
- Do capacities exist for carrying it through?
- Who needs to take what steps?
- How can other potential actors be drawn into the scenario?[2]

The important overall point is that sustained dialogue is a process—not just a series of meetings. Participants learn that what happens between meetings is at least as important in the process of changing relationships as what happens in meetings. Participants must internalize the process if it is to change them and their relationships.

As participants work their way through stages 2 through 4, they learn several important things:

They learn to create a cumulative agenda. Questions left unanswered at the end of one meeting are thought about between meetings and shape the agenda for the next meeting. Participants learn that the instrument for change is not a series of meetings but a continuous process in which change is happening within them and among them wherever they are.

They learn to talk analytically and empathetically in dialogue rather than argumentatively in debate. They learn a different way of relating— collaboration and thinking together rather than confrontation.

They create a common body of knowledge. This goes beyond simply learning what the other thinks and what her or his position is to learning what the other considers really important and why. This kind of knowledge opens new doors to solving problems because it opens doors to transforming relationships.

Individuals develop capacities to become boundary spanners in communities, internalizing both practical skills as agenda setters, speakers, and analyzers and relational skills in bridging deep human divides.

They learn to design change together with the particular purpose of reaching outside their dialogue space to engage necessary elements of the larger community. In engaging the community, they build networks. Participants in sustained dialogue take their design for change to a larger scale. In doing so, they recognize that they have learned to work change in their own group and that in order to influence the larger environment that constrains them or could open doors to new opportunities, they need to connect with other likeminded groups and engage elements of the larger community. They move from their dialogue space back into the community. In doing so, they may create new spaces. Training can be an integral part of engaging the community. Training can create spaces where much of the thinking and planning for collective action can take place.

EVALUATING

A group engages in continuous evaluation as an integral part of its process. Once participants start acting in the community, they will constantly ask themselves, "How are we doing?" As they assess their progress, they will adjust course or design additional actions. At this point, others—including involved catalyst organizations—may also assess what is being or has been accomplished. They may use the five stages—as well as their own objectives—as a framework for evaluation.

Notes

1. Harwood (2005, 9): "A time when many Americans have turned away from the public arena."
2. For a fuller presentation of the stages see Saunders (1999, 98–145).

3

SUSTAINED DIALOGUE IN ACTION

Harold H. Saunders and Priya Narayan Parker

SUSTAINED DIALOGUE has been developed and tested in many circumstances over more than two decades. We have used it in zones of conflicts as varied as the Soviet-U.S. relationship; the civil war in the former Soviet republic of Tajikistan; transitional South Africa; the stalemated conflict in the area of Armenia, Azerbaijan, and Nagorno Karabakh; the interaction between the Muslim Arab world and the West; Iraq; and U.S. colleges and high schools.

We in IISD have conducted some of these dialogues ourselves among international or intranational adversaries. In other cases, we have trained local organizations to conduct dialogues in their own settings at a community level. The issues have ranged from race relations and youth violence to economic development and nation building. Each may focus on different component of relationship.

As noted in the chapter 2, the starting point for any effective sustained dialogue process is a shift in mindset of at least one concerned citizen. On university campuses, each sustained dialogue program started with a shift in the way an individual student viewed herself or himself within the context of race relations on campus—a shift from being a victim or observer of a racialized system to being an actor within that system. For the IISD-conducted Arab-American-European trilateral dialogue, a concerned Arab American believed she could create a space to improve relationships and understanding between these major regions, and she embarked on a two-year "dialogue about dialogue," to create that reality. In Harare, a citizen's organization reassessed its own "instrument for change," specifically a massive media campaign against youth violence, and, after concluding that such a plan would not work, decided to learn how to implement sustained dialogue to address youth violence.

The initial or preparatory stage of sustained dialogue—the "dialogue about dialogue"—has varied enormously from case to case, and the initial framing of the issue has influenced the development of the further stages of the process. Because the projects differ widely, it is important to keep in mind what Teddy Nemeroff—an American asked by the Institute for Democracy in South Africa to integrate sustained dialogue into its programs—refers to as the "essence of Sustained Dialogue" (Nemeroff 2004). Reflecting on his experience with different communities in South Africa, Nemeroff recognizes the need to keep open the possibility of combining different methodologies simultaneously within the sustained dialogue framework so as to support and complement the process while preserving that "essence." He continues:

> Each potential setting for a dialogue may require very different techniques for getting participants to speak openly about and change relationships. They may even require the incorporation of entirely new methodologies, such as IDASA's use of Appreciative Inquiry. The key is not what techniques are used, but rather that the process is directed through a specific series of stages and that these stages are focused on a transformation of relationships.

As sustained dialogue is applied in a growing variety of contexts, practitioners are constantly adjusting the tools and moderating style they use and the type of training that seems appropriate. However, in all cases, sustained dialogue is a process that serves as what another colleague has referred to as an "incubator for social change" (Slim 2004a). Sustained dialogue creates the opportunity for people to come together, build relationships across lines of difference, and think and work together to transform relationships and design change.

NATIONAL AND INTERNATIONAL
IISD-CONDUCTED DIALOGUES

TAJIKISTAN

The Inter-Tajik Dialogue, was an initiative of the Dartmouth Conference Task Force on Regional Conflicts. The Dartmouth Conference was a group of influential U.S. and Soviet citizens that met periodically from 1960 through the end of the Cold War. In 1982, they formed task forces to meet between plenaries. After the dissolution of the Soviet Union in 1991, the Regional Conflicts Task Force continued to meet. One of their projects, designed in 1992, was to "see whether a group could be formed in the middle of a civil war—Tajikistan—that can learn to shape a peace process for their own country" (Saunders 2005, 127). Meeting for the first time in Moscow in 1993, the group then convened regularly in thirty-six dialogue meetings over the next ten years. Saunders, as cochair of the Dartmouth Task Force and comoderator of what came to be known as the Inter-Tajik Dialogue within the Framework of the Dartmouth Conference, describes the development of the dialogue group in four periods (Saunders 2005, 127–30).

First, the initial six meetings between March 1993 and April 1994 "played a significant role in opening the door to formal negotiations mediated by the United Nations in May 1994. Three participants in the dialogue became members of the negotiating teams while remaining in the dialogue." Second, when negotiations began, the group decided to focus on a developing political process for reconciliation among Tajikistani citizens. Some of the ideas they developed found their way into the peace treaty. Third, five dialogue participants became members of the National Reconciliation Commission, which was mandated by the peace treaty in 1997 to "work through detailed solutions to problems that had not been resolved in the peace agreement." "The Dialogue itself also became a space where senior members of the civil society and citizens closely associated with officials could talk informally about critical issues" (Saunders 2005, 129). In each meeting, they normally produced a joint memorandum on an important issue.

Finally, in 2000, the group formed its own nongovernmental organization, the Public Committee for Democratic Processes. It decided to institute a network of public issues forums; a national project to develop a curriculum, a textbook, and teaching materials for a course in resolving conflict and peace building; committees to tackle community economic development; and "mini-dialogues" in seven regions of the country to deal with "state, religion, and society" in the only country in Central Asia with a legitimate Islamic Party.

The Inter-Tajik Dialogue in the course of its thirty-six meetings, repeatedly cycled through the sustained dialogue stages, mapping and naming the problems and relationships in the country as they changed over time, selecting specific areas for change, and writing joint memoranda on the significant national issues of the moment. The participants truly became what Saunders often refers to as "a mind at work in the middle of a country making itself." IISD vice president Randa Slim (2004b, 4) reflects:

> The Public Committee in Tajikistan presents for us the best example of joint action [from a sustained dialogue]. It is an NGO that grew out of a sustained dialogue process and has now become an important and influential mediating organization in the peace-building process in Tajikistan. They make our best case for how an SD process became an incubator for social change at the national level through the founding of an organizational change agent that has taken upon itself the task of establishing tens of similar other organizations around the country that are dedicated to the same mission of transforming the character of the relationships in Tajikistan through dialogue and peace-building work.

One of the reasons for the Inter-Tajik Dialogue group's success was the work of the participants outside the dialogue group. Over the ten years of the process, participants in the dialogue were simultaneously involved with official national negotiation and planning processes and in general had the capacity to take what was spoken of informally to the formal political processes. During these peace negotiations, the comoderators shared their analytical memoranda with the UN mediator and with their foreign ministries. In 2006, the national dialogue was reconstituted with the president's approval to take stock of Tajikistan's social, economic, and political development and to set goals for the next seven-year presidential term.

ARAB-AMERICAN-EUROPEAN DIALOGUE

As mentioned earlier, the AAED started with an individual "who [was] concerned with the situation at hand and wanted to do something about it" (2004b, 5). She and others felt a need to open a dialogue channel outside government among influential citizens in these three regions regarding the relationship between Islam and "the West." "In the Middle East case, the preparatory 'dialogue about dialogue' went on for two years before potential participants agreed to attend the first dialogue session. During these two years, the conveners needed to educate some of the groups targeted for engagement about the sustained dialogue process" (2004b, 3)

The AAED has met for three days three times a year to focus on building relationships and discussing current issues most relevant to the political, social, and economic relations among the three regions. While stage 1, or "deciding to engage," went on for two years, the dialogue group spent one year in stage 2, downloading, venting, and sharing experiences and thoughts with one another regarding this relationship. As the group began mapping and naming the relationships among and within all three major regions, they established an executive committee to create cumulative agendas from meeting to meeting. These allowed the group to set a direction and begin to engage collectively in a deeper analysis of the nature of the relationships and issues. By the end of the second full year of dialogue meetings, group members were beginning to enter into the public realm, writing joint articles, visiting one another's countries for meetings with nonofficials, and thinking about how better to use their social capital as well as a nuanced understanding of the relationships in order to have an influence on the international debate.

The key to the initial accomplishments of dialogues like this is, first, change within and among the participants themselves. As relationships among individuals from key constituencies from somewhat conflicting, or at least perceived to be conflicting groups change, participants build what has come to be called "social capital." Social capital can be defined as the "norms and networks that enable people to act collectively" (Woolcock and Narayan 2000). Through convening over and over again citizens from different political backgrounds who have both legitimacy within strikingly different movements as well as the "ear of the government," dialogue processes are able to play an increasingly influential role in shaping the international discourse. Especially when relations and understanding between societies decline, sustained dialogues such as these create more open linkages outside of government to build the capacity to create new options in a growingly interdependent world.

COMMUNITY-LEVEL ISSUE-BASED DIALOGUES IN SOUTHERN AFRICA

In addition to conducting dialogues the International Institute for Sustained Dialogue works with citizen's organizations around the world to help them develop the capacity to conduct sustained dialogue programs in local communities. Between August 2003 and July 2006, for example, an experienced leader from the Sustained Dialogue Campus Network worked with the Institute for Democracy in South Africa to establish a peace-building program, called the Dialogue Unit, aimed at building the capacity of citizens to resolve their own conflicts in a way that supports the growth of democracy in Southern Africa (Nemeroff and Adams 2005, 2). The Dialogue Unit has used sustained dialogue as a way of engaging community leaders and has implemented it in a variety of mostly community-based contexts. Three of their most successful projects are described in this section: a sustained dialogue to help consciously explore the problematic relationship between legal and illegal traders in conflict over space and resources at a trading post; a project to address youth violence in Harare, Zimbabwe; and an initiative to examine the role of a process like sustained dialogue in economic development in rural KwaZulu Natal.

SUSTAINED DIALOGUE AT THE DENNEBOOM INTERCHANGE   The Denneboom Interchange is a train station in Mamelodi, a formerly black township just outside of Pretoria that serves as a major transportation hub for the area. A facility that was originally intended to host 380 traders has become a business area for approximately 1,200 informal traders or street hawkers (Nemeroff and Ratlou 2005, 2):

> The traders that have been allocated these stalls are officially registered with the government and are required to pay rent for their space. The rest are operating in the facility illegally and have taken up much of the available open space . . . the numbers of illegal traders have grown rapidly in the last three years . . . the consequences of these numbers has been a decrease in economic viability for all traders operating in the facility as the business with the commuters has spread thinner, a deteriorating business environment for other groups operating there, and an increase in crime and violence as ever more closely packed traders have come into conflict with each other or other facility users.

To make matters more complicated, the local government created the Local Economic Development department, whose role, among other things, was to regulate the activities of the informal traders, disrupting the formerly self-regulated system among the traders. "The distorting effects of government regulation broke down the community's ability to resolve its own problems by denying them ownership, and creating divisions based on interests" (Nemeroff and Ratlou 2005, introduction). The Institute for Democracy in South Africa worked with local community members to create a sustained dialogue group involving the key stakeholders in the community with the aim of helping "facility users (transport operators, informal traders, passengers, and local political leaders) and the government officials responsible for managing it . . . build more effective working relationships so that they can better achieve development and prosperity" (Nemeroff and Ratlou 2005, 2).

The Denneboom project illustrates the importance of an insider-outsider relationship. The dialogue was comoderated by the IDASA sustained dialogue project coordinator Teddy Nemeroff, an expert in sustained dialogue methodology but not a member of the Mamelodi community, and Richard Ratlou, a longtime activist and resident in Mamelodi with "extensive experience dealing with community level politics, public participation in governance, and conflict management" (Nemeroff 2005d, 1). Together they formed a strong moderator team by combining their areas of expertise with local knowledge and connections. Ratlou describes one such meeting:

> During that meeting the official was having trouble understanding Teddy's explanation of how SD could help the issues at Denneboom. He could understand the process but didn't see how it made sense for local conditions. I therefore broke in and explained how I understood many of the governance problems in South Africa and how SD could contribute to the facility and this made him willing to come on board. This allowed us to meet with other officials and politicians to secure buy in.
>
> (NEMEROFF 2005D, 2)

Ratlou describes the sustained dialogue process: "Because we don't take decisions but continue discussions, it allows us to see how people's opinions change over time. It also gives us time to understand how people operate, seeing whether they are honest and what agendas they are pursuing at the dialogue and in the community as a whole" (Nemeroff 2005d, 2–3). Having met over a sustained period of time, Nemeroff describes the progress at the beginning of 2006:

> Dynamic changes towards greater transparency and engagement at the Denneboom Interchange. . . . Through a series of both highly substantive analytical conversations and some very heated and emotional arguments, this process has secured a greater commitment by government to address issues and work with citizens at the facility, engaged previously marginalized

groups, exposed leaders that were not contributing productively to the situation, and identified a number of specific steps that can be taken to improve management. This dialogue has also opened the door for similar processes at other train stations in the Pretoria area.

(NEMEROFF 2005F, 13)

The Denneboom sustained dialogue was a good example of a sustained dialogue project that brought people together across lines of difference to focus on very immediate and practical issues facing the community. Through the sustained interaction, the participants themselves start interacting differently and their relationships begin to change. The process itself develops a better understanding between parties, as well as a greater capacity and willingness to want to solve problems that serves multiple interests and betters the community as a whole.

ZIMBABWE: YOUTH VIOLENCE A Zimbabwe-based organization wanted to address the problem of youth violence in that nation. Initially planning a countrywide media campaign to address the issue, they organized a coalition of fourteen local NGOs to support the program. However, as the program progressed, the organizers realized that their original plan for a media campaign was not going to be feasible in the current political situation, and they had to change course midway. The organizers decided that they would be most effective by working with the youth directly and wanted to create safe spaces for affected youth to come together to create new patterns of relationships and address the growing problem of youth violence.

In May 2004, three Zimbabwean nongovernmental organizations, an Italian international NGO, the Coordinating Committee of the Organizations for Voluntary Service, the Zimbabwean partner the Amani Trust, and the IDASA began an initiative to conduct sustained dialogue groups to address issues of youth violence in Zimbabwe. Together, they designed a sustained dialogue initiative that involved launching eight youth dialogue groups simultaneously throughout the city of Harare, to "reduce the political exploitation of youth and strengthen their self-reliance by engaging key local leaders in dialogue. . . . They have engaged 120 youth leaders in Harare, from across the socio-economic and political spectrum, to build relationships, better understand issues of concern to them, and to develop actions they can take to improve their lives and the lives of their peers" (Nemeroff 2005b, 1).

IDASA first conducted training with twenty-four activists who divided into eight "Initiating Teams," each of which set out to assemble a dialogue group of fifteen youths, based on specific criteria. The initiating period lasted four months, and once the group was formed, moderators were selected and trained by IDASA, which also created ongoing support and training systems for the moderators involved. Each youth group selected two of the following topics for discussion: unemployment, HIV/AIDS, the role of youth in nation building, political tolerance, and delivery of public services. They held monthly half-day meetings at venues in their communities. IDASA also conducted two further advanced training workshops for moderators during the project.

This project took place under extraordinarily difficult circumstances, but the groups continued to meet and progress through the five stages of sustained dialogue. In a summary progress report, Nemeroff cited the following project results: increased knowledge about issues discussed, increased sense of agency, strengthened relationships among participants and willingness to "agree to disagree," increased sense of the value of talking and knowledge of conflict-management techniques. Additionally, he notes, "these significant impacts on the participants have led to some important results for the youth communities they were drawn from, including increased youth leadership, the mitigation of community conflicts and youth violence, and the development of plans for addressing community challenges" (Nemeroff 2005b, 6).

In September 2005 the group organized an international conference in Siavonga, Zambia, to share findings and develop future action plans, which three members of IISD attended. As of this writing, the Committee of the Organizations for Voluntary Service has decided to continue the project and has gained funding for the next phase.

KWAZULU NATAL: ECONOMIC DEVELOPMENT   The idea of using sustained dialogue to focus on relationships affecting economic development in South Africa was first explored in South Africa's rural province of KwaZulu Natal. "This project was initiated . . . by two local organizations that realized past efforts at development had failed and they concluded that to successfully develop Ethalaneni and the surrounding villages they would first need to cultivate among residents a capacity to concert" (Nemeroff 2005g, 2).[1] Ramon Daubon and Harold Saunders discuss the importance of a dialogue process that engages citizens from within local communities to develop a "capacity to concert" around issues of importance to them. "People and their capacity to orchestrate their own development are the foundation of sustainability—that economic development is not only about economics but also about people's capacity to concert" (Daubon and Saunders 2002, 179). Realizing that outside funding and donors were, for the most part, not succeeding in reducing the level of poverty, some people began looking for new options to engage the poor in the decision-making and relationship-building processes of development. The idea now emerging is to have local community members engage in a dialogue around their own needs, desires, and relationships, meanwhile building the social capital that recent studies have shown to be necessary for long-term growth (Narayan 2000).

With this idea in mind, Nemeroff writes: "A group contacted us about this training because of its conviction that dysfunctional relationships and low level conflict were preventing the community from advancing. . . . Essentially, the community lacks a certain kind of social capital. Community members lack an understanding of the long term goals of development and a realization that cooperation is in everyone's interest."[2] Conducting a series of iterative trainings with village leaders, chiefs, youth, and women simultaneously, an insider-outsider team helped the community to begin building the bridges among the various groups and to better understand how they as poor people can become assets in development. It seemed that one of the biggest impediments to development was internal jealousies and an unwillingness to cooperate among different factions of the community with outsider-funded development initiatives. "Poor communities in which relationships are an obstacle to development often appear to lack the self-awareness to realize that is the case. . . . People there see each other as the problem rather than their way of relating."[3] The trainings, all conducted in Zulu, brought together all facets of the village, changing the power dynamics within the village itself as the dialogue participants recognized how destructive their relationships had been.

This project included a series of village-based dialogue groups in the rural Nkandla district. The dialogues led to a range of community-development projects as well as "a change of mindset about what is required to develop the community with a greater recognition of the need for local responsibility" (Nemeroff 2005f, 2).

SUSTAINED DIALOGUE CAMPUS NETWORK

The Sustained Dialogue Campus Network owes its growth to concerned students finding sustained dialogue a useful approach to effecting change on their campuses, specifically to improving campus racial climates. The mission of SDCN is to "help university and high school students create a healthy and open climate on their campuses. SDCN trains, mentors, and connects student leaders who work through dialogue to design cohesive, engaged and diverse communities nationwide" ("About SDCN," http://www.sdcampusnetwork.org/). As more students initiate programs on their campuses, SDCN, directed by former student leaders experienced in the process, facilitates the sharing of the common body of experience students have developed on how to initiate and moderate sustained dialogue. SDCN program directors enable students at each new school initiative to learn from previous mistakes, challenges, and practices. All of the materials created for sustained dialogue on college campuses, though based on the initial work and writings of Saunders in A *Public Peace Process* (1999), have been written by students who have started programs, including the moderator manuals, initiator guides, and training curricula.

The first student-run sustained dialogue began at Princeton University in 1999. Since then, students have assisted one another in starting new programs on eighteen campuses, as of the date of this writing. The SDCN was established in 2002 and now helps interested students learn the skills and tools they need to start their own sustained dialogue programs.

The "dialogue about dialogue" process on campuses is often much shorter than in other communities. Many students report that they heard about sustained dialogue as a useful "instrument of change" when they addressed concerns to a campus administrator or faculty member. Since administrators' inter-university networks are usually wider than students', the former are more likely to know about approaches at different schools, and. at this point, many have heard of sustained dialogue.

Once students have contacted SDCN for more information and have decided that they want to use dialogue as their tool for change, the students enter stage 1. SDCN program directors and graduate volunteers then train students in initiating the process, connect them to other student leaders, and coach them through the process of starting such an initiative. SDCN and student leaders also organize an annual national conference for sustained dialogue leaders, moderators, and supporting administrators from all campuses to come together for a weekend at a host university. The purpose is to connect, share, and learn about one another's efforts; to receive additional training; to help one another with current program challenges; and to improve the various programs.

The program directors, Clark Herndon and Tessa Garcia (2005, 2), wrote:

> Among the most important principles of the Campus Network's philoso-phies is the belief that students should be the ones who are the agents of change in their communities. SDCN takes very seriously its mission to train, mentor and connect, and draws a sharp line of distinction between providing a curriculum for students to follow and training them to do for themselves what only they have the power to do. This philosophy has shaped the way trainings are conducted, the way SDCN Program Directors interact with students, and the way the relationships between the organization and the program exist. Students are taught to analyze and internalize the SD theory so that they might be able to apply it to their situations however they see fit under the guidance (and not behind the *leadership*) of experienced SD practitioners.

Institutions of higher education share many features that make transfer-ring sustained dialogue from one campus community to another relatively straightforward. Typically, the sustained dialogue program has developed into a recognized student organization on campus that recruits students and administrators from diverse backgrounds to come together for an academic year of sustained dialogue, in most cases to address race relations on campus. The student leadership forms groups of twelve to fourteen participants based on a variety of criteria, with two trained student moderators for each group. The groups meet once every two weeks for two hours through the course of the year. Most programs develop similar patterns that correspond to the practicalities of the academic year. For example, leadership teams usually spend the summer and the first month of the school year in stage 1. Once students identify and recruit participants and form the dialogue groups, the groups meet regularly throughout the school year, each maintaining its own membership composition, exploring relationships and the dynamics of race on their campus. Toward the spring semester, groups begin thinking of ac-tion projects they can take to influence campus racial climate.

Sustained dialogue groups on campuses face a major challenge in that the student community in which they seek to make changes loses, and gains, one-fourth of its membership every year. Nevertheless, a number of different action projects have emerged from campus sustained dialogue programs, including education campaigns and forums, creative "mixed" social events that challenge students to change ingrained patterns of interaction, high school sustained dialogue mentoring programs, projects that address institutional memory and issues of retribution, and, of course, the creation of many more dialogue groups to involve as many students as possible in a new type of conversation and a new way to learn about race and racism—from one another.

RELATIONSHIPS IN ACTION

In sum, it is useful to come back to a point made briefly earlier: an important insight in the application of the concept of relationship as an operational tool lies in the recognition that in each situation where sustained dialogue may be used, different components of relationship may be uppermost among the causes of conflict. Nemeroff (2005a, 2) notes: "Perhaps the most significant distinguishing feature between one issue area and another is the relative importance of specific elements of the relationships being discussed. Different kinds of relationships require different techniques of moderating and are likely to yield different types of results from dialogue processes."

For example, a major focus of dialogues on college campuses surrounds identity, perceptions/misperceptions and stereotypes, and the sharing and exploration of one's racial identity. There is less focus on the parties' "interests," per se. On the other hand, in Denneboom the major focus was on interests and patterns of interaction. In that case, one of the major problems at the trading post was the underlying personal and professional relationship between the various parties—lack of trust. It was therefore vital to talk explicitly about the patterns of interaction and how each group interacts with and responds to others based, for instance, on who puts whose stand where. What are the rules of interacting in the market? In short, the concept of relationship not only helps practitioners better understand the dynamics of the situation; it also helps them focus the dialogue and shape its goals.

CHALLENGES

New challenges inspire new experiments and new solutions. As of this writing, there are four major challenges facing the practice of sustained dialogue:

1. How does a practitioner diagnose whether sustained dialogue is an appropriate instrument for change?

In discussing the work of sustained dialogue with practitioners of other instruments of conflict resolution, they often say, "You are doing the same thing we are doing." Our response is usually, "No, we are not, and it's good that we are doing different things. We need to understand better which approaches work best in different situations." As practitioners we need to increase greatly our capacity to diagnose a situation and determine the appropriate instrument for change. In the case of sustained dialogue, our goal is not to sell a tool but rather to provide an approach that will help citizens transform their relationships and develop the capacity to design change in their communities on the basis of a thorough understanding of what the situation calls for. It is a continuing challenge to determine when to present sustained dialogue as the tool to use and when to direct people elsewhere.

Sustained dialogue seems to be a useful approach in situations where relationships are strained or broken and people feel the need to work together across lines of difference to address issues of common concern so they can hurdle the relational obstacles to joint action. How can one determine whether indeed that is the problem?

One helpful approach is for an "insider-outsider" team to conduct an assessment of the community. To determine whether sustained dialogue is appropriate in a specific situation, the assessment team should include community "insiders" who have experienced and understand the dynamics of the current situation, and an "outsider" who is familiar with the sustained dialogue project and can be more objective about the specific community and its problems.

One colleague describes his thought process when diagnosing a situation to determine whether the situation is ripe for sustained dialogue: "I no longer think, will dialogue work in this situation? Rather I ask myself, how could we use dialogue in this situation and is it worth the time and effort, or is there another approach that would be more effective?"[4] It is sometimes easier to determine when sustained dialogue is inappropriate than when it is appropriate. For example, because dialogue demands a sense of equality within the group, it is extremely difficult for dialogue even to begin, or to create any sense of urgency that dialogue is worthwhile, when the power imbalance between two groups of people is too large. Those in control may see no need to talk to "them" or may see no need or have no desire to change existing relationships. People on both sides need to feel a sense of personal interest and some likelihood of change before they are willing to engage.

Currently, some time is being spent in South Asia reviewing situations in which people see no possible "political solution" and are seeking justice through the legal system, which is inherently confrontational. Some people argue that a dialogue process aimed at reconciliation can in fact be counterproductive for the community, depending on the timing of the initiative. We continue to learn from experience.

2. How can sustained dialogue be introduced in a way that strengthens citizens' capacity to sustain and enlarge their initiatives rather than drowning them?

People are usually attracted to sustained dialogue as an approach precisely because it is a *sustained* intervention.[5] However, any type of sustained effort takes time, resources, and commitment. Often, citizen groups decide to engage in dialogue because they realize their current efforts are not working because of relationships blocked within the group. In that case, the initiators must be careful in balancing internal processes of change with the need for external help. To date, the only experiences IISD has had in fully introducing and transferring sustained dialogue to another organization is with IDASA and—perhaps the challenge is similar—through SDCN.

3. How can the transformation of relationships in the dialogue room generate change in the larger community?

As a dialogue progresses and participants in the sustained dialogue group begin transforming themselves, they become aware of this dilemma. It usually arises when someone asks the question, "What can we *do* about it?" Participants begin to brainstorm different scenarios of action in stage 4. They discuss the interdependent steps members of the group might take in order to implement a plan. Finally, they develop their plan of action and have to take it into the community. Depending on the context, the groups often face a number of different challenges at this stage.

The first issue the group often has to address is what some refer to as "reentry." In many cases, the dialogue group can initially meet without many people knowing about it. But as soon as the group attempts to create change outside of its own circle, its members have to address their communities. Sometimes, the participants are seen as "selling out" to another community for engaging in the first place. Groups in conflict tend often to demonize the "other," and a dialogue process can threaten a group's sense of self-identity.

Many leaders resist engaging with other groups for fear of compromising their own group identity.

A second challenge in generating change in the larger community lies in the problem of scale. While the size of the community varies greatly (on college campuses it may be as small as 2,300, as in the case of Dickinson College, whereas in Tajikistan the group was influencing a process that affected a national population of about 7 million, and in the Arab-American-European dialogue, the "communities" are entire regions of the world), the size of the sustained dialogue group is still the same (about fourteen people). Groups have to think creatively to use the social capital they have been able to create through the sustained dialogue process in such a way as to effect change in the larger community.

There are several ways to address the problem of scale. One is to create multiple simultaneous dialogue groups. When the problem to be addressed lies broadly in the relationships among groups, this approach is often necessary, though it brings with it its own challenges. For example, at both Princeton University and the University of Virginia, after the first year of efforts, students engaged in the process decided that the best way to change the racial climate was to engage more students in the sustained dialogue process. Five years later at the University of Virginia the students had formed an organization that identifies, selects, and trains new moderators every year and currently runs fifteen to twenty dialogue groups. However, experience shows that it is difficult to maintain the quality of the dialogue groups and moderators as the numbers increase. The more groups the student leaders have to organize, the more moderators they have to train, and the less able student leaders are to monitor the groups and coach the moderators through the year.

Another way to address scale comes in the initial period of participant identification and group formation. Initiators should recruit participants who both reflect the different perspectives of the communities involved and also have wide "circles of influence." The wider the reach of each potential participant, the easier it will be to influence change on a greater scale. IISD vice president Randa Slim explains: "Each SD participant operates within a small circle of influence composed of followers/colleagues/constituents and we have by now firm evidence that learning and skills gained by the SD participant get shared with his/her immediate circle of influence" (Slim 2005, 6). During initiator training, we often tell people that stage 1 is the easiest to talk about and explain and the hardest to carry out effectively. In the Arab-American-European dialogue, Dr. Slim spent two years laying the groundwork for the group and building personal relationships with participants, just to convince them to engage in the process. In the case of Tajikistan, initiators interviewed one hundred Tajikistani citizens before selecting their first ten participants. While participants must by definition be actors *outside of government*, it may be important, especially in national and international dialogue groups, that the participants have the "ear of the government," as well as other influential groups.

4. How can it be shown that sustained dialogue works, that there are identifiable links between the process and specific changes in the community?

Conceptually, there are three ways of approaching the evaluation of sustained dialogue: by reviewing the conduct of the five stages in terms of their own objectives; by assessing the impact of the process on participants and their capacity as citizen actors; and by measuring the change that occurs in the community.

An example of the last would be an assessment of student racial climate on a campus before and after the sustained dialogue process; some work along these lines is underway. An inherent problem with developing evaluation tools is that the dialogue itself must be an open-ended process, without specific goals from the beginning. Goals must be generated within the dialogue itself. We have found that stating what effect the dialogue will have often limits the thinking of both the group and the moderators.

Within sustained dialogue we have separated the process into two separate approaches: monitoring and evaluation. We have defined monitoring as "an on-going systematic procedure for checking the effectiveness of dialogue implementation and to recommend changes to improve performance," and evaluation as "a systematic assessment of the design, execution and effectiveness of the dialogue process to address problems identified by the community" (Nemeroff 2005e, 1). While we have developed some tools to do both, there are major limitations, particularly on the evaluation side—it is notoriously difficult to attribute causation in social and political matters. There are, moreover, challenges in capturing data, high costs in making comprehensive assessments, and a danger that assessment will by itself disrupt the intervention. Current efforts focus on evaluating each phase of the process within a theory of change, i.e., how initiators create the space, how the space creates leaders for peace, and then how the leaders build peace in their community.

In any case, it is clear that both the evaluation and the monitoring system must be embedded into the design of the dialogue process. Ideally, moderators can be trained to self-monitor within the design of the project.

Any political process is the product of continuous experimentation. So it has been, is, and will be with sustained dialogue as we respond to these challenges—and hopefully many more to come.

Notes

1. Nemeroff refers to Daubon and Saunders (2002).
2. E-mail from Teddy Nemeroff to Hal Saunders and Ramon Daubon, February 7, 2005.
3. Ibid.
4. Conversation with Teddy Nemeroff, Pretoria, South Africa.
5. "Sustained Dialogue separates itself from other projects that seek to ameliorate ethnic and racial conflict in a very simple regard: it is sustained" (see Nemeroff and Tukey, this volume).

4

SUSTAINED DIALOGUE AND PUBLIC DELIBERATION: MAKING THE CONNECTION

David Robinson

THE KEY CONCERN in this chapter is the potential contribution of deliberation to building social capital. This topic involves three principal questions:

1. How to deal with situations where ordinary citizens (let alone those who are disadvantaged or marginalized) have lost the capacity to engage meaningfully in the process of making decisions about issues of concern to them.

2. What to do about situations in which people are isolated from the talk through which it is possible to make sense of the world and to effectively test norms and values and implement (positive and negative) sanctions, that is, when they have lost the ability to sanction others (individuals, groups or organizations). This function has largely been moved from citizens to the state sector and to a range of officials and professionals.

3. How ordinary citizens should respond to increasing diversity (in terms of ethnicity, culture, religion, and status) where this disconnection is repeated within each group and where there is also considerable lack of trust among groups.

Such disconnections are often experienced by members of the fragmented citizenry within an increasingly "organized" and "managed" society where their actions are constrained by two major influences: the political state, and "professionals." Residents of the United States have seen recently one of the range of responses in the "Tea Party" movement. Residents of Great Britain, France, Germany, and other countries, including New Zealand, have, from time to time, experienced similar disruptions. In a situation of complete (or more complete) social capital these disconnections tend to disappear. Encouraging a deliberative (and ongoing or sustained) form of discourse within and among groups marks a major step in moving toward more complete systems of social capital in which citizens can engage in meaningful decision making—a form of deliberative democracy.

For the better part of the past decade, our research group has been investigating the nature of social capital in Maori and non-Maori society in New Zealand. Our work has indicated that there are considerable differences in the way in which social capital is configured and used in Maori society. This reflects the different worldviews that exist in different cultural groups. This has helped us to understand the overall social environment in which people interact and where social capital is created and used.

The "free" space formed by civil society—which third-sector researchers are so keen on—within which people interact and where social capital is created, is constrained by culture and history.[1] These vary even within an apparently cohesive society such as New Zealand's. In this context, "culture" does not refer simply to ethnic groups. We are also concerned with "medical culture" and the culture of "professionals," that is, cultures that create and sustain norms and values that are dominant in particular situations.

Although social capital can appear to be a complex concept, in essence it is simply the outcome of networks of interaction and relationships: the social dividend gained from meeting, talking, and acting with others. There are numerous published definitions of social capital—though they all refer to some combination of norms and networks. The OECD defines social capital as "networks together with shared norms, values and understandings that facilitate co-operation within or among groups" (Cote and Healy 2001). The IPS says social capital involves "the collection of resources that an individual or a group has access to through their membership of an ongoing network of mutual acquaintance. Features of this social structure, such as relationships, norms and social trust, help develop co-ordination and co-operation for common benefit" (Robinson 1997).

Much of the emphasis by researchers such as Robert Putnam on the measurement of social capital has been on levels of membership in voluntary associations and associated networks. However, as the OECD and IPS definitions indicate, it is also important to understand the nature of those networks and how norms (and sanctions) change over time. This is why we have placed our interest in deliberation and sustained dialogue within a broader social capital framework. These networks cannot effectively maintain, build, and make use of social capital without the associated factors of knowledge, trust, and the certainty of sanctions (certainty that behavior will be appropriately rewarded or punished), that is, that people will behave as expected.

Social capital networks provide an opportunity for "checking out" such assumptions and for checking out risk—whether people are likely to act in the way that they promise or that is expected of them. What degree of risk is involved in taking a particular action? Using a social capital framework can lead to redefining some apparent externalities as desired outcomes and they can become internalized as intended effects of an action.

Aspects that we have considered within a social capital framework include the *functions* of social capital: the purposes to which networks and trust are put; the *activities* carried out in maintaining and using social capital: how it is built; the *places* where the maintenance and use of social capital happens; and the *processes* that best enable these actions to take place.

Four key functions of social capital include:

- Processing information
- Assessing risks and opportunities
- "Checking out" the trustworthiness of others (individuals and agencies) and assessing the legitimacy of their mandate
- Assessing, maintaining, and amending norms and sanctions

Activities carried out in building social capital include accessing and sharing information and interacting and engaging in dialogue in order to carry out the above functions. Activities that nurture social capital can occur in spaces created through both formal and informal interaction. The existence of a wide range of networks of association (including voluntary community organizations) is necessary to enable these activities.

A variety of social processes build and use social capital. One of the most important of these is dialogue. The existence of appropriate spaces and the interaction of people within them are not sufficient for the development of social capital. Forms of dialogue are required that enable an equal exchange of information and ideas, that reveal people's interests and provide the opportunity to build "public knowledge," that is, to move from public opinion (a collection of individual opinions) to public (collective) knowledge.

In our social capital framework we have identified the key elements or points within a social capital field. What is now required is better understanding of the most effective "connections" among these points. For example, what kind of communication most effectively enables the equal and open sharing of information and the revelation of interest and externalities?

A system with high levels of social capital provides the potential for the exchange of information and the accompanying dialogue that enables effective sanctioning and testing of norms. At the same time, deliberative processes, including sustained dialogue, provide the essential connections within the social capital field that are needed to enable the actualization of potential social capital.

Our understanding of social capital and the focus of our research has evolved and developed since the mid-1990s. We have gone from an initial interest in networks of voluntary associations with high levels of generalized trust to focusing on spaces for discussion and deliberation and relationships among actors that created a capacity to act and opportunities for interaction with the certainty of sanctions and the knowledge of interests. Most recently, our primary concern has been on forms of communication.

The growing emphasis on process rather than structure resulted in exploring how people interact; the social environment that these interactions take place in can be seen to consist of three key elements:

- The underlying worldview (based on culture, religion, and history) that influences how people see the world in which they act: their beliefs
- The overarching social, legal, and political environment that forms a kind of roof or shelter that encloses our interactions and sets and bounds the rules
- The intermediary processes that takes place (underpinned by our worldviews and constrained by the social environment) between them; the form of communication and discourse through which we interact with one another and with our environment: our behavior

These elements are interconnected both historically and in practice. To build, maintain, and use social capital requires input and a response at all three levels: beliefs, rules, and behavior. In considering the nature and importance of trust (defined as a form of belief or certainty), it is important to note that in practice trust is constrained by culture (including history and religion).While relationships and interactions are constrained within specific sectors of society (or within particular communities) by cultural factors, the social environment is likely to be contested both by differing worldviews and through different forms of interaction. So society is at the same time constrained (within groups) and contested (in terms of the forms of structure and rules).

Our work with Maori and in the health arena indicates that in New Zealand, society-wide "rules" are determined by the dominant (European) culture, which then imposes specific forms of structure (including appropriate or recognized forms of NGO or community association) on everyone in New Zealand society. This places the core of social capital (the networks and relationships) in the center of a struggle between differing worldviews constrained by a dominant set of rules. It is not clear how this social capital space can provide a way of negotiating between those worldviews and the dominant rules.

In this context, we have tested the use of a deliberative approach as a preferred form of communication and interaction, and we suggest it is most conducive to the growth of social capital within a system spread over several different localities and communities. Emphasizing deliberative communication is a way to build the confidence of participants and create a form of generalized trust. That is, confidence in one's ability (e.g., to have a seat at the economic-development table, to give oneself permission to participate) builds belief in the outcome of a process and trust that things will take place as expected.

At the 2002 ISTR conference in Cape Town I suggested that social capital could be envisaged as having the nature of a field within which actions take place (Robinson and Robinson 2002). Such a field requires connectors to enable the flow of social capital as well as nodes or places where it is generated (see figure 4.1). Complete social capital using a deliberative form of communication then can act as a "superconductor," providing instantaneous knowledge of others' interests. There are many ways in which information can be exchanged and through which social capital can be built.

Figure 4.1 raises a number of questions, including:

- What is the nature of the "lines" or "wires" that connect the elements of social capital in figure 4.1?
- What are the most effective forms of "talk" for each purpose?

As with electrical conductors there are varying forms of efficiency in these "conductors." With electricity there may be a loss in transmission, e.g., through heat buildup in an iron or copper wire, while a fiber optic cable may provide a more nearly instantaneous form of transmission. An amplifier

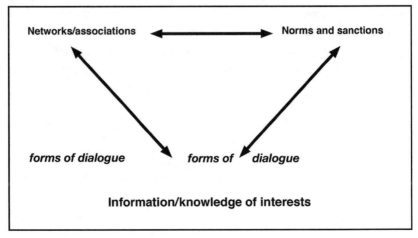

FIGURE 4.1

may be required to boost low levels of energy to the degree that they can be of use or a tuner used to remove static.

We can liken a deliberative process to a form of "filter" that carries out these functions in a social capital field. In order to move from absolute information (overload) to adequate and appropriate information from which the knowledge required to achieve a particular purpose can be constructed, the social capital current needs to pass through a "filter" that will enable the retention of only useful information. This filter (or tuner that can "tune out" the static and amplify the relevant data) can take the form of a deliberative community. The useful knowledge is extracted/created through this form of interaction.

Therefore we need places, participants, and a process for connecting the key social capital factors. As has been noted, much emphasis has been placed on the "place" where social capital is developed and used. Less attention has been given to exploring the nature of the processes through which it is transmitted, through which information is turned into useful knowledge, especially knowledge of others' interests. We suggest that the preferred form of communication, the most effective form of connector, is a deliberative form of discourse. However, although in an ideal (or complete) form of social capital, information would flow instantaneously and we would all have accurate knowledge of the interests of those we are working with and consequently would have good reason for trusting or not trusting other individuals or groups, in reality social capital is only present in varying degrees of incompleteness. These incomplete forms of social capital have been categorized by Michael Woolcock in his work at the World Bank:

- *Bonding* social capital provides connections to people "like you"; this is similar to but not synonymous with "strong ties"; it is also associated with survival ("getting by")
- *Bridging* social capital provides connections to people "not like you"; this is similar to but not synonymous with "weak ties"; it is also associated with mobility ("getting ahead")
- *Linking* social capital enables connections to people in positions of power. This is, Woolcock suggests, used in most instances to leverage resources

Each of these represents a different form of *incomplete social capital* within discrete systems; the incompleteness is revealed only when one system comes into connection with another. That is, social capital might be incomplete in terms of "content" (i.e., some of the factors are missing) or incomplete in terms of "reach" (i.e., the system itself is incomplete or out of balance in that the system or community in which the social capital is present and where it has been identified is not coterminous with the system or community in which the actors are engaged).

In his paper "Conceptualising Social Capital—Frameworks," my colleague John Cody raised this concept with reference to James Coleman's notion of a "perfect social system" in which "social capital is complete: all actors can interact with all others, each has full knowledge of others' interests in resources[,] and sanctions are certain" (Cody 2002, 7). Bringing together our work on social capital with that on deliberation and sustained dialogue leads me to suggest further that the type of discourse required in each case varies and that these variations are critical to their function.

High levels of *bonding* social capital require cohesion, moral trust, and shared cultural capital. This is a matter of shared norms, values, and sanctions or "keeping together." Bonding is internalized and depends on the reinforcement of existing cultural and moral norms and values. This requires discursive internal forms of discussion that involve all members of the group, that is, not hierarchical but broad based and deliberative discussion. However, this does not suggest that customary, previously bonded groups are internally static. Customary forms of talk allow for and enable change. The key issue is that that change is internal and is not imposed from outside.

The nature of custom is that it is endlessly changeable and adaptable—on its own terms.

Developing higher levels of *bridging* social capital requires opportunities to interact, generalized trust, and understanding of others' norms and values. This is a matter of structures that bring different groups in society together. It requires time to bridge the gap between moral and generalized trust. The time required to gain generalized understanding of another group means that an ongoing discussion in the form of sustained dialogue is preferable when building bridging social capital. This may be combined with a deliberative approach that develops and explores a range of views and options. The key is both the range of views and options and the ongoing nature of this dialogue. Bridging social capital requires a generalized connection between groups. Therefore, a form of sustained deliberation is suggested.

Further, a high level of *linking* social capital requires connectors to other levels in society. This requires individuals who act as connectors and structures that draw the "lower" or isolated levels into positions of participation. Such linking can be accomplished through select, mandated connectors. It is not necessary that many members of a group connect with members of another group; it is sufficient that key people (with a mandate from the group) make these connections and that they report information in an interactive, two-way manner.

This framework distinguishing these three forms of social capital highlights the importance of the availability of "time" as well as information, especially in the creation of bridging social capital. Time is needed not just to absorb and analyze information but also to gain an understanding of the others' norms and values, that is, to come to a shared understanding of who each group is. It is not necessarily to develop "shared norms"; "shared understanding" of each other's norms are enough. However, this can lead to the creation of a new, shared norm of "acceptance of difference."

THEORY AND PRACTICE

As indicated by other authors in this publication (see the introduction), in the exploration of deliberation and sustained dialogue the pracademic nature of our quest has been to ask, "This may well work in practice, but does it work in theory?" We are each working directly with communities and building a theory to help us understand their practice in using various forms of deliberative communication.

I would like to turn to three projects in New Zealand that we have been working with that illustrate the potential value of placing public talk in a social capital framework. These projects are being monitored through ongoing, participative, interactive, and reflective research:

1. The Iwi Fisheries Forum has been building both bridging and linking social capital ("*iwi*" is a Maori tribal group, akin to a village). The forum has been running for two years based on a customary Maori form of discussion — the *hui*. A formal protocol or ceremonial approach is used to enable people to get to know one another, to build respect, and to provide opportunities to understand others' points of view. This builds trust within individual *iwi*, among *iwi*, and with representatives from the Ministry of Fisheries. The process has prepared participants to talk seriously with one another.

2. The Porirua Health Cluster is implementing the approach espoused by the Healthlinks community-health group in their coordinator's job description and in their vision statement: "Encouraging and engaging in deliberation." The Porirua Health Cluster brings together people from the local community with hospital officials, general practitioners, and nonprofit associations to develop and implement policies and practices to deal with health issues, starting with diabetes.

3. A mental-health consumers group has been using a deliberative process with the goal of changing existing norms in the mental-health services and in the wider community. The goal is to move the perception of mental-health consumers from being considered subject to the decisions of others to an expectation that they will contribute to their assessments and treatment.

In each case there was a deliberate move to enhance the internal cohesion of a particular group of marginalized people (building their bonding social capital), to connect them with others in the community with similar concerns (bridging social capital), and to provide a connection to those in positions of authority (linking social capital).

The actual combination of these three factors varies from project to project, but in each case there is an emphasis on the most effective form of discussion. This has led to the use of deliberative forms of dialogue with a growing interest in evaluating their value and impact.

In each case, participants build on their considerable internal (bonding) social capital to link with those in decision-making positions. In this they have been successful in gaining specific policy objectives and amendments to working practices through dialogue and discussion. The participants are all concerned with increasing equality, which is defined as equal access to power or decision making.

However, to change existing community norms, a greater degree of bridging social capital, in particular, needs to be developed. This would enable a move from the enclosed space of "shared norms" within a group to "shared understanding" of norms and ongoing interaction between groups that may have substantial differences in culture, values, and access to power.

Each of the three cases that I refer to is concerned with bridging the divide between specific groups of citizens and those who make decisions that are supposed to benefit them. In each case the affected group has taken the initiative, has defined a deliberative way of working, and has gained access to some level of public funding to help carry out its actions. In some cases the groups appear to have been successful in changing the norms within their communities or to have established new terms of engagement that have changed the power balance among participants. For the mental-health consumers, such a change in norms is an expressed goal of the project. Although it is too soon to judge the degree to which this will be successful, the fact that this action is being undertaken is an indication of increased confidence in their ability to engage with those who have traditionally been in positions of power.

IWI FISHERIES FORUM

The customary Iwi Fisheries Forum is being conducted through an ongoing series of *hui*. The forum has been meeting on a monthly basis for two years. The meetings were initiated by Maori *iwi* and are organized and run by *iwi* with officials from the Ministry of Fisheries and others participating as invited guests. "Setting the scene" is an important part of the protocol at a *hui*. This process

- establishes who is present and whom they represent or are affiliated with;
- establishes and reaches agreement over the purpose of the meeting;
- allows the opportunity to "let off steam" and express strong views that might otherwise either disrupt the actual discussion or remain hidden and unacknowledged;
- acknowledges the history of the discussions, both of the people involved and of the issues being discussed; and

- establishes this as a reciprocal forum in which a range of views will be put forward and listened to with respect.

This is carried out through formal introductory speeches from the hosts and the guests and *waiata* (traditional songs) from each side. Together the speeches and *waiata* link the gathering with the past, bring the past into the present, and also link those at the meeting to "others" who are not present. The introductory session concludes with the giving of a *koha* (or gift) by the visiting group.

This formal welcome may be followed by refreshments before any actual discussion. This serves to cement the agreement to talk (rather than to fight) and is a sign of reciprocity—a response to the "gift of *koha*" with the "gift of hospitality." The welcome, the *waiata*, and the responses establish the situation and the conditions under which people are willing and able to talk with one another; that is, the welcome and response set the scene and establish that those present do, in fact, wish to talk with and listen to one another and that they are willing to respect an agreed protocol for such a meeting.

Participants of one such *hui* emphasized the need for localized organizations so that local people, including *hapu* (subtribe) and *iwi*, can create their own fisheries-policing systems. The intention is not just to implement regulations defined by and monitored by government but rather to develop a system of self-management within the broad parameters of a mutually ne-gotiated policy. For example, the encroachment of one *rohe moana* (tribal fishing ground) on another is up to the *iwi* forum to resolve, not the Ministry of Fisheries. A voice from the floor of the meeting said that in the past "the relationship between the Ministry of Fisheries and *iwi* has consisted of you telling us what you are doing—to me a relationship means sitting down and working together." Building this kind of relationship is what the forum has been doing.

PORIRUA HEALTH CLUSTER

The Porirua Health Cluster was established following an earlier delibera-tive forum that sought to identify how communities, health providers, com-munity organizations, funders, policymakers, and local government could work together to improve health outcomes for people who live in Porirua City.[2] At this forum the general manager of the City Council presented his view that the deliberative process provides an opportunity to ensure that all "voices" are heard, to clarify what the issues are, to develop a process of cooperation, and to give the community confidence that it will be listened to on future issues.

Participants recognized that previous models of service were not improving health outcomes and agreed that improvement must begin with a fundamental change in the way that services are designed and delivered. It was agreed that "users of services must be able to tell their stories and be involved at all stages of planning and design." As a result, the City Council, Healthlinks, Ngatitoa (the local Maori tribal group), and the District Health Board agreed to work together. The agreed goal was to support Porirua as a "Centre of Excellence in Healthcare" by "developing a unique opportunity for coordinated training in innovative models of care, based on cultural leadership and integration between prevention, primary and community care, secondary and specialist services."

The cluster has provided a forum for discussion on health issues. It has no formal constitution other than an agreement by the participants to work together to meet this goal. A crucial point is that it is not a service provider, its role is:

- To provide leadership for the development of the cluster
- Oversight of coordination across projects to deliver specific outcomes
- To broker access to resources to support projects
- To monitor results of projects and assess priorities for future projects

The cluster facilitates communication, collaboration and access to information, sparks innovation, and fosters interaction among such sectors as health, housing, education, and business. The deliberative process used has helped achieve the following emerging themes:

- A mandate based on community and clinical leadership
- A strong commitment to work together
- Putting people first
- Reciprocity
- Values and respect for diversity
- Community and organizational confidence and engagement
- Information sharing and gathering
- Supporting innovation

- Integration and collaboration
- Promoting continuous quality improvement

As a result, the cluster agreed to develop a Community Centre of Excellence in Healthcare. It held a further one-day deliberative workshop with users of services, families, community organizations, health providers, and others that identified diabetes as its focus. This is the most significant health issue in the city, particularly for Maori and Pacific Island people. Together the participants in the cluster have developed their own models of care, and there have been opportunities to work with other members and to build on one another's strengths. The key community group involved in forming the cluster is Healthlinks, which includes local Maori, Pacific Island, and community groups as well as health care providers. As I noted, Healthlinks includes "encouraging and engaging in deliberation" as a key part of achieving its vision, which is to provide leadership in articulating and realizing "health" for the peoples of Porirua. The cluster has provided the opportunity for people to interact free of the control of "officials." At the same time, some officials have also been given the opportunity to engage free of the constraints of the formal structures they normally work within. Action is only constrained by the will to engage and the acceptance of these actions by the community affected.

MENTAL-HEALTH CONSUMERS GROUP

This project uses a recovery focus, which means that the mental-health consumer will be seen and respected as a person who is (at the very least, potentially) capable and competent, able to learn, make life decisions, and act to create life changes—no matter how severe the symptoms of his or her mental illness. A recovery approach respects autonomy, the status of a person who is the author of his or her own life. Self-responsibility is a prerequisite: autonomy is meaningless if a person cannot be held accountable for actions that she has initiated. Self-responsibility, however, must be granted; it is not naturally possessed, thus, the priority given to self-responsibility in recovery-based models of care. Self-advocacy and support promote and reinforce self-responsibility. Two necessary conditions for exercising autonomy are *being informed* and *being permitted*. To *inform* adequately means more than just providing the information considered necessary for appropriate decision making; it is also crucial to listen, to provide any additional information or opinion requested by the consumer, to respond to any concerns expressed, and to repeat and explain again if asked. It also means acknowledging that the consumer knows what supports are necessary to make his own decisions safely, confidently, and credibly. Note that this describes clearly and concisely the key elements in the deliberative process.[3]

A key aspect of this form of deliberation is the focus on the importance of "permission." Permission is a necessary condition of autonomy and implies knowledge of the rules of the negotiation, the terms of engagement. Additionally, it implies the right to disagree, question, and, if necessary, challenge. It assumes an understanding of the relationship between clinician and consumer: the reason for it, the limits upon it, and, crucially, its intended outcome: what the consumer needs to achieve in order for the relationship to end (to be discharged from the service). Importantly, permission requires that the consumer feel self-confident, safe, and trusted.

Building on these concepts and his involvement in discussions on deliberation and sustained dialogue, and following a survey of mental health consumer groups in the Hutt Valley, Mike Sukolski (2002) proposed that "working groups of consumers be established and, working together with the Upper and Lower Hutt Community Mental Health Teams, develop and define a reciprocal understanding of and guidelines for the building of relationships which promote, protect and permit autonomy. This deliberative process will link into the current service-wide Models of Care and Clinical Pathways Projects." That is, Sukolski proposed a deliberative process to "change" the existing norms in the mental-health services and in the wider community from a situation where mental health consumers are considered subject to the decisions of others to one where mental-health consumers are expected to engage with and collaborate in their assessments and treatment. This is a major step toward becoming "autonomous."

UNRESOLVED ISSUES

There are a number of significant unresolved issues in each of these three approaches. High on the list is the reluctance of professionals and government agencies to take seriously the voices of the disadvantaged and marginalized. There is a tendency when matters of uncertainty arise to get a

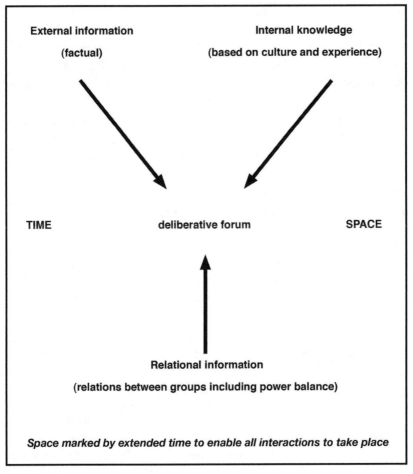

External information
(factual)

Internal knowledge
(based on culture and experience)

TIME   deliberative forum   SPACE

Relational information

(relations between groups including power balance)

Space marked by extended time to enable all interactions to take place

FIGURE 4.2

"second opinion" from a "professional" policy analyst, to "reprocess" these voices from the community into an acceptable form.

Local and central government agencies also have a habit of "noting" concerns but not acting. They often act in a self-satisfied and congratulatory manner for having "listened" without actually hearing what is said; as one forum participant said, "They have not *felt* what we are saying."

Identifying and developing the forms of dialogue that are most effective in building social capital requires a space for deliberation defined in terms of time rather just by space (see figure 4.2). Within this time/space the discourse should be open to all views, provide opportunity for people to share their internal information and experiences, and explore underlying relationships as well as access external "factual" information. Putting this process into practice makes a dual outcome likely: building both collective opinion and action on an issue and also the potential for a change in the norms of the power structure.

In each of the cases reviewed, the intended outcome has been to move decision-making power from residing exclusively with government officials, medical practitioners, or clinicians to a shared process where these technicians and professionals respond to and collaborate with those affected by the decisions. The ongoing engagement of actors from different sectors of the community indicates that these changes are, in fact, taking place.

Notes

This chapter draws on material from a research project with the New Zealand Institute for Economic Research on how the process of consensus is reached within different cultural groups in response to issues of globalization and technological change.

1. Editors' note: Such space is "free" in part by not being defined or constrained by political states or professional institutions.

2. Porirua City is a dormitory city on the outskirts of Wellington. The population is 54 percent European and 41 percent Maori and Pacific Islander. In eastern Porirua, 80 percent of homes are public housing and over 80 percent of the population is Maori and Pacific Islander.

3. My description of a recovery approach and of autonomy, information, and permission were provided by Mike Sukolski, an advocate for mental-health consumers and the former manager of the Wellington Mental Health Consumers' Union.

5

LET'S TALK: DIALOGUE AND DELIBERATION IN HIGHER EDUCATION

Lisa Bedinger

Educators come to Highlander and ask what is your method; what is your technique; what is your gimmick? . . . To get people to understand that education is a process and that whatever method or technique seems best in that given situation is the best one to use. This is better than a method that you clamp onto every situation and force people into it like you are torturing them. If they are not long enough, stretch them; if they are too long, cramp them up so they will fit your methods! Deform them anyway you can so they fit your methods.
—MYLES HORTON

IN RECENT YEARS, I have had the privilege of working with staff, faculty, and students from several Vermont college and university campuses. These individuals have been an inspiration for me. They have provided opportunities for themselves and others to engage their best thinking and speak from their hearts in order to take on some of the most problematic issues facing their campuses and the larger world. Most consistently, the dialogues initiated on each campus have taken on brave and needed explorations of how we as human beings have become separated from one another: dialogues on race, ethnicity, gender, sexual orientation, class background, and religion. Part of the pracademic challenge in this context is to put additional tools into these individuals' hands in order to give them more information and greater understanding of what is possible in guiding these dialogues and deliberations. This chapter also strives to assist them in meeting their own hopes and aspirations, the needs of various situations and groups—as Myles Horton speaks to in the epigraph—and assisting all involved in continuing to engage in desperately needed conversations.

INTRODUCTION TO THE FIELD OF
DIALOGUE AND DELIBERATION

This chapter has its basis in the field of dialogue and deliberation, an emerging field born in the cross-section of organizational development; conflict studies; education, both formal and popular; political science and democracy studies; psychology, social work, self-help, and personal growth; communication; and community activism and organizing, as well as rich religious and cultural traditions, such as Native American, Quaker, and Mennonite. Of particular interest to the dialogue and deliberation field are human interaction that is "high stakes, high risk and/or high benefit" (Glock-Grueneich) and theory and methodology that increase the likelihood of desired outcomes and decrease the likelihood of unwanted outcomes in these circumstances.[1] Dialogue and deliberation (D&D) is inherently goal-oriented and practical yet simultaneously contains the ability to transcend these original goals. D&D seeks to identify principles of discourse and improve upon them so that these guidelines can be replicated and taught. Thus, one goal of D&D is transforming the messy reality of human interaction into organized structures that create improved possibilities for planned interactions. A second and equally valuable goal is to develop our capacity as human beings to respond to the unplanned, which will always be part of human interaction. The field of D&D has developed both responsively and actively. It has responded to existing challenges and crises of human interaction and has recognized and created new opportunities for interaction that envision our world differently and lay a path to move in new directions. Ultimately, D&D is about systematizing the learning gained through the quest to understand and improve human interaction in order to increase the knowledge available for future interactions.

DEFINITION OF TERMS

In naming a field "dialogue and deliberation," we need to look also at what is meant by these terms.[2] Within the field itself, there are numerous definitions of dialogue. Some point to the goal of the interaction, and some aim to describe what happens within an interaction. It is not a goal of this chapter to propose a consistent definition of dialogue for the field. Instead, this chapter flags the inconsistency and invites practitioners of D&D to struggle with this inconsistency in order to see what understanding may emerge from this effort. Initially, I define dialogue as *a type of human interaction to which participants bring an intention to understand and learn.* This definition stresses listening for understanding and the potential for learning based on considering the viewpoints of others. It does not include trying to change others yet is enhanced and furthered when participants can remain open to the possibility of their own change. It assumes that although goals and objectives may be achieved, learning takes priority over task orientation.[3]

The term "deliberation" already carries much more consistency in its definition and use than "dialogue." Deliberation refers to the process of human beings carefully considering and critically thinking together. Thus, I define deliberation as *a type of human interaction to which participants bring an intention to critically explore avenues of thinking and action.* The consistency in the use of the term "deliberation" may be directly related to its limited use in common parlance whereas dialogue is a term most people assume they know the meaning of.[4]

Finally, in considering what will be useful information for those using dialogue and deliberation in the context of higher education, this chapter will be concerned with *social technologies* (Olson 1996). These are *named, structured processes developed over time and honed through repetition and refinement.* Social technologies are useful shortcuts to wisdom that others have gained through the trial and error.[5]

CONTEXT AND ASSUMPTIONS

There is no intent here to create structure where none is possible or to apply social technologies without flexibility, regard, or understanding the subtleties involved with each particular situation (Glock-Grueneich). Social technologies are tools that may be useful in order to take advantage of pervious good thinking, not to re-create structures when much good thinking currently exists. It is also my intent to support the use of D&D social technologies in ways that are flexible and responsive to unique circumstances through an exploration of design considerations.

Another assumption is that much of the important work that those on college and university campuses already do is in the area of civic engagement, *doing needed work in communities and in the larger world that is intertwined with learning and scholarship.* I believe that college and university communities are an enormous resource for change within our society. I hope these tools enhance the quality of human interactions and the outcomes from them that are part of this vast civic engagement effort.

The perspective inherent in the theory of dialogue and deliberation is that ordinary citizens have important thinking to offer, and each social technology outlines a process to elicit this thinking. Some authors also include methodologies to act on this thinking. A sometimes unstated assumption for a large subsection of the field of D&D is that there is a crisis in how democracy currently functions in the United States. One of the goals inherent in the theory is to increase civic engagement through collaborative dialogue as one method of participatory democracy. Ultimately, a goal of many of the social technologies is to increase citizen engagement in community, diversity, and public policy issues in order to effect social change.

Finally, in selecting social technologies for use by those on campuses, there is a preference for those in which people meet face-to-face. While online D&D technologies may also be useful, they are excluded from my consideration here in part because I have not experienced online technologies in higher education dialogue and deliberation and as such have no basis for judgment of them.

KEY DESIGN CONSIDERATIONS

Designing a successful dialogue or deliberation event involves much more than choosing a particular social technology and jumping in. This section will review what I believe to be some of the most important design considerations for increasing the likelihood of organizers' and participants' desired outcomes and for guiding the selection of a particular social technology to meet the needs of specific and infinitely varied situations.

There are two design considerations that can make or break dialogue and deliberation events: *alignment with the purpose for the event* and *diversity of participants in regards to this purpose* (Glock-Grueneich). Some aspects of these considerations are intertwined. In order to plan events that translate the initial, often one-sided motivating concern into a perspective that encompasses the wide variety of views related to this initial concern, a diverse, broad-based planning team is essential.[6] Forming a planning team that encompasses the range of views on the issue eliminates the possibility of the event's being owned, or being seen as owned, by advocates on any side of an issue. If an event is part of a course, campus club, or other preselected group, it is important to consider how to increase the perspectives available to frame the dialogue and the views present in the room. "Framing" is a term widely used to mean *identifying and articulating the focus for dialogue or deliberation.*

Including a range of views in an event enhances the quality of the dialogue, the creativity of ideas available, and the potential for learning for those involved. This diversity of perspective can be enhanced by, yet is not synonymous with, including individuals from a wide array of identities and experience: age, race, gender, education, sexual orientation, ability, religion, culture, position inside or outside the institution, and more. Which types of diversity are essential to include will depend upon the purpose and the issue addressed (Herzig 2006).

Once the issue is framed in a manner deemed acceptable to the perspectives represented on the planning team, invitations and the organization of the entire event can proceed in a manner that is consistent with this broad-based framing. An example of a narrowly framed issue that would likely exclude voices from the dialogue would be an invitation to talk about banning military recruiters from campus. An example of a more inclusive framing would be an invitation to a dialogue about how U.S. military policies affect our campus and what, if any, action is needed. In addition, the framing organizes why individuals would want to attend and can help with consistency in how people are invited as well as what participants can expect both during the process and in outcomes resulting from it. Giving participants sufficient information to understand what they will be participating in is essential. The failure to do this can result in confusion, frustration, erosion of good will, and reluctance to engage in subsequent events (Glock-Grueneich).

The purpose, *the goals of the event related to the issue,* is the key factor that needs to be in alignment with what a social technology best delivers and thus forms the primary basis for selection of a technology. We can sort purposes into four categories: exploration via dialogue, exploration via deliberation, taking action, and repairing relationships.[7]

The purpose of the dialogue or deliberation helps inform the *requirements for facilitation* and the *facilitator's role.* Events in which exploration is primary and other outcomes may or may not occur require less facilitation skill or experience. In other words, do participants primarily expect to have an opportunity to learn from others or to talk with people different from themselves, with no expectation of what will emerge from this exploration? When particular actions are anticipated as desired outcomes, the facilitation demands increase. Questions that identify action purposes include:

- Do participants expect to emerge from the event with a decision supported by the group?
- Do they want to develop an action plan?
- Do they expect their thinking to affect official policies?

The highest demands on the facilitator come from processes in which participants desire to repair relationships damaged by a history of tension, misunderstanding, volatility, or oppression. Decisions regarding the training needs for facilitators or whether to hire facilitators should be informed by an understanding of the purpose of the particular event and of the social technology that will be used. It is important not to place facilitators in situations for which they do not have the skills required. The group can be at risk if situations arise in which they need the facilitator to set boundaries to create needed emotional safety and the facilitator is unable to do so. Other facilitation considerations are:

- How many facilitators are needed considering the number of sessions, number of groups, and group size?
- Does the social technology usually include the facilitators as participants in the dialogue or are they expected to withhold their opinions?
- Might particular facilitators be perceived as biased because of views they have previously expressed on the issue at hand or related issues?

An additional consideration for designing a D&D event is *thinking about the particular group* of participants involved. Successful events often leave participants feeling well thought about throughout all aspects of their experience. In order to accomplish this, thinking about the group needs to begin well before they are in the room. Questions that can be useful in this regard include:

- How well do participants know one another?
- What is the participants' history with one another both as individuals and as parts of groups to which they belong?
- How much conflict can be anticipated?

- What can you anticipate their needs will be concerning guidelines and confidentiality?
- How can the room be set up to encourage relaxed participation?
- How can everything from the room selection to how topics are framed to the social technology selected be best thought about to meet this group's needs and expectations?

Resources in regards to funding, time, space, and leadership and their impact on logistics are a final category for design consideration. Resources constitute a real factor in designing the vast majority of D&D events.

Funding

- How can the the event best occur within whatever resource limitations are likely to exist?
- What would be ideal for this event if these limitations did not exist?
- What adaptations can be made to optimize resources while most closely achieving these ideals?
- Are financial resources needed, and, if so, where will they come from?

Time

- Is the length of the event or the number of sessions determined by resources?
- How much time does the conversation ideally need, and how much time can all involved give it?

Space

- Are spaces available that will hold the number of people needed in an arrangement conducive for dialogue?
- What arrangement of the room will foster the goals of the event?
- Can the space selected encourage the goal of including the range of perspectives represented?

Leadership

- Who will take responsibility for each of the leadership aspects: logistics, inviting, facilitating or recruiting facilitators, hosting, record keeping, and any follow-up?
- What are the limitations on these leaders' time?

Other Logistics

- Will the event be better served by meeting as one group or in multiple groups?
- A one-time event or successive gatherings? Face-to-face, online, or a combination?
- What group size will meet the needs of the participants? The facilitators? The event purpose?

SOCIAL TECHNOLOGIES FOR HIGHER EDUCATION

The following information is intended to give the flavor of each social technology, enough information to know whether it may be useful after reflecting on the design considerations. By their nature, social technologies have made decisions regarding some of the design considerations. The packaging of the particular group of decisions via a social technology may be useful as is or may need some modification to meet the needs of a specific situation. The order of presentation of these social technologies and in all of the tables begins with models requiring less technical experience on the part of the facilitator and concludes with models that demand a high level of facilitator expertise.

WORLD CAFÉ AND CONVERSATION CAFÉ

These two social technologies are grouped because they share several important qualities. Both most often occur in cafés or other informal settings and can be led by anyone with a desire to do so (see http://www.theworldcafe-community.org/ and http://www.financialintegrity.org/). The atmosphere can be enhanced by music, tablecloths, candles, flowers, or other creative means. Both require that someone host and advertise or otherwise invite dialogue participants, and both can occur in a single ninety-minute session. An organizer for a World Café proposes a series of questions on the framed dialogue topic and initiates rotations before each question. Participants are typically distributed among tables of four people each. Participant volunteers serve as table hosts for World Cafés by offering to stay at their table while the other three people rotate to other tables. Table hosts maintain a connection throughout the dialogue.

Conversation Cafés are more likely to involve larger groups at a single table and an organizer who initiates and facilitates the dialogue. In both café forms, all involved are encouraged to participate in the dialogue. Either of these social technologies can be organized quickly, and the minimal structure allows for a vast range of topic possibilities that can be highly responsive to events occurring in the world.

NATIONAL ISSUES FORUMS AND CITIZEN CHOICEWORK

These two social technologies are also grouped because of their similarities. Both use prepared discussion materials and distribute these beforehand to deliberation participants. NIF issue books tend to be much more extensive—as much as forty pages of background information on each issue—while Citizen Choicework discussion guides often contain a two- to four-page synopsis of each issue. Both contain three or four perspectives on the issue and arguments that explain, support, and challenge each perspective. Moderators, as facilitators are called, withhold their opinions from the deliberation. Both of these technologies can happen in a single two- to three-hour gathering. Subsequent meetings can also be planned but don't have to occur, depending on participants' needs and the event purpose. A goal of both of these technologies is to move the public conversation forward on critical public-policy issues and social problems, such as immigration, health care, gay rights, and dozens of others. Additional goals of Citizen Choicework are:

- Help citizens understand complex problems
- Involve those who are normally excluded from policy debates
- Promote productive public and leadership dialogue
- Create momentum for change by building common ground, managing differences, and creating new partnerships (Citizen Choicework 2010)

Issues that work best in these formats contain value differences at their core yet are not so divisive as to be too painful for participants to want to hear what others think. Deliberation is analytic and cognitive by nature and as such may not meet participants' needs when the value differences are deeply painful or involve estrangement from others who think differently (Herzig 2006). For NIFs, each participant's task, as guided by the moderator, is to explore the strengths, drawbacks, tradeoffs, and underlying values of each approach while noticing areas of common ground that develop as the forum unfolds. Some design principles important in Citizen Choicework include "inclusive participation—'beyond the usual suspects'"; "strategic follow-up that leads to more informed policies, new collaborations, and innovative initiatives"; and "a commitment to helping communities build long-term capacity for this work" (Citizen Choicework 2010).

STUDY CIRCLES

The purpose of the Study Circle approach is to "expand civic engagement and make it meaningful to all sorts of people" (McCoy and Scully 2002, 117). The Study Circle Resource Center has conducted research on how to best accomplish this goal. Leighninger and McCoy (1998) distill their findings into the following principles of what citizens want:

(1) To make a direct impact on the issue
(2) To know that their individual participation makes a difference and matters
(3) To start at the beginning
(4) To work in diverse yet harmonious groups
(5) To work together with others in way that overcomes feelings of isolation and powerlessness

The Study Circles model is based on these findings. Convening Study Circles requires a significant amount of effort—three to six months—from broad-based coalitions in order to bring together multiple groups of participants with the widest possible range of backgrounds and thinking.

Study Circles involve five gatherings. The first explores personal connections to the issue as a way to ground the conversation and develop safety within the circle. Subsequent meetings explore a range of views about the issue, consider alternative approaches for addressing it, create action plans, and then present each group's plans in a combined meeting of all the groups (Flavin-McDonald and Barrett 1999; McCoy and Scully 2002). The final meeting allows for more broad-based connections, including connections to government and policymaking officials. Issue-based materials exist, and training is provided to assist community volunteer facilitators through this progression. In addition, Study Circles Resource Center staff is available for consultation at no charge for large-scale community projects.

LEARNING CIRCLES

The community organizer Myles Horton developed what has come to be known as Learning Circles,[8] a method of collaborative self-education as a way to work with poor Southerners and Appalachians who had already taken action or were poised to take leadership within unions, on civil rights, or on other issues related to the poor (Glen 2006). Horton was a self-proclaimed "radical hillbilly" and felt it was critical to bring out the expert information of poor people to inform the definitions of the problems they face and their solutions.[9] Learning Circles pose a series of questions to the group that elicit storytelling based on each person's experience and insights and ends the process with the question, "What are you going to do when you go back?" (Horton 1989, 11). Horton's method of Learning Circles is inseparable from the retreat aspect of bringing activists from several communities together who are working on the same issue. Participants still travel to the Highlander Center in east Tennessee for at least two consecutive nights and sometimes for as long as two months. The resulting ongoing relationships that develop and the continued availability of assistance from Highlander staff in participants' political work are all integral to the model. In this model, the two facilitators participate in the conversation as people also invested in the issue as peers in the conversation.

INTERGROUP DIALOGUE

Intergroup Dialogue aims to explore cultural identities and differences, build deeper understanding of oppression and privilege, and create alliances across commonalities and differences for the purpose of social change (Nadga et al. 1999). Dialogue participants are organized by identities that have been polarized, such as men and women, blacks and whites, Protestants and Catholics, or Muslims and Jews (Clark 2002). In this approach, groups meet initially with others who share their identity. After appropriate preparation, the two groups combine. Two facilitators—one from each group represented—work together with both groups, share their stories and thinking in conversations along with participants, and pose questions that increase in risk over time (Clark 2002). For example, first joint meetings may explore the histories of each participant's name. From here the facilitators guide the conversations to explore commonalities and differences, areas of conflict (such as interracial dating), and, finally, action planning and alliance building (Alimo, Kelly, and Clark 2002). Materials assist facilitators in developing this progression, and there is no inherent need to rush termination. Some existing interracial and interreligious dialogues have been going on for years and even, in a few cases, decades.

PUBLIC CONVERSATIONS PROJECT

"Although PCP specializes in fostering dialogues about polarizing public issues, its methods have been effective in situations characterized by chilly disconnection and suspicious silence as well as in heated and noisy conflicts" (Herzig and Chasin 2006, front matter). The Public Conversations Project has roots in family therapy and began developing its methodology in the crucible of dialogue on abortion during the early 1990s.[10] Elements of PCP dialogues are (see Herzig and Chasin 2006, 3):

- Careful, collaborative planning that ensures clarity about what the dialogue is and isn't, and also fosters alignment between the goals of the dialogue and participants' wishes.
- Communication agreements that discourage counter-productive ways of talking about the issues and encourage genuine inquiry.
- Meeting designs that include supportive structures for reflecting, listening, and speaking questions that invite new ways of thinking about the issues.
- Facilitation that is informed by careful preparation and is responsive to the emerging needs and interests of the participants.

The materials created by the Public Conversations Project give a great deal of background information about design considerations, which creates the opportunity to apply their thinking and guidance to a wide variety of issues and in a wide range of settings (such as large and small groups and single and multiple sessions). They describe themselves as offering a general approach, not a strict structure or model (Herzig 2006). Nonetheless, PCP dialogues typically open with a phase of welcome and orientation to set the tone of the dialogue, followed by two or three structured rounds in which participants respond to carefully crafted questions. The purpose of the first question is "to invite participants to connect their views with their life experience" (Herzig and Chasin 2006, 112). "This begins a process of melting stereotypes and paves the way for later questions about 'what the heart of the matter' is for each participant and for sharing 'gray areas' as well as certainties related to the issue. After such a structured beginning, participants are invited to ask each other questions 'arising from genuine curiosity' and then to engage in a less structured conversation" (Herzig 2006).

VICTIM-OFFENDER MEDIATION

Victim-Offender Mediation developed as part of the field of restorative justice, an alternative to the traditional justice system.[11] In restorative justice the crime is seen in reference to the violation of the relationships involved and thus the needs of the people involved can be more directly addressed (Presser and Hamilton 2006). Facilitators meet serially with both those who have harmed another and those who have been harmed in preparation for the final face-to-face meeting. In order for VOM to be successful, all those involved must participate voluntarily, and the person committing the harm must be willing and able to take responsibility for the harm done and have a desire to make things right.

The preparation work involves talking through possible scenarios that may occur during the face-to-face meeting and providing emotional support for the difficult dialogue ahead so that no surprises occur for anyone involved when it comes time for the final meeting. One example is working with the offender to consider what it will be like if the person they've harmed is not able to forgive them. During the highly structured face-to-face meeting, the victim has the opportunity to explain the impact of the offender's actions, ask questions, and state what he or she needs to make things right. The offender has the opportunity to hear the impact of his or her actions, apologize, and commit to taking agreed-upon actions to repair the harm done. It is important that facilitators be able to honor all those involved in these painful incidents by validating their perspectives, needs, and experience. Both training and supervision for this social technology are advised because of the awareness and information needed to walk with others through such delicate events in order to avoid re-victimizing people who have been harmed and shaming those who have erred.

SUMMARY TABLES

Tables 5.1 and 5.2 give an overview of purposes and highlight the basic characteristics of each of these social technologies as well as offering suggestions

TABLE 5.1 Characteristics of Well-Known Dialogue and Deliberation Processes: A Project of the National Coalition for Dialogue and Deliberation

SOCIAL TECHNOLOGY	PRIMARY PURPOSES			SIZE OF GROUP	TYPE OF SESSION (EXCLUDING PREPARATORY SESSIONS)	FACILITATOR ROLE
	EXPLORATION VIA DIALOGUE	EXPLORATION VIA DELIBERATION	TAKING ACTION	REPAIRING RELATIONSHIPS			
World Café	X				Up to hundreds in one room at tables of four	Single event ranging from ninety minutes to three days	Participates
Conversation Café	X				Single or multiple small groups	One ninety-minute session	Participates
Citizen Choicework		X			Multiple small groups	One session, ranging from two hours to all day	Withholds opinions
National Issues Forums	X				Up to hundreds in one room at small tables	One two-hour meeting	Withholds opinions

Study Circles	x	X	x	Up to hundreds meeting in separate small groups; come together later for Action Forum	Four to six two-hour sessions	Withholds opinions
Learning Circles	x	X		Small group	Multiple sessions of the same group over three days; also one session adaptation	Participates
Intergroup Dialogue	x	X	X	Single or multiple small groups	Regular weekly meetings of two to three hours	Participates and teaches
Public Conversations Project	x		X	Single or multiple small groups	Ranging from multiple two-hour sessions to three-day retreats	Recommended to withhold opinions
Victim-Offender Mediation	X	X	X	Small group	Multiple two- to three-hour sessions	Withholds opinions and advice

Note: A lowercase x signifies a secondary purpose.

TABLE 5.2

SOCIAL TECHNOLOGY	BRIEF DESCRIPTION	ORGANIZATIONAL RESOURCES AND WEBSITES
World Café	World Cafés enable groups of people to participate in evolving rounds of dialogue with three or four others while at the same time remaining part of a single, larger, connected conversation. Small, intimate conversations link to and build on one another as people move among groups, cross-pollinate ideas, and discover new insights into questions or issues that matter in their life, work, or community.	www.theworld cafe .com
Conversation Café	Conversation Cafés are hosted conversations that are usually held in a public setting like a coffee shop or bookstore, where anyone is welcome to join. A simple format helps people feel at ease and gives everyone who wants to a chance to speak.	www.conversation cafe.org
National Issues Forums	National Issues Forums offer citizens the opportunity to join together to deliberate, make choices with others about ways to approach difficult issues, and work toward creating reasoned public judgment. Topical materials provided.	www.nifi.org
Citizen Choicework	Public Agenda's Citizen Choicework helps citizens confront tough choices in productive ways. Participants work through value conflicts and practical tradeoffs and develop a sense of priorities and direction. Key principles include nonpartisan local leadership, inclusive participation, and unbiased discussion materials that "start where the public starts." Topical materials provided.	www.public agenda.org
Study Circles	Study Circles enable communities to strengthen their own ability to solve problems by bringing large numbers of people together in dialogue across divides of race, income, age, and political viewpoints. Study Circles combine dialogue, deliberation, and community organizing techniques, enabling public talk to build understanding, explore a range of solutions, and serve as a catalyst for social, political, and policy change. Topical materials and assistance to communities are provided.	www.studycircles .org
Learning Circles	Learning Circles are based on storytelling and built on principles of popular education, allowing accessibility to the process for both readers and non-readers. In successive go-rounds, all participants (including the	Educators for Community Engagement: www.e4ce.org

TABLE 5.2 (*continued*)

SOCIAL TECHNOLOGY	BRIEF DESCRIPTION	ORGANIZATIONAL RESOURCES AND WEBSITES
	facilitators) tell stories in response to the facilitators' questions leading to the final question regarding next steps each person commits to taking.	Highlander Research and Education Center: www.highlander center.org
Intergroup Dialogue	Intergroup dialogues are face-to-face meetings of people from at least two different social identity groups. They are designed to offer an open and inclusive space where participants can foster a deeper understanding of diversity and justice issues through participation in experiential activities, individual and small group reflections, and dialogues.	Intergroup Dialogue, Education and Action (IDEA) Training & Resource Institute: http://depts .washington .edu/sswweb /idea/main.html Program on Intergroup Relations: www.umich.edu /~igrc/
Public Conversations Project dialogue	The Public Conversations Project helps people with different worldviews, values and identities to develop the mutual understanding and trust essential for strong communities and positive action. Their approach is characterized by a careful preparatory phase in which all stakeholders are interviewed and prepared for the dialogue process and by meeting designs that are responsive to participants' input before and during the meeting.	www.public conversations.org
Victim-Offender Mediation	Victim Offender Mediation is a restorative justice process that allows the victim of a crime and the person who committed that crime to talk to each other about what happened, the effects of the crime on their lives, and their feelings about it. They may choose to create a mutually agreeable plan to repair any damages that occurred as a result of the crime. In some practices, the victim and the offender are joined by family and community members or others.	www.voma.org

for where to find additional resources for each. The tables and resources were originally designed and compiled by the National Coalition for Dialogue and Deliberation (see http://www.thataway.org/) and are presented here in modified form, based on experience in using them.[12]

REASONS FOR SELECTION AND ADAPTATIONS FOR HIGHER EDUCATION

These social technologies may be most useful for time-limited campus community dialogues and deliberations, both on and off campus. The discussion includes reasons for selecting each technology, adaptations that others have made for use in higher education, and particular considerations or potential pitfalls. Table 5.3 summarizes current thoughts on this.

WORLD CAFÉ AND CONVERSATION CAFÉ

These two social technologies are relatively low risk, can bring an element of fun to dialogue, require minimal preparation, and are highly adaptable in terms of the issues they can address. Participants need to understand that no action may occur as a result of these dialogues. Simultaneously, organizers need to be prepared to support the momentum of participants if they initiate action. If desired, any room can be set up café style, and organizers can have fun doing this. Many D&D events require a level of seriousness in order to adequately address what is at stake; these social technologies allow the possibility of more lightness and as such may be more inviting for students or others for whom dialogue is new or unfamiliar. Because of moving from table to table, World Café is especially well suited for meeting a number of people and not well suited for topics in which participants need more time to get to know one another in order to speak authentically.

NATIONAL ISSUES FORUMS AND CITIZEN CHOICEWORK

The highly structured formats of these two social technologies—which address three or four predetermined approaches to an issue—allow for new facilitators to lead these deliberations. By presenting these approaches to participants for their reaction, they also create a low-risk avenue for those new to deliberation. Risk is reduced through preestablished, coherent, reasonable, and well-articulated perspectives, eliminating the need for participants to articulate their own perspectives or defend them. Developers of both technologies urge participants to make choices about how they think the issue should be addressed. Outcomes, such as sending the groups' thinking to NIF or to public officials should be determined beforehand so that participants know what, if anything, will be the results of their efforts. Simultaneously, organizers need to be prepared to support the momentum of participants if they initiate action.

Many faculty members have used these technologies in their classrooms either to address development of dialogue and deliberation skills or as a participatory means to address an issue related to course content. Courses have also been structured around the creation of new discussion guides. In addition, these technologies have been widely used to hold open-campus forums on issues of critical importance in the United States. These technologies are less applicable when the motivating concern of an event does not line up with any topic in the preestablished discussion guides. The process to create new guides is involved enough that it is difficult to use these technologies for new and immediate deliberation needs. These technologies can be used in community or mixed campus/community groups as well. Care needs to be taken regarding the length and accessibility of any written materials when community members are involved so as to not limit the diversity of perspectives based on reading ability.

STUDY CIRCLES

Study Circles can be particularly useful for campus/community collaborations, the involvement of new participants in engagement efforts, and for new and creative solutions to campus or community issues. The highly structured nature of this technology makes it accessible for new facilitators from a wide variety of backgrounds, while the ability to run several small groups simultaneously allows for the involvement of many participants and facilitators. Participants are recruited with the understanding that collaborative action will result. The model itself guides facilitators to achieve this outcome. When Study Circles are used in community contexts, written materials should be brief and highly accessible so as not to restrict the diversity of those involved.

LEARNING CIRCLES

Coming from a foundation in popular education, Learning Circles were originally intended for nonreaders in order to promote their inherent wisdom. Groups like Educators for Community Engagement have considerable experience in adapting this model for curriculum use in higher education. They have published few written materials but do provide facilitator training. The retreat format is often dropped in adaptations for higher education. Because the work that happens does not involve crosstalk, *responding to other participants*, participants' only opportunity to follow up with one another about what they said in each round comes during meals and breaks in the retreat format, which is often multisession. In adapting Learning Circles to a single-session format, opportunities for follow-up, exploration, and relationship development can easily be lost, which may cause frustration for some dialogue participants. Learning Circles can be particularly well suited to gathering campus, community, or multicampus activists and organizers working on the same issue. This use lines up well with the original intent of gathering people already in motion on the same issue so that each has the support needed to take the next step.

INTERGROUP DIALOGUE

Intergroup Dialogue was developed within the culture and goals of higher education and is particularly well suited for campus use, whether curricular, cocurricular, or extracurricular. Dialogues can be lead by faculty, staff, or students, but considerable training or life experience may be needed for facilitators. Learning across polarized identity groups through conversations of increasing risk of misunderstanding and conflict and attending to any emotional triggers that arise during the dialogue should be the key intended outcomes of Intergroup Dialogues.

PUBLIC CONVERSATIONS PROJECT

The materials available from the PCP are excellent general resources regardless of which social technology is selected. Many of the insights and methods discussed can be adapted to other technologies. When a PCP dialogue is convened for which considerable potential for conflict and volatility exist, as much support and encouragement as possible needs to be offered

TABLE 5.3

SOCIAL TECHNOLOGY	WHY SELECTED FOR INCLUSION	HIGHER ED ADAPTATIONS	LIMITATIONS AND CONSIDERATIONS
World Café and Conversation Café	• These dialogues can happen on campus or in the community on a wide range of topics, allowing adaptation to emerging needs for dialogue, e.g., Hurricane Katrina. • These two technologies can be hosted in a way that is light and fun, which can be well-suited to meet students' dialogue needs.	• To my knowledge these technologies have been used in higher education without adaptation.	• Organizers will need to match the expectations of participants to the outcomes of these dialogues so that participants' goodwill is not dishonored by unmet expectations of action or decision making when neither might occur. • Organizers need to be prepared to support any action that participants are inspired to take as a result of their participation. • World Café facilitates meeting others but is not conducive to more sensitive topics.
National Issues Forums and Citizen Choicework	• Both create a format for deliberation on policy issues that fosters participants' capacity for thoughtful disagreement in response to three or four approaches to an issue. • Because of their structure, both are accessible formats for new facilitators and those unaccustomed to participating in D&D.	• Because the deliberations are issue based, both the content and skills developed can be suitable for curriculum inclusion. • Courses can also be built around the creation of new discussion guides.	• The process to develop new discussion guides for these technologies for additional issues can be time consuming and involved. This can limit their flexibility when the topic needing D&D, such as Hurricane Katrina, is new and immediate. • Also see World and Conversation Cafes regarding setting expectations and supporting emerging action.
Study Circles	• When working to mobilize groups of people for collective action, Study Circles shine. • SC's high structure makes this an accessible technology for new facilitators. • The information in SC resources about best practices in convening is useful regardless of what technology is used.	• It is likely that SC's have long been used in higher education without adaptation.	• When working with community members, campus members will need to pay attention to how much reading is asked of community members in order for all to feel welcomed and to invite the most diversity possible.

(continued)

TABLE 5.3 (*continued*)

SOCIAL TECHNOLOGY	WHY SELECTED FOR INCLUSION	HIGHER ED ADAPTATIONS	LIMITATIONS AND CONSIDERATIONS
Learning Circles	• Offers the opportunity for those already in motion on a particular issue to meet with other organizers and activists to create the circumstances needed for each to decide what his or her next brave step will be.	• Learning Circles have been adapted as a structure for coursework on many campuses, often in a single-session format.	• Much less information exists about this technology, so gaining information and skills in its usage may be more difficult. • The three-day retreat format may be cost and time prohibitive. • The lack of crosstalk may be frustrating to some participants.
Intergroup Dialogue	• Offers conversations across polarized identity groups, allowing for rare and needed learning.	• ID was developed on college campuses and is well suited for course content in addition to the change it can create in campus culture.	• Training or experience of facilitators is needed so that they have a deep understanding of intergroup dynamics and potential emotional triggers in order to maintain the safety needed for these conversations.
Public Conversations Project	• PCP dialogues are one of the most flexible technologies, with applications for many types of conflictual conversations. • The depth of information included in PCP materials about what to consider in designing D&D events is essential regardless of what technology is used.	• PCP's general approach has been used in higher education settings. When pre-meeting conversations with all participants have been impractical, more work is done at the beginning of the event to ensure that participants are informed about what the event is.	• This model is intended to maintain as much confidentiality as possible for those involved in conflicts. Because confidentiality may be difficult to ensure on campuses, careful consideration will be needed to create enough safety to conduct PCP dialogues. As always, participants are encouraged to pass if not ready or willing to share; they are in charge of their level of vulnerability and openness.

TABLE 5.3 *(continued)*

SOCIAL TECHNOLOGY	WHY SELECTED FOR INCLUSION	HIGHER ED ADAPTATIONS	LIMITATIONS AND CONSIDERATIONS
Victim-Offender Mediation	• VOM offers the possibility of more thoughtful responses to situations when community members do things that hurt one another.	• Through systematic use of VOM, the potential exists to extend campuses' learning mission into the day-to-day interaction of campus community members through thoughtfully addressing these incidents in a way that promotes taking responsibility, healing, and learning.	• Facilitators of VOM need to be highly skilled and trained in order to negotiate the careful territory of harm and setting things right. • Much prework is needed with all involved before people are ready to be in the room together.

to dialogue participants in order to allow for new conversations. Altering the relational impact of existing conflict is a primary consideration of PCP dialogues.

VICTIM-OFFENDER MEDIATION

When applied thoughtfully and selectively to incidents of discrimination, vandalism, date rape, and other kinds of victimage, Victim-Offender Mediation had the potential to give those harmed a clear place to turn and a means to address these incidents, and it can create a shift in campus culture toward fostering community members' accountability to one another. Confidentiality is critical for the success of this social technology. VOM provides an opportunity for learning in community members' lives outside the classroom, encouraging holistic institutional learning goals. Because of the highly sensitive nature of these dialogues, extensive training for facilitators and oversight of a coordinated campus VOM program is needed.

[Editor's Note: This is an area in which deliberation and dialogue directly overlap with clinical and therapeutic models of group practice and family therapy. It is clear that both social work faculty and advanced students have contributions to offer to their campuses in this area, and our hope is that in the future, social work practitioners in these areas will begin to explore more fully the interface with Victim-Offender Mediation methodology in the same manner that the Newfield and Newfield chapter in this volume explores the interface between family therapy and sustained dialogue.]

PERSONAL QUALITIES OF DIALOGUE AND DELIBERATION LEADERS

The primary focus of this chapter has been on event design and matching event purpose with an appropriate social technology. For those who find they have a passion for dialogue and deliberation work, there is another integral aspect of the field: developing personal qualities that support dialogue and deliberation work. Patricia Wilson (2004, 3) says:

> An effective process leader knows the social technologies for civic engagement and when best to use them. But more importantly, she or he has done the deep inner work necessary to be 'strong like a mountain and spacious like the air'—to be centered in the face of conflict and emotion, to connect with the other's humanity without judgment or defensiveness, and to be aware of the invisible energy field of the whole.

As the dialogues we lead require increasing skill from us and increasing risk by participants, these personal qualities aid in creating the needed safety. Safety must not be equated with participants' or conveners' comfort. Overall, a high level of safety in a deliberation or dialogue is needed in order to enable potentially uncomfortable conversations where real risks exist. Some particularly useful qualities are our desire and ability to:

- Understand the reasonableness inherent in each individual's perspective
- Be present and responsive to the individuals and the group in front of you amid changing dynamics
- Avoid being the center of attention

- Do your homework to understand the life experiences of others different from ourselves
- Be a full, imperfect, real human being in leadership
- Know and understand our own triggers and how to reduce their impact on those with whom we work
- Admit what we don't know to ourselves and to those with whom we work
- Ask for help

For those in the role of instructor, additional challenges can occur in leading dialogue and deliberation events. These two hats can be difficult to transition between because of the different goals of each, particularly the role of judging competency as an instructor and encouraging individual expression and thinking and possibly personal risk as a dialogue and deliberation leader. Because of this, particular care will be needed in determining whether instructors offer their opinions as they lead.

Many other qualities of dialogue and deliberation leaders exist in addition to those listed above. How to place your feet upon the path of intentionally developing these qualities can be found in others' writing, particularly the writings of those who've developed D&D innovations. Development of these inner qualities and habits is a critical complement to our skills as facilitators and is crucial to increasing our capacity to respond to the unplanned human interactions we encounter every day. Our individual development of these qualities is essential to being "the change you wish to see in the world," as Gandhi suggested.

CONCLUSION

This chapter is primarily intended to be a useful resource for individuals within higher education who are planning dialogue and deliberation events for their campus or the wider community. It is offered as a beginning map to point readers in directions that will be useful for both design and implementation of deliberation and dialogue events. A great deal of further information on the entire field of dialogue and deliberation can be found on the National Coalition for Dialogue and Deliberation's website (www.thataway .org) and other sources.

Notes

1. My definition of the field has been expanded and enhanced through my collaboration and conversations with Nancy Glock-Grueneich as part of writing this chapter. This description has been greatly influenced by Nancy's thinking.

2. Within dialogue and deliberation literature, debate and discussion are sometimes defined as less valuable than dialogue. I do not hold this assumption and view each kind of human interaction as valuable and necessary.

3. Bohm, Factor, and Garrett (1991) define dialogue as only occurring when shared meaning is developed and when no agenda exists for the interaction. My definition challenges this assumption that dialogue can only occur when goals are absent.

4. Also, I agree with Pearce and Littlejohn's (1997) observation that we in the United States have an underdeveloped vocabulary in regards to how we communicate.

5. Editor's note: Lohmann's commons theory of association, discussed in a later chapter, deals with social technologies as one type of action repertory.

6. For more information about developing a broad-based planning team, refer to materials from the Study Circles Resource Center (SCRC), such as "Basic steps in creating a community-wide study circle program" in the appendix of *A Guide for Training Study Circle Facilitators*. SCRC materials are the most comprehensive I have encountered on this critical design aspect. Another excellent resource for many design aspects is *Fostering Dialogue Across Divides* from the Public Conversations Project.

7. The following section identifies the purposes of each social technology based on these categories.

8. Myles Horton did not actually refer to this social technology as Learning Circles (Glen 2006). He did not name it at all as it was secondary to and a means to achieve his primary societal-transformation goals. This label came later as educators have focused on his technique.

9. Horton's theoretical framework parallels that of Paulo Freire ([1970] 1973). The two had a meeting of the minds after each had independently developed his popular education theories and methods (Glen 2006).

10. For a consideration from the standpoint of family therapy, see the Newfield and Newfield chapter in this volume.

11. Victim-Offender Mediation is sometimes called Victim-Offender Dialogue. With my experience in both mediation and dialogue, I believe dialogue more accurately categorizes this social technology.

12. NCDD's original information is found in one table. Their original table is separated here for formatting purposes.

6

DELIBERATION, DIALOGUE, AND DELIBERATIVE DEMOCRACY IN SOCIAL WORK EDUCATION AND PRACTICE

Roger A. Lohmann and Nancy Lohmann

THE INTERRELATED THEMES of public talk—deliberation, dialogue, citizen participation, and organizational democracy—figure importantly in contemporary social theory and political philosophy (Barber 1988; Elstub 2008; Cohen and Arato 1992; Gutmann and Thompson 2002; Habermas 1984) and a number of other disciplines, including public administration (Morse 2006; Stivers 2009; and the Williams and Ludeman/Gelles chapters in this volume). What may be less clear is the original emergence of many of these ideas in earlier forms as part of the formulation of social work as a field early in the twentieth century. Closely related ideas of public talk were of central importance in the settlement house, neighborhood, and community-centers movements and in the establishment of social group work, community-organization, and social-administration perspectives in social work education and practice.

For several decades early in the twentieth century, the handling of these ideas in social work was what is described throughout this volume as pracademic, as practitioners such as Jane Addams and Mary Parker Follett (as well as hostile opponents such as Walter Lippman and more traditional elements of the "ivory tower" academy) engaged academic philosophers such as John Dewey and George Herbert Mead on these questions. The result was a rich and powerful strand of thought and action that continues to nourish and enrich social work today.

Each year, numerous proposals are put forth in social work journals, at the Annual Program Meeting of the Council on Social Work Education, and in other forums for the development of new forms of social work education and practice in new arenas. For some in social work, proposals for active citizenship through greater integration of public deliberation and sustained dialogue into social work may appear to be just another case of such pro-posals. Such a conclusion, however, would be in error. For one thing, any such proposals that are to go anywhere will inevitably be filtered through processes of deliberation not unlike those considered here. In social work such proposals also fit easily into a long tradition of similar efforts. A more important difference, however, is that proposals regarding deliberation and dialogue are actually a return to a rich chapter in the social work tradition.

Far from representing any departure from a nondeliberative social work past, greater attention to public deliberation and sustained dialogue in social work education and practice represents an embrace and continuation of a well-documented past: an affirmation of important parts of the history of the field and expression of some of its most basic principles. One telling bit of evidence is the way in which the social work formulation of "the individual in her social environment" not only brings together psychological and so-ciological perspectives but also explicitly incorporates an important civic or civil-society dimension. That dimension, together with social work values on human growth and development, explicitly connotes the idea of a citizen-individual in a civic environment of rights and responsibilities that directly fits the conception of a self-regulating (or "autonomous") individual in a self-regulating (or "democratic") community. This is the very essence of the "civic republican" formula that some in political philosophy find to be an important recent innovation. Yet this configuration is so basic and so deeply embedded in the core of the social work worldview that there is no need to label or make constant reference to it. Fundamental notions of deliberation and dialogue are so deeply woven into the fabric of social work education that it would take a major reconstruction of the field to remove them.

Modern social work theory and practice are built in fundamental ways on a base of several early models of deliberation and dialogue, together with several distinct models of group process and at least two models of deliberative democracy that arose during the Progressive Era (1889–1918).[1] Ever since that time, diverse individuals and groups within social work have continued to build on this deliberative base in various ways. Some of these contributors were more successful than others; several have suffered from serious neglect; and some are very difficult to properly assess and integrate fully into the contemporary profession of social work.

In some respects, social work's interest in the full range of civil rights movements for racial and ethnic minorities; women; the mentally ill; handi-capped and disabled persons; gay, bisexual, and transgendered people; and others has simultaneously been an effort to give civic voice to those who had been silent. Most such efforts have also had a strong deliberative core. In social work, the issue was never just what our elected leaders can do differently to better serve us. It was always a question of what we, as active, engaged citizens and community members, can do to make our world a better place. This may involve advocacy, of course, to influence elected and appointed officials. But, as the long history of interest in workplace democracy in social work attests, it is frequently also a question of more active forms of civic engagement, including deliberation and dialogue.

For example, although the "maximum feasible participation of the poor" and welfare-rights initiatives of the 1960s (both of which were partly deliberative in nature) have been widely and loudly condemned as failures by neoconservatives,[2] many of the associated ideas of participation, involvement, and the empowerment of clients, customers, and citizens have continued to exercise a strong motivating force for many people in social work and for those in other fields who have recently become interested in citizen participation and deliberative democracy issues (including all of the contributors to this volume not affiliated with social work).

Various commitments to deliberation and dialogue have not always been an unmixed blessing for social work. The continuing deliberative base sometimes lends an air of instability and incoherence to social work that not only has obscured its purposes and projects but also demonstrates some of the very theoretical problems that remain unresolved in deliberative democracy theory.[3] For example, the continuing flow of proposals for new forms of social work practice and new client groups far outstrips the ability and resources of social work to respond fully to such an abundance arising from so many directions. In this context, ideas are seldom rejected; most just generate insufficient interest. This brings to mind criticisms of the alleged inability of deliberative democracy to reach definitive decisions.[4]

Social work has never been an applied field in the sense of a consumer of deliberative ideas developed elsewhere, however, as practice models positioning it as a consumer of more basic social science and theory would imply. In fact, several of the most fundamental ideas associated with deliberative democracy theory arose directly out of social work practice experience and continue to function in different forms within contemporary social work theory and practice. In contemporary social group work and community practice, one can easily find self-conscious continuity with some of the earliest theoretical traditions.[5] But these traditions are also deeply woven, in ways almost too numerous to identify, into the basic culture of the contemporary profession and practice of social work.

BASIC APPROACH

The remainder of this chapter will point to the role of deliberative perspectives in early-twentieth-century social work and highlight the ideas of a few key people from whom much of the deliberative posture in social work is derived. It will also show that these early initiatives have continued to define and inspire many in contemporary social work. Central to the emergence of these ideas were intellectual leaders of the intertwined community centers, social group work, and settlement house movements who, even as they inspired others outside social work,[6] also contributed to the rise of a distinct pracademic environment that has continued to foster and nurture crucial ideas on dialogue and deliberative democracy to the present day.

Beginning in the first decades of the twentieth century, important ideas about the nature of social groups and group process, the importance of communication as something more than simple message transmission, and a fundamental group-democratic orientation arose and were blended with the pragmatic idealism of such seminal figures as Jane Addams and Mary Parker Follett, as well as dozens of their supporters, followers, and contemporaries.[7] While it would be easy to reconstruct this history as the emergence of practice from the theoretical work of philosophers—notably John Dewey but also Josiah Royce and a bevy of idealists such as T. H. Green and Bernard Bosanquet associated with the origins of the welfare state—reconstructing this history as a one-way transfer from theory into practice seriously distorts it and downplays the independent creative contributions of Addams, Follett, and other pracademics, who thought long and hard and wrote much about their own and others' practices. It should be clear that the democratic nature of group process has been fully and fundamentally realized over a longer period of time in social work than in any other discipline, profession, or field of practice.

Unfortunately, the response to the social work record in this regard in the wider academic and intellectual community remains mixed. One can search high and low in political philosophy and social theory for anything more than hesitant, half-hearted, and grudging acknowledgment that anyone even remotely associated with social work ever gave a moment's thought to these questions. Characteristically, such recognitions when they do occur are often encapsulated into a single sentence or phrase. For example, it is frequently noted in passing that Mary Parker Follett's *The New State*, a major work of deliberative political theory, was grounded in her experience—nine years of experience—in the community-centers movement.

At the same time, some of the implications of dialogical perspectives continue to prove challenging for social work education and practice, and not everyone in the profession is altogether comfortable with embracing this legacy.[8] One question that proves especially vexing for contemporary social work education is whether there can be a single preferred "method," technology, or proper protocol that defines the right way or best practice for a free and enlightened group of people to engage in dialogue or deliberation.[9] Is the choice of how to conduct a discussion entirely up to the members in a particular group setting? Or can someone outside the situation (whether a methodologist, philosopher, theorist, or professional "best practices" panel) prescribe the correct way for citizens to engage one another in deliberation or specify the criteria deliberators ought to use to evaluate their own performance? Certainly, room must be allowed to learn from past experience. However, the line between benefiting from past experience and proscribing future conduct proves to be a difficult one to draw.

A question that perplexed Jane Addams, among others, and remains unresolved today is the extent to which any robustly deliberative democracy worthy of the name can be said to be the unique province or professional base of any group or profession.[10] This is true not only for ideas but for people as well: major questions arise about the extent to which exclusive labels such as "social worker," "sociologist," "adult educator," or "philosopher" can be successfully pinned on several of the historic figures in this area, including Jane Addams, Mary Parker Follett, John Dewey, Eduard Lindeman, or the still largely unknown L. J. Hanifan, whom we introduce and discuss in this chapter.

PRACADEMIC ORIGINS

We can easily identify several original pracademic formulations of the ideas of deliberative democracy in social work history. The question of getting beyond traditional representative democracy was not first posed and answered by social or political theorists or academics as so much current theoretical work on the topic appears to suggest.[11] It arose instead in the early-twentieth-century context of Progressive Era social work practice and education, from key figures seeking to put their own ideals into practice and to reflect upon, understand, evaluate, and explain their resulting practice experiences.[12] Important pracademic work on deliberation and dialogue by Jane Addams and numerous other less well known figures, including Mary Parker Follett, Robert Woods, and L. J. Hanifan, proceeded from a consistent desire to identify and practice new forms of democratic behavior and to build new democratic institutions. This work occurred simultaneously with and influenced the philosophical writings of John Dewey in particular (Dewey 1993; Westbrook 1991). This pattern is quite different from the theory-into-practice flow of later practitioners and more abstract and general political or social theory on the subject.

For those attempting to work out theoretical answers to the most fundamental questions of deliberative democracy, the highly original work done within Progressive Era social work should constitute an important resource. Instead, the context in which the insights of Jane Addams arose, for example, has been almost entirely ignored by both practitioners (including, in some cases, social work educators and researchers seemingly unfamiliar with their own traditions) and, until recently, theorists.[13] The reasons for this are unknown. They may be nothing more substantial than indifference, sheer lack of familiarity, or that the sometimes florid and idealistic language in which Addams and Follett, not to mention the British idealists and others of the period, expressed themselves runs counter to the flat realism of today and often grates on the modern ear. This is probably connected, for example, to long-standing claims that John Dewey is "difficult" to read and Jane Addams is naïve and romantic.

Nowhere is this neglect more disconcerting than in Mary Parker Follett's highly original theory that links group, neighborhood, and the political state; those few who acknowledge her work agree that this theory grew directly out of her social work practice experience in the community center of the Roxbury neighborhood of Boston from 1900 through 1908 and is linked to her later, equally original work on organizational democracy. Instead of using Follett and her community-center experience to get a leg up on their own interests, contemporary theorists of deliberative democracy making many of the same claims appear to believe (or wish their readers to believe) that theirs is entirely original work. For example, nearly eighty years after Follett first laid out much the same point in *The New State*, recent work by a political theorist (Elstrub 2008) highlights secondary associations (e.g., groups) as a suitable infrastructure for deliberative democracy—without a single mention of Follett or *The New State*. If Elstrub is correct in drawing this connection (and we believe she is), then so was Follett, and that deserves mention.

Even Jürgen Habermas, whose work is otherwise deep, wise, and thorough, cannot be entirely excused from the tendency to overlook this earlier work, nor can contemporary social work. A great deal of Follett's highly original point of view has been incorporated into the core of contemporary social work and social administration theory, but almost completely without attribution.[14]

Sadly, neglect of the contributions of Progressive Era social work to deliberative democracy theory has been so complete and thorough that it might require an entire volume just to document the omissions. At the same time, the contemporaneous orientation and lack of historical insight among practitioners of deliberation and dialogue are no different from what is found in practice in other arenas. For example, the "core principles" of public deliberation identified by a group of practitioners in 2008 endorse principles that any assembly of group and community social workers would have been completely comfortable with seventy-five years ago. (See the appendix in this volume for the text of this code.)

The next section briefly recounts the contributions of Jane Addams and Mary Parker Follett as deliberative theorists. Finally, we will note in passing the roles played by John Dewey and a forgotten progressive education reformer named L. J. Hanifan, who has been recognized only within the past decade as the original American source of the concept of social capital.[15]

CONVENTIONAL WISDOM

The conventional wisdom on Addams, Dewey, Follett, and even Hanifan is instructive: Addams is currently an iconic figure in American culture as well as in social work, although many inside social work and beyond seem uncertain as to why she is important and it is not unheard of for students to assign her joint responsibility with Mary Richmond for the development of social casework. Her role as a pracademic is internationally recognized. She is one of only a handful of modern public intellectuals to invent a distinctive political/civic institution (the settlement house). Dewey, over much of his sixty-year public career was *the* quintessential American philosopher, the twentieth-century equivalent of Emerson, who nevertheless fell into obscurity shortly after his death and remained there for nearly half a century. Social work was one of numerous fields for which Dewey played a major defining role before he largely disappeared from public view. He is more or less singlehandedly responsible for the original problem-solving perspective, for example. His work only began to be reconsidered as of major importance forty years after his death, after it drew the attention of such European intellectuals as Habermas. Follett and Hanifan, like most of the social work figures cited previously, have been consigned more or less permanently to the recycling bin of history. Hanifan is currently making a cameo appearance in connection with his pioneering work on social capital, while Follett appears to have gone through several cycles of being recalled and forgotten again.[16] When she is remembered today, it is most often as a pioneer of management theory. Her early career is often presented as a set of academic and theoretical contributions, beginning with a study of the U.S. House of Representatives (1896) and her theory of what she termed the "New State" (1918), followed by her "mature" pracademic work in management and business organization (1941).

In connection with his research on the role of social capital in civil society, Robert Putnam discovered the completely neglected Hanifan and his early formulation of the theoretically important concept of social capital (Putnam 2000, 19). What Putnam did not note is the degree to which Hanifan's contribution was also a pracademic one within the same tradition as Addams, Follett, and Dewey. He was a functioning state education official (an "education bureaucrat") supervising rural schools in West Virginia and seemingly energized by the same set of progressive ideas about neighborhoods, groups, community action, education, and democracy that energized the other three thinkers. This connection alone should be enough to forge a strong theoretical link between social capital as trusting relationships and networks, the civil society tradition, and deliberative democracy theory.

In addition, Hanifan appears also to have been the first to note in print that schools are the community centers in rural communities—one of the most powerful and generally accepted principles of contemporary rural social work (Hanifan 1916; Lohmann and Lohmann 2005). Despite the continuing vigor of the ideas he first presented, Hanifan remains unfamiliar to most people in social work, who may not be aware of Putnam's rediscovery.[17]

JANE ADDAMS

Political philosophers, social scientists, historians, and other non–social workers have in recent decades rediscovered Jane Addams in many guises. In addition to the many claims made on her by social work, she has been said to be a Chicago School sociologist (Deegan 1984, 1988), feminist theorist (Fischer, Nackenoff, and Chmielewski 2009), public administration theorist (Stivers 2009), pragmatist philosopher (Menand 1997), public intellectual (Lasch 1986), social philosopher (Lasch 1965), and peace theorist (Elshtain 2002) to name just a few. In Fisher, Nackenoff, and Chmielewski (2009) Addams is "an extraordinary activist and thinker in many ways ahead of her time" (1). Reasonable (albeit anachronistic) cases can be made for each of these claims, and in Addams's case they are certainly not (as some of their advocates appear to suggest) mutually exclusive.

Unfortunately, too much of the Addams renaissance distorts the pracademic Addams and distances her from social work even as it succumbs to the priority of theory. Was Jane Addams all of the things these authors suggest? Yes, almost certainly. But did she also have a deep and abiding commitment to the social work practice community of her day? That, too, should be undeniable. And as part of the overall package Addams had a strong record of commitment to deliberation and dialogue and her own unique blend of deliberative democracy theory that for several decades after her death in 1935 was dismissed by philosophers and others outside social work as naïve and idealistic, but in which new generations have found interest.

The very project of the young, educated, bourgeois "urban settlers" Addams, Ellen Gates Starr, and the others who followed them in establishing residence in inner-city neighborhoods of poor immigrants was fundamentally dialogical: Hull House residents sought to speak, listen, learn, and teach. Certainly, they did other things as well (although a great deal less "relief," casework, and family visiting than many contemporary social work students are comfortable with).

According to their own reports, one of the first things that Addams and Ellen Gates Starr did upon moving into the Hull House in 1889 was to hold a salon (or "open house") for the purpose of meeting and talking with residents of the neighborhood. One would be hard pressed to find a comparable example of a theoretically informed dialogical democracy initiative anywhere at the time. From the very start, Hull House was tied to a basic model of deliberative democracy. This is evident in the three "ethical principles" that Addams and Starr endorsed at the beginning: *"to teach by example, to practice cooperation, and to practice social democracy, that is, egalitarian, or democratic, social relations across class lines"* (Knight 2005, 182). Hull House was not an experiment in policy advocacy or lobbying Congress or the Illinois legislature, nor did its residents aspire to organize charity, like the Charity Organization movement, or "practice cooperation" like the Roycrofters by forming a production cooperative. We have the testimony of the founders that Hull House was, from the start, an effort at cross-class dialogue as part of a larger experiment in cooperation as conflict reduction and equality and social democracy in social relations.

This Hull House model of deliberation and dialogue continued to evolve throughout Addams's long career. The Hull House model, like Deweyan ideas on social democracy and Follett's model articulated in *The New State*, also influenced the development of social work education and practice with respect to groups and the desirability of face-to-face group interaction of people with differences, and in the basic commitment to group and organizational democracy.

JOHN DEWEY

Cause and effect are almost impossible to tease apart in the case of Addams and her longtime friend and colleague John Dewey. Both through Addams and on his own, Dewey was also a major contributor to the early (and contemporary) social work model of deliberation in addition to his contribution of the social work problem-solving model. Until well into the 1970s, social work texts routinely cited a number of Dewey's articles, notably "How We Think" (1910). Dewey began his long career in the nineteenth century as a Hegelian idealist but early in the twentieth century began to emerge as one of the founders of a distinct American pragmatism. Festenstein (2009), in the online Stanford Encyclopedia of Philosophy suggests a number of characteristics that survived this major transition in Dewey's thought: "holism about the individual; anti-elitism; democratic participation as an aspect of individual freedom; and *the unconventional view of democracy as a form of relationship inherent not merely in political institutions but in a wide range of social spheres*" (emphasis added).

It should be immediately apparent that these are deeply embedded in social work and laid the groundwork for the social work model of deliberative democracy. Festenstein might have added to this list the importance of evidence-based social experimentation, personal growth grounded in education, and a strong commitment to the kind of communication-based social relations that Habermas and other more recent political theorists also redounded from Dewey. These same beliefs are also attributable to Addams, Follett, Hanifan, and much early social work. Although Dewey is still difficult to read and interpret half a century after his death, there can be little doubt that his influence upon the evolution of social work education and practice was strong, and that a distinctly Deweyan model of deliberative and democratic social relations, derived in part from his relations with Addams and Hull House, was an important part of that influence.

MARY PARKER FOLLETT

The evidence in support of Mary Parker Follett (1868–1933) as an early pracademic of deliberation and dialogue is equally decisive, even though she is even less known and celebrated than her contemporaries Addams and Dewey. Follett's career is often divided into two phases, pre- and post-management. Her unique contributions to deliberative democracy become more clear and convincing when it is divided, as Mattson (1998) does, into three periods, each marked by one of her three principal publications. Her career began with a conventional period of academic study of history with — like Dewey, the theorists of the British welfare state, and her mentor, Josiah Royce — a strong emphasis on Hegelian, idealist philosophy. In 1896 Follett authored a solid and well-received institutional analysis of the Speaker of the U.S. House of Representatives. Following her inability to secure an academic appointment, the second period in Follett's career began with nine years of community social work practice (1900–1908) and culminated in her second and most remarkable book, *The New State: Group Organization, the Solution of Popular Government*, published in 1918. In the third and final phase of her career, Follett concentrated on applying insights gained from her social work phase to democratizing business organizations, as evidenced in her collection of essays published posthumously in *Dynamics of Administration* (1941).[18]

Since her death two years before Addams, Follett has remained a major figure in administrative and management theory, but both the pivotal importance of her social work experience and her status as a political philosopher of deliberative democracy periodically fall into anonymity. To understand her enduring contributions, we need to look more closely at Follett's contributions to deliberative democratic thought.

Follett's 1896 House study (and her even less known biography of Henry Clay) "conformed to a developing consensus in professional political science" to accept the growing power of the national government and the declining relevance of older forms of popular self-government like New England town meetings (Mattson 1998, xxxiii). In short, like other Progressives (notably Herbert Croly and Walter Lippman), the early Follett argued that the civil society of local communities observed by de Tocqueville was obsolete, necessarily pushed aside by a representative democracy of elected officials and administrative experts deemed more suitable for an industrial society in which citizenship consisted principally of voting in elections and watching. In this she should be seen as a precursor of important parts of the urbanization-industrialization thesis later made famous by Wilensky and Lebeaux (1965) and the Dahl (1963) pluralist policy-process model that still form the basis of prevailing social work perspectives on policy and advocacy.

In her second phase, this representational view was not only modified but completely upended in ways that still have implications for social work education and practice. Those most familiar with Follett's career generally agree there is only one factor to explain her radical shift away from representative democracy to the view expressed in *The New State*, and that is her involvement in community social work. "By the 1910s," Kevin Mattson, editor of the 1998 edition of *The New State* says, "Follett had radically changed her political ideas. . . . The same woman who had once written that 'the democracy most to be desired' was the 'representative assembly,' now argued that 'representation is not the main fact of political life; the main concern of politics is *modes of association*'" (Mattson 1998, xxix). She also wrote: "you cannot establish democratic control by legislation . . .; there is only one way to get democratic control—by people learning how to evolve collective ideals" (xxix).

Follett's nine years of social work practice (1900–1908) in the Boston community-center movement are generally acknowledged as the sole motivation for this profound shift in her theoretical orientation. Mattson tells us that

Mary Parker Follett followed in Jane Addams' footsteps, always working within the parameters set by a society that allowed only a circumspect involvement of women in public affairs. Ironically, Follett's lack of academic opportunities provided her with new forms of experience *that radically altered her intellectual ideas about democracy.* Experience taught Follett a great deal more about politics than a career in academia ever could.

(MATTSON 1998. XXXV–XXXVI, EMPHASIS ADDED)

It is important to note that Follett was not an urban settler in the Addams mode. Instead, she worked in Boston in the community-schools movement founded by Robert A. Woods in Rochester, N.Y. (Woods [1929] 1971), which sought to redefine schools as community centers open to the social and civic participation of neighborhood residents. This was the same movement that influenced our fourth (and least known) figure. L. J. Hanifan was engaged in similar community-school efforts as superintendent of rural instruction in West Virginia (1912–1920).[19] Before looking further at Hanifan, however, we need to look closely at Follett's *New State*.

THE NEW STATE

Benjamin Barber, political philosopher of deliberative democracy and author of *Strong Democracy: Participatory Politics for a New Age* (1984) which is itself a major theoretical contribution to deliberative democracy theory, calls Follett's *The New State*

an extraordinary paean to a stronger more participatory form of American democracy that was *drawn in equal parts from Follett's academic acumen as a student of democratic theory, Royce and Hegel as well as Laski and Cole, and from her own personal experience in local democracy and community organization.*

(BARBER 1984, XV)

In other words, like Addams and Hanifan, Follett also has solid pracademic credentials, although the social work connection is not mentioned explicitly. Barber goes on to offer this assessment of the book:

In *The New State*, she writes what must be regarded as an American classic of participatory democracy. She keeps arms length from nationalist accounts without falling into parochialism, and she distinguishes deliberative, education-grounded forms of direct democracy from mob-rule caricatures first drawn and then assailed by Lippman and other liberal critics of too much participation.

(BARBER 1984, XV)

As Mattson observes, "For Follett, as with other social centers activists, the democratic citizen was committed to public dialogue" (Follett [1918] 1998, 313). As part of her transformation, Follett replaced her earlier nationalist emphasis with a local/community orientation still recognizable by social workers: "In a neighborhood group," Follett insisted, "you have the stimulus and the bracing effect of many different experiences and ideals" (Follett 1918, 196).

Yet rather than signaling the beginning of a major shift in thinking about American democracy, both the community-centers movement and Follett's (as well as Hanifan's) contributions came at the very end of the Progressive Era and soon were ignored, unread, and largely forgotten. Thus, her career took yet another turn. "After the decline of the social centers movement after World War I—a decline due largely to the mistakes made by activists and thinkers in the movement itself—Follett became interested in modern business management" (Mattson 1998, lviii).

The essence of Follett's perspective on deliberation was a clustered hierarchy of associations, beginning with neighborhood-based face-to-face groups practicing deliberation and democratic social relationships. Her nested-institutions view (groups within organizations within neighborhoods within communities within society) is still evident in the social work education models of today. Yet even as Follett went on to radically transform theories of business administration and organizational life, her contributions to a strong and vital social work–based original perspective on deliberative democracy fell from view.

L. J. (LYDA JUDSON) HANIFAN

We turn now to the final example of a pracademic contemporary of Addams, Dewey, and Follett who also played a role in the pracademic conceptualization of deliberative democracy that was lost to history for decades, and whose major contribution to deliberative democracy and social work may yet lie in the future. L. J. Hanifan (1879–1931), from his position as superintendent of rural instruction for the West Virginia Department of Education, authored a number of books and articles that enable us to place him squarely in the same community-centers movement as Follett (Hanifan 1916). They also establish him, as Putnam noted, as *the* original American pracademic to formulate the concept of social capital, a concept tied by Robinson and others in this volume to deliberative theory and practice.[20] From the vantage point of social work, he may also be the first in print to give voice to a principle still fundamental to rural social work practice: that local schools are the vital centers of rural communities.

More than seventy years after his death, Hanifan's writings on social capital and community centers were rediscovered by Robert Putnam, who discussed them in *Bowling Alone* (2000, 19). The known facts of Hanifan's life and career as a West Virginia progressive are still sketchy and need not be repeated here.[21] Hanifan's writings are clearly those of a pracademic (he was one of eight original members of the West Virginia Department of Education and involved in policy efforts setting high school curriculum requirements for the state). He was also clearly writing in the context of the same community-centers movement as Follett. Between 1912 and 1920, Hanifan authored ten known articles, chapters, and reports that not only are the first publications identifying the concept of social capital but also link him with the community-schools movement and position him as a potential source in rural social work. In all, five of Hanifan's ten known publications, three journal articles and two books, deal with neighborhood (in his case, rural rather than urban) and the concept of schools as community centers.

Hanifan's (1916) definition of "social capital" reflects not only an orientation similar to Addams, Dewey, and Follett but also an affinity for, if not direct organizational ties to, a social work orientation:

> The tangible substances [that] count for most in the daily lives of people: namely good will, fellowship, sympathy, and social intercourse among the individuals and families who make up a social unit. . . . The individual is helpless socially, if left to himself. If he comes into contact with his neighbor, and they with other neighbors, there will be an accumulation of social capital, which may immediately satisfy his social needs and which may bear a social potentiality sufficient to the substantial improvement of living conditions in the whole community. The community as a whole will

benefit by the cooperation of all its parts, while the individual will find in his associations the advantages of the help, the sympathy, and the fellowship of his neighbors.

(QUOTED FROM PUTNAM 2000, 19)

Social work is only beginning to take notice of the idea of social capital, and to date there has been no discussion linking social capital to the deliberative interests of the field. But making that connection is a very small intellectual leap.

CONTEMPORARY SOCIAL WORK AS A DELIBERATIVE ENVIRONMENT

The ideas of Dewey, Addams, Follett, Hanifan, and others of the settlement house and community-centers movements have been so deeply engrained in social work that the entire profession is organized as a democratically constituted, deliberative body, where decisions are seldom made by voting but on the basis of emergent consensus following organized group discussion. There are many groups, organizations, and focused publics[22] involved in the social construction of contemporary social work as an activity, programmatic enterprise, and institution, and each is concerned in its own way with issues of definition, identity, and boundaries of professional education and practice. The very fact of this plurality means that important elements of dialogue and deliberation are built into the theory and practice of modern social work to an even greater degree than in other disciplines and professions.

Social work in the early twenty-first century both as a profession and as an academic discipline has established itself more securely than ever before. It is at least partly in the nature of the civic republican conception of professions and disciplines that the various organizations and entities that define modern social work can be seen as autonomous, self-governing collectivities of autonomous, self-governing people.[23] Indeed, from a deliberative-theory perspective, social work professionals can be seen as autonomous people working within a self-governing profession, and clients can be seen as people wishing to achieve greater personal autonomy. This is a key element of the (service- or supply-) worker side of the social work emphasis on human development and the social environment. In order for social workers to make sense of what they are doing, as well as evaluate when they have done it successfully, there must be some measure of widespread agreement on the nature, scope, and dimensions of the activity of social work. While for many "authorities" this is seen as a preliminary—and one-time—consideration, the reality is that deliberative and dialogical processes focused on two disarmingly simple questions—What is social work? Who is a social worker?—have been matters of almost continuous dialogue and deliberation within the field for at least the last century.

The institution of social work in all of its diverse manifestations has grown to include a bewildering variety of licensed and certified professionals, clients, volunteers, and paraprofessionals, at least some of whom are organized into various self-governing membership organizations and mutual-aid and self-help groups. The contemporary social work profession is a highly complex entity. It includes not only the 167,000 or so members who belong to the National Association of Social Workers but also a large number of non-NASW members licensed for the practice of social work by their states, and all of the graduates of the nearly 200 MSW and more than 500 BSW programs in colleges and universities accredited by the Council on Social Work Education. Moreover, social work practice and education in the United States have become the working models for the organization of social work in many other parts of the world through such organizations as the International Association of Social Work, the International Association of Schools of Social Work, and assorted national and regional professional and academic associations in different countries.

Because there are so many groups, organizations, and focused publics involved in the social construction of professional social work as an enterprise and institution and each is in some way concerned with managing the definition, identity, and boundaries of professional education and practice, important elements of dialogue and deliberation are built into the very warp and woof of modern social work.

The delegate assembly of NASW, the accreditation commission of CSWE, and the diverse state licensing bodies are routinely involved in fundamental concerns of defining and elaborating what is regarded as legitimate practice and preparation for practice. Dialogue and deliberation are also fundamental to the constitution of social work education and practice. A thoroughgoing value commitment—indeed, one of the core social work values in the view of social work educators and the official code of ethics established by NASW—is the idea of self-determination, for the profession as well as for clients.[24] However, social work practice and all of the assorted international, national, state, and local associations that support it are highly complex and contingent matters, and the coherent, ongoing operations of the profession are dependent in part on continuous, on-going discussions.

In all of these senses, dialogue and deliberation in their general meanings are built into the very organizational efforts that go into creating, identifying, and sustaining the institutions of modern social work. It is important to note, however, that the adjectives "public" and "sustained" in the subtitle of this book are important: not all of the deliberations that construct social work are public and not all of the dialogue is sustained. Some are the proprietary talks of specific organizations and interests, and some are sporadic and short-term.

However, careful reading of the other chapters in this book will make clear to most readers that the specific models of public deliberation and sustained dialogue have many applications in social work. Perhaps nowhere is this more evident than in the long and continuing history of discussion of that momentous question: *What, exactly, is social work?* Practitioners, academics, employers, students, the NASW Delegate Assembly, and many others have periodically revisited this question through deliberations over most of the past century. This is also true in the case of creating and sustaining public understanding of the rationales for the profession and for professional practice and for resolving some of the many existential dilemmas that arise in application of the values of the social work profession to daily life on an ongoing basis.

CONCLUSION: IMPLICATIONS FOR CURRICULUM

Given the role of social work curricula in specifying the nature and parameters of social work practice, one might ask how deliberation and dialogue have been addressed in the curriculum of accredited social work education programs. In order to fully appreciate that relationship, it may be appropriate to briefly describe how the curriculum influences social work practice.

One of the changes over the last few decades in the field of social work is the increasing requirement that people identifying themselves as social workers be licensed as such. While the requirements for licensing differ from state to state, one common thread is that to be eligible for licensure, a candidate must have graduated from a program accredited by the Council on Social Work Education. Thus, the expectations for accredited programs influence who is recognized as a social worker and the kind of practice he or she may be prepared to do. Now and in the future, engagement with deliberation and dialogue by social workers will be, to a significant degree, influenced by some measure of recognition of these processes in accredited curricula. The curricular requirements for all accredited programs are found in the Educational Policy and Accreditation Standards of the Council on Social Work Education. The most recent standards, adopted in 2008 are available online at http://www.cswe.edu.

While neither the current nor the preceding standards explicitly use the words "deliberative" or "dialogue," it is clear from some of the standards that there is a continuing legacy of Jane Addams and Mary Parker Follett and that some measure of deliberation and dialogue is expected in social work education. One such example may be found in Educational Policy 2.1.10. In that section, one finds such statements as, "Professional practice involves the dynamic and interactive processes of engagement, assessment, intervention, and evaluation at multiple levels." The terms "dynamic" and "interactive" certainly refer to processes that are a part of deliberation and dialogue. It is also clear from social work's involvement with broader cultural values, social problems, and social policy that these multiple dynamic and interactive processes also apply to group and community deliberation and dialogue processes. For example, the engagement of the campus sustained dialogue movement with issues of racism, as described by Saunders and Parker, Tukey and Nemeroff, and Van Til in this volume, is an obvious extension of social work concerns.

Subsections of Educational Policy and Accreditation Standards also describe a specific deliberative process. Section 2.1.10 (a), "Engagement," includes, "Develop a mutually agreed on focus of work and desired outcomes." Section 2.1.10 (b) indicates the need to "develop mutually agreed-on intervention goals and objectives." Neither of these would be possible without engagement in processes of deliberation and dialogue.

The continuing importance of deliberation and dialogue for social work education may also be found in Educational Policy 3.0, which refers to "the culture of human interchange; the spirit of inquiry; the support for difference and diversity" among other qualities that inform a student's learning and development. Thus, while the terms "deliberation" and "dialogue" do not appear in CSWE accreditation standards, it is clear that such activities are compatible with and even expected by the standards.

The expectation of dialogue is demonstrated in several ways as a student progresses through the social work curriculum. First, it is likely demonstrated in the classes taken by a student via the interaction among faculty members and students. Such classes typically place an emphasis on students' providing feedback on the concepts introduced. In fact, to facilitate such feedback, it is not uncommon for students and the faculty member to sit in a large circle as a means of enhancing dialogue. The use of this kind of seating arrangement also demonstrates equality among the participants in the discussion.

Social work education often makes use of group assignments in classroom work. This is not a matter of accident or coincidence but a direct result of the continuing recognition in social work education of the importance of group process, a recognition that is directly traceable back to Jane Addams, Mary Parker Follett, and others. As Follett observed in *The New State*, group process inevitably requires deliberation and dialogue among the participants. While students sometimes object that work is not evenly distributed among group members when such groups are used, their continued use indicates the importance placed on dialogue and developing the skills needed to engage in it.

The most recent CSWE accreditation standards also incorporate the concept of a signature pedagogy for social work: field instruction. The use of field instruction, grounded as it is in the historic insights of Dewey, Addams, and Follett, also emphasizes the importance of deliberation and dialogue among students and field instructors and classroom faculty. In recognition of this, many undergraduate and graduate social work programs have adopted the model of the *field seminar*, in which aspects of the students' experience are engaged, assessed, and evaluated in an educational intervention. The process begins when the student and his or her field instructor develop learning objectives for the field experience. Through that process, they discuss both the curricular expectations and the strengths and learning needs of the student. Thus, field expectations for a particular student reflect deliberation and dialogue about that student's strengths and limitations.

The dialogue also continues outside the seminar when the student and field instructor meet periodically to discuss the student's progress. Those meetings may result in consensus that a given field objective has been met. They may also, however, result in extended discussions about the progress a student has achieved in a given area. Similar discussions would occur between the student and field instructor about the student's clients and their programs. Such discussions inevitably involve deliberation and dialogue.

Field experiences also involve a more formal, written assessment of student progress. While the particular methods used may vary from social work program to social work program, it is not uncommon for both the student and the field instructor to rate the student's performance in specified areas and then discuss where their individual ratings agree and disagree. As these few examples indicate, the signature pedagogy of social work, in both the classroom and the field, involves significant deliberation and dialogue.

Notes

1. We will deal in this chapter with only two of the most fundamental models of deliberation and dialogue. Others, including Robert Woods, Eduard Lindemann, Gisela Konopka, Alan Klein, Murray Ross, Gladys Ryland, Gertrude Wilson, Ralph Kramer, and a large group of other community-organization, group-work, and education theorists, are not at all hard to identify. The biggest problem for this or any other publication, in fact, is simply the length of the list.

2. "Certifying" these failures was one of the important dynamics in the writings of early neoconservative intellectuals like Irving Kristol, Daniel Patrick Moynihan, and Nathan Glazer and in neocon publications, particularly *The Public Interest*.

3. Elstub (2008, esp. chap. 2) offers a careful and extensive consideration of the theoretical weaknesses and problems of deliberative democracy theory.

4. Elstub (2008) speaks of this as the "infinite regress" of "preference formation."

5. The social work literature is rich with insights into this continuity. In the group-work area, for example, see Gitterman (2004). Gitterman cites three sources that he says "provided group work with its philosophical base": Mary Parker Follett (both the 1924 and 1926 editions of *The New State*), Eduard Lindeman, a social work faculty member widely regarded as the "father" of adult education, and the Progressive education movement, inspired by the philosopher John Dewey, with its emphasis on group process and peer learning.

6. See, for example, Fischer, Nackenoff, and Chmielewski (2009)

7. "Pragmatic idealism" refers to the multiple, subtle, and at times vague and even inchoate ways in which several generations of social workers translated into practice their understandings of the philosophical idealism of Hegel; the British idealist tradition of Thomas Hill Greene, Bernard Bosanquet, and

others; the American idealist tradition of Josiah Royce and the early John Dewey; the pragmatism of the later Dewey as well as assorted Marxian and Freudian perspectives; and the sociology of Tönnies (community), Weber (organization), Parsons, and dozens of others. This Rube Goldberg mélange of a discipline sometimes leaves purer theoreticians of the older traditions of the academy agog, but it yields workable combinations in practice. This unique mix enlivened early social work and still characterizes (and in some respects, one is tempted to say, haunts) contemporary social work thought.

8. These elements and the associated qualitative, interactional, and constructivist tendencies of the social work tradition have been particularly vexing for those who have sought to separate social work from its tradition and move it "forward" in behaviorist, positivistic, or "more scientific" directions, such as current "best practices," "performance management," and "evidence-based practice" initiatives. A broad tolerance for apostasy is one of the characteristic features that contemporary social work inherited from its deliberative tradition.

9. This issue is important for more than social workers. Others, such as members of the interdisciplinary (and, in some respects, nondisciplinary) National Conference of Deliberation and Dialogue confront similar questions regularly. A logically and theoretically consistent answer would be that it is not, that a consistent deliberative stance requires that genuinely free groups must be free to select their own processes and criteria.

10. Gutman and Thompson (2002) offers a major political-theoretic analysis that speaks directly to this issue.

11. Even in the current era, pracademics continue to be important on this topic, often in the guise of "public intellectuals." Thus, for example, Jürgen Habermas has, for the past four decades, not been content to speak only to philosophers and sociologists but has also been a major public force in German (formerly West German) public opinion through many newspaper and magazine articles, public speeches and lectures, and other media (as far as we know, Habermas was not a blogger).

12. Program-evaluation methodology, of course, is a more recent invention. I mean to suggest here evaluation as the psychological and social process of reflection and thought which characterized the work and writing of Progressive Era social workers.

13. It is hard to know the extent to which writing social work out of the deliberative democracy tradition has been purposeful. Some of the alternative explanations that come readily to mind are rather egregious and unflattering: It might be caused, for example, by lack of learning and unsound scholarship or, perhaps, by remarkable degrees of disciplinary parochialism. Just to cite two of many possible examples: although groups get more than a dozen mentions in the

index of Elstrub's *Towards a Deliberative and Associational Democracy* (2008), Jane Addams, Mary Parker Follett, and social work completely fail to make the index, and John Dewey gets one brief, passing mention. The terms "social work" and "social welfare" also do not appear in the index of Fischer, Nackenhoff, and Chmielewski (2009), *Jane Addams and the Practice of Democracy*, even though the latter does appear in one chapter title.

14. There are, of course, also exceptions to the neglect of Mary Parker Follett's unique contributions scattered throughout social work publications since her time. Gitterman (2004) has already been mentioned. Further, Myron Weiner's *Human Services Management* (1990) devoted a whole case study vignette to Follett's work in both editions of that book. Understandably, the emphasis was primarily on her third-career management efforts. As often occurs, however, *The New State*, with its endorsement of deliberative democracy is mentioned but neither highlighted nor elaborated. We also cited her in our book *Social Administration* (Lohmann and Lohmann 2002).

15. Stereotypes can be very strong, so strong in fact that the improbability of a vital, active rural progressive movement in West Virginia before the economic devastation of the 1930s through 1980s was probably an active factor in the loss of Hanifan from the historical record.

16. The "new editions" (reissues, really, since the author is deceased and has not made any revisions) of *The New State* in 1965 and 1998 seem to have temporarily brought her back into view before she slipped into the mists yet again.

17. In late 2007, just before the first author of this chapter posted a brief biographical statement about Hanifan on the Citizendium.org website, a Google search produced not a single online mention. (Someone has to be well-forgotten to produce o Google hits!) As more information has became available, a fuller entry based on archival research—complete with picture—has been posted on the Citizendium site. In 2010, as of this writing, the number of search engine hits on Hanifan had risen to just over 11,500, which is still well below the numbers generated by many obscure American writers who were his contemporaries, like Lafcadio Hearn and Ole Rølvaag.

18. Conceivably, one might suggest another phase in her career associated with Follett's 1924 publication of *Creative Experience*, although this is probably best assigned to her final business-management phase, just as the early (unpublished?) biography of Henry Clay is easily assigned to her representative-government phase along with the 1896 study.

19. The clearest evidence of the affinity with the Woods movement is found in Hanifan's writings on rural schools as *community centers*.

20. Hanifan's 1916 journal article and a chapter in his 1920 book entitled "Social Capital" mark his contribution many decades before academic theorists such

as Pierre Bourdieu (1986), James Coleman (1988), and others cited as originators in the theoretical literature.

21. Everything currently known about Hanifan is published at http://en.citizendium
.org/wiki/L.J._(Lyda_Judson)_Hanifan.

22. A focused public is defined here as a body of people sufficiently large that
members are not personally known to one another but would under most circumstances have some sense of mutual recognition and who do not all belong
to the same organization yet share some common values, mission, or interests.
In this sense, the professional community of social work identified in the first
paragraph of this article is a focused public, and the American Association of
Retired Persons is not even though it involves more people and is similarly purposive. The term is often used in conjunction with at least one more adjective,
as in consumer-focused public, science-focused public, new-focused public,
and a wide variety of topic-focused publics.

23. The civic republican tradition in political philosophy tends not to be acknowledged by name in contemporary social work but is deeply embedded in the
self-definition of the profession in many ways; none is more fundamental than
the social work model of personal growth and development influenced by the
social environment. This model is completely consistent as a matter of political philosophy with the civic republican model of a democratic community
made up of self-directing individuals in self-governing communities. This is
attributable in large measure to the influence of several generations of writers
and thinkers, including Jane Addams and Mary Richmond and many others
in the charity-organization society and settlement house movements and the
more recent movement to define and articulate the profession. It goes without
saying that the civic republican (small R) element in social work is no more a
matter of partisanship or party than the equally deep professional commitment
of social workers to democratic (small D) community.

24. Self-determination in this sense might be seen as merely the civil, apolitical
aspect of what the political theory literature treats as self-governance or autonomy (see Elstub 2008).

SECTION II

SUSTAINED DIALOGUE IN PRACTICE

Introduction

THIS SECTION CONSISTS OF FIVE chapters that examine the practice of sustained dialogue in several different contexts: race relations on campus; the conflict in Derry, Northern Ireland; social justice at West Virginia University; and situational policing and public safety in urban neighborhoods.

The student sustained dialogue movement on U.S. campuses began in the late 1990s when two Princeton undergraduates, David Tukey and Teddy Nemeroff, met Hal Saunders, an alumni who was then a Princeton trustee. "Diving In: A Handbook for Improving Race Relations on College Campuses Through the Process of Sustained Dialogue" is a handbook in which Tukey, who has since earned his doctorate in neuroscience, and Nemeroff, whose subsequent work in South Africa is discussed by Saunders and Parker, explained to their fellow students seeking to become involved with sustained dialogue the workings of a viable campus process. Social workers and others familiar with group process will find much that is recognizable in their discussion of the process, which was written as a student-to-student account of how to initiate a campus sustained dialogue process.

After more than thirty years of violence, the conflict in Northern Ireland was finally ended with the Good Friday Agreement (Comhaontú Aoine an Chéasta) in 1998, although grievances and misunderstandings remain on all sides more than a decade later. In "Derry Exceptionalism and the Organic Model of Sustained Dialogue," Nick Acheson of the University of Ulster and Carl Milofsky of Bucknell University explore the social conditions for the emergence of dialogue in Derry/Londonderry in the wake of that famous accord.

West Virginia University was among the first American universities to establish a viable institution-wide social justice program for faculty, staff, and students. When the Nova Institute sought to establish a student sustained dialogue effort in the Tukey-Nemeroff-Saunders mode on the WVU campus, one of the first places organizers turned for help was to the Office of Social Justice. In "The Role of Dialogue in Achieving Justice at an American University," the executive officer for social justice, Jennifer Macintosh, and Charles Morris, a staff member in the Office of Social Justice, review the development and operation of that office in light of its continuing role in facilitating dialogue on campus.

Another of the contexts in which sustained dialogue is making inroads is in community policing, thanks to the work of James Nolan, associate professor of sociology and his colleagues at WVU. Jim is a former police officer and FBI agent with a long interest in community policing who, together with his colleagues and students in sociology, conducted two important studies of the role of dialogue. The first of these, presented in the chapter by Nolan, Norman Conti, and Corey Colyer, "A Public Safety Process: Sustained Dialogue for Situational Policing," lays out "a structure for policing that begins by conceptualizing a practical end state that the police and community can work toward (i.e., neighborhood development) and then provides a blueprint for achieving it." The second study, presented in the chapter by Nolan, Ronald Althouse, and Jeri Kirby, "Facilitating Neighborhood Growth: A 'Commonsense' Public Safety Approach from the Relational Paradigm," reports the results of their studies of community responses to a dialogue-based approach to community policing on the North Side of Pittsburgh, Pennsylvania.

7

DIVING IN: A HANDBOOK FOR IMPROVING RACE RELATIONS ON COLLEGE CAMPUSES THROUGH THE PROCESS OF SUSTAINED DIALOGUE

Teddy Nemeroff and David Tukey

INTRODUCTION: WHAT IS SUSTAINED DIALOGUE?

THIS HANDBOOK IS LARGELY ADDRESSED to potential moderators. In our first year of implementing Sustained Dialogue,[1] moderators participated in a training session with a developer of the process. While this session was vital in energizing and informing the initiators of Sustained Dialogue on our campus it was not a prerequisite for establishing dialogue groups. The tips and helpful hints presented throughout these pages should provide an adequate knowledge base for an interested group of students to successfully establish sustained dialogue on their college campus and generate discussion on how the process can succeed.

Sustained dialogue is a process for improving relationships within a community that are strained along racial or ethnic lines. Its approach focuses on probing the dynamics of troubled community relationships to better understand them and formulate actions for improving them.

A relationship exists between two groups of people when one group positively or negatively impacts the lives of the other over time. By bringing together concerned community members from all sides of contentious relationships, Sustained Dialogue, under the guidance of a moderator, allows participants to explore their problems in a non-confrontational setting. This is not a form of mediation or negotiation in which two sides attempt to come to an agreement.[2] Instead, it is a cooperative exercise in which all participants share their own views and experiences and attempt to learn from others.

This does not mean that conversations are tame or that the emotions are blunted. Indeed, for many participants, sustained dialogue provides their first opportunity to share with representatives of a perpetrating group the experiences that have caused them pain. Meetings can, in fact, be quite heated, but the purpose of the dialogue is to deepen the group's understanding of the relevant problems.

Sustained dialogue is not just talk; rather it is talk with a purpose. Participants are attempting to work through the dynamics of relations so that they can formulate actions to improve them. Though all participants are present because they see an interest in addressing the issues on the table, these conversations are not just preaching to the choir. By working through a community's problem, the sustained dialogue group becomes a new source of power within the community that can provide solutions.

As a methodology, sustained dialogue works through five stages. These five stages as outlined by Dr. Harold Saunders are meant to represent the natural phases through which discussions pass among groups in conflict. These are not rigid steps that must be followed but a gradual process through which groups pass. This passage is not a linear progression, and groups should expect to move back and forth as needed.

In the first stage, interested students should develop a plan for establishing dialogue groups on their campus and gather participants for those groups. Once individual groups are formed, the group's leaders should ensure that each participant understands the process. Then, groups move into stage two, and conversations begin. This stage is often called the downloading phase, as it is typified by participants sharing personal experiences and seemingly getting things off their chest.

The moderator will notice a change in the character of conversations as the dialogue progresses into stage three. Here, participants are beginning to understand each other's experiences with race and are able to link each individual's experience into a web of concepts that enables a better understanding of racism. With this understanding of the problem, the group then moves into stage four, where they generate possible solutions to the problem. In stage five, the final stage, group members turn suggestions into action. (See Appendix 1 for a visual presentation of the stages.)

It is important to note that these stages are a conceptualization of human experience and by no means represent a rigid framework. Rather, the stages are presented here in order to give a moderator some guidance on how the dialogue should be directed in order to reach the most desirable ends. As will be described throughout the following pages, the moderator has the difficult duty of facilitating both the emotional satisfaction that participants gain from the sharing of personal experiences and maintaining a pragmatic perspective of the direction in which the conversations need to move. In the end, however, our experiences show, you can see some very beautiful results.

STAGE ONE: DECIDING TO ENGAGE

It is important to note that attempting to begin sustained dialogue on a college campus will be time-consuming and often frustrating. As you set out, you must recognize that without patience, perseverance and energy the dialogue will not get started. In the course of our work we found that there were times when it appeared that our efforts to establish groups would fail. Just remember that demonstrating your own commitment through constant efforts will also affirm others' faith in the process. Also, the rewards that come from your efforts will certainly make them worthwhile.

The primary goals of stage one are to (1) be sure that potential group leaders are comfortable moderating a sustained dialogue group, (2) find a group of 8 to 12 potential participants who represent key viewpoints or constituencies on campus, (3) agree as a group to commit to regular meetings every 2 to 4 weeks throughout the school year, and (4) agree to the rules of the dialogue.

This section describes the issues and questions that you must confront as you begin the dialogue process. Chronologically, you will need to think about:

- How to initiate the dialogue
- The dialogue leaders
- Recruiting participants
- How to gain commitment from participants in the process
- Identifying and gathering resources
- Building trust

I) INITIATING THE DIALOGUE

You must first decide who will initiate a sustained dialogue on your campus. As a concerned student, you have enough weight or authority to begin the process on your own! At the same time, the efforts required for beginning the dialogue are so great that you might find it useful to form a coalition from the very beginning. A group of concerned students from different backgrounds and with different reasons for being interested in addressing the community's problems can be more effective than an individual. This is not just because of the greater quantity of able bodies, but also because a greater number of initiators can offer a wider network of contacts, in turn increasing effectiveness in convincing potential participants.

A coalition of concerned organizations can be quite effective in initiating the dialogue because they can lend both physical resources and prestige to the effort. On our campus, dialogue groups were convened through a cooperative effort by the Undergraduate Student Government and the office of the Dean of Student Life. It is important to remember, however, that regardless of who initiates it, sustained dialogue must have a life of its own and must exist independently of any organizations that initiated it in order to maintain its credibility once it gets started. Participants emerge as individuals speaking only for themselves. They do not represent any organization, although they, of course, reflect the perspectives of the groups they identify with. The coalition that begins the dialogue must therefore be prepared to merge with other participants once the dialogue begins. This will be discussed in great depth later in this section.

II) THE DIALOGUE LEADERS

As you move toward establishing sustained dialogue groups, you need to begin to think about who will take the lead through the process. A well-balanced and well-run group will proceed through meetings without any one person dominating the discussion. At the very beginning, however, the group needs to agree upon who will play the role of the moderator.

The moderator need not necessarily be one of the initiators of the dialogue, but this person does need to be familiar with the process. Thus, at least one of the moderators generally will be among the originators. She/he should be well respected by the group and willing to take on the additional burdens of both organizing the meetings and molding the dialogue in a number of ways. Generally, the moderator's responsibilities include:

- Facilitating discussion within the group both overtly and covertly in order to keep the group on track.

- Evaluating the composition of the group; without a cohesive group dynamic and a variety of perspectives, the group will seem to lack direction and energy
- Leading conversation when necessary
- Giving out homework assignments
- Scheduling meeting times and locations in consultation with the group
- Helping to insure that group rules established in the beginning are followed

Because the moderator is often also a participant in the dialogue, it may be advantageous to have more than one moderator. That way, these co-moderators can alternate taking the lead when one of them is too personally engaged in the discussion to provide guided leadership. In our dialogues, we supplemented student moderators with interested non-students (members of the administration) who could provide more objective perspectives at times.

Try to think about engaging the entire group in running itself. Moderators or other leaders within the group should not become so bogged down in administrative details that they cease to gain from the process. Delegation is key, and simple tasks like taking notes and emailing them to the group can serve to further engage participants.

It is important that newcomers to the dialogue feel that the group as a whole values their input into the direction of the dialogue. Initiators must, therefore, be willing to relinquish control to the entire group.

III) RECRUITING ADDITIONAL PARTICIPANTS

Once you have created a coalition of concerned students to initiate the dialogue, you must turn to the task of finding participants. Sustained dialogue can only be successful if the participants represent all key viewpoints within the campus community and if these people are relatively well respected among their respective groups. Dialogue groups that are most successful have enough participants that no important perspective is excluded, but are small enough that everyone can take part. From our experience, between 8 and 12 is the optimum number of people for a group. As you begin finding participants, you should first sit down and think about which groups should be represented and any individuals who might be particularly qualified to contribute.

The most important aspects of finding participants are flexibility and personal contact. We began our process thinking very institutionally. As such, our first targeted participants were leaders of student organizations that represented different interest groups on campus. This approach was successful in that it gave us solid leads for attracting a diverse and concerned group of people. What we found, however, is that the leaders of these organizations, while well placed to take part in the dialogue, were often too busy with their own activities to make a steady commitment. In the end, it was only by casting our nets wide enough and telling as many people as we could about the initiative that participants emerged. Often the names of these people came as recommendations from other student leaders. In some cases, they came to us as volunteers who had heard about Sustained Dialogue along the way. In the end, the best way to begin finding participants was to be as open minded and inclusive as possible and not be afraid of following unconventional leads.

Once you have a list of potential participants, however, you must get them to agree to participate. Our suggested method for doing this is to begin sustained dialogue on your campus with a retreat of some kind. As one approaches students about engaging in a dialogue on race relations that meets on a consistent basis one immediately encounters two major reasons for resistance. First there is some issue of time commitment. On any college campus students are going to be busy with other responsibilities. Classes and responsibilities to teams or student organizations take up valuable time, making it understandable that students are often reluctant to give up additional time for further undertakings. This is the reason that will most often be given by students and it is often also used as a substitute to cover up the second reason—that race relations are a difficult subject to talk about. It is not surprising that many people will be reluctant or afraid to make themselves vulnerable by talking about experiences that have caused them paid with groups that they possibly perceive as responsible for it. At the same time many students will be unwilling to talk about race relations because they do not see a problem. This is also to be expected in a situation where insular groups or a self-perceived campus mainstream are not conscious of the existence of the strained dynamic among other groups on campus.

Approaching potential participants with the invitation to a retreat rather than a request for commitment is an easy way of initiating a dialogue because it offers potential participants an opportunity to test drive sustained dialogue before they make a final decision. Students concerned about time commitment are more likely to agree to attend a day of meetings at first than to join an entire process. Once at the retreat, it is likely that they will be drawn in by the strength of the process and thus be more willing to make a serious time commitment.

In the same way, students reluctant to talk about race relations for a variety of reasons may be willing to attend one retreat. Once there, students unaware of a problem will have a chance to see first hand that their peers believe there is indeed a problem. At the same time, students reluctant to talk about their experiences will see more clearly the benefits of dialogue and be more likely to commit.

Our retreats have generally been four to six hours long and organized in two parts. We have begun with a description of sustained dialogue as a process. Sustained dialogue is a very complex methodology and while it is possible to describe it in a brief conversation with potential participants, it generally takes a longer discussion of the underlying process to equip students with the knowledge to engage in it. In our experience, we were lucky enough to have had Dr. Harold Saunders, one of the creators of the process, as a motivational/informational speaker at the beginning of the retreat. We then have turned the retreat over to the potential participants and asked them to reflect on their own experiences and relationships. The initial engagement has generally been what has won over many initial doubters. (For a sample retreat agenda, see Appendix 3.)

The ultimate goal of such an opening event has been to present people with a process and instill in them a sense of hope that their engagement can make things better. By taking people out of their everyday environment and throwing them together, you place them in a situation where they can be inspired. Think about ways that you can make people's initial exposure to sustained dialogue one that creates hope. One possibility would be to bring in outside speakers that carry with them authority by experience.

Regardless of how you decide to initiate sustained dialogue on your campus, you need to be willing to pound the pavement and make contact with as many people as possible. Your commitment will make others willing to try it out. Tell students what sustained dialogue is and what it will address. We found the best way to talk to our peers was to use vivid examples. If you are having lunch with a potential participant, for example, and she/he is unwilling to acknowledge the existence of a problem, you can point to the dining hall and ask the students why all the tables are racially segregated.

IV) BUILDING COMMITMENT

Once you have the participants engaged, you need to figure out how to keep them. Commitment is something that must be built up like momentum. Hopefully, if you have chosen to hold some kind of an initial event, you will have built up a base of interest that you can work from. In our case, we then set the first meeting following the retreat as the day by which people needed to commit for the year. In order to build momentum you need to think about how you can decrease the kinds of inconveniences that will give people reasons not to attend while deepening their personal investment in the process.

The first part can be largely accomplished through intelligent logistical planning in order to fit the dialogues to the needs of the group. We worked hard to make sustained dialogue as convenient for its participants as possible. Because dinner is a necessary expenditure of time, our meetings were all scheduled to take place during meals. Participants came to meetings knowing exactly when they would end and time limits for meeting were strictly enforced. The simplest thing that we did to maintain commitment was to never leave a meeting without scheduling the next one. By having the entire group present when the next meeting date is set, participants can plan ahead and the group makes a collective commitment to see each other again. It might be useful to agree at the beginning on one given day and time and frequency per month when participants will meet. (See Appendix 4 for a sample meeting agenda.)

Creating personal investment in the process will be discussed in greater depth in the next section. It is important to remember that this is something that must be done at every stage. In the beginning, you should make participants relate their involvement in sustained dialogue to their own experiences. This is a chance for them to explore pain that they have experienced. Only when they are making the process their own can they proceed through it. In addition, as will be discussed below, initiators of the dialogue should be wary of making the process seem too much theirs. You should be willing and ready to let new participants take a leading role.

V) IDENTIFYING AND GATHERING RESOURCES

Before you jump into the dialogue you will also need to worry about the mundane logistical details that must be considered to make sustained dialogue possible. Retreats, meetings, and other efforts require a commitment of time and other resources. Something you will need from the beginning is a safe space where you can hold regular meetings. It is very important that whatever space you select offer privacy and intimacy. Participants should feel as if they can speak freely there and it should be set up in such a way that everyone is physically included in the conversation. If you choose to meet during meals you need to consider where food will come from. In addition, as you move into later stages you may wish to have funds at your disposal to hold a public event or have a special meeting.

From our experience, we found that the idea of sustained dialogue largely sold itself to administrators willing to provide resources. Dining halls were willing to provide meals and special rooms to meet in because our dialogue added to the character of the space. In addition, our major advantage from the beginning was that we began as a coalition between two institutions on campus that already had access to funding. As you get further into the process it will be easier to get help from different organizations on campus. You should put some thought in the beginning, however, into where your start up investments will come from.

VI) BUILDING TRUST

In order to facilitate the transformation of viewpoints that take place through dialogue, it is important for the chosen moderator of the group to begin building trust among group members immediately. As the group moves into later stages of the dialogue participants will need to feel that they can share their viewpoints and experiences in an environment that is safe. Stage one is where building this trust must begin.

It is probably best for this to be done in both spoken and written form. We accomplished this by first talking about the importance of confidentiality within the group. Not only did this start to build trust within the group, but it also gave a necessary warning to group members that ensuing conversations were to become very personal. In order to stress fully the importance of confidentiality, group members were required to sign a Covenant.[3] (See Appendix 2 for a sample covenant.) This agreement is a written guarantee stating that nothing said within the group will leave the group unless participants agree. With the Covenant or some similar agreement serving as a starting point, participants will be ready to begin building deeper levels of trust with each other in the dialogue process.

LOOKING FORWARD

Now that you have agreed to begin the dialogue you may proceed into stage two. You should, however, continue to consider throughout all stages of the dialogue the problems you faced in the beginning. In particular, commitment to the group and to the process must be maintained in order for it to succeed. Be flexible as you move forward and be willing to adjust some of the decisions you have made during this initial phase.

It is important to make sure that the feeling of group ownership you have created is preserved. If you are successful, it will only deepen as you move into the next phase of Sustained Dialogue.

STAGE TWO: MAPPING AND NAMING PROBLEMS AND RELATIONSHIPS

Once interested people have been assembled and logistical matters have been addressed, the dialogue itself can begin. This is stage two. It is important to remember that the stages do not have any concrete boundaries. Individual conversations often have the characteristics of more than one stage, and it is likely that it will be necessary occasionally for a group to move back one stage as a result of premature advancing.

The overall purpose of stage two is to instill experiences into broad concepts that can be used to move toward the tangible products of the process. At the beginning of this stage, the different members of the group undoubtedly will express dramatically different viewpoints on race and its effects on individuals. By the end of this stage, as a function of openness within the group, each person should be closer to understanding how their own and others' experiences have shaped them. In turn, this new mindset empowers the group to discuss effective strategies for combating the problems of racism.

In stage two, participants will (1) set the tone and habits of the dialogue; (2) present to the group important problems that will need to be explored; and (3) identify the connections that link these problems.

This section will delve into and describe:

- How to set the tone
- The importance of documentation through the process

- How to begin the discussion
- Using the power of human experience
- The process of creating a comfort zone
- Dialogue as power building

I) SETTING THE TONE

During the first meeting, it is important to set the tone for the dialogue with some very important judgments and statements.

First, the moderator should make plans for future group meetings. We found that it was effective for the group to have a short discussion about when and where they would like to meet. The moderator should make it clear that the group should meet over a meal about once every two weeks. Although this seems like a small time commitment, it can be very difficult to have a group of eight to twelve busy college students and adults commit two dinners a month to any process. As such, in order to affirm the group's commitment to the process, the moderator should demonstrate his/her own commitment to Sustained Dialogue. The effectiveness of this message can be augmented by discussion of Sustained Dialogue's success in the past, by stating the group's obligation to take racism into their own hands on their campus, and/or by the moderator sharing some of his/her own experiences with race in an attempt to illustrate exactly how important the process is to him or her.

In our experience, students were very skeptical to commit time to a process that was yet unproven.[4] Some campus leaders claimed the sustained dialogue just wouldn't work. Invariably, one will encounter such pessimism in potential participants. After all, racism is one of the most longstanding problems in the human experience, meaning that many do not believe that there are any solutions. Here it is necessary to realize that sustained dialogue is not trying to make everything perfect; instead, the process aims toward one improvement at a time. We confronted skepticism by simply working harder to make sustained dialogue work, actively recruiting more participants and holding more events to draw attention to the process. At about the two-year mark of our work, we saw a change in the way people saw Sustained Dialogue. Mainly, given the award Sustained Dialogue won on our campus and the publicity it enjoyed in various publications, it became a relatively well-known organization among students. This led to many students approaching us and indicating they were interested in participating. Beyond that, the time we had spent making the process work had afforded us the ability to speak passionately, concisely and convincingly about the strengths of Sustained Dialogue. In short, given the eloquence of experience and the credibility of public recognition, we now see that potential participants are now much more willing to commit time to the cause.

We found that another tool for ensuring that group members stayed committed to sustained dialogue was to stop each conversation at an agreed upon time. This deadline was adhered to regardless of where the group stood in conversation.[5] Invariably, people had things they had wanted to say but lacked the time to do so. Thus, excitement about sustained dialogue is maintained. It is important for the moderator to force the group to get into the habit of doing this at the very first meeting because it also creates a more businesslike atmosphere for the process. Participants that find the time commitment for sustained dialogue predictable and reliable will be more willing to make a reliable commitment to it. (See Appendix 4 for a sample meeting agenda).

Additionally, the moderator should be open to the possibility of having a co-moderator, possibly someone whose leadership presence in the first meeting demonstrates potential to make a very valuable contribution as an official leader of the group. We found that having co-moderators was an important part of the success of Sustained Dialogue only partly because it both lessened the logistical burden on the single moderator. In addition, it gave the moderators the chance to bounce ideas off one another in preparation for the individual sessions. Further, co-moderators from different ethnic backgrounds will assure distinct perspectives in front of the group and provide a greater number of possible avenues for discussion.

Because this process does work toward an end, it is also important for each stage of the process to be carefully documented. Moderators can review notes as the stages progress and look for pervasive themes in order to carefully direct conversation toward the goals of the dialogue. After signing the Covenant, a note-taker can be chosen. This appointment need not be permanent, as the responsibility of taking notes should be accompanied by the responsibility of compiling them into readable form and distributing them to the group. In our experience, we found it was best to have a different person take notes at each meeting. Another possibility along these lines would be for the group to compile a logbook. Such a book would contain notes on each week's session and would allow for all records to be centralized. In terms of the notes themselves, it is probably a good idea to record people's names in conjunction with the statements they make. Given the confidentiality of the dialogue, it is safe to note each person's thoughts. This can help the moderator and the group as a whole in understanding the pervasive themes of the dialogue as they work through the dialogue process.[6]

II) BEGINNING THE DISCUSSION

At this point, a dialogue on race can truly commence. The moderator can get the conversation started in a number of ways. In our experience, we found it was often most effective to be very direct: Let's talk about our experiences with racism. Silence usually followed such a statement, providing what was something of an awkward situation. This, however, is not necessarily something to be afraid of. During such initial periods of silence, participants are often sizing each other up and thinking for the first time about the situation. Do not be afraid, if necessary, to let the group sit until someone speaks up. We found in our initial meetings that courage and a passionate desire to talk about race outshown any shyness.

If silence persists for too long, however, the moderator may wish to take action. In our experience, we found that a very effective means of breaking silences was for the moderator to say something that provokes feeling and/or thought. Of course, something like this can take many forms. We found it was most effective for the moderator to express a view or anecdote that he/she knew would garner immediate feedback from group members. Your imagination and experience can synthesize a great number of possible statements. For example, a moderator could bring up a controversial current event that involves race and ask people to share their opinions. Another possibility would be for the moderator to courageously share a serious personal experience that he/she has had with race. Statements such as these, because they frame the discussion around the concrete and human experiences of the people sitting in the room usually are most effective in making participants speak freely. Additionally, if group participants witness the moderator taking personal risks, they will be more likely to take risks themselves.

Another means of breaking silence is simply requiring everyone to say something. The moderator can pose a question about race and ask the group to go around the room and answer it. Such an exercise, by nudging people to engage, can break the tension in the meeting air and allow the group to move into a comfort zone. This is probably the most effective and common method we used to promote participation.

In subsequent meetings the moderator can do a number of things to initiate conversation. We found that it was very effective to assign participants thought exercises as homework that participants could then discuss at the beginning of meetings. Such exercises could range from something that occurred on campus to a recent national or international event. After discussing individual feelings toward the event, it proved very effective for the group to discuss the relevance of a national or international event to their own campus and their own experiences. Without fail it would become easier to facilitate discussion after the first few meetings of the group. Participants will become more comfortable with each other and speak more freely. Sustained conversation on racism affords participants an increased sensitivity to incidents of racism in their everyday lives, in turn leading to more sharing of experiences and more fluid conversation.

III) TOWARD A "COMFORT ZONE"

When you think about moving the group toward a comfort zone do not expect that to mean the dialogue will become less intense. Indeed, truly effective dialogues will be very probing as they help participants to grow by testing the limits of their individual comfort zones. The real goal is to generate an atmosphere in which participants are comfortable being honest with each other. Agreeing on a covenant is the first step toward doing that. It is most important to pull people in by drawing upon their own individual experiences.

At first, sharing experiences will be much like story time. Still being unfamiliar with each other, participants will be very careful with their responses to each other's experiences. Usually, people at first will venture only a Hmmm or Yeah or Wow in response to others' stories. After some time, however (perhaps as soon as the end of the first meeting) people will start to discuss each other's experiences. Gradually the dialogue will begin to probe beneath the surface of a participant's story. Whereas initial shared experiences centered on events individuals had heard about on campus or on the news, discussion upon reaching a certain comfort zone, took on a much more personal and substantive character. Participants were no longer afraid to ask personal questions and provide their own personal insights about the stories that had been shared. In later stages, these individual stories are linked into a larger web of concepts underlying racism.

Creating an environment conducive to the sharing of such experiences is very important, but usually relatively difficult. We have used several different techniques in attempting to create the desired atmosphere. One approach was to organize events in which participants are able to interact outside the dialogue setting. An example of this was a trip to a pizza parlor located off campus where the people involved were brought together by sustained dialogue but conversations centered on topics other than racism. Such a setting allows participants to become more comfortable around each other, thus facilitating more sharing when everyone returns to the dialogue.

Another possible technique for promoting a comfort zone is for the moderator to recognize participants who seem like they have something to say, and approach them outside the dialogue to talk to them more intimately. Often, within the dialogue setting, you will notice participants who make obvious that they have had experiences pertinent to the discussion but are not comfortable enough in the environment to share them. If you have trouble imagining this, place yourself in the participant's position and think about how you would act. Once a person eager to share is identified, it is important for the moderator to make an extra effort to make them feel comfortable in the dialogue group. Usually this can be accomplished simply through a pleasant one-on-one conversation.

Finally, the creation of a comfortable environment for personal exploration is contingent upon the tone set among the participants. The moderator should lead by example in this aspect, and be sure to address each participant in as respectful and caring a tone as possible. Additionally, he/she should be sure to subtly urge each person to address one another with respect as well. The more openness individual statements are met with, the more likely it is that individuals will share their most personal experiences.

Once a comfortable environment is created and participants are able to reach a comfort zone for sharing personal experiences, participants can download their experiences until each individual is thinking about race on virtually the same plane.

IV) USING THE POWER OF HUMAN EXPERIENCE

It is likely that some moments during this downloading phase will be breathtaking. As group members become more comfortable with each other, they will share experiences that unconditionally captivate each person in the room. Individuals often allow emotions that have been pent up for years to flow out in the form of a dramatic release of feeling. Such expression is sometimes vitriolic, sometimes didactic, and nearly always cathartic. Moments of emotion like these in our dialogues have been called magical, breath-taking, and awe-inspiring. Invariably, moments like these facilitate dramatic realizations in participants from all racial and ethnic backgrounds. Individuals have often admitted that it is humbling to realize exactly how little they knew about human experience.

These are moments that will draw the participants personally into Sustained Dialogue. Assuming a proper setting, moments like these will happen, and they inspire group bonding and a commitment to think more carefully about and probe more deeply into the issue of race than they had ever done before.

At times like these, the dialogue has a mind of its own. The moderator (usually as engrossed as everyone else) will simply sit back as the conversation determines its own path. In its course, it grabs a tight hold of each group member and inspires a sense of hope that will prove very necessary in identifying underlying concepts behind racism and possible solutions to them in the later stages of the process.

V) DIALOGUE AS EMPOWERMENT

Much of the success of sustained dialogue is contingent upon what happens underneath the surface, among the relationships of group members. The moderator has two primary responsibilities: to tend to logistical matters and to direct the conversation toward the desired end of the dialogue. In order to fulfill the latter duty, it is necessary to recognize and analyze the various dynamics among the group members in order to decide how best to direct the conversations. These dynamics will always change as group members become more, or possibly less, comfortable sharing with each other.

As the relationships change, so does the power of the group. As people become more comfortable with each other, the group dynamic is more cohesive. Individuals build off of each other's energy and the group becomes able to accomplish very exciting things as a whole. Perhaps more importantly, word of the dialogue is bound to find its way back to the organizations that the participants come from, giving them greater credibility with which to speak to their constituents about race relations. In addition, sustained dialogue serves as an avenue for networking among campus leaders that may not otherwise have the chance to come together around the issue of race.

On our campus, we have observed other very positive effects of the power of cohesive sustained dialogue groups. As Sustained Dialogue has grown in size and in credibility, students around the campus have gotten word of the program and become more prone to tackle the sensitive issue of race in casual conversation. Beyond that, Sustained Dialogue as an organization has now gained the credibility to make statements about racism on our campus, as will be described below.

LOOKING FORWARD

The key to stage two is patience. The moderator should not look to advance to stage three in two meetings. Instead, it is better for the group to dwell on stage two. In past dialogues, stage two has gone on for years. Some group members will be more willing to share experiences than others, but it is important that the group benefits from each person's experiences. Speaking about one's race in relation to one's identity is one of the most difficult things a person can talk about. As a result the moderator should be sure to give each person (and therefore, the group) time to get everything off her/his chest concerning experiences with racism. It is only then that the group can look objectively at the specific problems that lead to racism on their campus. It is important for the moderator to periodically test whether or not the group is ready to move on to stage three. To do this, it is important to realize that the primary criterion for readiness at this point is that each participant understands each other participant as much as possible, given the different ranges of experiences.

STAGE THREE: PROBING PROBLEMS AND RELATIONSHIPS TO CHOOSE A DIRECTION

The purpose of stage three is to effectively sharpen the picture of the dynamics of racism on campus and to identify an approach to combat the problem. Once sufficient downloading has occurred in stage two, the character of the dialogue will change. This transition is very difficult as the moderator must be sure that he/she has given enough time for downloading, allowing the group to become ready to move to a deeper level. Individuals will begin to speak with each other instead of to each other. The discussions that previously centered on statements of What? now probe deeper into individual experiences to answer the question Why? Accordingly, the personality of the dialogue moves from anecdotal to philosophical.

It is important to note that it is almost always necessary to revert from time to time to stage two from stage three. Participants must better understand each other's experiences in order for the group to stand on equal footing while assessing the problem of racism. Once that unity is achieved, the group can begin to pinpoint the specific reasons why their campus' racial climate has taken its current form.

In stage three, the group will (1) probe more deeply the dynamics of troubled relationships that cause problems, (2) assemble individual experiences into a web of conceptual understanding and (3) identify choices for addressing these problems. This section will explore and describe:

- Creating concepts that pinpoint the problem
- Maintaining a will to change
- Moderator trouble-shooting to keep the dialogue moving along

I) CREATING CONCEPTS

In this stage, the group should aim to unify the experiences previously described into named concepts that explain the overall problem. Participants will have already told their personal stories about racism. With the raw material on the table, stage three will begin when the group starts making connections between these stories and attempts to explain the factors behind them.

This does not mean that the story telling ends at this stage. Rather, participants begin retelling their own stories and each other's in order to test connections and build them into concepts. The isolated nodes created by the experiences related in stage two become a web as the group reinterprets them. A phrase that embodies the beginning of this state is: "In thinking about it, it seems like the way [Person X] felt in [story A] is actually quite similar to how I felt in [Story B] and this is because of [Concept C]. As concepts emerge from the experiences that have been offered, new stories will be added as participants think of other situations that further illustrate the group's ideas.

Building up a macro picture, these concepts will explain why racial problems exist. They can range from specific campus events that have shaped students' viewpoints on race, to general characteristics of the campus, social climate and dominant features of the American landscape. Regardless, the concepts should be formulated so that participants can say: If we take steps to overcome this problem race relations will be significantly improved along these lines.

II) MAINTAINING A WILL TO CHANGE

After identifying the concepts that underlie racial tension on campus, the group can choose a general approach to combating race relations as the analysis moves in a specific direction. Pushing the level of detail in concepts continually further, the group can better understand the problems at hand, thus paving the way for the later action-oriented stages. Yet a very important aspect of stage three is that the group generates a will to enact change at the same time that it identifies the concepts that must be addressed. The moderator and the other participants must therefore always have it in the back of their minds that this analysis must serve an ultimate purpose.

Unfortunately, this stage of the discussion can often lead to frustration within the group. Individuals may deem the problems and their obstacles insurmountable and, as a result, begin to lose faith in the process. A common complaint, as participants begin talking but not yet discussing, is that the group is preaching to the choir and therefore not accomplishing anything. Moderators must, therefore, take a more important role in this part of the process, preventing the group from getting off track, preserving high morale and thus helping to generate a desire to enact change.

Stage two can be far more personally fulfilling for group members than stage three. In stage two, individuals have an opportunity to talk about experiences that had major impact on their lives and that they may never before have had a forum in which to share. Most likely, they receive feedback that leads them to think differently about race and can leave each meeting with the warm glow of personal insight and growth.

Once the group enters stage three, the dynamic changes from me to we. The dialogue no longer serves the same role that drew participants in to begin with and thus individuals may not receive as much personal satisfaction from the process. As the work becomes more difficult participants may begin to lose interest in the process and the group may get stuck. Yet without continued commitment from each member the group's dynamic and hence its goals will likely suffer.

Accordingly, it is the moderator's responsibility to keep participants from avoiding the difficult analysis that furthers the dialogue. Of course not everyone will avoid delving deeper but the moderator should be prepared for it nonetheless. Expect that some members of the group will resist placing their own experiences into context with the other stories told by participants and that it will be hard for some to express how they felt or what they were thinking in a given situation. For some there may be a tendency to claim that their stories speak for themselves and therefore require no looking into. Others may simply dwell on continual narration of additional stories rather than seriously addressing what is already on the table.

Yet these are the places that the moderator should focus on because they often conceal the deepest insights. If participants show resistance to analyzing experiences, it could mean that they are grappling with underlying feelings that they would rather not admit. As participants reach stage three, they relate their personal feelings to larger forces. For some, this means admitting feelings of absolute frustration and disempowerment. For others stage three is a time when they come to terms with their own racism and roles in perpetrating an unfair system. It is necessary to remember that each individual has become involved in sustained dialogue for her/his own personal reasons. Some individuals may simply have wanted to find an audience to listen to his or her experiences, while others become involved in the process with the distinct hope of changing the racial climate of their community.

Seeing these different desires fulfilled by different stages of the dialogue, it is the moderator's responsibility to help ensure that the group's interest in the proceedings evolves as the purpose of the discussion changes. An effective method of keeping abstract discussions on the personal level is always to relate the abstract concepts on the table to experiences that have already been described.

The moderator can lead the way by being the first to offer new ways to think about past experiences and to relate them to broader ideas. Challenge participants to analyze how a particular concept may have been working underneath an experience that was painful for them. Taking it from the other side, ask participants to tell new stories from their lives that can add new illustrations of concepts at work. Increase empathy within the group by helping participants to see how their different experiences with racism placed them each in the same position.

A key aspect of unity and trust that should hopefully have developed by now is that the members of the group piggyback off of each others' ideas. The group dynamic by this point should have progressed to a point where individuals feed off one another's energy. There is a definite appearance of a sense of people who have grown together and are now working toward a common purpose. If you find that such a dynamic is not present, and the conversation seems to be stuck it may be necessary to investigate possible means to get the conversation moving again.

III) TROUBLE-SHOOTING HINTS

In order to do this, you can use some of the techniques discussed in stage two. You can try making statements that provoke feeling and thought or you can ask each person to speak on a certain topic in turn. However, as was also mentioned in the discussion of stage two, the moderator's duties go beyond simply moving the course of the conversation. You should move toward pinpointing exactly why the group is stuck. As previously noted, identifying the reasons that people are hesitant or slow in moving forward at this stage can speak volumes about underlying issues.

If the dialogue appears to have lost direction another strategy would be to take a step back, asking the group what each person hopes to get out of the process. When the character of the conversation changes, participants may need to rethink their interest in the process in order to continue attending. Placing this topic on the table can serve as an inspiration to those that may have lost enthusiasm and can help everyone to settle for themselves why the later stages of the dialogue are necessary. In doing this the tone for the rest of the dialogue will be set.

Yet if pointed questions and pep talks are insufficient for keeping the group on track, the moderator should also consider whether the voices represented at the table reflect a diverse enough set of viewpoints to make the conversation meaningful. Though an important aspect of this entire process is building group dynamics, adding new and particularly vocal participants can often jumpstart dialogues that have gotten bogged down. If the group appears unresponsive to the suggestions made above, adding individuals with fresh enthusiasm and new perspectives may reinvigorate everyone else as they are forced to think about problems in new ways and address new questions.

LOOKING FORWARD

In this stage the group begins to discuss race from a more philosophical or analytical standpoint in order to diagnose the causes of racial conflict on their campus. In effect, the group builds its experiences into concepts. The moderator should be careful that the group does not get ahead of itself and attempt to create solutions at this stage. It is important that a complete list of concepts be generated. Following this, the group should identify the specific direction in which they want to move to combat the problem. Ideally, after getting to this point the group shares a will to change that will be pivotal to their progress in later stages.

STAGE FOUR: SCENARIO BUILDING

By the time your group begins the fourth stage of sustained dialogue you will have spent almost all of your meetings talking about problems. The dialogue group's relationships will have dramatically changed in the process as participants have learned to view the problems discussed from each other's perspectives. This is the stage at which the group needs to start thinking constructively about positive steps they can take. The understanding of complex problems needs to transfer into the power to address them.

Moderators should realize, however, that like stage three the fourth stage is not something that the group can be pushed into. Rather it is one that the group will find itself in when it is finished analyzing a problem in stage three and ready to solve it. In our experience, we found groups floating between stage four and the other stages throughout the course of meetings. You should know that when your group reaches the stage in which it is ready to begin formulating solutions it will have developed the kind of bond and awareness that discussions will have a life of their own. Because the problems your group will be discussing by now will be particularly distinct, this section will not attempt to act as a roadmap. Rather it will attempt to show through experience a path that your group may take as it moves from a stage of analysis to creation.

In stage four participants will attempt to (1) list obstacles to change, (2) develop actions and strategies for overcoming these obstacles and (3) identify the individuals and groups that can take the necessary steps. This section will describe:

- The change to thinking positively about problems
- The process of designing exercises to evaluate problems
- The importance and challenges to maintaining commitment through this stage

I) THINKING POSITIVELY

At this point the group will have spent so much time talking about the challenges the community faces that participants may be feeling a sense of hopelessness. A major change that takes place in this stage is that participants will turn from the problems that the community is facing and begin to talk about what will work. When you sense that the group is ready to start talking about solutions, you may need to help facilitate this change. Try encouraging the group to think about actions and strategies that have been effective in the past. This is a lot harder than it sounds. People have a natural tendency to take past successes for granted and to gloss over what about them made them work. Generating a list of even the simplest set of actions and strategies that have an impact will provide you with valuable tools for deciding upon future steps.

In the case of our own experience, the transition happened when one of the participants simply got fed up with talking negatively about the problems and said "Alright guys, what actually works?" The conversation that followed was one in which fellow participants, peers, and friends listed effective solutions that already existed on campus and then distilled from these solutions what made them effective. The group was left with a list of ways to solve problems.

You should also know that thinking positively about the problems does not just serve the purpose of bringing forth new strategies. A less obvious benefit of taking this asset-based approach is that it can serve to rebuild the group's confidence. Seeing that there already are options for the group to follow will help invigorate faith that the group can make a difference.

II) DEVELOPING EXERCISES

Another way in which groups can move forward in developing scenarios is through the application of thought exercises that allow participants to address elements of particular problems. We found it particularly useful at times to apply information that we gathered in order to solve hypothetical problems. The relevant questions to be asking are: What does one do in this situation? Or How can we reach someone in that position? Role-playing may be a useful tool as you begin to formulate scenarios. You may also think about developing simulated problems and asking participants to solve them.

To give a sense of the options open at this stage we will provide a description of one exercise that we found quite effective and systematic. During one of our meetings, the group was attempting to brainstorm strategies for reaching different kinds of students within the campus community. We were struggling with the problem that some students contribute to the overall problem because of ignorance of the problem, while others do so because of a lack of tolerance, while still others contribute because of a combination of both.

The various permutations of such a discussion were mind-boggling and the group was beginning to get frustrated. Then, out of nowhere, one participant suggested plotting it all on a four-quadrant graph. By making one axis level of awareness and the other level of tolerance of racial diversity we could pinpoint different types of personality by degree and then decide which kinds of approaches we had distilled during our discussion of things that worked might be applicable to each.

The modeling we did through this exercise was somewhat clumsy and it involved using some gross generalizations about campus personalities. This made it still difficult for some participants to get into. The major obstacle was that the problem of racism simply defied satisfactory reduction to a working model and the group should, therefore, not try. Gradually, however, we were able to work out most of the frustrations with the framework we were using so that everyone was willing to continue. In this case, it simply took some real patience on the part of the moderators and a few participants to push the group to accept the limitations of modeling. Once we got into it, we found the simplification of the exercise very powerful in matching tools we had described to situations and personality types with whom they would be effective.

Regardless of whether you or your group choose to use such overt methods of scenario building, the basic question you should be asking at this point is: What if? At this stage you are testing out possible solutions in the controlled environment of the dialogue room. Do not be afraid to discuss the most radical or obscure scenarios. Innovation can come from the strangest places and the creativity of this process comes from participants' ability to build off and adapt to each other's ideas. It is impossible to predict how conversations will proceed so just try to make sure that the group is staying on task.

III) MAINTAINING CONTROL

As you work through stage four you need to be extremely sensitive to the level of commitment on the part of the group. A problem you will have already encountered in stage three is that the function of the dialogue will have changed fundamentally from what it served in stage two. Rather than venting its past experiences, the group will now be straining itself intellectually to develop solutions. This means that the aspects of sustained dialogue that will have earned many people's commitment in the beginning will have disappeared. Do not be surprised if you find that some of the participants took part in sustained dialogue primarily for its therapeutic function rather than to solve campus problems and disappear at this point.

You may also face resistance at this stage because the task has become much more difficult and complex. Confronting the issues on the table can be extremely daunting and even imagining solutions may be frightening. In addition, the group may become frustrated as you discuss possible actions because no solution seems adequate.

As you move through stage four you should therefore remember that patience is the key. First, resistance on the part of some participants to discussing solutions may come from the fact that they have not fully worked through earlier stages. You should, therefore, always be ready to go back and explore other problems. At the same time, you should be wary of the group's level of frustration. After exploring challenges for a number of weeks the group may feel itself facing obstacles that are impossible to surmount. In order to keep the group committed to the process this may be a good time to begin thinking positively. Also as you dive into making scenarios you should remind participants that if perfect solutions already existed for these problems, they would not be problems. The task of the group is to accept the obstacles and think about what actions would serve to improve the situation rather than attempting to make it perfect.

LOOKING FORWARD

You will know you have completed stage four when you have selected actions that can be taken and identified people or groups that can take these actions. Commitment will be crucial as you move into the final stage of Sustained Dialogue. Many participants may feel that they have gotten what they want out of the process. Others still may feel that the costs of taking the actions described are too great to make them worthwhile. Stage five will only truly begin when members of the group tire of talking and decide to act.

STAGE FIVE: ACTING TOGETHER

Through the course of the last four stages we have emphasized the importance of patience with the process. To a large extent the moderator is powerless in controlling the pace of the group's progression and only at the proper time can a group move through the stages. This, of course, takes time and as you think about moving into the final stages of sustained dialogue a major logistical concern you will be having is whether there will be enough time in the school year to complete the process. We suggest that you do not feel obligated to get through the process in a given time limit. Having tried at times to push our groups faster than they were prepared to go, we can tell you that it creates more trouble than it is worth.

It is therefore important that you not rush into the acting stage of Sustained Dialogue. If you need to, close the school year with the agreement that the dialogue will continue next year. What is important is that any action your group takes is its own. They should be actions that come from the analysis that the dialogue has fostered. Avoid the pitfall of taking action simply for the sake of taking action Because the decision to act and the choice of actions must come from the participants, this section is not meant to provide suggestions for actions. Rather it is intended to offer a few considerations to take with you as you decide to act.

In stage five participants will (1) decide whether the situation within their community is such that scenarios developed in stage four are workable, (2) determine what resources and capacities can be used to realize them, and (3) act. This section will discuss:

- The significance of the four year cycle
- Possibilities for outreach
- The diversity of forms of action that arise from the dialogue process
- The value of spreading opportunities to engage in dialogue

I) THE FOUR YEAR CYCLE

As described in the introduction to this handbook, you have an advantage in working to change campus culture over other environments because a college student body has a life cycle of about four years. This creates a naturally truncated institutional memory and a rapid process of acculturation. Experiences that a class may have as freshmen can cause a change in campus culture by the time they are juniors or seniors. This means that actions you take now can improve the overall campus climate in a fairly short period of time. Memory of incidents, particular social structures and traditions that were anemic to race relations can more easily fade away and new traditions can be more readily established. The mutability of campus culture as compared to culture in other communities is one of your greatest assets as you choose to act. The ways in which you impact the way freshmen perceive campus culture this year will in turn impact the way the entire student body perceives it as that class rises to leadership within the student body. It also means that race relations among students can deteriorate just as quickly, but that should be viewed as additional reason for action rather than an obstacle to it.

II) POSSIBILITIES FOR OUTREACH

During the process your group will have grown together. Interpersonal relationships within the group will be dramatically different in character and intensity from how they were at the beginning. This dynamic is not something that can be predicted and thus the group course at this point will be entirely a function of the specific events, activities and ideas that have carried them together through the process.

While each group's path and action will be unique, we can advise a few possibilities for action. In order to change the racial climate of a community, outreach is necessary. To that end, groups in stage five will most likely be looking for ways to share their experiences with those within the campus community whose experiences with race (or lack thereof) have rendered them either intolerant or ignorant of the issue of race.

Naturally, this can be done in a variety of different ways. For one, the group as a whole can reach out to others. A very effective program that we conducted was showing the movie "The Color of Fear" in a small theater on campus. This is a very provocative movie that can have dramatic effects on members of the views of the members of the racial majority on the issue of race. Each dialogue participant was required to recruit three friends who normally would not think about race. Following the movie, two group moderators led a discussion among everyone in the audience. The people who took part in this event were obviously moved by the movie and took different opinions of race back to their residence halls, hopefully to be shared with others. A number of group outreach activities such as this one can be imagined. Another possibility for outreach is for each participant to reach out individually. Individuals can make concerted efforts to start discussions about race with many different people. However, not all action needs to center around people in the dialogue group. Instead the group can look to enlist the services of other students on campus to carry out projects that move toward greater awareness, tolerance and in turn change. Race relations on campus, in our experience, are something that the majority look at as a non-issue and that minorities look at as an immutable unpleasant aspect of campus life. As such it is usually necessary to do two things in order to make an initial action effective: build awareness and build hope.

III) DIVERSE FORMS OF ACTION

As the group begins steps to take action remember that the most effective actions address the problems at hand in their own terms and not through any particular formula for action. This is important to recognize because the most effective actions coming out of sustained dialogue may not necessarily take place as an official action of the dialogue group. As an example on our campus, Sustained Dialogue led one participant to produce a report for administrators asking for specific steps to improve life for minorities on campus. Additionally it was the inspiration of two dialogue members from the class of 2001 to have their class honor Judge Bruce Wright, an African-American admitted to Princeton in the 1930s but who, upon arriving, was immediately sent home because the administration discovered he was black. The dialogue also led the president of the student government to initiate standing committees to report to the administration on the state of women and minorities on campus.[7]

All of this is included to show that the actions coming out of our Sustained Dialogue organization are often taken by individual participants who recognize the process as their reason for acting, but do so because they see themselves in the most effective position to initiate change. At the onset of our process, we imagined quite one dimensionally that the actions coming out of our dialogue would be enacted by the groups as a whole working as a single body. This conception, however, did not recognize that our greatest assets for taking positive action were the positioning and influence of individual campus leaders who participated in the sustained dialogue process. It was when these students took their conceptual understandings of problems, plans of actions and conviction that they had gained from the dialogues back to their public positions that the action stage really began.

As such it is important to remember the nature of expected action when beginning in Stage One. Ultimately, the action stage of sustained dialogue will be greatly facilitated if you can begin the process with current or rising campus leaders in the room. This of course goes back to the idea of the dialogue as an exercise in empowerment. Dialogue places leaders in contact who may never have been in touch with one another before. From these contacts partnerships form for improving race relations that can lead entire organizations to work together for the first time. In addition, leaders hoping to take action within their own networks or organizations can use their participation in the process as an additional source of credibility, lending greater authority to the steps they want to take.

Sustained dialogue can also initiate change through action committees devoted to taking immediate material steps to improve the current situation on campus. Such groups may include different participants from actual dialogue groups but are aided by the ideas and strategies coming out of Sustained Dialogue. In our own case, this took place when a separate group of concerned students began their own Action Oriented Race Dialogues, partly in reaction to the more deliberative form of Sustained Dialogue. Their goal was to tackle aspects of race relations at weekly public meetings, attempting to brainstorm at every meeting about steps that they could take to improve the current situation.

From the beginning Sustained Dialogue participants on our campus took part in these other discussions and we found the groups' roles to be quite complimentary. The Action Oriented talks marshaled popular enthusiasm to initiate action and change but lacked the perspective on deeper systemic and social issues that was originally necessary to formulate deeper and more innovative actions. In contrast, the sustained dialogue process of probing for conceptual explanation generated a large quantity of ideas but the groups' willingness to deliberate slowly on these issues meant that they also did not have strong activist energy for immediate action. Thus with overlapping membership and recruiting, participants in the two efforts were able to lend each other ideas and power to act. You must also be aware by now that in a smaller community like a college campus the process in and of itself can represent powerful action. Your dialogue will impact its participants. In doing so, these people from different subgroups on campus will transfer their accumulated knowledge and perspectives to others. Remember this as you evaluate the success of the process in your own mind. In addition the value of the dialogue for the people engaged in it makes it a more than worthwhile endeavor. This is meant to serve as a reminder and not a substitute for the other ways of taking action discussed above. It should however be reason for confidence and patience. If you are engaged in dialogue your are positively impacting race relations on your campus. Be proud of that and think about how your experiences can benefit others.

IV) PROLIFERATION

Seeing that the process itself is an action, a goal of sustained dialogue should be to expand to as many people in the community as possible. As mentioned above, each time a person is moved by a conversation and each time a new, more understanding, viewpoint is engrained in another student, race relations within your community have been improved. Such is the case with the formation of each new dialogue group.

Initially, two pilot dialogue groups were started on our campus. Almost everyone involved with these groups was moved by increased understanding toward action. With each person involved in the original groups then fluent in the process of Sustained Dialogue, our efforts the following year were expanded to four full groups and the program continued to expand in following years. It also spread to the University of Virginia and other campus under the leadership of Priya Parker and others. Experienced individuals from all of these groups can continue to spread the world of sustained dialogue to underclassmen and upperclassmen alike. Dialogue groups have thus continued to proliferate long after we have left Princeton and this hope assures us that the process is productive, regardless of what action manifests itself in stage five.

While word of mouth is integral to the success of Sustained Dialogue, group members should also use other means to further community knowledge of the process and its fruits. We have benefitted from publicity by bodies such as the school newspaper and by having our efforts talked about by members of the campus in various contexts. Also, as mentioned previously our Sustained Dialogue organization was awarded the Daily Princetonian award for distinguished service, an honor that furthers the awareness and credibility essential to the success of our campus efforts. In order to gain such positive publicity, it was important to have each person involved in the group to articulate what sustained dialogue is and exactly how promising the process can be. Such optimistic words about race relations are received well by practically everyone in the campus community and, as such, can be counted upon to spread.

IV) CONCLUSION

The methodology we have outlined and the tips we have given serve as our own interpretation of the success of Sustained Dialogue on our campus. It is only a model however with some concrete examples provided to better illustrate the different aspects of the process. Other student groups on other campuses can tailor their sustained dialogue efforts to fit the needs of their own communities. Though it would be beautiful to see sustained dialogue efforts pass from stage one to stage five in practically the same fashion in which it has been outlined in the preceding you should remember that the experience your group will have and the insights participants will learn from each other will be distinct. When you have downloaded, pinpointed the problems and their obstacles and formulated your own solutions, you will realize that you have learned more about human relationships than you could have in any classroom. At that point, you too can sit down as we have and try your hardest to share this amazing process with other people who can benefit from it.

APPENDIX 1

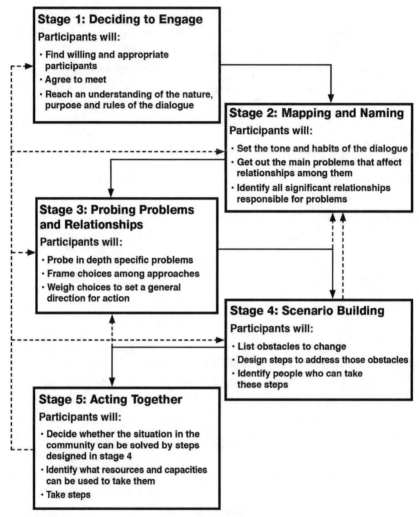

FIGURE 7.1

APPENDIX 2: SAMPLE COVENANT

- The purpose of this dialogue is to work on changing the relationships among the groups with which participants identify.
- There will always be two items in the agenda: the particular problems participants need to talk about and the underlying feelings and relationships that cause these problems.

- Because of the importance of this work, participants commit themselves to meet approximately twice per month, at least two hours per meeting. The duration of the series will be open-ended. Participants will wait until they are well into the dialogue to agree on when to finish the series of meetings.
- Participants represent only themselves. They reflect views in their communities, but in these dialogue sessions, they do not formally represent any organizations or groups.
- Participants will observe time limits on their statements to allow genuine dialogue.
- Participants will speak from their hearts as well as their minds.
- Participants will interact civilly, listen actively to each other with attention and respect, not interrupt and allow each to present her or his views fully.
- Because participants will need to speak about feelings and relationships behind specific problems that bother them, feelings will be expressed and heard with mutual respect. Participants will try to learn from these expressions.
- Participants will try to respond as directly and as fully as possible to points made and questions asked. Each will make a real effort to put herself or himself in others' shoes and speak with sensitivity for others' views and feelings.
- To facilitate serious work, participants will listen carefully to the issues and questions posed by the moderator and try to stick to them.
- Nobody in the dialogue will be quoted outside the meeting room.
- No one will speak publicly about the substantive discussion in the dialogue unless all agree.

FROM *A PUBLIC PEACE PROCESS* BY HAROLD SAUNDERS

APPENDIX 3: SAMPLE RETREAT AGENDA

1. Morning Refreshments
2. Icebreaker
   A brief activity allowing people to become comfortable with each other the meeting room and situation.
3. Student Panel
   Students speak in front of the retreat, talking about how race has affected them, indicating the need for a program like sustained dialogue on campus.

4. Speaker on the sustained dialogue process

Ideally someone from outside the campus community with experience with sustained dialogue to introduce the process. Speaker should address both the theoretical aspects of sustained dialogue and its past applications to communities.

5. Lunch

6. Division of groups; beginning of dialogue

Retreat participants are divided somewhat randomly into their dialogue groups for the year. Groups meet briefly to discuss date for first meeting.

APPENDIX 4: SAMPLE MEETING AGENDA

1) Meeting Convenes (Participants have already agreed on a set time and place for the meeting.)

2) Pre-Discussion Business

   a. Schedule next meeting time and place

   b. Agree on a time to end discussion

   c. Choose person to take notes and forward to group

   d. Participants make any announcements that are relevant

3) Discussion

   a. Conversation generally begins with a discussion of the previous homework assignment

   b. Participants explore topics of interest from previous meetings or new ones

4) Ending the Meeting

   a. Discussion ends when the agreed upon time is reached

   b. Participants agree upon a homework assignment for the next meeting

APPENDIX 5: THE CONCEPT OF RELATIONSHIP

Social and political life is a multi-level process of continuous interaction among significant elements of whole bodies politic across permeable borders. We use the human word relationship to capture that dynamic process of continuous interaction. The concept of relationship is both a diagnostic and an operational tool: diagnostic as it helps form a picture of a relationship from unfolding and confusing exchanges in dialogue; operational as it helps us get inside an interaction to change a relationship.

Relationships combine five elements. The overall mix of continuously changing interactions characterizes a relationship. Changes in any element and changes in the combination of elements explain why a relationship changes Each is a point of entry in efforts to change conflictual relationships.

Identity. Each party in a relationship is described most simply in terms of physical characteristics: a group's size, ethnicity, demographic composition, resources. But it is also essential to understand what human experiences have shaped a person's or a group's mindset and ways of acting in relationships with others. We often define ourselves in terms of who we are: parents, enemies.

Interests. We have commonly defined interests in material terms: how much money or property we need, what positions we want to control. But interests are defined in human terms as well. Our need for acceptance, inner security, dignity.

Power is defined normally in physical terms: greater economic resources, military force, institutions controlled, and as one's ability to force another to do what it takes not want to do power over. But citizens without these raw forms of physical power have come together to change the course of events: the sit-ins and marches of the civil rights movement, the anti–Vietnam War movement, Wenceslas Square, Solidarity, the Vote No campaign against Pinochet. Citizens generate power by acting together.

Perceptions, misperceptions, stereotypes familiar to us all often define relationships. Because you have black or white skin, you are likely to act in a predictable way.

Patterns of interaction confrontational collaborative, combative, argumentative, problem-solving become characteristic of any relationship. As we understand identity and interests, we may limit interactions to respect them.

Once we analyze interactions between or among groups using such headings, we can actually change interactions through dialogue. Identities don't change, but respect for another's identity can become real no longer mindless hatred fueling deep-rooted conflict. Realization of others' interests can reveal shared interest. People can see how they need each other to fulfill their own interests. People stop talking at each other and begin talking with each other to solve a problem and actually work together.

FROM *A PUBLIC PEACE PROCESS* BY HAROLD SAUNDERS

Notes

The original version of this handbook was written in 2001, when the authors were seniors at Princeton University.

1. Editors note: In this discussion, Sustained Dialogue (in capital letters) refers to the specific organization founded by Nemeroff and Tukey at Princeton University, while sustained dialogue (in lower case letters) refers to the general process.

2. Editor's note: It is also not the type of deliberation in which different sides attempt to reach consensus on a particular position or endorse a particular platform.

3. Editor's note: As part of the process of building trust and commitment, small changes to your prepared covenant will sometimes be sought by participants. Generally, you need to be aware that sometimes these changes have the potential to disrupt, interfere with, or circumvent the sustained dialogue process, but ordinarily they will not and can be seen as signs of growing engagement and commitment from participants.

4. Editors' note: Despite widespread effective use of similar group process approaches for many decades, the process will always appear "unproven" for beginners and those unaccustomed to working in groups.

5. Editors' note: Keeping this deadline further adds to a sense of sustained continuity and on-goingness.

6. Editors note: As part of their covenant, some groups may elect not to keep notes or recorded records of conversations.

7. Editor's note: This committee was still functioning at the time of this chapter was finished, although because of the revolving nature of the student body described in this section, current members may be completely unaware of its origins.

8

DERRY EXCEPTIONALISM AND AN
ORGANIC MODEL OF SUSTAINED DIALOGUE

Nick Acheson and Carl Milofsky

SUSTAINED DIALOGUE is a model of peacemaking articulated by the diplomat Hal Saunders (Saunders 1999) that deemphasizes negotiations between either political leaders or professional diplomats. Rather, it involves the creation of regular discussion meetings or retreats between emerging leaders from the different communities that engage in violence in conflict-prone societies. The examples Saunders describes are self-conscious, sponsored meetings organized by an experienced facilitator such as Saunders himself, and they occur on a regular, periodic basis over a span of years.

Through this mechanism the leaders develop strong, trusting, cross-community relationships, and they also gain a deep knowledge of the culture, beliefs, interests, and contested claims of the other side. As these younger leaders move into more prominent leadership roles, conflict is reduced. Misunderstandings that otherwise might continue and renew long-standing conflicts are less likely to occur. Furthermore, when difficult negotiations must occur, strong relationships, established trust, and deep knowledge of the opposing culture make it easier for discussions to be realistic and productive.

From our point of view, the sustained dialogue model has two weaknesses: a strong, outside leader must be a key player, and the process must be designed in a self-conscious way. These imply that sustained dialogue only works because it is intentional and guided by the wisdom of experience from key figures. We argue, in contrast, that sustained dialogue is most effective if we see it as a model of the kinds of relationships and the styles of interaction that are necessary for conflict to be transformed into peaceful relationships and coexistence. The integrative dynamic that Saunders describes that creates cross-community networks and the form of dialogue that allows people from contesting, sectarian groups to work with one another in a respectful, trusting way comes from a certain kind of social structure. That social structure occurs naturally or, put differently, as the consequence of certain sociological rules of group and intercommunity dynamics. A facilitator is useful and might launch this process where it would not otherwise occur. But we can find examples of sustained dialogue emerging out of community life and leading a situation of intense, overt conflict into one of cross-community cooperation, dialogue, and peaceful community development.

We make our case by offering as an example Derry (we will follow the growing local custom and call it Derry rather than Londonderry, the official name used by the minority Protestant population), Northern Ireland. When people in Northern Ireland talk about the peace process and the barriers to reconciliation that exist in many parts of the country they often point as a counterexample to events in Derry. A common response from the audience when these examples are offered is a sigh of frustration and the comment, "Yes, but Derry is exceptional." Our purpose is to explain Derry exceptionalism, which grew out of a natural process of sustained dialogue. The consequence is that One of the most violent communities during the troubles of the 1970s and 1980s became a place where the Catholics and the Protestants could work together to peacefully resolve deep, enduring conflicts between the two groups.

THE DERRY STORY

Derry was one of the original points of the conflict in Northern Ireland, which began in 1968 and continued in its violent form until a ceasefire in 1994. The conflict in Derry was intense and led to the demolition of most of the downtown section of the city. Nearly as dramatic was the process of peace building and reconciliation, led by a burgeoning collection of community-based organizations. The peace was the product of important changes in the conflict strategy by paramilitary organizations and also by effective diplomatic initiatives from England, Ireland, the United States, and the European Union.

Our argument, however, is that peace never would have happened had there not been leadership both in Derry and at the regional Northern Ireland level that followed a variety of strategies to build ties between community organizations. These ties generally involved work on specific projects, but for the participants the larger significance was the formation of personal relationships with the other side. These relationships required leaders from both groups to examine long held personal prejudices and acknowledge the good intentions and humanity of people (such as priests, bishops, fraternal order leaders, and paramilitary leaders) who presented symbols of office that were genuinely hateful and terrifying to the participants. It also required nonleaders to form cross-community relationships and in so doing come to terms with horrific personal losses. Only if people could achieve personal reconciliation when they had lost a loved one or suffered a disabling injury could cross-community partnerships proceed.

These partnerships at both the leadership and the citizen level were essential. Because effective dialogue and cross-community working partnerships developed and were expanded over the decade of the 1990s, there emerged a palpable, community-wide commitment to peaceful coexistence. There were important projects that would serve the collective well-being of the city, and this required working cross-community relationships.

This happened, however, in a climate where cross-community tensions and hostility have remained intense. They also happened in concert with a process of systematic residential segregation of the Protestant and Catholic communities. The point of our narrative is to show that an organic process of sustained dialogue emerged in Derry and made civic-reconstruction projects possible. This was a process of community organization that we can describe analytically and whose effects we can assess. It led to relative peace in the city, but it did not end the conflict. This chapter seeks not only to assess the contribution of organic sustained dialogue but also to recognize its limitations as a peace process.

THE CONFLICT

Derry is the second largest urban center in Northern Ireland, with a population of 90,736 in the 2001 census. Almost 78 percent of the population is from a Catholic background. It is situated on the northwest margins of Northern Ireland with the international border with the Republic of Ireland more or less running along the city boundary to the west. It has long been the main urban center in the northwest corner of Ireland, with well-established economic and social ties linking it to County Donegal, from which it was summarily cut off at the time of the partition of Ireland in 1922. From that time until the eruption of the violence in 1969, Derry was run by its Protestant minority through gerrymandered elections and a housing policy that corralled most Catholics into one electoral ward in the city, reducing the political impact of their majority numbers. This background gave it a crucial practical and symbolic role in the emergence of the "troubles."

Events such as Bloody Sunday and the Battle of the Bogside are engraved in international consciousness. They were significant moments in the transformation of what had been a peaceful civil rights movement modeled on the American nonviolent protest efforts of Martin Luther King into an armed revolutionary struggle. Derry became a center of Irish Republican Army organizing and is the home of Martin McGuinness, a key IRA leader who became a leading Sinn Fein politician.

The walled city that makes up downtown Derry is also a focus of Protestant Loyalist sentiment—the Loyalists being that part of the Protestant community most determined to retain the status quo and opposed to any unification with the Irish Republic. The name Londonderry is associated with the original initiative by London guilds to finance and settle "plantation towns" in Northern Ireland at the start of the seventeenth century. The city was financed and built by these guilds much like the contemporaneous English colonies on the Eastern seaboard of what is now the United States. Derry is the only city in Ireland that retains a complete walled center, which dates from that time. Apprentice boys from the London guilds were central players in 1689, when James II, the deposed Catholic king of Britain, took his campaign to restore his crown to the mainly Catholic Ireland. The city fathers in Londonderry were at the point of surrendering to his army when, slamming the doors to the city, the apprentice boys of Derry (now the name of an important Protestant fraternal society) brought upon themselves a siege that lasted through six months of death and starvation. The ultimate liberation by William of Orange is one of the focal cultural moments in Protestant history. Each year the dates on which the siege began and ended are marked by Protestant marches that often are associated with rioting and the most important marches are around the top of the Derry city walls. Its colonial origins are important for an understanding of the recent conflict; in the Protestant community there remains an important sense of being a besieged settler population surrounded by hostile and untrustworthy natives.

PRECIPITATING EVENTS Although there is a long history of conflict in Northern Ireland the beginnings of "the troubles" is usually traced to 1968, when a coalition of college students, sympathetic politicians, and community leaders targeted substandard housing as a primary problem for the Catholic community. This prompted a series of political actions. The actions were modeled on the American civil rights movements and included sit-ins, public protests, and marches through contested areas. At the beginning there was some cross-community participation in the movement. It also quickly ran into a violent response from the Royal Ulster Constabulary and their support force, the B-Specials. This police force was entirely composed of Protestants. While there was police violence, more important is that some elements from the Protestant community met protesters with violence while the police did nothing to interfere.

Despite this violent response and a steady, low-level response from Catholic young people, who threw rocks and did their best to harass the police, the early movement apparently had only a small formal revolutionary component. The Irish Republican Army is the historical name for revolutionary fighters in the Irish rebellion leading up to independence in 1921, but the organization had not been active since and did not receive much support in the early years of the troubles. Nonetheless, anger from civil rights protesters at police violence seemed to lead government officials to fear an organized IRA presence, and stern police enforcement was partially justified on these grounds. The Irish government protested police violence against Catholics, which led the British to assign paratroopers to Northern Ireland. The paratroopers' major concern was for an organized, violent Catholic presence.

These fears seem to have been an important component in the events of Bloody Sunday, January 30, 1972, when British paratroopers killed thirteen Catholics and injured another fourteen in reaction to a huge civil rights march.[1] The civil rights protests had become larger and more militant as police violence continued and government resistance provided continual targets of protest. The January 30 march was pronounced illegal by the government but proceeded anyway as more than 20,000 people marched down the hill from the Creggan Estates to the Bogside. There were the usual rock throwing teenagers, and the paratroopers thought they heard some gunshots before they opened fire.

Civil rights leaders comment that the small, embattled IRA gained nearly unanimous support overnight from the events of Bloody Sunday.[2] The conflict rapidly escalated as the conviction grew in the Catholic community that the only solution would be some form of independence from the government regime. A resident of the Bogside, recently returned from Berkeley, California, and its People's Park protests, painted a now famous sign that said, "You Are Now Entering Free Derry." Barricades were erected across the streets, and neither police nor paratroopers were able to enter the neighborhood. The barricade could be maintained because a high-rise housing block at the intersection gave petrol bombers a way to attack the police without allowing an effective means of counterattack. Open warfare continued for four days until the police finally broke through. The consequence was open acceptance on both sides that a violent revolutionary war had begun.

An interesting aspect of the Battle of the Bogside was that the combatants were mainly British paratroopers, the Royal Ulster Constabulary, and the Catholic community. At the beginning, members of the Protestant loyalist community were bystanders. Conditions changed rapidly, although from the Protestant side the incentives for conflict seemed to be mostly symbolic. Protestants who sympathized (by attending the funerals of Bloody Sunday victims, for example) were ostracized. Families of policemen certainly felt the effects of Catholic anger and violence. There also was a certain amount of violence against minorities in both predominantly Catholic and predominantly Protestant neighborhoods.[3] At that time even the Bogside had a significant number of Protestant residents, and modest housing integration was the norm in Derry. That has changed today, especially in working-class neighborhoods, which are uniformly homogeneous.

The conflict escalated throughout the 1970s. The government sought ways of controlling resistance, and their methods of control—such as arresting suspected IRA members without objective evidence, a process called internment—provoked increasingly intense opposition. The IRA became increasingly militaristic and hierarchical in its organization. Initially organized on a battalion structure based on geographical areas, it was rescued from near defeat in the mid-1970s through tight organization and effective central control of the projects and targets of action, which became a hallmark of the organization (Maloney 2002).

The peak of the conflict came in the early 1980s in terms of both violence and the effectiveness of symbolic actions. The IRA and its members in prison argued that they should be treated as military prisoners, but the government insisted on calling them common criminals. This led to a dramatic hunger strike that resulted in ten deaths, an action that has particular symbolic power in the Catholic community because of its tradition of martyrdom.

Meanwhile, Protestant militants became increasingly emphatic in their demands that the British government not be conciliatory. They were effective because their members controlled operational centers that governed daily life, especially in Belfast. When higher-level governmental officials sought to introduce and implement cross-community peace initiatives, Protestant workers would take direct action by, for example, shutting down the electrical power system and paralyzing the cities. Thus, in the early 1980s, opposing paramilitary movements prevented effective progress on peace by fighting with each other and by creating effective actions that blocked larger government resolutions of the conflict.

THE SHIFT FROM VIOLENCE This changed in 1985 when the Anglo-Irish Agreement, strongly backed by American influence, created a framework wherein national governments agreed to no longer support violent movements. The Irish agreed not to try to incorporate Northern Ireland nor to allow the IRA to use Irish soil as a staging ground for attacks. The British government agreed to control Protestant paramilitaries and to work toward more equitable government services for Catholics. The Americans agreed to provide substantial funding for peace initiatives while also applying political and economic pressure in London and Dublin.

This macrolevel story was significant in Derry because it became increasingly apparent to the IRA leadership that it could not win a military victory and that a unified Ireland would not happen (at least not until there was a Catholic majority in the north). Power within the movement became centered in its political arm, Sinn Fein. A critical moment in this consciousness shift occurred when the leader of the peace-oriented Social Democratic and Labour Party, John Hume, wrote a secret letter to the Sinn Fein leader Gerry Adams and the two began cooperating on a Catholic political initiative.

These events took place against a marked drop in the level of violence. The 1970s were the most violent period, with 1972, the year of Bloody Sunday, by far the worst. By the end of the 1970s, the worst was over, although there was a clear rise in violence that coincided with the period of the hunger strikes in 1981 and 1982 before the rate settled to fewer than ten deaths a year. By the mid-1990s deaths relating to the troubles were very rare in Derry.

LINKING THE MACRO-STORY TO MICRO-EVENTS

The shift in IRA strategy away from armed insurrection and toward electoral politics was slow but quite clear. It was accompanied by a reduction in the levels of violence and by political developments that were to lead to the peace process of the 1990s. Senior republicans in Sinn Fein have always downplayed its significance, but it is apparent that a key role in reducing tensions in Derry in the early 1990s was played by a local organization, the Peace and Reconciliation Group. Two English Quakers had been particularly important in opening a channel of communication between the IRA and the British army and helping them negotiate deescalation in a process that was dubbed "the Derry experiment" by the British authorities (Maloney 2002). It seems certain that the IRA was open to these contacts as a result of the universal condemnation they experienced, including from their own support base, for their use of "human bombs" in 1990. On October 24, 1990, Patsy Gillespie, a Derry Catholic, was forced to drive a huge bomb to a British army base on the outskirts of the city; it was then detonated, killing him and five soldiers. The soldiers were the last army personnel to be killed by the IRA in Derry.

The effective end of the IRA "war" in Derry was a necessary but not sufficient condition for what happened next. It provided the context in which leaders from both the Protestant and Catholic communities were able to emerge and begin dialogue.

In between macrolevel developments and microlevel events in Derry itself were a series of meso-level initiatives that had the effect of, first, legitimizing community development and then, second, reducing resource constraints that might otherwise have made it difficult if not impossible for community leaders to move dialogue forward. This process was in turn assisted by coincidental changes in the approach of the European Union, both to its relationship with civil society and in its funding streams. Put together, they provided a powerful set of opportunities and incentives for engagement and change on the ground. Three aspects of these meso-level developments are worth noting.

The first was a 1993 change in policy by the direct-rule administration in Northern Ireland that recognized the value of community development to positive social and economic change, in marked contrast to policy development at the time in the rest of the United Kingdom. The roots of this change lay partly in successful lobbying by community activists who in 1989 had created the Community Development Review Group. This group was able to engage with senior civil servants, who were in turn able to influence the government ministers responsible (Acheson and Milofsky 2004). The Community Development Review Group came into existence partly because of a relaxation of attitudes in government toward Sinn Fein and its community-based support that followed secret negotiations between government and elements in the IRA that can be traced back to 1986 (Maloney 2002).

Second, these changes had an important impact on the symbolic level as they legitimized community activity in new ways. Importantly, an influential policy community developed that involved community activists, civil servants, and officials from the European Union Commission who were looking for ways in which European institutions could support the fledgling peace process. Changes in European Union social policy at the end of the 1980s had brought the idea of using civil society as an instrument of policy into the mainstream (Acheson, Harvey, and Williamson 2005). As a result, relatively large amounts of EU money became available for developing community-based organizations after 1994. These two sets of circumstances helped to highlight a view of community development that saw it as having a central role in peace making through combating social exclusion (Acheson and Milofsky 2004).

The third set of relevant circumstances relate to a government-funded training and employment initiative, designed to address the high levels of long-term unemployment that had emerged in Northern Ireland in the 1980s as a result of the collapse of much of the industrial base. The Action for Community Employment scheme was a wage-subsidy scheme that at it height in 1992 provided short-term employment to 10,000 unemployed people and cost 50 million pounds a year. It was delivered entirely through voluntary and nonprofit organizations, many of which were established for the purpose. The ready availability of labor and the preference for nonprofit delivery provided a crucial opportunity for the emerging community leadership in Derry to make a rapid impact on the physical fabric of the city through the rebuilding of its bombed-out historic core.

THE HEROIC PERIOD OF PEACE BUILDING

These meso-level changes set the stage for Derry leaders to undertake several initiatives that transformed the city. Our data are fragmentary, but in historical interviews with key players three initiatives are particularly significant: First, business and institutional leaders sought funding and undertook a project to rebuild the central city in a way that incorporated significant community participation and also provided a bricks-and-mortar infrastructure for civil society organizations. Second, several cross-community partnerships developed among local organizations in which direct-action strategies for peace were used to reduce the frequency and intensity of conflict. Finally, Loyalist Protestant leaders negotiated with leaders of the Catholic community so that marching could be carried out peacefully, in a way that would not be disruptive for the (largely Catholic) business community in the center city or excessively provocative to residents of nearby Catholic neighborhoods. The particular changes were important but the combination created a larger impact, a sense of commitment across the community to maintaining peace in the city.

REBUILDING THE CITY CENTER   Central Derry was seriously damaged by bomb blasts during the troubles, and a heavy police and army presence made it almost impossible to use the main shopping district for normal commercial purposes. For the city to return to normalcy this area had to be rebuilt. Grants became available for this work from government and from the International Fund for Ireland,[4] which allowed for the construction of shopping centers and public arenas of the sort that usually are elements of urban economic-renewal schemes. A partnership formed among an emerging community leadership, business leaders, and the leading bishops of the Catholic church (Edward Daly) and the Protestant Church of Ireland (James Mehaffey).

Believing that lack of economic opportunity was an important cause of violence, this leadership group sought to develop job-training programs for the building trades in which young apprentices would rebuild the central city as their training work. According to Bishop Daly, the leaders figured that if the young people built the buildings they would be less inclined to blow them up, and this has proven to be true.[5] The availability of the Action for Community Employment scheme as a means of subsidizing the wages of the labor required was crucial to the success of the venture. A community leader from the Bogside, Paddy Doherty, established the Inner City Trust as a vehicle for the purchase and renovation of derelict sites. Its success helped trigger private investment in new shopping malls and other infrastructure that has transformed the central area of the city. As structures were rebuilt, space was provided for civil society organizations. The result is a remarkable density of organizations in a small area, and this helped encourage partnerships and dialogue through the creation of neutral space.

BLOSSOMING OF CIVIL SOCIETY ORGANIZATIONS   When we visited Derry at the end of the twentieth century with the intention of placing students for study experiences in community-based organizations, we found remarkable the number, variety, and creativity of organizations in the square mile that makes up the walled city. Some of the largest and most impressive organizations are arts organizations that seek to draw people from both communities by focusing on work that has no immediate sectarian focus. The Nerve Centre supports young rock musicians and develops community video projects. The Verbal Arts Centre celebrates writing and attempts to teach writing by drawing young people from Catholic and Protestant schools. There is a program to involve developmentally disabled adults in cooking and selling food. Although not located in the city center, one of the most effective cross-community organizations is the hospice, which is primarily supported with voluntary gifts and supports people from both sides.

There also are several peace-oriented organizations that undertake direct action to further peace. An important recognition was that rumors develop and spread rapidly during times of tension and that they are an important factor inciting violence. Leaders of one community group were concerned about rumors of police violence so they kept a police radio. When they heard news of a civil disturbance they would go into the center of the trouble and try to get arrested. This would allow them to calm down both those arrested and the police. It also would allow them to provide an accurate and trusted account of what had happened so that exaggerated stories would not escalate violence.

Another group that included Catholic and Protestant women developed the practice of seeking out growing groups of teenagers agitating on opposite sides of an interface zone between communities. As rumors developed the women, equipped with cell phones, would call their opposite number across the flashpoint, get accurate information, and use this effectively to calm the crowds. A different group would approach the groups of young people, identify the leaders, and take them off in vans for fishing trips or vacations, thus cutting off the leadership of civil disorders. These "youth diversionary schemes" have now become a regular part of the work of many community-based organizations and have helped to manage and reduce tensions in interface areas.[6]

Another initiative has been concerned with reconciliation. Several organizations have followed the idea that in the wake of trauma individuals tend to find emotional response so difficult that they forget violent and personally damaging events. It is believed that this suppressed trauma leads to depression or excessive violence in families and communities. A variety of groups have brought people into groups and worked with them to remember past events and to publicly tell their stories. Simple expression of these past pains helps people to manage their emotions in a more self-conscious and constructive way. Groups also encourage storytelling between people from the different sectarian communities as part of an effort to recognize that there were losses on all sides. The feeling is that effective peace requires that people give up anger at the other side and accept that ending conflict and violence is the highest priority.

LOYALIST RECONCILIATION   Since Derry is majority Catholic, members of the working-class Protestant community tend to feel especially embattled. Peace projects that have their origins in this community are therefore especially striking. One of the most dramatic efforts has come from the leadership of the Apprentice Boys of Derry, one of the main fraternal marching societies in Northern Ireland. The Apprentice Boys runs large marches in July and the other in Decemberto commemorate the beginning and the end of the siege of Derry. These generally bring thousands of people to the city and comprise bands and many marchers. These events have been provocative for the Catholic community and often were associated with violence.

In the late 1990s the business and religious leaders of the group that had led the reconstruction of the city center approached the Apprentice Boys and tried to convince them to negotiate to find an alternative that would be less violent and disruptive. Since the walls of the city themselves are sacred historical structures for Protestants and the Apprentice Boys Hall is an ornate building perched on the walls overlooking the Catholic Bogside neighborhood, the marching problem seemed intractable. This is especially the case because within the Protestant community marching is a particularly important expression of community solidarity. Because Protestants are fragmented religiously they do not easily join together into expressions of community, and so it is felt that the fraternal societies and public expressions of their sectarian identity are important for Protestants to maintain a distinctive social and political identity in a situation where their group is threatened.

Although sentiment from within the Protestant communities across Northern Ireland was strongly against compromise, the Apprentice Boys leaders agreed to discuss their marching traditions with Catholic leaders since ongoing violence created real dangers for the tiny Protestant community. The only Protestant community that remains on the city side of

Derry is the Fountain, a small housing estate nestled against the city walls. (The river Foyle divides the city, and the east side, called the Waterside, has a substantial Protestant presence—about 40 percent of that community.) A high fence surrounds the Fountain, and many afternoons Catholic children come to throw rocks at the buildings. One of the main community resources for residents of the Fountain is the bar in the Apprentice Boys Hall, two blocks away, and so provoking Catholic hostility creates an ongoing threat to routine life for Protestant residents.

Convinced that they had to retain their cultural traditions related to marching in a way that would be more peaceful, the Apprentice Boys leaders began an extended series of conversations with Catholic community leaders, businessmen, priests, and bishops.

The narrative of this negotiation effort is dramatic because for many people in Northern Ireland segregation of their world is nearly complete.[7] Not only are there few cross-community social relationships, but the symbolism and leadership of the Catholic Church were also powerful and scary symbolic elements for the working-class Protestant men who led the Apprentice Boys. Yet through coming together and negotiating, a climate of mutual respect developed. The Catholics acknowledged that marching was an important and valid part of the ethnic identity of Protestants, and the Protestants acknowledged that the timing (in the middle of the Christmas shopping season), language, and noise of their marches could reasonably upset the Catholic community.

The Apprentice Boys agreed to move their December march to a Saturday earlier in the month, to restrict the number of groups from outside the city that could march, and to temper the style of the march. In return, Catholics sought to prevent young people from confronting the marches, and a general effort was made to present the marches as a historical tradition of the other community. The Apprentice Boys as an organization sought to reframe their mission, presenting themselves as a historical preservation association. They even went so far as to have St. Patrick's Day celebration where they presented historical displays accepting that a shared Irish identity was important for both communities (an especially distasteful acknowledgment for many Protestants, who strongly deny that they are Irish).

It is hard to overemphasize the symbolic importance of this accommodation. Community leaders have expressed the view that it has modeled the viability of negotiation over conflict in ways that have made it easier to reach more accommodations in other areas of the city.[8] Viewed from areas outside Derry where such conflicts have often proved insurmountable, the success of the Derry negotiations has contributed in no small measure to the perception of Derry exceptionalism.

DERRY AND ORGANIC SUSTAINED DIALOGUE

Several things stand out about the Derry experience and link it to Saunders's (1999) ideas about sustained dialogue. Derry was a center of conflict throughout the troubles, and its internal relationships added fuel to the conflict at key points. Bringing the hostilities of that period to an end required fundamental change in Derry. Macrolevel changes made key parties less committed to warfare, which made resources available for community building. But that community building could only happen when local community leaders acted aggressively and with vision.

Critically, the process started with a small number of leaders who, within their own frames of reference, created cross-community ties—ties between the bishops, between specific business leaders, among politicians. What seems to have begun as relatively specific, perhaps pair-based relationships expanded in the late 1980s into a small leadership group. This group then undertook strategic projects meant to create a context for cross-community relationships, then build strong community initiatives for cross-community relationships, and then finally address certain recurrent conflict issues. Out of this came a generalized community commitment to peace. People want to sustain peace even when cross-community tensions remain high.

SUSTAINED DIALOGUE

We find the framework of sustained dialogue helpful for understanding developments in Derry because it implies a strategic plan and clear stages of development. What strikes an observer in Derry is that there is a definite story with key actors, a process of development, a specific vision, and a denouement of a local civil society committed to nonviolence. Sustained dialogue is conceived as a process with stages, and it will be helpful to frame the Derry story in terms of these stages.

1. DECIDING TO ENGAGE Hal Saunders has experienced sustained dialogue as a powerful diplomat, an individual with great personal influence who enters a national conflict and seeks out leaders who are willing to meet people from opposing communities and to spend time over a span of years getting to know them. In polarized communities, simply meeting people from the other side is usually difficult, dangerous, and unappetizing. Saunders argues, however, that peace can only be accomplished if the combatants choose not to fight and for this to happen citizens must be involved in the process. Saunders is careful in whom he chooses since he can foster only a small number of cross-community relationships through his personal intervention; he often sets up a process of regular meetings or seminars that continue for years. Thus, he concentrates on emerging leaders with the expectation that they will become significant national figures in years to come and bring an understanding of the opposing culture and strong person ties into the political roles.

In the 1980s key Derry leaders reached across community boundaries to form relationships and often strong friendships with parallel figures on the other side. It is important that these relationships began as private gestures and that dialogue began in intimate terms, person to person. People shared small challenges in their work and in their private lives, and from this they came to trust one another and enjoy one another's company.[9] Once these relationships were formed, people wanted to move forward.

2. MAPPING AND NAMING   Once people have formed relationships, they then more easily begin talking about what provokes conflict and why it continues. There is a tendency to interpret the sources of conflict in terms of broad issues and dissatisfactions and the need for sweeping government programs or a general willingness of one group to give in to the demands of another. Sustained dialogue may bring macro-influences to bear on the sources of conflict, but the main emphasis is on conflict as participants experience it. Thus it is well suited to conceptualizing the sources of violence in a particular place and to link conflict to specific causes that might be ameliorated.

In Derry, leaders developed a clear agenda around 1990. The physical condition of the city and the living situation of many residents were obvious problems that had to be dealt with. The city had a geographic advantage since a large river divided most of the Protestants and Catholics. But the iconic stature of the walled city itself and the defensive situation of the Protestants would set up continual provocations. It was important that the city is small and that most of the community activists knew one another. Some of the leaders had a longstanding commitment to peace, and thus it was important to underwrite their efforts to organize.

3. PROBING PROBLEMS AND RELATIONSHIPS

4. SCENARIO BUILDING   These are the action phases where leaders lay out possible courses, look for strategies that would address endemic problems, and develop a general direction for proceeding. What Saunders offers as two stages, necessary when the target is a large country with diverse problems, was collapsed in Derry into a burst of action concentrated in a few years. This is the stage where external government programs become important because they can provide resources for new initiatives. This also may be a stage when outside leaders with vision can play a role in the development of local programs.

In Derry mobilizing to rebuild the city and simultaneously working to fund and support new civil society organizations were critical steps. It was important that the European Community was making funds available for these purposes, but it was equally important that leaders could access those funds and imagine effective ways of putting them to work. This happened in terms of large-scale economic-infrastructure development: rebuilding the city and building a new bridge across the river. But there was also strong community and voluntary leadership, evident in particular in the emergence of the North West Community Network, whose leaders were able to channel resources to specific organizational development projects. There was a clear plan for Derry's social and physical redevelopment, and the cohesive leadership group both conceived the vision and brought the means to bear for the plan to move ahead.

5. ACTING TOGETHER   With the problems defined, possible resources identified, and plans laid out, the final stage for Saunders is for people to finally act together. This is often a slow and difficult process since coalitions fall apart, resources disappear, and new coalitions have to be formed.

Since Derry is a small place, action happened rather quickly there. One thing we see, however, is that larger, more visible projects could be completed in a matter of a few years. Other projects were difficult because they required personal decisions to give up anger or established cultural traditions of separation and hostility. Storytelling and reconciliation groups take years to develop because individuals must be encouraged to give up their reluctance to confront violent assaults from the past. They then must gain further security and understanding in the narrative process. This emotional unfolding can have dramatic effects, as happened with the Apprentice Boys. The willingness of leaders from both sides to engage an enemy that they truly saw as evil required a challenging process of personal reflection. This can only happen once the peace process becomes established and is so convincing as a reality that people feel compelled to take the personal risks associated with acceptance and reconciliation.

LIMITS TO PROGRESS

The sustained dialogue framework fits the historical developments in Derry. The model helps us to bring into sharper focus the way the changes in Derry represented a concerted, self-conscious effort and also the significance of strong, cross-community friendships that developed over a number of years. We have the sense that there is a "Derry story" that is definite and unique and important, and this uniqueness makes the progress in the city somewhat at odds with other political developments in Northern Ireland. It is hard to use as a model for other places because Derry is simply exceptional, and we think it is the structure of sustained dialogue that emerged organically from the town's civic life that defines this quality.

Derry is also a frustrating place, however. There is a civic commitment to peace and a remarkable number of strong, innovative civil society organizations. There is also enduring tension and hostility and an emphatic pattern of segregation between the communities. There may be no bullets or bombs, but longstanding observers of the city suggest that really nothing has changed from the time of the troubles. Derry continues to be an economic backwater and does not benefit much from the economic boom occurring a few miles away across the Irish border. The political system is dysfunctional for national reasons and because there are deep divisions between champions of community organizations and the political and economic sector controlled by people who are unenthusiastic about participatory democracy. An important consequence is that all politics remains sectarian and there is little room for special identities to have their voices heard—"minority" identities such as the women's movement, the disabled movement, the integrated education movement, and the youth movement.

To an important extent the Derry story is a period piece, referring to the golden years of the 1990s—the heroic era, as we have called it. Looking back after several years, we are convinced that the mechanisms of sustained dialogue were present and that they really worked. They were extremely important for the period of Northern Irish social and political history that led in the peace process and the 1998 Belfast Agreement. But what happens after peace breaks out?

One consequence in Derry is that there has developed a robust civil society comprising organizations that grew out of the peace business. Once the funding disappears, will those organizations die? This is a double-edged question. One aspect is whether civil society organizations and cross-community friendships really are the strong engine for peace that Saunders believes them to be. They may be a significant force for ending overt conflict, but does that mean they are also an effective instrument for changing a society's basic structural elements, which many observers argue are the primary motivations for conflict? If the goal is long-term peace perhaps the main objectives should be economic reform and political inclusiveness. Should limited resources, limited time, and limited political capital be spent on community-process projects or on widening the road from Belfast to Derry so that true economic development can happen (Cunningham 1998)? Many would argue that structural changes must happen in order to reduce the enduring grievances that motivate conflict in the first place.

On the other hand, for peace to be enduring people must feel that they are citizens of a country where their needs are recognized and their interests can be expressed. Civil society organizations like those in Derry make people feel involved in and responsible for their communities. They also link them to identity-building organizations that could support pluralistic representation in a democratic society. But for that to happen, civil society organizations have to be connected to the political system in an enduring way. Northern Irish political culture today distinguishes between representative democracy and participatory democracy, and professional politicians prefer the representative variety—after all, as representatives they are given autonomous power. As long as politicians run the country, sectarian divisions will be maintained because they form the basis of the party structure that elects government officials. The prospect for continued relevance and vitality, therefore, are possibly grim for civil society organizations of Derry.

Notes

Originally presented as a paper at the Association for Research on Nonprofit Organizations and Voluntary Action, Washington, D.C., November 17–19, 2005.

1. http://cain.ulster.ac.uk/events/bsunday/bs.htm.
2. Some data for this paper come from videotaped lectures provided to students in the Bucknell in Northern Ireland program over a four-year period. These comments by civil rights leaders come from a panel that included Ivan Cooper, Eamon McCann, and Bernadette Devlin McCalsky, held at Magee College, Derry, on May 30, 2003.
3. Neighborhood violence seems to have taken the form of occasional vigilante violence against selected members of the opposite sectarian group. Residents who were part of mixed marriages report that they were accepted and well treated in both communities. There was a real threat of vigilante violence as people were attacked returning home alone from work late at night. Fear of violence caused people to give up and move out to communities of their own sectarian group. In Derry, one Protestant community, the Fountain Estates, remained. Nestled against the outside of the city walls, these Protestants were determined to stay so that they could hold on to their claim that the city walls were part of their community. The community is dramatically fortified and is a regular target of attack from rock-throwing children.
4. The International Fund for Ireland was largely funded by the U.S. federal government with contributions from other states, including Australia and New Zealand. It was established in 1985 at the time of the Anglo-Irish Agreement and has focused primarily in repairing economic infrastructure. Private sector investment was also made available from the United States through the "Derry Boston link," established by John Hume. U.S. involvement in the reconstruction of Northern Ireland was heavily promoted during the years of the Clinton presidency.
5. This account comes from a videotaped lecture from June 6, 2002, by Bishop Edward Daly to Bucknell in Northern Ireland. In the first part of the lecture John Hume explains the economic focus of peacemaking efforts. Bishop Daly and Bishop Mehaffey, in a lecture to Bucknell in Northern Ireland on June 10, 2005, expanded on their experience with this project.
6. Interviews with community leaders conducted by Acheson in May 2005
7. This account is informed by a videotaped lecture by Apprentice Boys leaders to Bucknell in Northern Ireland, May 30, 2002, and May 23, 2003, and a personal conversation between Milofsky and leaders on March 10, 2003, for which we have field notes.
8. Interviews by Acheson, May 2005
9. We have particularly detailed accounts of how this happened between Bishop Daly and Bishop Mehaffey in their lectures to Bucknell in Northern Ireland, June 4, 2003, and June 10, 2005.

9

THE ROLE OF DIALOGUE IN ACHIEVING SOCIAL JUSTICE AT A LARGE PUBLIC UNIVERSITY

Jennifer McIntosh and Charles Morris

THE OVERALL FOCUS OF THIS volume on the practice of democratic deliberation and sustained dialogue can be brought into considerably sharper focus by concentrating on the applicability of these perspectives to a single institution, in this case, a comprehensive, land-grant university, and a single program focus, the social justice program at that university.

West Virginia University, located in Morgantown, West Virginia, enrolls approximately 27,000 students and is a comprehensive, land-grant institution. The Carnegie Foundation for the Advancement of Teaching classifies WVU among doctoral institutions as a Research University (High Research Activity). WVU has an interesting and unique history of addressing the broad issue of social justice. In the 1980s, the university established an office specifically charged with providing leadership in the area of social justice; it would handle all issues related to compliance, diversity, and universal opportunity. Named the President's Office for Social Justice, it is led by an executive officer and is responsible for the university's compliance with requirements of affirmative action, equal-opportunity employment, the Americans with Disabilities Act, and section 504 of the Rehabilitation Act of 1972. The office investigates all discrimination and harassment complaints and conducts related training. It also administers the Office of Disability Services, which aids students with disabilities in obtaining reasonable accommodations for their university experience. In addition, the office promotes minority opportunity, administers the university's Mediation Program, and supports efforts to promote opportunity for all in an atmosphere of dignity and respect.

This broad approach may seem unexpected given the limited amount of diversity and activism in the state. About 95 percent of West Virginia's population is white, non-Hispanic, and the majority of the minority population is located in fewer than ten of the state's fifty-five counties. This makes West Virginia one of the least diverse states in the country. However, the university community in Morgantown is considerably more diverse than the state. Less than 90 percent of WVU's students identify as white. Minority students and international students make up nearly 12 percent of the student population. Although this is not a large percentage compared to some institutions in other regions, it is more than double the state's minority population. Similarly, roughly 10 percent of the full-time employees of WVU on the Morgantown campus identify as members of a racial or ethnic minority group. Again, this is approximately double the representation that these groups have in the rest of the state. Given the homogeneity of West Virginia's population, the university can be held up as a good example of the benefits and challenges of increased diversity.

Beyond racial diversity, other dimensions of diversity are important in day-to-day life at WVU. Announcements in one issue of the student newspaper, the *Daily Athenaeum*, captured a snapshot of the diversity at WVU. Students were notified of an initial meeting of the Association of American Muslims (in addition to a Muslim Student Association, which has been a recognized campus organization for many years) and meetings for at least five Christian groups, the WVU Students United for the Separation of Church and State, Democrat and Republican student groups, the Female Equality Movement, two environmental groups, gay and lesbian student organizations, the Japanese Animation and Manga Society, and "Spanish Tables," in addition to a Celt Fest. Other organizations, centers, and programs of study address a wide range of employee and student needs and interests.

For many years, strong leadership from faculty and administration has brought focus and direction to promoting understanding between disparate groups, seeking the benefits of a diverse environment and assuring equal opportunity for all.

SYSTEM DEVELOPMENT THROUGH DIALOGUE

Dialogue has played a critical role at pivotal times in the university's history: it was prevalent when noteworthy progress was made and was essential in developing a system to achieve a more socially just environment. At the inception of the Office for Social Justice, various constituents from across the university community played a pivotal role in defining the scope of this concept of inclusion.

In later years, an important example of the role of dialogue came with the development of the "Strategic Plan to Achieve Social Justice at WVU." Relevant dialogue began well before the idea for the plan was formulated. In 1999, the executive officer for social justice position became vacant. As one might expect, various interest groups developed agendas based on their expectations and perceived needs. In this climate, President David C. Hardesty Jr. held discussion sessions with a variety of campus leaders. He listened carefully and crafted his thoughts into a personal position paper. This work preceded the appointment of a new executive officer and set the stage for critical actions during the coming years.

The outgrowth of those discussions included merging the positions of director of affirmative action/equal opportunity and executive officer for social justice and appointing Jennifer McIntosh to this combined role. President Hardesty at this time also announced expectations of developing a strategic plan and a Social Justice Visiting Committee. These steps would have profound impact on the direction of social justice within the university system and were based on dialogue that took place to advance social justice.

In order to develop a strategic plan, a series of listening sessions were held. More than twenty opportunities were provided for students, faculty, and staff to discuss both the process and the content of the plan. In some sessions, participants espoused views that were met with resistance by others. Sometimes emotions were as much a part of the discussions as the content expressed. Some participants seemed to react to past concerns while others took a futuristic, proactive view. Based on these discussions, drafters identified common themes and created a preliminary plan. The university then discussed the draft plan and provided feedback. The drafters prepared a second version, which they ultimately submitted to the president for his acceptance.

The "Strategic Plan to Achieve Social Justice at WVU" has proved to be a solid foundation. The plan documented an all-encompassing vision for the future, identified the university's core values, named the functions of the President's Office for Social Justice, and established criteria by which to evaluate social justice initiatives. In addition, the plan was the first systematic approach to a cohesive direction for social justice on all the regional campuses, which include WVU–Parkersburg, Potomac State, WVU–Institute of Technology, and WVU.

Concurrent to the development of the plan was the creation of a Social Justice Visiting Committee. Visiting committees have existed at WVU for many years and have characteristics similar to advisory committees. The president selects their members from constituency groups external to the university. Thus, the committees bring insight and perspective to the institution from a wide range of experiences and work to promote the college or unit they represent.

From the time of its inception, the Social Justice Visiting Committee provided a meaningful contribution to both the Office for Social Justice and the university community as a whole. At their first meeting, the committee made valuable suggestions about the strategic plan, including making it a priority to equip students with "social justice competencies" to prepare them for the world and workplace. The committee is valuable because its members are individuals with backgrounds of passion and experience with social justice topics; the diverse and sometimes contradictory ideas that emerge in the committee's continual dialogue make the group effective. One of the university's goals is to equip both its students and its employees to function effectively in communities that are increasingly shaped by diverse global forces. Whether they remain in West Virginia or live and work halfway around the world, the skills to interact productively with people from diverse backgrounds are essential. The Visiting Committee members, with their grounding in the world outside of higher education, model these skills in the way they participate in the life of the university community, continually bringing it to engagement with dialogue that extends beyond its boundaries.

The university's climate of exploring new ideas, challenging the status quo, and bringing together divergent views in an atmosphere of reason and trust has set the stage for important developments related to social justice. An excellent example of this is the development of graduate study opportunities for minority students. The concept began in a meeting with state education leaders when a state college president commented that the system needed WVU to encourage minority doctoral students to consider pursuing faculty careers in West Virginia. WVU leaders considered the suggestion carefully and sought ways to be responsive to a legitimate state need. From the dialogue between education leaders and WVU campus administrators, the WVU Academic Partnership for Minority Teaching Fellows was created. This partnership affords minority doctoral students at WVU an opportunity to become teaching fellows at a public or private college or university instead of serving as a teaching or research graduate assistants on the WVU campus. Participants gain valuable teaching experience while finishing their degrees. In addition, colleges and universities in the region are afforded a more competent and diverse faculty than would otherwise be available. We discovered that in several instances this was the first time that students had ever been instructed by nonwhites or non-Americans. This cultural interchange was an unintended consequence; students at the colleges were positive about the opportunity of having a teacher from Trinidad and Tobago or Colombia or even just an African American.

The success of this partnership spawned the need for further dialogue and innovation. The demand for teaching fellows was greater than the number of available students. Through discussion with education leaders, the Office for Social Justice established a Colloquium for Aspiring Minority Doctoral Candidates. This annual event, funded through a special allocation from the chancellor of the WV Higher Education Policy Commission and with strong support from WVU's provost, Dr. Gerald Lang, affords potential minority doctoral scholars the opportunity to learn how they can pursue graduate studies at WVU. After the first four colloquia, approximately 60 of the first 140 participants are enrolled in a graduate program. The ultimate impact will not be seen for several years.

These recent examples of using dialogue to build a system to address social justice needs are a continuation of a long-standing tradition of dialogue at WVU. During the 1960s, numerous interest groups emerged on campus. Over time, each group went through transformation, with the strongest, most viable groups continuing. In addition, new groups organized to meet emerging needs. By the mid-1980s, university administrators recognized the need to integrate formally many of these groups into the university system. This was one of the motivators involved in the establishment of the Office for Social Justice.

By the time the "Strategic Plan to Achieve Social Justice at WVU" was prepared, the pattern of dialogue within these groups and between these groups and the institution was well established. Institutionalized groups include:

- *Social Justice Council:* The SJC brings together relevant campus offices and constituents to promote communication among these groups, provide a forum to address issues of mutual concern, and serve as an ongoing venue for dialogue between the groups and university administration. In addition to the executive officer, who chairs the SJC, standing representatives from the Deans' Council, the Office of the Provost, the Office of the Director of Graduate Education, the Health Science Center, and the Office of Student Affairs participate. In addition, twenty or so representatives from various campus groups regularly participate. Every representative group is afforded the opportunity to place items for awareness on the agenda. Meetings are held monthly.

   ▪ *Council of Women's Concerns*: The CWC promotes equality of women in the academic and local communities. The council was founded in 1977 and has maintained a presence throughout the evolving response to women's issues. The CWC has continued to sponsor or cosponsor conferences and activities that highlight the concerns and accomplishments of women, such as the Mary Catherine Buswell Award, the Women of Color Day Luncheon held during the annual Diversity Week celebration, and Take Our Daughters and Sons to Work Day. It has also promoted institutional development via the Center for Women's Studies, Social Justice Council, Affirmative Action Office, Sexual Assault Prevention Program, and Child-Care Programs. The CWC has a wide representation of women and men within the university community and the broader Morgantown community.

   ▪ *Council on Sexual Orientation*: The purpose of COSO is to provide a visible, accessible presence in the university community for gay, lesbian, bisexual, and transgender and questioning people. The council seeks to improve the social, political, and educational climate for these people and to engage the university in achieving this goal. The group deals with campus climate issues of inclusion, safety, and diversity. Dialogue between this group and the Office for Social Justice is sustained through regular meetings and participation by COSO on the Social Justice Council.

   ▪ *Council on African and African American Affairs*: The CAAA is a community of individuals representing the needs of African and African American faculty, staff, and students. The CAAA provides the university with a proactive voice on issues relevant to the black community. The CAAA's seeks to enhance the university's commitment to diversity, advance the careers of black faculty and staff, be a resource to university administration on issues of mutual concern, encourage black students to achieve academic and personal success, and address contemporary issues critical to the black community. The council has maintained a strong presence on the campus since the 1970s.

   ▪ *Social Justice Liaisons*: Liaisons are appointed by the executive officer for social justice based on recommendation from their administrators. There are about seventy volunteers who serve as links to a wide range of issues across the university. They meet four times a year to discuss topics of mutual interest and to receive ongoing training. Their role is to be a resource within their individual units and the greater campus community. They are trained to provide information to faculty, staff, and students on institutional resources and how to report sexual harassment and discrimination, facilitate communication on social justice issues within a department or college, and cultivate an atmosphere of respect and civility.

The system of councils and liaisons provides an ongoing structure to facilitate dialogue and ensure grassroots involvement when critical decisions are made. They provide invaluable assistance to the executive officer as a communication link with the institution. The Visiting Committee enriches the process by bringing additional perspectives and competencies into play. Individuals on the committee from disparate constituencies allow dialogue that leads to creative thinking.

INDIVIDUAL NEEDS AND DIALOGUE

Not only students but also staff and faculty come to higher education from many places and bring many forms of baggage with them. This is true geographically and socially as well as personally. Many students at West Virginia University are the part of the first generation from their families to attend college and come from relatively homogeneous environments (whether inner-city neighborhoods in Pennsylvania and New Jersey or the fabled "hollers" of Appalachia). An active approach to social justice requires that each student be treated as an individual as well as appreciation that people are often more alike than they are different.

WVU faculty come from a wide range of races, nationalities, and religions. They have been raised and educated all over the world and bring their varied cultures and expectations with them. Staff, on the other hand, are a mixture of what have been characterized in the sociological literature as "cosmopolitans" and "locals." Moreover, the university exists in a small urban setting where differences between "town" and "gown" are always present, on the surface or deep in the psyches of those involved. Obviously, in such a context a great deal of social justice–related dialogue is necessary on a continual basis for the community to survive and grow. Attending to the individual needs of students, faculty, staff, and townspeople is an important dynamic of ongoing dialogue.

ORGANIZATIONAL NEEDS AND DIALOGUE

In the modern American university, ongoing dialogue among the various constituencies is an organizational necessity. It is through this dialogue that institutions grow from good to great. When institutional leaders make the opportunity to listen and take the opportunity to hear, organizations will thrive.

Successful identification of organizational needs can be made at many levels of an institution. Bringing various constituents to the table to help identify problems and, even more important, help find solutions contributes to organizational well-being. Yet this can only be accomplished in an environment where discussion and involvement are welcome. When people feel invested they are far more eager to put in time and energy. Dialogue provides an opportunity for that involvement, gives people a voice where they thought that they had none, and gives them a feeling of participation where they felt marginalized.

CONCLUSIONS AND OBSERVATIONS

Several observations are apparent from the foregoing history of achieving social justice through dialogue:

- Maintaining dialogue does not mean that all parties will agree on decisions. Rather, it means that all parties will be heard and discussions will occur both before decisions are made and afterward.
- Dialogue alone will not always bring resolution or change. However, without dialogue, decisions are less likely to be effective and more likely to face rejection.
- The involvement of all relevant parties is essential. This includes senior leadership, those who often feel left out of the process, those with special competencies, and representatives of all interested parties.
- Dialogue must be ongoing. For example, had the dialogue that created the "Strategic Plan to Achieve Social Justice at WVU" ceased after the plan's

release, programs that resulted from it, such as the WVU Academic Partnership and the Colloquium for Aspiring Minority Doctoral Scholars, might not have been created.

- A perfect environment for dialogue probably never exists. Some groups or interested individuals may feel neglected, or new interests may be too slowly assimilated. But dialogue must occur.

10

A PUBLIC SAFETY PROCESS: SUSTAINED DIALOGUE FOR SITUATIONAL POLICING

James J. Nolan, Norman Conti, and Corey Colyer

Take the case of the United States. . . . We can see clearly that they are facing some kind of moral crisis. They are either increasing their police force or seeking some other technical solution to their problems. Unless some positive developmental change occurs in each individual's heart, or unless there is some transformation there, it is very difficult to control external forces

—HIS HOLINESS THE DALAI LAMA, 2001

THIS CHAPTER EXPLICATES A CONCEPTUAL framework for a *public safety process* that is a synthesis of Saunders's *public peace process* (1999) and *situational policing* (Nolan, Conti, and McDevitt 2004, 2005). While Saunders's public peace process emerged from "a mix of experience and concepts pragmatically—not theoretically—defined" (Saunders 1999), our public safety process was developed with a strong theoretical orientation. A public safety process is based upon the recent work that analyzes the relationship between crime and group development in neighborhoods (Sampson and Raudenbush 1999; Sampson, Raudenbush, and Earls 1997). While Saunders's framework focuses on dealing with deep, longstanding, *intergroup* conflicts, such as Arab-Israeli relations, our model focuses on overcoming *intragroup* conflicts in a way that promotes "normal" group development and enhanced public safety. From this foundation we have designed a structure for policing that begins by conceptualizing a practical end state that the police and community can work toward (i.e., neighborhood development) and then provides a blueprint for achieving it.

Our central presupposition is that neighborhoods are not just aggregates of individuals and families living in close proximity to one another but are in fact "groups" with identifying characteristics that are different from, and many times greater than, the sum of their parts. The central characteristic that qualifies a neighborhood as a group is what Lewin (1948) described as an "interdependence of fate." In other words, it is not the fact that the individual residents are similar in physical, political, or social thought or attributes that makes them a group but the fact that they live near one another and experience fear and safety in the public space they share. In addition, residents share the common goal of personal security, which further ensures their interdependence of fate and frames the neighborhood a group (see Sampson and Raudenbush 1999). The public safety process has the unique feature of establishing neighborhood as the unit of analysis for any criminological policy evaluations.

Like other groups, neighborhoods are "dynamic wholes" and have a mentality that either enhances or inhibits their ability to ensure public safety. At any one time a neighborhood can be psychologically *dependent* on the police to solve all its public safety problems, in *conflict* with the police because they are not able to adequately attend to public safety, or prepared to work *interdependently* with the police to effectively solve neighborhood problems. Sustained dialogue is introduced as a means for helping neighborhoods overcome the obstacles to this development. Developing a psychological state of "interdependence" or "collective efficacy" enables neighborhoods to participate more fully and effectively with the police and others to provide safety and security in their own local public sphere.

THEORETICAL FOUNDATION

NEIGHBORHOOD AS UNIT OF ANALYSIS

As mentioned above, the unit of analysis in our public safety process is the neighborhood. Shifting perspective from the individual to the group is essential in order to understand social phenomena related to local public safety efforts. Lewin (1943) notes that groups have qualities that are separate and distinct from the individuals that compose them:

> In physics, we are accustomed to recognize that an ion has different properties from the atom of which it is a part, that the larger molecule again has specific properties of its own, and that a macroscopic object like a bridge, too, has specific properties as a whole. . . . The organization of a group is not the same as the organization of the individuals of which it is composed. . . .

That a social unit of a certain size (in our case "neighborhood") has properties of its own should be accepted as a simple empirical fact.

Shifting the focus to the neighborhood as a whole enables us to see opportunities for a public safety process that might otherwise go unrecognized.

THE NEIGHBORHOOD MENTALITY

A central point in our model is that, like groups, neighborhoods have a shared consciousness that affects their ability to function effectively. This is not meant to imply that there is a "group mind" that transcends the individual residents. Instead, it means that the neighbors think about community issues in parallel ways at corresponding times. Examples include responsibility for protecting the neighborhood from crime and disorder and whether there is cohesion and trust among the residents and a shared willingness to intervene in public safety matters. Recent sociological research on crime and disorder in the city of Chicago demonstrated that neighborhood-level collective efficacy is strongly associated with crime: low levels of collective efficacy predict high crime rates and vice versa. Collective efficacy was defined by the researchers as the "cohesion among residents combined with shared expectations for the social control of public space" (Sampson and Raudenbush 1999, 612–13). Taylor (2001) points out that the concept of collective efficacy and its relationship to crime has been of interest in sociology, community psychology, and environmental psychology for over thirty years. In the past it was called "willingness to intervene," "social disorganization," "territorial functioning," "attachment to place," "sense of community," "organizational participation and neighboring," "informal social control," and "local social ties." The related concept "social capital" has also been connected to violent crime (see Putnam 2000).

The concept of a group mentality is not new. In his pioneering work on group behavior, Bion (1959) observed this same fact. His research revealed that in any given task-oriented group, two distinct groups were actually present, a "work group" and one of three "basic assumption groups." The work group is the facet of group functioning that pertained to the job to be completed. Mentally and physically, members of the work group were fully engaged and were "at one with the task" (Rioch 1975). The "basic assumption group" refers to the aspect of group functioning that either interferes with or enhances the activity of the work group. While working on a task sometimes group members behave "as if" such and such were true. For example, sometimes the members of the work group seemed overly dependent on the leader to tell them what to do. They behaved "as if" the leader was omniscient or omnipotent. This "dependency" on the leader to guide group activities severely interfered with the functioning of the work group, especially when the leader was unable to live up to the expectations of the group.

Bion (1959) made the point that group mentality can and does exist. As group members work collectively on a task, they can begin behaving in ways that imply a shifting group mentality that either helps or hinders effective group functioning. In a similar way, a neighborhood mentality, such as a dependence on the police to solve all the local problems of crime and disorder, can get in the way of the public safety efforts of the neighborhood

DEVELOPING NATURE OF NEIGHBORHOOD MENTALITY

The development of a neighborhood mentality is part of a natural process, and there are structures and mechanisms that either inhibit or enhance this psychological progression. In their study of Chicago neighborhoods, Sampson and Raudenbush (1999) identified several obstacles to the development of collective efficacy. Conditions such as concentrated disadvantage, residential instability, population density, and mixed land use (private and commercial) were external structural obstacles to the development of collective efficacy.

Lewin (1948) suggests that social scientists should examine the dynamic movement of group mentality in an expanded social field. In this way, one could more easily see what Lewin called the "space of free movement." This means that in a particular social field, groups have boundaries that enable or prevent certain movements. It is useful to consider this concept in terms of a group's social or physical movement. For example, a family's wealth may make certain opportunities available that might not be open to families of lesser economic standing; or consider pre–World War II Europe, where ghettoized Jews were subject to limitations in both physical location and social status. Lewin stresses that it is not only the physical and social motion (or "locomotion," as he calls it) of groups that can be restricted by boundaries and obstacles but also their mental movement. For example, a group mentality such as collective efficacy could be blocked by fear among residents of a street gang or drug dealers who have a hold on the neighborhood. Collective efficacy could also be blocked in neighborhoods where residents work two or more jobs. These obstacles to collective efficacy are "social facts" (Durkheim [1895] 1982) and must be dealt with as such.

Building on these theoretical and empirical observations, sociologists and social psychologists have introduced the idea that group mentality develops in a sequence much like the development of an individual from childhood, through adolescence, and into adulthood. Children are *dependent* on adults for care and protection. As adolescents they move into a state of *conflict* as they seek freedom from the oppressive oversight of parents who may still see them as young children and treat them accordingly. Adults form new relationships with their parents that are based more on mutual respect and *interdependence*. The conceptual framework for a public safety process suggests that the mentality of the neighborhood evolves in a parallel fashion: from *dependence* on the police to solve all problems, through *conflict* with the police because they are unable to meet these unrealistic expectations, to *interdependence* with the police (and the larger body politic) to keep the neighborhood safe. We demonstrate this process in a slight modification of Wheelan's (1994) model of group development.

STAGE 1: DEPENDENCE In stage 1 of neighborhood development, community members want the police to solve problems related to public order, and the police are willing, and sometimes able, to do so. At this stage the police are viewed as competent and respected by most residents. As long as the police are able to solve the problems of community disorder, the community members will remain satisfied with their services and continue to depend on them. In this stage, the police may view the neighborhood as unable or unwilling to care for itself, so they fully embrace their mandate to act as the sole protectors of the community (see Manning 1977). If the police are not able to meet the neighborhood expectations, the community moves into the next stage of development.

STAGE 2: CONFLICT When the police are unable to "enforce away" community problems, residents become frustrated and dissatisfied. Residents in this second stage still see the police as having the primary responsibility for maintaining order and ensuring safety, but they believe the police are simply not doing a good job at it. Individuals might decide to take action on their own because they view the police as ineffective and the neighborhood has yet to develop the structures, mechanisms, and trusting relationships that would inspire collective action. Dissatisfaction and frustration in the community may result in formal complaints against the police. In defending themselves the police may consider new and innovative programs, such as high-visibility foot or bike patrols, in order to appease the residents and try to regain their confidence. At this point, the police may feel vulnerable; they are asked to meet unrealistic expectations within the prescribed (and finite) resources.

In order to move out of stage 2 toward interdependence (and collective efficacy), the police must give up the notion that they alone can protect the neighborhood against public disorder (Conti and Nolan 2005). Both the police and the residents must come to recognize the importance of collective action and informal social controls in restoring and maintaining order in the neighborhood before the neighborhood can move toward stage 3. Indications by the police that they will work harder or deploy more officer power to the location serves only to move the neighborhood back to stage 1, instead of toward stage 3.

STAGE 3: INTERDEPENDENCE Once the community and the police come to recognize their mutual responsibilities for restoring order and safety, each begins to develop the social networks and processes needed to make this happen. As neighbors and the police continue to work interdependently, they will develop stronger and more trusting relationships. In this final stage of development, strong, trusting community networks emerge in order to maintain control over neighborhood order and safety. The police will start to play a less prominent role in the maintenance of public order as they work with the community in order to deal with situations that are beyond the scope and capability of residents.

In this developmental model, we do not intend to imply that a neighborhood must pass through all these psychological stages before it is able to achieve any level of interdependence or collective efficacy, or that the neighborhood is exclusively in any one stage. Instead, this model should be viewed in terms of how the neighborhood is expending *most* of its finite time and mental energy. The model also explains how mature mental states, such as collective efficacy, evolve.

DIALOGUE FOR NEIGHBORHOOD DEVELOPMENT AND PUBLIC SAFETY

A few things are immediately clear in this model of neighborhood development. First, when the police are able to solve all the neighborhood problems, there will be no conflict between the police and the residents. Police efficiency, then, serves to *maintain* the collective mentality of *dependence*. Later, if crime and disorder reach a level where the police are unable to resolve them, *conflict* between the police and the residents develops. The important thing to recognize is that *conflict cannot and should not be avoided*. It serves a vital purpose in this developmental process. Working successfully through the conflict stage is an essential step to achieving the more mature mental state of interdependence and collective efficacy. However, when conflict is avoided, such as when the police promise to try harder or deploy more officers to a particular neighborhood, the unintended consequence is that they create an obstacle to the normal psychological development of the neighborhood. Finally, it is obvious that the police do not intend for this to happen, but the fact remains that effective and efficient police service in maintaining public order helps to keep the neighborhood locked in the mental state of dependence. So why does this happen and how should the police respond when it does?

Freire ([1970] 1973) helps us to see more clearly why this situation exists and how it can be resolved. He described a conflict in Brazil between the *oppressed* (i.e., poor and dispossessed peasants) and *oppressors* (i.e., government and ruling class) that resulted from an unjust social order in that country. He recognized that the resolution to this conflict could only come when the oppressed could see "the reality of oppression not as a closed world from which there is no exit, but as a limiting situation which *they can transform*" (Freire [1970] 1973, 31; author's emphasis). The *reality* that existed in this situation was not objective. Rather, it was the *subjective reality* of the oppressors, a reality that served to justify and perpetuate an unjust social order. Political action and educational policies that simply "deposit" government services or "expert knowledge" encourage passivity and foster fear and continued oppression. According to Freire, the only solution was for both the oppressed and the oppressors to see the objective reality of the situation so that they could transform it together. Effective political action in a community can only happen by changing the *consciousness* of all involved so that they can work together for change. The only way this liberating change can happen is when the politicians and citizens engage in a sustained dialogue based on humanistic principles and practices. Further, for educational and political systems to be liberating and transformative they must be based on honest dialogue in order to reveal the true nature of the mechanisms holding the social conditions in place.

In her work with small groups, Wheelan (1994) observed group-level phenomena similar to those observed by Freire. She recognized how oppressive, autocratic leadership could keep group members passive, disengaged, and "dependent" on the leader, just as the oppressive institutions worked to keep the poor and dispossessed "dependent" on the government in Freire's Brazil. Wheelan also observed that in order for the members of small groups to move out of this psychological state of *dependence*, they must begin to perceive the true *reality* of the situation. In other words the group must achieve a change in consciousness. Furthermore, she observed that this evolving consciousness creates confusion and conflict within the group and that only open and honest dialogue can resolve this conflict and move the group into more mature psychological states such as interdependence (or collective efficacy). Through dialogue group members engage in critical thinking about the group's task and their ability to accomplish it. They also begin to recognize their own capabilities and participate in setting goals and agreeing to roles and responsibilities. Once these are established, stronger, more cohesive relationships form, and more effective ways of working together are developed. When new members or new leaders join the group, the group may go back to earlier stages of development, i.e., dependence or conflict. However, a commitment to dialogue is the way to quickly return to the more mature and humanistic stage of interdependence.

The description of this developmental process is much easier to imagine in a small group than in a neighborhood, where there are many obstacles. For example, within neighborhoods there are subgroups that are sometimes in conflict with one another. Racial and ethnic groups on a higher rung of the socioeconomic ladder may, out of either fear or bias, not want to work with other, less-affluent residents on public safety issues. The reverse is also true. At the community level, these intergroup relations can be additional obstacles to the normal psychological development of the neighborhood. However, Saunders's (1999) public peace process used sustained dialogue as a means for dealing with these types of intergroup conflicts. Sustained dialogue, then, may serve as a method of dealing with both intergroup conflicts that divide communities and the intragroup conflicts that result from the normal psychological development of neighborhoods.

NEIGHBORHOOD TYPES

Since our model is a public safety process, it is important to explicate the conceptual link between neighborhood development and crime. By conceiving of these two dimensions (crime and neighborhood development) along horizontal and vertical axes we establish four neighborhood types: Strong, Vulnerable, Anomic, and Responsive (see figure 10.1). In a Strong neighborhood crime is low, and psychological development is high (i.e., "interdependence" relating to public safety issues). In Vulnerable neighborhoods crime is low, and so is psychological development (i.e., they are dependent on the police to solve most public safety problems). As long as the police have the resources and ability to solve these problems, citizens will gladly turn over their responsibilities to them. However, as disorder and crime grow beyond the capacity of the police to deal effectively with them, residents become dissatisfied and a conflict will develop.

A Vulnerable neighborhood is analogous to a person who is not yet sick but has a weak immune system and so is highly susceptible to illness. In contrast, Anomic neighborhoods are high in crime and low in development. In these neighborhoods, residents are typically both dependent on the police to take care of community safety problems and dissatisfied because of their lack of success. In Anomic neighborhoods, the police are called to respond to excessive numbers of neighborhood complaints, far beyond their ability to handle them successfully, resulting in tension and frustration between the police and the community. Finally, Responsive neighborhoods are those that are high in crime and disorder, but are working with the police to resolve them. Figure 10.1 illustrates the four neighborhood types.

SITUATIONAL POLICING

The literature on policing styles generally refers to a standard mode of operation for a particular police agency. These policing styles reflect both the organizational culture and the trends of the times. For example, in recent years many police agencies have moved away from the professional crime-fighting model of policing—where emphasis is placed on rapid response time, special investigations, and arrests for serious crimes—to the community-policing model, where community involvement, problem solving, and eliminating disorder are emphasized. However, policing styles should not be selected based on a police organization's standard mode of operation but should instead match the conditions of the neighborhood. In this regard, we refer back to the four neighborhood types and match these with four preferred policing styles: Supporting and Recognizing, Substituting and Selling, Securing then Organizing, and Systems Planning and

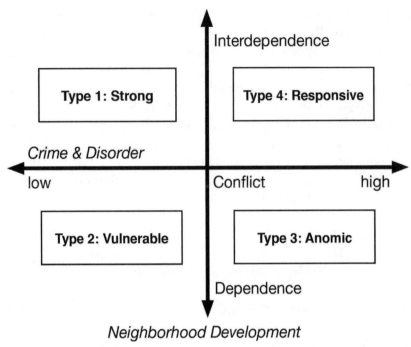

FIGURE 10.1 Neighborhood Types

Response. The relationship between neighborhood type and policing style is depicted in figure 10.2.

POLICING STYLE 1: SUPPORTING AND RECOGNIZING Residents of Strong neighborhoods are not concerned about crime and disorder because they are not present to a degree that seems problematic. Police officers assigned to Strong neighborhoods should support indigenous, community-based efforts to organize. Additionally, they should work to expand neighborhood access to resources and decision making and broaden the involvement of neighborhood members. The police department might also want to recognize individual community members or groups of members who have had particular successes.

POLICING STYLE 2: SUBSTITUTING AND SELLING Crime and disorder are not serious problems for residents of Vulnerable neighborhoods. This fact makes it difficult to motivate residents to organize around these issues. However, in Vulnerable neighborhoods residents have other concerns that

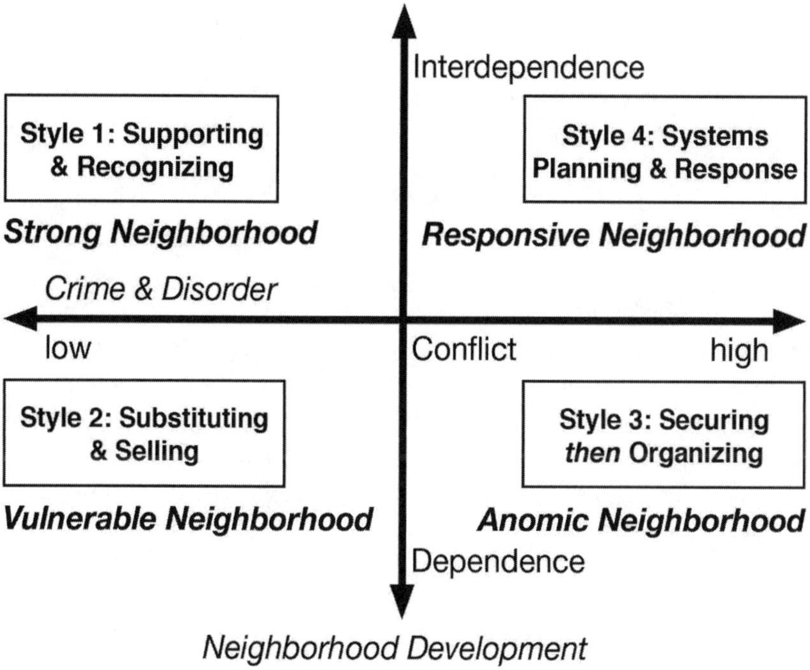

FIGURE 10.2 Policing Styles

could motivate them to work together, such as educational issues, other government services, the closing of a local fire station, and so on. Policing Vulnerable neighborhoods involves broadening the definition of public safety to include other problems that might not normally fit into the public safety framework.

POLICING STYLE 3: SECURING THEN ORGANIZING In Anomic neighborhoods crime and disorder are rampant, and the residents are disconnected, frustrated, and fearful. Collectively, residents in Anomic neighborhoods are dependent on the police to help them. In these neighborhoods the police are called to action to secure and protect the residents. Traditional law-enforcement practices such as drug raids and sweeps, undercover operations, and strict enforcement of relatively minor crimes are examples of some appropriate first steps in dealing with crime and disorder in Anomic neighborhoods. Once police have demonstrated to residents that they are committed to working together with them by temporarily resolving some of their most significant problems, the police must participate in organizational efforts. The police do not necessarily need to be the community organizers but must make sure that community organizing is going on and support it. This is the only way for an Anomic neighborhood to become a Responsive one.

POLICING STYLE 4: SYSTEMS PLANNING AND RESPONSE In Responsive neighborhoods, residents are organizing and working to regain control of public spaces. However, many of the social problems that are associated with crime and disorder lie far outside their expertise and abilities. Other resources must be brought to bear on the problems in the Responsive neighborhoods, e.g., city and state public safety and social services, the public school system, local advocacy groups, urban planners (especially focused on economic development), and other neighborhood-based services. These groups must create a vision for change and develop a coordinated response to make it happen.

SUSTAINED DIALOGUE AND SITUATIONAL POLICING

The situational policing model provides a conceptual framework for the police so that they can see both a desired end state, i.e., a strong neighborhood, and are equipped with a blueprint for achieving it. In this model, for example, if a police officer were to find herself assigned to an Anomic neighborhood (high crime and dependent residents), she would know that the right response would be to secure the neighborhood through standard law-enforcement practices and follow up with neighborhood organizing. What our model does not show, however, is exactly how this could or should be accomplished. In other words, the process for developing a neighborhood from Anomic to Responsive and then into Strong has not previously been defined. This is where Saunders (1999) makes an important contribution to the process. He provides a strategy for the police to help move neighborhoods through the stages of psychological development so that the residents can work more effectively with one another and the police in order to respond to and prevent crime. While Saunders believed that conflict was often the result of a "breakdown of state and local authority" (1999, 21), among other causes, we see it as a stage in the *normal* development of neighborhoods. In other words, when problems of crime and disorder grow beyond the ability of the police to handle them, *conflict arises naturally*. When this happens it puts a severe strain on the police, who are trying to deal with both the crime problem and the rising neighborhood conflict. From our conceptual framework, it is tempting for the police to reduce conflict by moving the neighborhood back to the stage of dependence where little conflict exists. This regression can be achieved by promising the deployment of more police officers or more city or state resources. In many neighborhoods, this feedback loop can go on for decades.

One of Saunders's insights from over thirty years inside and outside government, working with foreign states, communities, and neighborhoods, is that the "absence of shared purpose among citizens can paralyze effective government action" (1999, 23). On this issue Saunders wrote: "Governments face problems they cannot deal with alone, and citizens outside of government have the potential to develop an array of capacities to creatively deal with problems human beings confront" (7). Saunders coined the term "public peace process" to describe a methodology for citizens outside of government to come together in dialogue in order to change the nature of their relationships so that peace between them would be possible. This public peace process is built around the idea of "sustained dialogue." The aim of sustained dialogue is to change relationships over time. It is a political and psychological process that first addresses the relationships within a small group that is a "microcosm of conflictual relationships in the larger body politic" (Saunders 1999, 89). The small group, then, designs a political process to change the conflictual relationship in the larger community.

Saunders's model of sustained dialogue unfolds in five stages. First, individuals from the communities in conflict agree to come together and engage in conversations about the dynamics of the conflict and possible ways to reduce it. Once a representative group is formed, participants begin their conversation by sharing their insights about the causes of the conflict and how it has affected them. The goal of this second stage is to "encourage people to talk broadly enough about the conflict so that they can 'map' its larger and deeper dimensions—both the surface issues and the relationships that caused them" (Saunders 1999, 89). In the third stage, a moderator or facilitator probes the group to identify the most important problem that it faces and to recognize the dynamics of the relationships that causes it. In this stage the group also explores multiple directions to take in order to solve the problems and then converges on a single direction. In the fourth stage the group works together to identify both the obstacles to solving the problems and also the solutions for each obstacle. Specifically, members build a

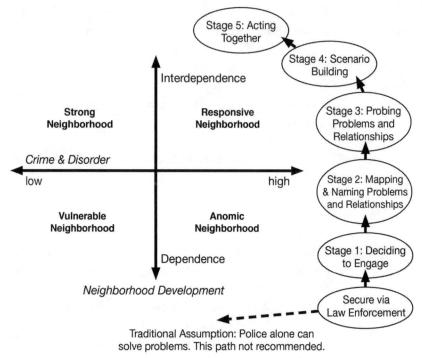

FIGURE 10.3 Sustained Dialogue for Situational Policing

scenario in which they implement solutions to all the obstacles. In stage 5, the group carries out its plan.

Saunders's model of sustained dialogue graphs perfectly on to situational policing and provides a "how to" for police who embrace our conceptual framework. Figure 10. 3 is a brief example of how sustained dialogue could work, beginning in an Anomic neighborhood.

STAGE 1: DECIDING TO ENGAGE

In Anomic neighborhoods residents are mostly dependent on the police to respond to public safety matters. Police are called for even small things like barking dogs, kids skipping school, loud music, groups of youths hanging out on the corner, and other forms of disorder. The roots of many of these public safety problems are beyond the capabilities and resources of the police. The only thing the police are equipped to do is to respond to calls for service and attempt to treat the presenting "symptoms." When the police can no longer keep up with the number of calls, the residents become frustrated with the police, and conflict develops. The situational policing style identified with this situation is "secure then organize." From this perspective, the police should use the resources the have available in order to secure the area so that residents will feel safe enough to get involved. In addition, they must begin to identify existing neighborhood subgroups (if there are any) or find individuals in the neighborhood who would be willing to engage in a dialogue with them about both the public safety issues facing the neighborhood and their strained relationship. Establishing a group willing to engage in sustained dialogue is a crucial first step in moving the neighborhood out of the psychological state of conflict but away from dependence and toward interdependence.

STAGE 2. MAPPING AND NAMING PROBLEMS AND RELATIONSHIPS

Once a representative neighborhood group is identified or formed, the police (or a third party) can facilitate a discussion aimed at mapping the public safety problems, including intergroup relations and the relationship between the police and the community. The purpose of this discussion is to "develop a picture of the whole situation from as many viewpoints as possible" (Saunders 1999, 119). It is likely that many social problems, such as unemployment, poverty, racism, and the like, that affect (if not cause) the public safety problems will be identified. It is also likely that the police and other government officials will be blamed or accused of incompetence because they cannot solve these problems. However, it is important to remember that the goal at this point is not to "fix anything," but only to "name" the problems and talk about their impact on community members and the neighborhood as a whole

STAGE 3. PROBING PROBLEMS AND RELATIONSHIPS TO CHOOSE A DIRECTION

In this stage the problems that have been identified are examined in more detail. The examination includes an analysis of the effects on the relationships of individuals and groups in the neighborhood. In this stage the group also talks about strategy. They ask, "What are the different directions for solving this problem?" This question is important because it allows the police to respond directly to dependent residents. Since the community members will undoubtedly want the police to take some action and just "solve" the problem, they might identify solutions such as "add more police officers" or "arrest more criminals." The members of the group (including police officers) must begin to see that solutions such as these, while desirable, are not practical because they do not really solve the underlying problems and may actually create more and different problems. Through an honest exploration of the different directions the group could take to resolve the public safety problems and their underlying root causes, the group will begin to see what Freire referred to as "objective reality." It will take a commitment from the whole body politic (government, quasi government, nongovernmental organizations, and residents) in order to solve the neighborhood problems, whatever they may be. At the close of this stage, group members must pick a direction and express their level of commitment to the course of action.

STAGE 4. SCENARIO BUILDING—EXPERIENCING A CHANGING RELATIONSHIP

From our conceptual model of neighborhood development, we see group members entering this stage in a psychological state of interdependence. Ideally, participants are no longer dependent and have progressed beyond viewing "more police" as the solution to neighborhood public safety problems. From the psychological state of interdependence the group can develop more realistic and effective solutions to chronic and complex social problems, particularly those associated with public safety. Working together they describe what the neighborhood (and perhaps an extended area) could look like. From this vision they are able to build realistic scenarios for making it happen.

STAGE 5. ACTING TOGETHER TO MAKE CHANGE HAPPEN

In stage 5, group members work together to carry out commitments to effect the desired changes. In order to do this they must go outside the small group and engage other residents and stakeholders in the body politic. This is important because the change in relationships that occurred in the small group must be transmitted to the larger community. It is also true that the group will need to draw on resources from inside and outside the neighborhood.

In stage 5, "acting together" may involve another round of planning that includes a more expansive group of stakeholders from the body politic.

These members might include social-service agencies, educational workers (principals, teachers, etc.), businesses, other government agencies, and hospitals, to name just a few. Neighborhood groups could draw on strategies for "whole-system planning" to carry out more comprehensive action plans. Planning processes such as Future Search have been implemented successfully in many places around the world and have been fully documented (see Wiesbord and Janoff 2000). Such strategies could help neighborhoods access resources from the whole body politic when they are prepared to do so interdependently.

CONCLUSION

While sustained dialogue was originally intended to resolve conflict between groups, it has further application in the development of strong neighborhoods. In this chapter we have explained how sustained dialogue fits into the situational policing framework and allows police to play a key role in the cultivation of strong communities. We are calling this synthesis "a public safety process," and it begins with the presupposition that interdependent neighborhoods are the best defense against crime and disorder. Sustained dialogue is included within the process as a central mechanism for developing these communities. This focus positions the neighborhood as the unit of analysis based on the notion that it holds public safety opportunities that go unseen in smaller or larger units (i.e., individuals or cities).

Within our framework neighborhoods are conceptualized as groups with fluid mentalities that unfold in stages. From this perspective it is easy to see how both social and physical variables can inhibit or enhance psychological development. Sampson and Raudenbush (1999) found that external structural variables such as concentrated poverty and mixed land use obstruct the development of interdependent neighborhoods. In neighborhoods where trust, cohesion, and the willingness to intervene in public safety issues are not present, residents have to depend on the police to solve the problems. Where the police are not able to solve the problems, conflict develops. Our model portrays this as a normal developmental process and suggests ways to overcome the types of structural obstacles discovered in Sampson and Raudenbush's Chicago study.

Sustained dialogue bridges the gap between the theoretical goals of situational policing and the practical realities of building efficacy within neighborhoods. We have argued that situational policing is a valuable model because it contains a clear vision for an end state of effective policing that has not heretofore been present within public safety discourse. However, sustained dialogue makes an important contribution to the situational model of policing by detailing a strategy for managing the internal processes involved. The addition of this approach significantly improves the theoretical framework of situational policing and further demonstrates the inherent logic of Saunders's process.

11

FACILITATING NEIGHBORHOOD GROWTH: A COMMONSENSE APPROACH TO PUBLIC SAFETY FROM THE RELATIONAL PARADIGM

James J. Nolan, Jeri Kirby, and Ronald Althouse

FOR THE PAST SEVERAL YEARS, we have been studying the effects of competing policing strategies on neighborhood safety. Specifically, we have focused on neighborhood-level dynamics and their impact on police-community relations and the prevalence of crime and disorder. Recently, we have spent some time with neighborhood residents and police in the Northside neighborhoods of the city of Pittsburgh, Pennsylvania. By way of citizen interviews, police focus groups, and participant observation, we have gained an appreciation for the complexity of the problems there. Our purpose in this research was primarily to understand, not to "fix," the problems associated with rising crime and deteriorating police-community relations. Our findings do, however, help us see how things could improve. In this chapter we will examine our findings through the lens of the relational paradigm and the logic of sustained dialogue, which have been described in the Saunders and Parker chapters. Through this review we intend to make transparent some commonsense approaches to public safety problems in Pittsburgh neighborhoods.

In this chapter we use the adjective "commonsense" to characterize a pragmatic public safety approach to crime and disorder. As social scientists we are careful about using a term such as this because it can lead to problems of understanding. It is generally used today to refer to practical judgments that are not based on any special training, experience, or knowledge, and it is often regarded as naïve by those who do, in fact, possess special knowledge beyond that of the average person. In this chapter we use "commonsense" to characterize group judgments that are based on collective everyday experiences employed in an examination of the issues. This involves integrating two kinds of knowledge: the intuitive, emotional knowledge and the thinking, cognitive knowledge of the neighborhood as a whole. In other words, collective judgments are not ineptly naïve but may be sound and based on knowledge gained through a collective exploration of the issues. We hope to make this distinction clear as we proceed.

THE RELATIONAL PARADIGM

Sustained dialogue was introduced in chapter 2 as "a *process* for transforming dysfunctional and conflictual relationships." Saunders and Parker explain this process in the context of what they call the "relational paradigm," a *"multilevel, open-ended process of continuous interaction over time engaging significant clusters of citizens in and out of government . . . to solve public problems."* For a social scientist studying phenomena from this perspective, the minimum unit of analysis would be two people, i.e., a dyad; however, as Saunders and Parker describe, sustained dialogue has been used more commonly to help larger groups of people resolve deep, longstanding conflicts that have stretched the social fabric to its tearing point. To understand and appreciate the logic of sustained dialogue—as both a means and an end in terms of political action—one must make the mental shift to the relational paradigm. One way to observe this shift is to juxtapose the relational paradigm with the current business paradigm, viewing government as a business and citizens as customers. In the mid-1990s phrases such as "no wrong door" or "streamlining services" were cliché in government service, reflecting the perspective that governments wanted to provide friendly, high-quality services to citizens and that anytime a citizen-customer entered a government building, he or she would get the assistance needed (see table 11.1).

According to the business paradigm the focus of government is to generate a service or product niche. The government provides trained experts and service providers to the citizen-customer. The relationship dynamic is that of expert to client in that government officials view themselves as dedicated professionals who care for their citizen-customer-clients. In the public safety arena, the police view themselves as warriors in a battle between good and evil. They are organized to respond quickly to calls for service in order to protect the "helpless" citizen-customers. In contrast, a primary focus of government from the relational paradigm is building strong relationships with a participative citizenry. In this view, citizens are not customers but

TABLE 11.1 A Comparison Between Government Service Paradigms

	BUSINESS/SERVICE PARADIGM	RELATIONAL PARADIGM
Focus	Finding product or service niche and serving customers (citizens)	Building strong relationships between and among citizens and government
View of citizens	Recipient of services	Active participants in problem solving
View of government officials	Experts and service providers	Partners in problem solving
Relationship dynamics	Expert-client	Expert-expert
Public safety perspective	Police "protect and serve"	Police help communities protect themselves
Police view of themselves	Warriors	Stewards
Police view of citizens	Helpless	Essential

active participants in community action and problem solving and prevention. Citizens view government officials as true partners in governance and share a relationship that can be characterized as expert to expert. From the point of view of public safety officials, police see themselves as stewards, with special training and equipment to help residents help themselves create safe, secure environments. From the relational paradigm, citizens are not helpless recipients of police protection but, in part, are essential players in keeping one another safe.[1]

METHODS AND FINDINGS

In 2005, we met with the chief of police for the city of Pittsburgh and told him of our plan to study neighborhood-police relations in that city. The chief was interested in promoting improved police-community relations and showed us a police district that had accommodated a diverse tract of neighborhoods. The chief introduced us to the precinct commander, who welcomed us and helped us establish linkages into these neighborhoods.

The second author made several ride-alongs as the district police officers showed us around the Northside neighborhoods. Patrolling along the local streets in and out of city blocks among these neighborhoods, police pointed out what they considered the "good areas" and the "bad areas." They shared their knowledge and opinions about routine surveillance and noted areas open to drug traffic and prone to violence. During an early encounter we were introduced to an officer assigned to the Northside communities; he offered his assistance, which led us to community meetings and helped us grow contacts within each area. At some meetings we were included on the agenda; at others we talked about our work; but with most encounters, we usually requested assistance and asked for volunteers.

After making rounds of meetings with residents, we identified four local neighborhoods of interest, two of which will be briefly described in this chapter. Over nearly six months, we attended community meetings, conducted interviews, faced focus groups with community members, made intermittent ride-alongs with police, and conducted face-to-face interviews among cooperating police officers assigned to the target neighborhoods. In the following sections, we briefly summarize some of our findings. For a more thorough coverage see Kirby (2006).

PITTSBURGH'S NORTHSIDE

The Northside area of Pittsburgh has seventeen identifiable neighborhoods patrolled by the Zone 1 police command.[2] This description of the Northside comes from a now-archived website that had been developed and maintained by Northside residents:

> The flat lands of the North Side cover a handful of residential and commercial neighborhoods that once formed a separate town—Allegheny City—until it was annexed by the City of Pittsburgh in 1907. The land, originally given as payment to Revolutionary War veterans, eventually turned its attention to production of goods—rope, iron and textiles.
>
> The latter is what attracted a weaver by the name of William Carnegie to immigrate to Allegheny City from Scotland in 1848. His wife Margaret stitched shoes for an Allegheny City cobbler. Their son, Andrew Carnegie, changed bobbins in an Allegheny City cotton mill. He went on to build an industrial empire and left a personal legacy with his gifts of libraries, museums, church organs and music halls.
>
> (SEE HTTP://PITTSBURGH.ABOUT.COM/LIBRARY/WEEKLY/AA050101B.HTM)

The Northside is known by some as the location of Heinz Field and PNC Park, the homes of the Pittsburgh Steelers and Pirates, respectively. The stadiums brings people to the area, which allows for some growth and prosperity but also places a heavy burden on the Zone 1 police officers. The Northside routinely confronts policing issues relating to crime and disorder, such as open-air drugs sales, prostitution, youth gangs, and graffiti. Some neighborhoods, more specifically certain areas within the neighborhoods, are more heavily burdened than others with violent crime and drugs, but nearly all of the neighborhoods in the Northside battle urban problems related to crime. Table 11.2 provides a comparison of Northside neighborhoods in terms of Part 1 crimes.[3]

The police officers assigned to the metro Northside tell us that they are "working against the odds." It is not at all uncommon to be informed that financial cutbacks have shaved the department to the bone, leaving the officers feeling vulnerable with little support. One officer said it this way: "Zone 1 is 29 percent understaffed, more than any other zone in Pittsburgh. The city, as a whole, took a 49 percent decrease in manpower. Pittsburgh suffered bankruptcy a few years ago, having to make major cutbacks to survive. The police seem to feel as if they have taken the hardest hit within the city. Manpower and budgets are the biggest enemies of police."

The police tell us they are suffering not only from budget cuts but also from the pressures of the city bureaucracy, mostly brought on by elected officials. One officer put it this way, "You can't do anything unless you're in charge. You have to address the citizens' concerns," expressing the feeling of frustration held by officers who believe they simply respond to the whims of elected officials. By and large, officers believe they have the knowledge, discipline, and ability to "do what's right for the area." They say their ideas come from the experience of working within the neighborhoods, and they want to be acknowledged by the administration and the residents. At a neighborhood group meeting an officer expressed it this way: "We need more community problem-solving officers; they need to be able to help address and control where money is spent in the neighborhoods. The residents need to ask us, 'Where should the playground be built?'"

THE MANCHESTER NEIGHBORHOOD

Manchester is a designated historic district, which requires many houses to be maintained in a specific way to ensure its historic cultural appearance. Many blocks show upkeep and are maintained, but others are not, with

TABLE 11.2 Northside Neighborhood Crime Statistics: Number of UCR Part 1 Crimes by Neighborhood

NEIGHBORHOOD	1989	1990	1991	1992	1993	1994	1995	1996	1997	1998	1999	2000	2001	2002	2003	2004
Allegheny Center	354	385	317	254	193	188	148	166	172	101	158	152	161	135	165	130
Allegheny West	167	153	194	198	162	187	103	144	121	133	98	97	133	92	132	80
Brighton Heights	253	277	281	366	333	299	276	254	241	183	208	240	283	280	344	303
California-Kirkbride	148	121	147	140	120	103	108	111	92	78	69	94	76	73	68	88
Central Northside	442	493	464	458	510	449	398	490	403	357	411	306	287	292	387	246
Chateau	141	156	179	137	135	152	119	98	103	89	85	79	88	94	86	79
East Allegheny	384	415	355	454	504	408	377	391	388	407	386	334	340	293	331	261
Fineview	195	167	204	190	219	178	163	153	170	159	174	175	116	102	166	110
Manchester	246	239	279	239	201	186	166	203	184	131	154	171	130	122	83	88

Marshall-Shadeland	342	321	363	354	356	295	338	284	241	279	251	235	329	305	293	318
North Shore	177	166	204	258	279	237	112	145	220	170	136	179	148	126	149	142
Northview Heights	212	248	196	193	221	213	183	124	109	89	76	119	111	125	154	102
Perry North	229	233	211	222	213	236	189	175	156	129	150	144	215	191	172	178
Perry South	525	441	470	403	386	360	365	344	322	254	266	322	296	232	293	284
Spring Garden	87	71	76	76	121	111	97	78	123	115	103	79	97	110	78	87
Spring Hill	162	182	164	172	185	191	119	125	170	162	152	183	161	199	185	142
Summer Hill	35	48	34	36	46	42	22	22	28	24	34	16	19	11	14	16
Totals	4099	4116	4138	4150	4184	3835	3283	3307	3243	2860	2911	2925	2990	2782	3100	2654

Source: Pittsburgh Police Department.

TABLE 11.3 Northside Neighborhood Crime Statistics: Number of UCR Part 1 Crimes by Type of Crime

CRIME	1989	1990	1991	1992	1993	1994	1995	1996	1997	1998	1999	2000	2001	2002	2003	2004	2005
Homicide	6	7	4	5	18	10	9	9	9	7	5	8	6	7	15	11	9
Rape	28	40	52	34	38	40	20	40	37	24	24	24	26	24	36	14	11
Robbery	298	375	405	396	422	336	332	243	242	225	247	249	237	210	271	219	124
Aggravated assault	256	320	206	192	224	216	185	167	142	217	204	269	229	331	315	355	153
Burglary	1066	851	1005	859	721	712	599	587	594	514	459	442	554	472	532	488	210
Theft	1392	1466	1568	1593	1729	1720	1595	1766	1774	1525	1485	1431	1446	1361	1449	1242	613
Motor vehicle theft	969	1002	826	1020	982	754	514	458	395	322	465	473	458	355	468	309	142
Arson	84	65	72	51	50	47	29	37	50	26	22	29	34	22	14	16	2
Total	4099	4126	4138	4150	4184	3835	3283	3307	3243	2860	2911	2925	2990	2782	3100	2654	1264

Source: Pittsburgh Police Department.

visible signs of urban blight and disorder. On the ride-alongs with police, there were passages made through areas with heavy drug and gang problems. The Manchester neighborhood is 86 percent African American, and perhaps the plurality is long-time residents.

Yet Manchester is a neighborhood where people can at times act together. Residents join community meetings and help out in the neighborhood—or at least they will tell you about doing so. We witnessed some residents, having willingly joined together to fight drug dealers, standing on the street corners, holding hands, and praying so as to make a visual spectacle of the street action in an attempt to pressure the drug dealers and their customers to leave. Manchester residents claim they feel safe in their neighborhood and don't doubt their fellow residents are watching out for them.

The problem in Manchester, they say, is the relationship between how the residents perceive assistance and the regard that the police express toward Manchester. Ask residents when and what things they call the police for, and they tell you this: "To get shot, that is all they are good for. The police around here are not trustworthy—we don't call them." The feeling of distrust is not held back. The police perceive that the residents are not calling them, and their presence is not wanted in Manchester. When Manchester residents need to communicate, they apparently signal the police through the Manchester Community Group leadership. The Manchester Community group is a strong entity. It would like the police to participate in public vigils and other, less volatile responses, but experience tells it that this is not possible. So it hardly ever calls for assistance.

Officially, the police hold that Manchester is "a neighborhood in decline that doesn't possess the ability to police itself." There is clearly a disjunction between the Manchester residents and the police. The residents feel the police are not interested in what the area really needs but only in arrest statistics. For example, the residents would like the police to come and help develop activities for their juveniles in an attempt to keep them out of trouble but instead feel the police are only interested in bullying and arresting local youth.

Figure 11.1 depicts the relationship in Manchester as one in which residents are angry with police because of routine aggressive and coercive crime-control tactics. This conflict is passive in the form of *avoidance*. Interaction between the residents and the police is in one direction, symbolized by the arrow. The police argue that they will help Manchester combat the crime problems, but "they never call us."

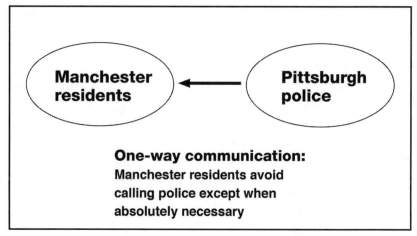

One-way communication:
Manchester residents avoid
calling police except when
absolutely necessary

FIGURE 11.1 Conflict Between Police and Community Manifests as Avoidance

THE FINEVIEW NEIGHBORHOOD

Pittsburgh is a city on hills, overlooking the confluence of two important rivers that form the mighty Ohio. The Fineview neighborhood also has a scenic overlook,—simply called the Overlook—that offers a stunning view of the city. The neighborhood is densely populated, packed with housing and parked cars. As one leaves the Overlook, a block of new townhouses comes into view. These homes are investments made by the Fineview Community Group.

The FCG regularly meets on housing issues and community fund-raising and even sponsors cultural events intended to bring the residents closer together. Conspicuously missing from the FCG meetings are representatives from the "Dwellings," i.e., the federally funded public housing projects. The membership of the FCG is predominately white, while residents of the Dwellings are mostly African American.

Although Fineview has a relatively low crime rate, the area is described by the police officers as "a drug thoroughfare." Fineview also is home to one of the most economically problematic jitney stations (black market cabs) on the Northside.

The residents of the Dwellings were relocated from other areas a few decades ago when Pittsburgh implemented a housing plan that moved public housing projects out of densely populated, high poverty areas and dispersed it throughout the city in order to link (i.e., integrate) with comparatively more established, resourceful communities. The Dwellings creates considerable fear among residents of Fineview. Stories of shootings and other violent crimes in these projects illustrate this. One FCG member told us, "I viewed three men shot out my front window and one of them died right there."

Usually, Fineview residents regard the police as a source of routine surveillance, expect a forceful response when they enlist the police, and voice no especial concerns about calling the police for any issue that may arise. One resident made this clear: "If I see something, I'm telling [the police]." Although the neighborhood ranks below the median of the Northside neighborhoods for reported Part 1 crimes, many Fineview residents continue to expect crime. Even if they are not directly threatened, residents certainly are fearful; one noted, "I'm afraid. I don't feel safe. There is a lot of noise and violence in the area." Neighborhood residents with whom we spoke share the belief that most of the noise and violence emanates from the Dwellings.

While residents regard police as a defense against crime, they are also viewed as ineffective. One resident told us, "I would take the license plate numbers of cars coming to a house near me for drugs, I would take the license numbers straight to the police station, they would say, 'Call narcotics,' and narcotics would say, 'Call your state representative.'" By the time our interviews in the neighborhood were over, it was clear the residents felt the police could be doing a better job, and, not coincidentally, we found police willingly "cool out" (see Goffman 1952) neighborhood dependency this way: "They voice their concerns—I respond to the problem. We address the issue."

Zone 1 police officers also are aware of the physical boundaries and racial and class divisions between many Fineview residents and their neighbors in the Dwellings. As one officer stated, "It is more than geographic boundaries that divides Fineview and the Dwellings. Those people [residents of the Dwellings] stay over on their side. I don't think they care what the people in Fineview think; they don't give a thought to Fineview. The Dwellings and Fineview are two different neighborhoods." Police acknowledged heavy drug and gang problems among those living in the housing projects, even suggesting they often used the homes of some Fineview residents for surveillance of the Dwellings.

Police performance in the Northside neighborhoods is perceived as a direct outcome of political processes—"politics"—that dominate budget management in the city. Zone 1 officers in Fineview, like those in Manchester,

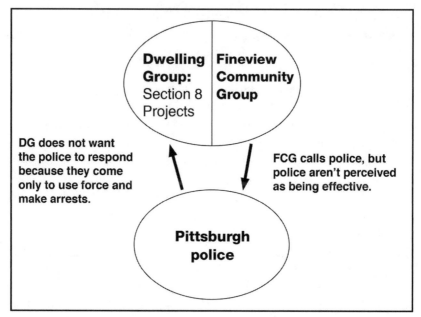

FIGURE 11.2 Fineview Neighborhood

say they are pressured to work harder because of the recent budget cuts since Zone 1 was one of the "hardest hit" areas in the city. As one officer stated, "You can't give people a level of service they become accustomed to and then just take it away," suggesting that they had been providing preventative services to the community but must now resort to reacting to calls for service.

The police told us that community members are unaware of or do not understand how budget cuts have politicized the department. One officer said, "Community members have to understand and gain knowledge that being ordered to deal with minor problems in the area might make us miss the bigger problems." But the officers must respond to all calls for service in order to keep some residents from "calling the chief of police and complaining." This is obviously frustrating for the officers; one said, "Community groups are no more than a voting block. They get what they want by influencing the elected officials." The police told us that they believe they are being pulled away from serious problems to address issues that should be handled by residents themselves.

Figure 11.2 diagrams the relationship among the community members and between the residents and the police. At the top, the circle is split to indicate a division between residents of the Dwellings (who are mostly black) and the Fineview Community Group (and then residents they represent, who are mostly white). There is little or no communication between these groups. FCG is depicted with a one-way arrow pointing toward the police, which indicates FCG does, in fact, contact the police and provoke enforcement. The police find that FCG calls them for social problems that are not "crimes" or, at least, are not serious enough to involve police, and so Zone 1 police treat "police-citizen" contacts half-heartedly. FCG members seem to notice this and consequently do not really think the police are effective, possibly finding them actually inadequate. In the Dwellings, police are "crime fighters." They maintain surveillance of the Dwellings to interrupt felonies in progress. The arrow pointing from the Pittsburgh Police to the Dwellings indicates that police contacts with residents of the Dwellings are principally initiated by the police, not residents.

A CONCEPTUAL FRAMEWORK

Before we present our thoughts about public safety in these Pittsburgh neighborhoods, particularly as they relate to sustained dialogue, we would like to present an organizing theory within the relational paradigm to provide a framework for this discussion. We would also like to explain what we mean by "neighborhood growth," the main thesis of this chapter.

SYSTEMS THEORY

From general systems theory (von Bertalanffy 1968) we know that in every living system there exists a hierarchy of isomorphic subsystems that "are energy-organizing, self-correcting, and goal-oriented" (Gantt and Agazarian 2004, 150). In other words, every human system exists in the context of a higher system and provides the context for a lower system. For example, a college system exists within the context of the university system and provides the context for a school or department system. The term isomorphic means that the subsystems are equivalent in form and function and that the knowledge of one subsystem can provide information about the other systems in the hierarchy (von Bertalanffy 1968). From the relational paradigm we think it makes sense to consider which subsystem in a systems hierarchy provides the most effective place to build relationships in order to make positive

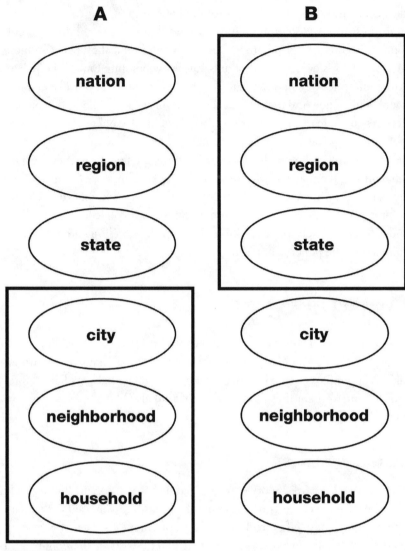

FIGURE 11.3

changes. Gantt and Agazarian (2004) respond to this dilemma by introducing system-centered theory, which identifies the concept of a core system. This begins by first identifying three levels in a living system. In figure 11.3 one can see a hierarchy of systems that range from the family or household level up to the national level. The rectangular boxes on sides A and B represent the core systems. On side A, the core system includes the city, neighborhood, and family/household. In this core system, the neighborhood exists in the context of the city and provides the context for the household or family subsystem. On side B, the core system includes the nation, region, and state, where the region provides the context for the state and the nation provides the context for the region. From the system-centered theory, the core system provides a conceptual framework for identifying the most effective points to effect change. Changes made to the middle system provide the most immediate impact on the entire core system. Whereas the core system for sustained dialogue has been identified at various levels in the hierarchy, our focus has been in the city of Pittsburgh where neighborhoods are the middle system.

NEIGHBORHOOD GROWTH

Growth from immaturity to maturity is a characteristic of life. Immaturity on the part of the individual or the group is marked by *dependence*, which we view as a positive attribute because it implies a social orientation. Independence, on the other hand, implies a lack of social capacity and is inversely related to dependence and interdependence. In other words, the more independent one becomes the less social he or she will be.

As Nolan, Conti, and Colyer (this volume) point out, neighborhood growth is defined in terms not of physical growth but of psychoemotional growth. Although this word "psychoemotional" is somewhat awkward and ambiguous, it is used here to refer to group cognitions (beliefs) and group emotions (feelings). For example, immature neighborhoods are dependent (emotion) on the police for protection because they believe (cognition) that the police are willing and able to protect them. The belief creates the emotion of dependence at the neighborhood level. Even though the facts may show that this is an unrealistic and naïve belief, dependence is characteristic of immature groups at the beginning of the growth process. An observer might recognize the psychoemotional state of dependence in a neighborhood that has just experienced a series of burglaries. Fearful, the victims contact the police and report the crimes, expecting to find out that the offenders will soon be caught. The reality of the situation is that the police rarely solve these types of crimes. According to the FBI, only about 12 percent of burglaries nationwide are cleared (Federal Bureau of Investigation 2001).

When immature or dependent neighborhoods begin to realize that the police are not as effective and efficient as they had hoped, the emotional state of *conflict* is produced in the neighborhood. This movement from dependence is actually a stage in the growth of the neighborhood. Just as adolescence may be a stressful time for a family, this conflict between what the residents expect and what the police deliver can also be emotionally stressful. While the neighborhood is still immature, residents share unrealistic assumptions about the police. In order to grow toward the mature psychoemotional state of interdependence, the neighborhood as a whole must realize a shift in its collective mindset toward the view that private citizens together with the police can make a difference. Saunders and Parker (this volume) note that "it is critical that their subconscious worldview includes the possibility that their action can make a difference." In the group and neighborhood literature relating to crime, this worldview or psychoemotional state is referred to as "collective efficacy." In recent sociological research, collective efficacy has been found to have a strong inverse relationship with crime and disorder. In other words, in neighborhoods where there are high levels of collective efficacy, there are low levels of crime and disorder, and vice versa (Sampson and Raudenbush 1999).

CONCLUSIONS

As mentioned at the outset of this chapter, it was not our intention to fix the public safety problems we found while researching the dynamics of neighborhood-level phenomena in the Northside area of Pittsburgh. Rather, we sought simply to understand the nature and extent of these problems. The relational paradigm presented by Saunders and Parker (this volume) provided a way of looking at our findings that enabled us to see "commonsense" solutions. The neighborhoods we observed, Manchester and Fineview, were qualitatively different in terms of the types of conflicts present within the neighborhoods and between the residents and the police.

MANCHESTER

In Manchester, the residents were very cohesive and worked together to solve neighborhood problems such as open-air drug dealing and youth gangs. Although the residents were cohesive in some regards, Manchester was in a state of conflict with the police over contested terrain, i.e., whether the neighborhood is a home or a patrol area. This conflict could be observed in the residents' passivity, calling the police only when it was absolutely necessary.

According to the police, the residents lacked the ability to use informal controls to curb crime and disorder. The police saw themselves as the solution to the neighborhood public safety problems, but the residents wanted the police to get involved in less aggressive, more peaceful, preventative activities, particularly ones aimed at juveniles. Although Manchester would like to deal with the crime problem in its own ways, it lacks the resources to be successful. The police, as representatives of city government services, could provide these resources; however, because of poor police-community relations, these city resources are never proffered in any meaningful way. In terms of its neighborhood growth, the Manchester neighborhood seems to be in the psychoemotional state of conflict. In order to continue its growth toward interdependence, the police and the community must resolve this conflict. Sustained dialogue as described by Saunders and Parker (this volume) could be the mechanism to facilitate this neighborhood growth by recognizing and addressing the latent conflict between the police and the community. A dialogue could also serve to change the mindset of the police in terms of its role in dealing with Manchester's crime problems.

FINEVIEW

The residents of Fineview have a different connection to authority than the residents of Manchester. The neighborhood is actually split in two groups: one, middle class and more white than black, is represented by the Fineview Community Group. The other group, mostly black, lives in federally funded housing projects called the Dwellings. These two groups are physically adjacent to each other, but they are worlds apart. The FCG members call on the police to provide the services they want and need. Because these services are not considered "real police work," the police lack the requisite enthusiasm for the job and, therefore, are viewed by FCG as friendly but virtually ineffective. In the Dwellings, the police patrol like warriors. It is a high-crime area, but residents avoid calling the police. The conflict between residents of the Dwellings and the police is similar to that in the Manchester neighborhood. The FCG often calls the police for meetings and such and sees them as partners of a sort but does not see them as important. The dysfunctional relationships within the neighborhood and between the neighborhoods and the police could be resolved by way of a process like sustained dialogue. What the two resident groups don't seem to see is that they need each other. The residents of the Dwellings could benefit from financial investments made by the FCG, and the FCG would benefit from the assistance and perspective of the residents of the Dwellings. Building strong, cohesive relationships between these two groups could reduce crime and the fear of crime in the Fineview neighborhood. A dialogue between these groups and the police could be structured to help the police see alternatives to law-enforcement solutions to public safety problems.

When examining crime in the city of Pittsburgh from the relational paradigm, one might wonder where best to focus relationship-building efforts. From systems theory and, in particular, the core systems configuration, we can see that the importance of the neighborhood as a focal point for effecting positive change. Using a process such as sustained dialogue to facilitate neighborhood growth from the immature state of dependence on the police to the more mature state of interdependence with the police could provide positive results in both of these Northside neighborhoods.

Finally, from the relational paradigm, we see that the role of the police should be more that of stewards than warriors. Stewardship means to hold something in trust for another. Historically, the word was used to mean "protect[ing] the kingdom while those rightfully in charge were away, or more often, to govern for the sake of the underage king" (Block 1996). From the relational paradigm and the conceptual framework presented in this chapter, one can see that the just role of the police is to protect neighborhoods only until they grow and mature to the point where they can protect themselves. Sustained dialogue is a process that could facilitate this neighborhood growth and provide for commonsense public safety approaches.

Notes

1. We think it is relevant to note that while this chapter was being written the governor of West Virginia changed the state's motto on signs displayed at various points of entry to the state. The signs had read, "Wild and Wonderful." The new signs reflect the mantra of this administration: "Open for Business." This new slogan refers to the present administration's plan to run the state like a business.

2. The city of Pittsburgh is divided into 5 police zones (or districts). The Northside neighborhoods in this study are all within Zone 1.

3. Part 1 crimes are those crimes the FBI identifies as most likely to come to the attention of the police. They include murder, rape, robbery, aggravated assault, burglary, theft, motor vehicle theft, and arson.

SECTION III

PUBLIC DELIBERATION IN PRACTICE

Introduction

IT IS NOT AT ALL uncommon for students in social work and other social sciences such as sociology, political science, and public administration to be interested in a wide variety of different forms of deliberation and dialogue. This section demonstrates something of the range of interest in deliberation and dialogue, with contributions from journalism, family therapists and public administration.

David Ryfe at the University of Nevada, Reno, is a well known author on public deliberation. In his chapter, Ryfe looks closely at what he terms "the deliberative posture," a kind of applied micro-sociology or a social psychological analysis of the act of deliberation. "In this essay," Ryfe writes, "my goal is to reduce the fuzziness that envelops the concept of deliberation."

In "Public Deliberation and Dialogue in Public Management," David G. Williams, emeritus professor of political science and public administration at West Virginia University, lays a theoretical groundwork for public deliberation as a managerial tool or strategy in the public sector. His perspective is as applicable to public social services as to any other form of government service. "Public deliberation and dialogue" Williams says, "can contribute significantly to effective public management. While some public managers have been pulled unwillingly into various types of public deliberation, it is critical to recognize that there are some important and legitimate management functions and needs met by such deliberation."

In chapter 14, one of the editors (Lohmann) explores "the social dynamics of citizens in public spaces" through certain convergences between deliberative democracy theorizing and commons theory. The chapter concludes with two "messages": For adherents to the rational choice paradigms, he notes, "There is more to life than the unfettered display of naked self-interest." And, he says, the message to "true believers in deliberation and dialogue" is that "deliberation and dialogue do not automatically lead to reconciliation in all circumstances, and even when they will, getting there can be sweaty, exhausting hard work."

In "Question Mapping: A Tool for Organizing and Sustaining Dialogue," Richard Ludeman, of Carta Nova Consulting in Portland, Oregon, and Erna Gelles, of the Department of Public Administration in the Hatfield School of Government at Portland State University, pursue a particular management application with their exploration of a group process technique. "Question mapping" is a "process for defining the central issue while identifying related issues and their relationships to the central issue."

The final chapter in this section is by a pair of family therapists, Neal and Susan Newfield. Neal is an associate professor in the Division of Social Work and Susan is an associate professor in the School of Nursing at West Virginia University. As they note in their chapter, several key assumptions of family therapy closely parallel those of deliberation and dialogue.

12

THE DELIBERATIVE POSTURE

David Ryfe

WHAT IS DELIBERATION? How is it different from other kinds of talk? At first blush, answers to these questions might seem obvious, even easy. But try for a moment to answer them off the top of your head. I think you'll find that the more you focus on them, the fuzzier the answers become. I've asked these questions of many people who have participated in deliberative forums. Typically, people say something like, "Midway through the conversation, I had this *aha moment*, a kind of epiphany about what we were doing here." This aha moment is when people feel like they are deliberating rather than just talking. When I ask what they mean by "aha," people invariably describe the moment as one of civility, inclusiveness, or some combination of the two. That is, they say something like: "I don't have an opportunity to talk seriously [or civilly] about public issues with others very much, and I thought at that moment that we ought to do more of this"; or: "I had never thought about the issue that way before, and it was a really neat experience"; or: "I had never heard an opposing view stated so reasonably and rationally." But when I ask how this is different from other kinds of conversation—many of which contain civil exchange about different points of view—they are stumped.

The same kind of fuzziness pervades academic thinking. Most work on deliberative democracy does not focus on deliberation per se but on "democratic" deliberation or "public" deliberation. And of the two parts of these terms, more attention is devoted to the former than to the latter. The literature is filled with discussions of the conditions necessary to achieve "democratic" talk: that society exhibit equality, for instance, or that democratic citizens display tolerance. But most scholars working in the field say little about what makes the ensuing talk particularly deliberative. Most stipulate that deliberation is a kind of reasoned conversation (for recent reviews, see Chambers 2003; Freeman 2000; Ryfe 2002). This seems plausible on its face, until one applies it to actual instances of deliberation. Studies of deliberation show that few people deliberate using reasoned talk (for reviews, see Delli Carpini, Cook, and Jacobs 2004; Mendelberg 2002). This finding makes it all the more odd that even if they do not deliberate, at least according to the standard definition, people nonetheless sometimes secure the benefits of deliberation, i.e., they become more informed, tolerant, civil, and so on. (cf. Burkhalter, Gastil, and Kelshaw 2002; Ryfe 2005). How people can get deliberative benefits from nondeliberative conversations is something of a puzzle. If nothing else, it casts doubt on whether academics have a good grasp of what deliberation is.

In this essay, then, my goal is to reduce the fuzziness that envelops the concept of deliberation. Pursuit of this goal requires that I set aside, for the moment, questions about the democratic or public character of deliberation: issues such as equality, inclusiveness, and the like. These are important concerns, of course. But they stand one step beyond my interests here. Before deliberation becomes a form of political communication, it is simply a form of communication. We should not lose sight of this distinction. Thinking about deliberation separate from its political manifestations may help us to see it in a new light. It may also be of benefit to our thinking about second-order issues like equality.

As a beginning, then, I wish to suggest that we focus not on what deliberation is, but on what people do when deliberating. The idea has roots in the work of Wittgenstein (1953), among others; he argued that linguistic meaning is firmly rooted in its use. It also has affinities with the ethnomethodological perspective associated with Garfinkel (1967) and, more distantly, with Goffman (1974, 1981). Put crudely, Garfinkel and Goffman argue that meaning inheres in practice. Part of this practice is sociological in that it involves learning socially shared frames that define an activity. Part is psychological and ontological, learning how to adopt the role—or become the character, to use Goffman's dramatic metaphor—that is appropriate to a practice. The sociological and the psychological come together in practice. People, in other words, learn what deliberation is by doing it. Adopting this perspective, I think, leads us to the view that deliberation is a distinctive *posture*—an attitude or mindset—set within a specific context of interaction. By using the word "posture," I mean to reference the essentially social and performative nature of deliberation. It is a pose toward the world taken up in interaction, with its own logic, rules, and preferred contexts.

I flesh out this approach to deliberation in two parts. In the first, I sketch the posture of deliberation in finer detail. In the second, I suggest a method for identifying the posture in actual instances of deliberation. As a conclusion, I consider a few implications of this definition of deliberation. For reasons of space, my discussion throughout is more exposition than argument. However, where appropriate I refer to writings in philosophy, communication, and deliberative democratic theory. My object throughout is to assist ordinary people, practitioners, and academics to identify deliberation as an activity distinguishable from all the other ways in which people might interact.

DELIBERATION AS POSTURING

When defining deliberation, scholars often seek a set of universal rules that apply to any instance of its use. Of these rules, none is more important than the notion that deliberation must entail argumentative markers, such as the presence of claims and the provision of evidence (cf. Chambers 2003; Delli Carpini, Cook, and Jacobs 2004; Fishkin 1995, 41; Gastil 2000, 22). The idea is that, fundamentally, deliberation is a kind of argument. Markers of argument, therefore, serve as something like rules that help us to know deliberation when we see it. Any instance of deliberation will follow these rules. As a general strategy for defining the term, this seems as sensible as any other. However, in his later work Wittgenstein (1953) suggests that the logic of this strategy is flawed. In *Philosophical Investigations*, Wittgenstein tries to ascertain how words gain meaning. For a long time, philosophers had assumed that words gain meaning when, in using them, speakers abide by fixed rules; that is, the meaning of words inheres in their rules of use. The problem, as Wittgenstein sees it, is that any use of a term can be justified by any abstract rule. Imagine, for example, that I insist the proposition "I feel good today" is an instance of deliberation. You counter that it is not deliberative because the proposition "I feel" is missing a key marker of deliberation, namely, evidence. Absent external evidence of my feeling, the proposition "I feel good today" cannot, by definition, be deliberative. To this assertion, I might respond that my feelings are, in fact, evidence of a kind, and, therefore, the proposition is deliberative. Wittgenstein realized that you and I have no logical way of resolving this dispute. Whether the rules apply in this instance will depend not on the rules themselves but on my ability to convince you that they do, in fact, apply. Either way, the rules only gain meaning in their context of use. Thus, appealing to the same set of rules, I might convince you that just about any utterance is deliberation. And, as we know, if a definition can apply to any utterance, it applies to none.

For Wittgenstein, the consequence of this fact is that one ought to avoid abstract definitions for the meaning of words. Instead, definitions ought to be sought in descriptions of how words are actually used. He sometimes calls the resulting method "therapeutic" (1953, para. 133; also see McGuinness 2002). Therapy in Wittgenstein's sense entails a dialogue in which one examines concrete examples of a term in use. The idea is to discover which uses of the term make sense. Can I use the term "deliberation" in such and such a way and be sensible to others? The product of this investigation is a set of statements that define the context within which a term gains meaning. These statements take the form of "what one would say to justify the belief that an object is X." The legitimacy of such statements rests not on a general form of logic but on the recognition by others that they are sensible, that is to say, recognizable, statements of fact.

Let us apply Wittgenstein's therapeutic strategy to deliberation. One of his favorite uses of the method is pedagogy: the act of teaching others the meaning of words. So imagine that you were charged with the task of teaching deliberation to a novice. This person knows how to speak, of course, in all the ordinary ways, but has never heard of deliberation, how to do it, or what it entails. How would you proceed? It seems sensible to begin with something your novice does know. She knows how to have a conversation, for instance. As a form of interaction, conversation bears some similarities to deliberation. You might tell her, then, that deliberation is "like" a conversation between two people. Your novice immediately says, "Great! Since I know how to have a conversation, I must know how to deliberate." But this isn't quite right. Deliberation is not merely a conversation. What do you say now? How is deliberation not like an ordinary conversation? Another way of asking the question: What would one say to justify a belief that an interaction is deliberative and not merely conversational? What is it that people do when they deliberate that they do not do when merely conversing?

Here it is useful to reflect on the kinds of situations in which people might deliberate. Engaging in such reflection, I think, shows that people deliberate when they face a decision about *what to do*. Think of any instance when one would deliberate, and you will find that it is motivated by some version of the question, "Should (I, we) do X or Y?" Choosing is central to deliberation.

Now, suppose you bestow this insight on your student. "Well, that's easy," she says, "I choose X." Has she then deliberated? Clearly not. But the fact that she can make the mistake shows that there are different kinds of situations involving choice, and not all of them are deliberative. Consider the following scenario: you have dinner out with a friend. Your friend is notorious for engaging everyone around the table in a deliberation about every menu item: Should she have the chicken? What about the veal? This understandably drives you crazy. But think for a moment about why your frustration is understandable. It is understandable because you and others assume that the choice of what to have for dinner should not be difficult and, in any event, is not particularly consequential. It's just dinner, you say to yourself. There is an insight to be had here: deliberation is more appropriate for choices that are especially momentous. If choices are relatively inconsequential, we expect people to make them quickly. As an initial statement then, we can say that deliberation is distinguished from other kinds of interaction by the fact that, in deliberation, one faces consequential choices. We might call this the basic sociological context of deliberation.

What of its psychological state? What posture is appropriate to a deliberative situation? In part, it is a posture of ignorance or, at the very least, a lack of surety (see Barber [1984], which applies this point to democratic politics generally). This should be self-evident. Deliberation would be unnecessary if one already knew which choice to make. Since the point of deliberation is to make a choice, one cannot know in advance which choice is best. Therefore, one must come at deliberation from a posture that one does not know, or is not sure of, which choice to make. Having said this, a deliberative posture involves more than ignorance. Faced with a difficult or complex choice, and admitting ignorance, one is as likely to punt as deliberate: I don't know so I refuse to choose. A deliberative posture couples ignorance with responsibility: even though one is not sure, in a deliberative posture one remains committed to choosing.

Ignorance coupled with responsibility puts individuals in a peculiar position vis-à-vis one another. Since they have to choose and do not possess information or knowledge to do so, individuals are naturally led to seek information outside themselves. Deliberation, in other words, is a posture of engagement with the outside world. It invites individuals to rely on others, to seek out information that they do not themselves possess. Again, this is nothing more than common sense. After all, if I already knew what to do or had sufficient information to make that determination, then I would have no reason to deliberate. I would simply choose. Notice, however, that nothing in this common sense implies a particular *way* of engaging the world. As I have noted, scholars sometimes like to claim that deliberative engagement requires logic, reason, or argument. Anything less, they assert, is not strictly deliberative. But this notion is simply incorrect. One might engage with the world via storytelling, confession, instruction, debate, and, yes, argument, among other modes of talk. I will say more about this later, but no criterion exists for generally favoring one of these modes of talk over others. Any might be reasonable in a particular situation.

To sum up: what have we taught our student? That deliberation is a practice of choice making. It is choice making in which individuals have a stake. In other words, the choice matters to them. It must matter, or they would feel no need to deliberate. Moreover, people come at this significant choice with the mindset that, at least at the outset, they do not know which choice is best. But because they have a stake in the choice, they have a responsibility for addressing it despite their ignorance. Responsibility and ignorance lead them to engage with the world in a search for information, data, or knowledge that might help them choose. This, in a nutshell, constitutes the deliberative posture.

Before moving on, let me just say a word about two related issues: the relationships deliberation has to implementation and to justice. All this talk of choosing can make it seem like deliberation also includes talk about how to achieve a particular outcome. It is not only about choosing but also about implementing a choice. However, we should not conflate choosing with matters of implementation. Consider this scenario: a married couple must decide whether and where to move. They have a choice to make, and the decision is clearly significant to their lives. They spend months deliberating and finally make a decision. At this point, they must now move. Moving is clearly different from choosing. The first activity involves the act of physically moving boxes, furniture, and so on from one household to another. The latter involves information seeking and filtering. Clearly, these practices are organized along different principles and involve different postures. The upshot is that deliberation should not be conflated with implementing choices.

However, if deliberation is not implementation, it nonetheless has definite consequences. As such, it is political at every step. All aspects of deliberation, from the creation of a "we" who deliberates, to naming problems and framing choices, to, finally, choosing itself, involves a distribution of symbolic and material resources. Every "we" defines a "not-we." Every problem confronted means that other potential problems will be ignored. Consideration of some choices necessarily means that others will not be discussed. And any choice will recommend some actions and not others. In practice, this means that deliberation raises issues of justice: rights, obligations, and duties. Suppose, for example, that my wife and I face a choice of where to go for dinner. Suppose further that we have adopted my choice the last five times we went out to eat. Should this fact enter into our discussion? Does she have a "right" to choose this time? Am I obliged to acquiesce to her wishes? You can see that justice issues arise even in the most mundane of deliberative situations. While deliberation may not involve action itself, elements of justice figure prominently into deliberative situations. And since it inevitably involves issues of justice, deliberation is an intrinsically political form of interaction.

You might now recognize that despite our best efforts at clarity, in the midst of actual events things can get quite murky. Consider again the example of the couple facing a decision about relocating their household. Although they face the basic choice of moving or not moving, they also face a string of choices along the way: which movers to use, which of their belongings to keep, whether to take their pets, etc. Any one of these decisions could be significant enough to require deliberation, and all might engender questions of justice. In the course of events, it can be difficult for an analyst to categorize these situations as deliberative or nondeliberative. This raises a question: How can one identify deliberation amid the complexity of actual events?

KNOWING DELIBERATION WHEN WE SEE IT

In my discussion so far, I have referred to the elements of deliberation—choices, ignorance, justice, and the rest—as if they were objective things in the world. In fact, however, as scholars have found, every element of deliberation is contingent on interpretation: whether one has a choice (Eliasoph 1998); whether that choice is consequential (Taber, Lodge, and Glathar 2001; Tetlock 1983, 1985); whether one is ignorant of the relevant issues (Kuklinski and Hurley 1996; Zaller 1992); whether matters of justice are at stake (Gamson 1992); and finally, whether one adopts a social identity congruent with a deliberative posture (Tetlock 2001; Walsh 2004)—all of these questions must be answered by individuals in real contexts of interaction. And their answers determine whether they adopt a deliberative posture. The elements of deliberation, then, are socially constructed, not self-evident.

We might say that deliberative situations are *framed* by those involved. The concept of a frame has strong roots in psychology and sociology (for reviews, see Druckman 2002; Levin, Schneider, and Gaeth 1998; Scheufele 1999). Differences between these approaches can be important. However, for our purposes it is enough to note that both psychologists and sociologists define frames as similar to stories. For example, Gamson and Modigliani (1989) define a frame as a "central organizing idea or storyline that provides meaning to an unfolding strip of events, weaving a connection among them." Put this way, we might say that a deliberative posture hinges on the kind of story that individuals apply to the situation they face. Does the situation require a choice? Is it a consequential choice? Do those involved feel capable of, and responsible for, making the choice? A frame is embedded within answers to these questions such that whether individuals adopt a deliberative posture becomes a matter of the frames—the storylines—they build to make sense of the situation.

This notion provides a tool for identifying deliberation. Analysts know people have adopted a deliberative posture when they have framed a situation as peculiarly deliberative, i.e., when they interpret the situation as one involving a consequential decision, a decision they feel unsure of but responsible for making. How does one know such a frame when one sees it? Framing analysts have suggested several fruitful answers to this question. For example, Gamson and Modigliani (1989) suggests that, as narratives, frames contain such devices as metaphors, exemplars, catchphrases, depictions, and visual images. These devices organize information into plots by making reasonable (i.e., causal, consequential, or principled) connections between discrete pieces of data. Pan and Kosicki (1993) is more specific. It suggests that frames are composed of several structures that lie at different levels of meaning: syntactical structures ("stable patterns of the arrangement of words and phrases in to statements"); script structures ("established and stable sequence(s) of activities and components of an event"); thematic structures (hierarchies of propositions leading to conclusions); and rhetorical structures (stylistic or word choices such as Gamson and Modigliani's metaphors, catchphrases, and the like). Finally, in a discussion of frames in conversational talk, Tannen (1993) is more specific still. It lists sixteen linguistic cues of frames:

- Omissions: what is included and excluded in a story
- Repetitions: reinforce the point of a story
- False starts: statements immediately repudiated or changed
- Backtracks: fill in information to repair/correct a story
- Hedges: a measurement of storylines against what is expected
- Negatives: a statement often used when an affirmative statement is expected
- Contrastive connectives: denial of an expected statement
- Modals: (must, should, etc.) reflect judgment of appropriateness
- Inexact statements: help to determine what information is significant in a story
- Generalizations: often triggered by knowledge left implicit in the frame
- Inferences: statements that cannot be known simply from information before the participants
- Evaluative language: (adjectives, adverbs, etc.) often reveals comparison to expectations
- Interpretations: assign value/significance to events and characters
- Moral judgments: reveal storyteller's orientation to events and characters
- Incorrect statements: reveal assumptions that lie within a narrative frame
- Additions: further evidence of story's expectations

Taken together, this literature suggests that one knows a frame when one sees it because it arranges information in a particular order. A frame connects information through inferences (rational, consequential, or principled) for which reasons can be provided. It characterizes information with distinctive language. In the process of integrating diverse information into a coherent storyline, a frame necessarily omits some and stresses other data. It encourages individuals to adopt a particular attitude toward the information it includes and excludes. It privileges certain identities and roles. And it offers an opportunity to make generalizations, inferences, assumptions, interpretations, and conclusions on the basis of its storyline.

An example may help to clarify how one might apply framing to deliberation. The following snippet of interaction comes from a videotaped National Issues Forum on the subject of campaign-finance reform. The discussion began as many NIF conversations begin, with a brief conversation about what the issue means to the participants personally. Several people have offered their views of the "problem," and then a participant whom I will call Neal offers this comment:

1. I guess to me it's—it's kind of sad in a way, umm,
2. I think sometimes people kind of use this issue as an excuse not to get involved.
3. I mean it is a major issue
4. and—and I think it needs to be addressed
5. but on the other hand especially in Oregon, ummm, of all the places I've lived in this country
6. I think that our politicians are more accessible than any other place I've ever lived before
7. and with or without money and with or without money
8. in most cases our politicians are open to listening to their constituents.
9. And I think many people think of the fact "well I don't have any power
10. I don't have any influence I don't have any money so I'm not even going to get involved
11. I'm not even going to make an attempt to contact my legislature, err, legislator or representative."
12. And I think people kind of use that as an excuse not to get involved not to be active

Though he equivocates at times—"it's kind of sad" (line 1); "people kind of use" (line 2)—Neal nonetheless offers the group a distinctive frame of campaign-finance reform. The frame is identifiable in such markers as the examples (lines 5–6) Neal offers, the propositions (line 6) he makes, the characters he animates (lines 9–11), and the generalizations (line 12) he offers to the group. Notice, for instance, that the central protagonist in Neal's story is not a nefarious lobbyist or a venal politician. Rather, it is the apathetic citizen. According to Neal, the problem with politics today is that people are not politically active. This is the central point of Neal's comment. The generalization he takes from this frame is that campaign-finance reform is an "excuse" (line 12) rather than a problem in and of itself. It is, in other words, a camouflage for the "real" issue, namely, the fact that so many people are willfully apathetic.

Neal's frame exemplifies how it is possible to talk oneself out of adopting a deliberative posture even when deliberation is the explicit goal of the occasion. The central idea or storyline of Neal's frame is that Americans are apathetic, and if this problem were resolved campaign financing would cease to be an issue. The proposition may or may not have merit. But the issue of voting patterns among the American public is clearly not a choice confronting this group. In other words, it does not conjure a deliberative situation for these participants, and they would (and did) have great difficulty in spinning this frame into a deliberative conversation. For our purposes, the point is that analysts may know deliberation when they see it by focusing on how individuals and groups frame the situation. These frames—revealed in such linguistic markers as generalizations, inferences, characterizations, and the like—provide signals as to how individuals understand the purpose of their interaction.

A framing approach to deliberation has many advantages. Perhaps foremost among them is that it does minimal damage to the complexity of actual verbal interactions. People accomplish many things in interpersonal interactions (for a review, see Ryfe 2005). They negotiate issues of politeness. They establish rules of etiquette. They adopt roles. They seek to persuade. The more people involved in an interaction, the more complex these issues become. At one moment an utterance may be directed at managing politeness issues. But in the midst of doing so, participants may become deliberative and then at a subsequent moment fall out of a deliberative posture. Or hearers may interpret an utterance that on its face seems deliberative in nondeliberative ways. Or, finally, participants may be unwilling to admit ignorance in a conversation with a group of people whom they have just met. However, later they may reflect on the other views expressed in the group and at that point adopt a deliberative posture. In other words, they may adopt a deliberative posture in private rather than in public. My point is that the meaning of verbal interactions is complex. The tools of framing analysis are a useful way for untangling these complexities as they occur in natural conversations.

Let me end this section with a brief discussion of a specific kind of complexity: the role of persuasion in deliberation. Most observers assume that persuasion is key to deliberation. After all, how are groups supposed to reach judgment if no one is willing to urge them toward a conclusion. Persuasion, in this sense, is a driving force behind the act of choosing. But persuasion has a double-edged quality for deliberation. Consider the following snippet of interaction, again from an NIF conversation. This NIF concerns the issue of public schools and was held in Durham, New Hampshire, a few years ago. From what they reveal about themselves, it is clear that the participants are extraordinarily knowledgeable about public schools. Many are teachers or former teachers. Several have served on local or state school boards. Most have had children in the public school system. Not surprisingly, the conversation is marked by its intelligence, insight, and persuasive appeals. But are these appeals deliberative?

1. [Speaker 1]: Well, umm, I guess, umm, from the perspective of a single parent having one daughter
2. who just started college this year and another one who is a junior in high school
3. what I've seen I guess with their education sometimes has been disturbing to me.
4. I don't suspect it's a lot different from one high school to another
5. but that the way kids are graded these days is disturbing in that there seems to be less emphasis
6. on at the end of a—a—a semester what their testing results have been, umm,
7. as opposed to whether or not they had completed all of their homework
8. so I would think that raising the standards is a pretty important thing.
9. [Speaker 2]: Yes, umm, with regard to raising standards
10. I think we have to ask what are—are standards actually
11. are they academics grades or are we looking for whole person
12. and in my—my particular position I own an education book catalogue
13. but I've also been a special ed. teacher
14. and as a parent of three I've noticed a—from all points of view a couple of things
15. and one of the things is I feel that if we start very early on in kindergarten teaching children organizational skills number one memory skills . . . the earlier you can start these real life skills
16. the better it can be . . . I really think we have to take a good look at what is true success.
17. [Speaker 3]: I say no to standards
18. and I say that because I don't want you to hide behind standards
19. but rather let's use some words like excellence and the outcomes.
20. [Speaker 4]: Well when I think about this issue one of the things that I'm concerned about
21. is who sets the standards who's responsible for setting the standards
22. do they come from the top down or from the bottom up?

23. [Speaker 5]: Uhhh, can I tell you where they came from in New Hampshire?

24. Uhh, I was I chaired the assessment steering committee

25. that put together the original frameworks

26. that set the standards for the children in the state of New Hampshire

27. the testing for the third, sixth, and tenth grade

28. and I can tell you how that happened . . .

29. [Speaker 6]: Well, umm, gosh a lot's been said since I raised my hand

30. but this choice does probably scare me the most

31. because of some of the things I said earlier

32. and [referring to moderator] when you were describing this choice

33. you I know you were reading from this booklet but you said two things

34. that made me uncomfortable and that was "make all students"

35. and the other was "hold all students to the same standards,"

36. and the thing that just strikes me or concerns me about standards is sort of this rigidity . . .

37. I don't like "hold all students" and "make all students"

38. because when I hear that I hear "high stakes testing"

39. and what they say in the education community that I'm a part of

40. is that high stakes aren't for kids, high stakes are for tomatoes.

41. [Speaker 7]: If I could say one thing about standards for a second real quick

42. I'm Betty and I'm a latecomer, sorry.

43. I had a really interesting experience about the testing

44. first of all because I know someone who was real involved in it very well I know a fair amount about it

45. and I've read them and our school district actually distributes them

46. and our teachers at the beginning of the year at open house talk to you about them.

47. I'm not sure if everyone here discussing them has in fact read all of them

48. and they're not particularly frightening.

It took about twenty minutes for the seven participants to make these statements. Two other participants, whose comments I have left out here, spoke at the end of this interaction, and then the group went on to consider a different choice. In other words, these seven utterances compose nearly all of this group's discussion of standardized tests.

Most of the utterances are persuasive. Speaker 1 is clearly in favor of standards because her children might have benefited from them (line 8). Speaker 2 is for the concept of standards but offers a broader, "whole-person" definition of the term. Speaker 3 is emphatically against standards. Speakers 4 and 5 wrangle over the question of who ought to set standards. Speaker 6 dismisses standards as a form of "high-stakes testing" (line 38). And speaker 7 suggests that standards are not as frightening (line 48) as previous speakers have made them out to be. By talking in such terms, the speakers clearly understand themselves to be participating in a deliberative situation. This is to say, unlike Neal in the first example, these seven individuals take seriously their responsibility to discuss whether standardized testing is a good choice about what to do with respect to public schools.

For the most part, however, the discussion is not deliberative, at least as I have defined the term. Recall that a deliberative posture implies ignorance. In a deliberative pose, people approach an issue from the perspective that they do not know what to do. This leads them outward, beyond themselves, in a search for new information. In this light, while it is clear that the speakers in this example are mulling over a choice, it is equally clear that most of them have already chosen. This is to say, having judged the issue of standards for themselves, they now seek to convince others of the rightness of their views.

A framing approach helps us to get at this layer of the conversation. As a potential frame, each utterance represents a kind of narrative that arranges information in particular ways and offers particular character types for general consideration. In this context, one might notice that all of the utterances include references to personal biography. Speaker 1 constructs herself as a mother of two school-aged children (lines 1–2). Speaker 2 reveals that she owns an education-book catalogue company and has been a special education teacher (lines 12–13). Speaker 5 talks about his experience serving on a state steering committee that set standards in the state of New Hampshire (lines 24–25). Speaker 6 notes that she is connected to an education community (line 39) and, in a part of her utterance that does not appear here, relates a story about visiting a Washington, D.C., school as an expert observer. And speaker 7 indicates that she "knows a fair amount about" standards, both because she knows someone involved in creating them and because of her role as an interested mother of school-aged children (lines 44–45). Speaker 7 even goes so far as to accuse others in the group of being ill-informed— despite their efforts to construct themselves as knowledgeable (line 47).

What are we to make of these biographical details? They can, of course, serve many, including deliberative, purposes in a conversation. Here, it seems to me that they serve a specific purpose. Put simply, they constitute an appeal to authority. They are a way of signaling that hearers may trust the veracity of utterances because the speaker is this or that kind of person. In itself, this does not make the utterances nondeliberative. However, their meaning becomes clearer when coupled with the fact that none of the speakers takes into account information provided by previous utterances. Speaker 1 begins from the perspective of a "single parent." Why not just a "parent?" Because being "single" implies that she is raising her children by herself, thus cannot monitor every aspect of her children's education, and, therefore, must rely on school administrators to set high standards. Rather than build on speaker 1's utterance, speaker 2 offers a completely different perspective. Speaker 3 ignores both previous utterances with the flat claim that he is against standards. Speaker 5 does address speaker 4's comments. But even here speaker 5 does so to educate, to "tell her" how standardized testing has been crafted in New Hampshire, not to engage with the meaning of speaker 4's words. What one finds then, in this conversation, is a set of self-contained persuasive appeals that violate a simple yet central element of the deliberative posture: ignorance.

Though it is difficult to convey in words, it is clear from the videotape that the group as a whole understands the persuasive "game" being played by speakers. A certain tension ripples through the group as the seven individuals fail to engage with one another's concerns. People are slightly taken aback with speaker's 3 flat statement against standards. Speaker 4 is clearly frustrated with speaker 5's efforts to educate her (the camera shows her folding her arms and grimacing as she listens to speaker 5's contribution), and others pick up on her feelings. When this segment of the conversation ends, there is a sense that the group has been cut short. Time has run out, and the group has failed to adequately deliberate about the issue under discussion.

Persuasive appeals, of course, can be deliberative. What makes them deliberative, though, has less to do with their linguistic structure than with the intention that motivates them. For instance, one can imagine a hypothetical speaker 8 who, after listening to the previous utterances, responds with something like: "From what I have heard it seems to me that 'standards' is often equated with testing schemes . . . perhaps we ought to embrace a different definition of standards, as speaker 2 suggests, and a different scheme for evaluating them?"

Like the other participants, our hypothetical speaker seeks to persuade, but it is a kind of persuasion that lies outside the egoistic self. The appeal is not to what "I" know but to what "we" know. The speaker, in other words, has listened to and incorporated the views of others. This is a subtle but crucial difference. As a posture, deliberation is a delicate performance. In the stream of conversation, people may quickly fall into and out of it. One moment can seem deliberative and then suddenly people find themselves debating, and, what is more, are unable to say precisely why. By focusing on how participants build meaning in a stream of conversation, framing analysis preserves the complexity of human interaction.

IMPLICATIONS

To briefly sum up: deliberation is a practice of choice making. But it is choice making of a particular kind. People tend to deliberatively choose when they feel that they have a stake in the outcome; when they feel responsible for making a decision, and when they are unsure of which choice is best. These conditions are not objective facts but are intersubjectively conjured in interaction among people. Deliberation, in other words, is a socially constructed activity. Whether potential deliberators face a choice, are responsible for that choice, and so on is determined in interaction. In the act of conjuring a deliberative situation, individuals adopt a disposition that takes them outside themselves. Committed to choosing a course of action but unsure of which course is best, deliberators become especially attuned to the world around them. I have called this disposition a deliberative posture.

A definition of deliberation as posture has many implications for both theory and practice. Limited space prevents a deep discussion of all of them, but let me end by highlighting a few of the more interesting. A first, perhaps counterintuitive implication is that deliberation may occur after conversation. This follows from the fact that deliberation is a practice, a way of engaging with the world. In the stream of conversation, it is sometimes difficult to know what to say at a given moment or what to make of new information. We have all had the experience of continuing a conversation in our head after it has ended. Individuals may make up their minds (that is, make a choice) in the car on the way home, during a recollection of the event with a spouse, or in the shower the next morning. We might take this to mean that deliberation can happen in private. This is, in a sense, true (Goodin 2003). People have the ability to privately review and parse new information. But recall that the animating impulse of deliberation is the recognition that one does not possess information necessary to make a particular choice. Thus, the natural posture of a deliberator is oriented outward, beyond the self. This remains true even in an instance of private deliberation. I know of no such studies, but a natural empirical question arising from this observation concerns differences between private deliberation and that involving conversation between two or more people. For our purposes, the important point is that, strictly speaking, deliberation concerns choice rather than talk. It does not necessarily have to occur in a face-to-face interaction.

A second implication is that deliberation is a learned rather than innate activity. Practitioners of deliberative democracy like to claim that anyone can deliberate (cf. Mathews 1994; Yankelovich 1991). In a context of elite suspicion about the political competence of ordinary people (see, for instance Delli Carpini and Keeter 1996), one can certainly understand the claim. But arguing that everyone can deliberate is not the same thing as saying that all can do so equally well. Anyone can stand on a mound and throw a ball toward home plate. Not everyone can do so like Roger Clemens. The point is that deliberation can be done inappropriately or poorly. Several scholars have picked up this insight to argue that learning to deliberate should be seen as a process of apprenticeship (cf. Burkhalter, Gastil, and Kelshaw 2002; Rosenberg 2002; on learning as apprenticing, see Lave and Wenger 1991). However, it is important to ask: apprenticeship in what? I have no thorough answer to this question. However, I think a key part of the answer is the art of learning to choose well in contexts of uncertainty. Recall that insecurity is an important prompt for deliberation. We deliberate when we must choose without full information. It is the recognition of partiality that leads us to adopt a deliberative pose. Thus, I would argue that learning to deliberate involves an effort less to acquire political knowledge than to choose in an environment that is resolutely uncertain.

This point brings me to what I consider a crucial implication of the view that deliberation is a socially constructed posture. It is simply this: even the most reasonable deliberative exercise does not guarantee good, or even democratic, outcomes. In part, this means that reason giving cannot serve as an evaluative benchmark for deliberation—a notion that contradicts a longstanding conventional wisdom. Since Aristotle, observers have associated deliberation with reason giving. This association follows from the observation that human access to the world is filtered by language: our abil-ity to "know" the world is necessarily mediated by the linguistic concepts we devise for describing it. From this observation, it follows that humans ought to be very careful in how they use language. It is simply too easy for language to distort our understanding of the world. Since reason giving is the most logical form of language use, it is most likely to comport with the "facts," or the "way things really stand" out there in the world. In other words, reason is taken to give humans the best hope of escaping from the "prison house" of language. This notion lies at the base of a good deal of our conventional wisdom about deliberation. To the extent that deliberation is grounded in reasoned argument, the thinking goes, it is more likely to offer an accurate picture of reality. Or, put more simply, we are likely to make better choices the more our language conforms to the rules of reason.

However, according to the view of deliberation as posture, deliberation is a socially constructed practice. The rules for its use, therefore, are social, not linguistic. Contrary to the conventional view, which assumes that language represents the world, my perspective suggests that the meaning of language arises from the practices in which it is embedded (on the broad point, see Hanna and Harrison 2004). This does not mean that the meaning of lan-guage is relative or that it is impossible to evaluate its consequences. As I have shown, practices like deliberation have a commonsense integrity. One can deliberate in ways that are unrecognizable to others. But the criteria for "wrongness" lie within the practice. It is perfectly possible, therefore, to de-liberate well and still make a bad choice—or to deliberate poorly and make a good choice. Indeed, examples of poor deliberative decisions abound in the literature (see Button and Mattson 2000; Hendriks 2002; Holt 1999; Kuk-linski, et. al. 1993; Mendelberg and Oleske 2000). In each of these examples, people behaved in a deliberative manner and nonetheless made choices that, in hindsight, were not particularly good. How do we know that they were "bad" choices? There are many ways this might be ascertained. It may be, for instance, that the choice had unintended consequences or turned out to be difficult to translate into action. Or it may be that, from the perspective of another practice—say, technocratic decision making—the choice has fatal flaws. Notice that in all of these cases our criteria for evaluating the conse-quences of choices lie not in the relationship of language to the world but *in the relationship of deliberative practice to the world.* The best deliberative exercise may produce the best outcome. Then again, it may not.

A corollary to this thought is that it is difficult to justify deliberation by claiming that it produces, or is likely to produce, better outcomes than other decision-making practices. As a general proposition, this is untrue (see, for instance, Surowiecki 2004, on the merits of voting as a decision-making practice). As one manner of engaging the world, the deliberative posture may be better in some contexts than in others. It seems reasonable, for example, that easy political decisions can be made more efficiently through voting or some other decision mechanism. This is, of course, an empirical question, one that has not been answered as yet by the literature. In the absence of answers, it is perhaps more appropriate, as Mark Button and I (2004) have argued elsewhere, to focus on the socialization benefits of deliberative practice. According to this view, deliberation is preferable to other decision-making practices because it invites us to adopt a pose toward the world that is beneficial along some measure that we value. I think here not of the typical democratic values—tolerance, civility, and the like—but rather of the possibility that the deliberative pose may help us to live as individuals and communities more easily and democratically with political uncertainty. In a complex world, many if not most political choices are complex and difficult. Yet they must be made, even when individuals and groups feel unsure of their ability to do so. Perhaps the great benefit of deliberation is that it invites us to sustain ourselves and our bonds with one another through this experience.

13

PUBLIC DELIBERATION AND DIALOGUE IN PUBLIC MANAGEMENT

David G. Williams

MANAGERS AND OFFICIALS AT ALL levels of government must interact with various publics. Various forms of deliberation, involvement, participation, and dialogue are a fact of managerial life, and effective managers must increasingly be skilled in participatory approaches. The arena for deliberation may be either external (hearings, citizen participation in planning, etc.) or internal (participatory management, task forces, committees, etc.). The interaction may be required by statute or regulation (as in much of the Great Society legislation), or it may be elective (to gather information and build acceptance). It may be structured (as in citizen comment periods in city council meetings) or open (informal discussions in various venues). The deliberation may be collective (working with associations and groups, particularly their representatives) or individual (either with separate groups or individuals). Regardless of the type, involvement, discussion, and dialogue have become integral aspects of how public managers must manage.

IMPROVEMENTS THROUGH PUBLIC DELIBERATION

Public deliberation and dialogue can contribute significantly to effective public management. While some public managers have been pulled unwillingly into various types of public deliberation, it is critical to recognize that there are some important and legitimate management functions and needs met by such deliberation. In this sense, public deliberation is a managerial tool or strategy.

The following discussion delineates the benefits of participation and involvement for public managers, particularly in the improvement and implementation of decisions. This limited focus on managerial benefits is not intended to negate or overlook the other significant concerns and rationales arising from democratic values, equality, individual dignity, moral responsibility, and citizenship. Indeed, many of the best reasons supporting public deliberation and dialogue stem from strengthening our democracy, responding to Barber's point that our democracy is often too "thin" (Barber 1984, 151). However, if the discussion can highlight the narrower managerial benefits in deliberation, then it may be helpful in encouraging more public involvement by public managers when they have a choice and more meaningful interaction when public input is required. That is, there are managerial reasons for public deliberation and dialogue.

MANAGERIAL REASONS FOR PUBLIC DELIBERATION AND DIALOGUE

1. *Understanding of decisions is increased greatly increased* when there has been involvement and participation. In both external groups and subordinates, there is a more thorough grasp of the factors, judgments and reasons in a managerial decision or public policy. The better and fuller the dialogue, the better the sharing of information and rationale.[1]

2. *Acceptance of decisions is enhanced.* People (both internal and external to the organization) tend to accept the decision more when they have participated in the process and understand better the factors and constraints involved. Sometimes involvement only provides opportunities for catharsis, a satisfaction of having had a say, or a chance to protect interests, but the reaction to the decision is often more positive. Of course, full public deliberation and dialogue should be genuine and not manipulative (which often backfires).

3. *Valuable information and perspective is added* through deliberative processes. Public managers are not always expert in every area, and important information could brought to the decision from other sources. The old aphorism that "two heads are better than one" has some merit. If nothing else, it is important to understand the viewpoints and desires of those affected.

4. *Public decisions and policies are improved.* Inherent in the previous points is the idea that public policy and decisions can be markedly improved by public deliberation and input. There is refinement as more information is gathered, more viewpoints are considered, and more effects are understood. The competition of ideas and views will lead to more and better choices—a fundamental assumption on which democracy is based. The

expertise, information, and analytical skills of all are directed to the issue at hand. Frequently, the result of a deliberative process is superior to the alternatives available before the deliberation began.

5. *Participation creates greater commitment and deflects opposition.* Participation leads to greater identification with decisions and to greater commitment to implement them. Acceptance is increased. Involvement may deflect opposition to the decision when implemented. Fuller deliberation, as anticipated in sustained dialogue and public deliberation, will often result in positive acceptance rather than just negative deflection because the decision will incorporate elements important to the parties involved. In some cases, the policy or decision developed through participation may not be any different than the one the manager would have made alone, but the acceptance will be enhanced.

6. *Implementation is improved through participation.* Policy and decision mean little; the process has just started. It is in the implementation that policy and decision have an impact and are further interpreted and defined. People internal to the organization who have been involved in deeper discussions will better understand the objectives and the policy needs as they carry out the policy or decision. People external to the organization who have been part of a deliberative process will find the implementation easier to understand, will be able to influence the policy as applied, and will perceive the rationale of various actions.

7. *Participatory involvement will encourage the growth and development of those who have been involved.* People internal to the organization who have been involved in deeper discussions will have better motivation, will understand and develop decision skills characteristic of the next hierarchical level, and will be more effective in task accomplishment. People and groups external to the organization who have been part of a deliberative process will learn to participate in more effective and mature ways, will be motivated to cooperate, and will understand better various perspectives and needs.

8. *Social pressure is increased for others to accept the decision.* When decisions and policies are the result of genuine deliberation and dialogue, then there is social pressure for dissenters to accept or at least comply with them.

9. *Deliberative involvement lends greater legitimacy* to the resulting policy or decision. The legitimacy can also be important in working with groups or individuals who were not part of the deliberative process, such as the general

citizenry. Of course, those with a stake in the outcome should be part of the deliberative process.

10. *Team identity is enhanced through involvement.* Successful deliberative efforts can lead to a "we" mentality rather than an "us versus them" mentality. Dialogue and participation lead to group feeling and team identity. That is, coordination and cooperation are established and lead to further coordination and cooperation. Small involvements can lead to larger successes and common effort directed to more intractable issues.

Of course, some limitations and disadvantages connected to public deliberation and dialogue should be recognized. It often takes longer. It can increase stress and risk. Sometimes leaders are wrongly seen as less strong. Group discussion can diffuse responsibility (see Powers and Powers 1983, esp. 205–7). While these concerns have some merit, they can be ameliorated in most participatory approaches. The key with respect to sustained dialogue and public deliberation is that solitary methods do not rise to the level of the significant issues facing public managers. To deal with these issues and concerns requires a methodology beyond a well-meaning but solitary public manager.

FACTORS IMPORTANT IN PUBLIC SECTOR DELIBERATION

It is too simple to argue that there should be public deliberation and discussion in all situations and that public managers will accrue some benefit from such. Two factors are critical to effective public deliberation and dialogue. First, the degree of participation can range from an autocratic style with no participation or discussion, to consultative styles, to full involvement where the decision-making power is shared. Second, the important contextual factors relating to deliberation and dialogue will present different requirements depending on expertise, available information, constraints, relevant publics, the probability of conflict or cooperation, the importance of the decision, shared or diverse goals, and so forth. These factors will prescribe different approaches to and degrees of participation in different situations or contingencies.

A decision tree can be constructed that lists most of the various contextual factors and identifies the participatory approach and degree that meet those factors. Vroom and Yetton (1973) develops a well-known and widely used model in the literature on small-group decision making that allows one to sort through most contextual factors to select the appropriate degree and type of involvement. This model has been adapted to public participation in public management decisions in Thomas (1995). The model helps to determine when and how much participation is appropriate.

Participation Types for Managers

1. Autonomous managerial decision
2. Modified autonomous managerial decision
3. Segmented public consultation
4. Unitary public consultation
5. Public decision

The Thomas model for effective and appropriate participation in public decision making has five managerial decision-making choices. First, in the *autonomous managerial decision*, the manager makes the decision alone with no public involvement. In situations where the decision has minimal impact on the public and the public has little to add, there may be little public need or desire to participate (e.g., whether agency trucks be blue or white). Second, in the *modified autonomous managerial decision*, the public manager or official seeks information from the public but retains the right to make the decision, which may or may not reflect group influence. This is consideration of public points, but the next step moves into fuller consultation. Third, in *segmented public consultation* the manager or official shares the issue separately with various segments of the public and gets their input, ideas, and recommendations and then makes a decision that reflects group influence. This approach deals with elements of the public separately. There can be significantly different dynamics in meeting with elements separately or together. This collectivity is reflected in *unitary public consultation*, which is participation and deliberation in a single assembled group, again getting input, ideas ,and recommendations and making a decision that reflects group influence. Fifth, in *public decision* the issue or problem is shared with the assembled public and together the manager and the public attempt to reach agreement on a solution. This end of the continuum is where the fullest expression of sustained dialogue or public deliberation would be found; however, elements can certainly be found at the other points (Thomas 1995, 39–40).

TABLE 13.1 Contextual Factors Determining Type of Participation

Quality Factors	Acceptability	Kind of Public
1. Quality requirements that must be incorporated	4. Degree to which acceptance is critical to implementation and degree of acceptance if manager decides alone	5. Structure of the relevant public and type of public organization
2. Sufficiency of information		6. Sharing of goals of manager and public
3. Problem structure and openness of alternatives to redefinition		7. Likelihood of conflict

In the Thomas model, the decision approach is determined by various contextual factors or characteristics of the issue or concern at hand (Thomas 1995, 41–71). One can work through a decision tree to the proper approach, as reflected in table 13.1. The first three questions deal with quality concerns. First, *What are the quality requirements that must be incorporated in any decision?* Particularly in the public sector, there are technical, regulatory, and budget constraints on the nature of the eventual decision. Public influence will have to be within these limitations. Second, *Do I have sufficient information to make a high-quality decision?* More information, ranging from the technical aspects to public acceptance, can improve the quality of a decision. Public participation can add much in some circumstances but little for other concerns. Third, *Is the problem structured such that alternative solutions are not open to redefinition?* Decision latitude and options are often circumscribed by statutory and executive prescriptions. Often, alternatives are limited and deliberation cannot aid some decisions.

The fourth question deals with acceptability: *Is public acceptance of the decision critical to effective implementation? If so, is that acceptance reasonably certain if the manager decides alone?* Of course, a principal reason for involving the public is to increase acceptance. In some cases, acceptance will not have much impact on implementation, but in other critical situations the fullest outcome of the intended decision or policy can only be achieved through public acceptance.

The last three questions think through and define the relevant publics who should be involved and the way in which the process should be structured: *Who is the relevant public? And does that public consist of an organized group, more than one organized group, an unorganized public, or some combination of the three?* Some publics are well represented by a defined group, but in other cases a small group can dominate while other larger but unorganized publics do not seek involvement. The way the participation

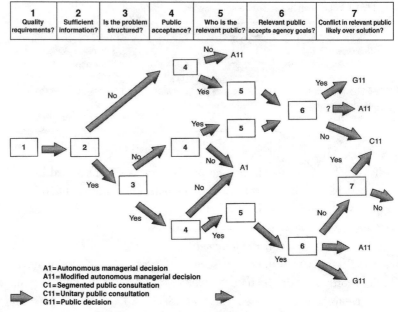

1	2	3	4	5	6	7
Quality requirements?	Sufficient information?	Is the problem structured?	Public acceptance?	Who is the relevant public?	Relevant public accepts agency goals?	Conflict in relevant public likely over solution?

A1 = Autonomous managerial decision
A11 = Modified autonomous managerial decision
C1 = Segmented public consultation
C11 = Unitary public consultation
G11 = Public decision

FIGURE 13.1 Effective Decision Model of Public Involvement

will be structured can depend greatly on the array of publics. Next, *Does the relevant public share the governmental or agency goals to be obtained in solving the problem or dealing with the issue?* If the public shares the goals then full and thorough involvement is enhanced, but if the public has different aims than those imposed by statutory and administrative direction, participation can be problematic for the public manager. Next, *Is there likely to be conflict with the public on the preferred solution?* Group dynamics are such that there are different advantages and disadvantages for meeting with segments separately and meeting with all together. Input can often be greater and individuals and groups can speak more fully when they participate separately and without domination by some. On the other hand, acceptance, awareness of other perspectives, and bridge building may be enhanced by a common meeting. The structuring of the process may better manage chaos and conflict.

The Thomas model is intended to help the manager think through some of the most important contextual factors and to ally them with the participatory styles or degrees. The complete "Effective Decision Model of Public Involvement" (Thomas 1995, 74)can be presented as a decision tree (see figure 13.1). In the model, one can move through the decision tree by asking and answering the contextual questions. They then lead to the appropriate participation approach (at the end of the branch) that meets the contextual factors. At a minimum, the public official or manager would consider some important points in structuring public involvement and deliberation.

The contribution of the Thomas model to sustained dialogue and public deliberation is the recognition that there are appropriately different degrees of participation and involvement and a consideration of important contextual factors that will influence deliberative structure and approach. Sometimes it is better to "deliberate" separately and sequentially (as in the shuttle diplomacy cited in the Van Til chapter in this volume). Sometimes the matter will not benefit from deliberation. Sometimes there are significant statutory and regulatory constraints that influence deliberation. Sometimes the matter can be given fully to the public to decide where there is goal agreement, but other times the public official or manager must maintain more control of the decision or process. These issues become especially important when sustained dialogue and public deliberation are used in the governmental arena and by public managers.

THE IMPORTANCE OF TRUST IN PUBLIC INVOLVEMENT

There is another factor in deliberation and participation as it is applied to the public official or manager. In the first chapter of this book, Van Til starts with a short definition of sustained dialogue and public deliberation and an identification of two major forms of such interaction. Van Til posits that dialogue must be based on a "belief that it may succeed" and the need for a "'profound love for the world and for people.'" This is critical in applications to the public sector. This element might best be termed "trust."

Empirical research by Kaifeng Yang shows that "public administrator's trust in citizens is a relevant and valid construct and a predictor of proactive citizen involvement efforts" (2005, 31). Survey research indicates that public managers have a relatively neutral view of citizens; in fact, they were largely neutral—neither strongly positive or negative—on citizens' knowledge, integrity, honesty, benevolence, and general trustworthiness. However, trust is a significant predictor that leads to greater levels of citizen participation.

Of course, Yang notes, citizens should "possess civic virtue, show authentic citizenship and be trustworthy, but it is more an imperative and responsibility for administrators to serve as trust initiators, to initiate the process to restore and maintain the mutual trust between government and citizens." Yang continues: "Public administrators have to be trustworthy in order to win citizens' trust, believing in local knowledge and action, listening to citizens' voices, sharing power with citizens, displaying trust and respect in the administrative process, and educating and engaging citizens" (2005, 283)

Yang has it right. Trust is important, and public officials and managers need to lead to those goals inherent in public deliberation and dialogue. There is much here to help society and governance progress, but—as shown in his article—there is much to benefit public managers in effectively accomplishing their responsibilities. This is the classic win-win: it is good for the public manager and good for the public to use public involvement and participation as appropriate to various circumstances.

GOVERNANCE AS AN EMERGING PARADIGM

There is a distinctive development in the field of public administration toward participative methods with broader publics—the kind of development sought in public deliberation and sustained dialogue. This development is often found in the literature under the terms "civic engagement" and "governance."

Civic engagement is understood to mean "people participating together for deliberation and collective action within an array of interests, institutions and networks, developing civic identity and involving people in governance processes."[2] The lead journal in the field, the *Public Administration Review*, featured a symposium on civic engagement in its September/October 2005 issue. A conference on the topic organized by the Civic Engagement Initiative of the University of Southern California focused on developing both a practical and scholarly agenda centered around civic engagement.

A broader definition of governance includes the ideas of expanded participation with expanded publics. In this concept, governance is broader than government. The term is widely used in United Nations agencies and reports to mean involvement of a broader range of individuals and groups (public sector, third sector, and private sector) in considering governmental, civil society, economic, and social concerns. These efforts are also found in various nations with governance institutes, from Canada to South Africa. Boyte (2005) states that governance, so defined, intimates a paradigm shift in the meaning of democracy and civic agency, particularly in the broadening of who addresses public problems and concerns. The "shift involves a move from citizens as simply voters, volunteers and consumers to citizen as problem solvers and cocreators of public goods; from public leaders . . . as providers of services and solutions to partners, educators, and organizers of citizen action; and from democracy as elections to democratic society" (Boyte 2005, 536).

Bingham, Nabatchi, and O'Leary (2005) reviews the practices and processes for participation in government and states that "practice is leading theory in developing processes for the new governance." The authors call for more teaching and research on this topic and for further developments to meet what they call the watchword for the next millennium: governance.

Good and substantial reasons exist for public managers to use public involvement and to expand participation. Contextual factors and degrees of involvement and control must be considered. Effectiveness is related to trust and relationship in making these processes work in the public sector. And there is heightened awareness in public administration, both academic and practical, of these trends, often termed civic engagement and governance. It is in this soil that the efforts and experiences of sustained dialogue and public deliberation—and similar approaches—will grow and bloom. These initiatives fit well in the public and governmental sector.

Notes

1. The list in this section is developed partly from points made by Yukl in his discussion of participatory management. See Yukl (1981, esp. 208–9).
2. Abstract to the Civic Engagement Symposium, *Public Administration Review* 65 (September/October 2005): 534.

14

DELIBERATION AND DIALOGUE AND COMMONS THEORY

Roger A. Lohmann

THIS CHAPTER IS AN EFFORT to bring together two separate strains of recent social theorizing. One is concerned primarily with the social dynamics of citizens in public spaces while the other is focused on the conditions and structural arrangements of public spaces themselves. The principal purpose of the chapter is to superimpose the practice of deliberation and dialogue, which has generally been focused on interpersonal communication, on a strain of nonprofit organizational theory known as voluntary action, using the lens of the commons theory of association (Lohmann 1992a, 1992b). Programs of public deliberation and sustained dialogue, I suggest, are in their essential characteristics temporarily constituted knowledge commons, and this insight can be used to understand some of their most important features.

In formulating the commons theory of association (1992a) I chose to defer consideration of questions of practice and policy until a basic outline of the nature of the commons itself had been set out. This was in part because it was clear that the theory did not point easily in the accustomed direction of conventional and utilitarian nonprofit management—attention to outcomes and accountability to outsiders, more resources, better volunteers, more effective boards, and the like—but in other directions entirely. This chapter is one step in an effort to reengage the practical issues set aside earlier and focus on what is most directly related to deliberation and dialogue.

Commons theory is a body of interdisciplinary insights from history, economics, sociology, political theory, and decision, environmental, and social sciences that is grounded in insights drawn from the metaphor of the medieval English commons, pastureland not held privately ("enclosed") but shared by a group of collaborators, or commoners. One key aspect of commons theory—the notion that enclosure of agricultural lands in late-medieval England led to a massive upsurge in poverty—was first introduced into social work in the 1970s by Richard Cloward and Frances Fox Piven (Piven and Cloward 1993) Different aspects of the idea of the commons have been introduced in other contexts both earlier and more recently. (Hardin 1968; E. Ostrom 1990; Ostrom, Gardner, and Walker 1994; V. Ostrom 1997; Hess and Ostrom 2007; Ryle and Richards 1988).

The commons metaphor, knowledge and information commons, the tragedy of the commons and free-riding, and the concept of carrying capacity have been influential far and wide because of how they synthesize both the possibilities of collective effort and the subversions of group intent that can come about, for example, through the free play of individual self-interest. The carrying capacity of a discussion, for example, might be the number and length of comments that could be made during a given session, or the number of propositions that could be discussed. "Free riding" points to an apparent instability or paradox in all collective action (Olson 1965). The most obvious free rider in a deliberative or dialogical context would be the person who insists on doing all of the talking, does not listen, and expects that only the others will change. And one possible "tragedy of the commons" would be that such egoists would inevitably provoke all other discussants to similar behavior, at which point the discussion would effectively cease although the noise level would be considerable.

At its most pessimistic, the tragedy of the commons appears to suggest that all voluntary cooperation is doomed to failure and that only unfettered individual self-interest can be effective in the long run. Closer examinations, however, have consistently shown that group interests in common are more stable than the tragedy hypothesis would suggest. In particular, it is now apparent that groups that formulate effective rules of collaboration can successfully ward off collapse in the face of individual selfishness—something that social workers accustomed to working with groups have known for decades. Two of the most thorough and sophisticated statements of commons theory to date are Elinor Ostrom's *Governing the Commons* (1990) and Yochai Benkler's *The Wealth of Networks* (2006). In environmental studies, the "tragedy of the commons" has been applied to the problems of wetlands, ocean fishing grounds, and global warming. In copyright law, authors responding to the "Creative Commons" initiative of Lawrence Lessig have created completely new forms of copyright that emphasize sharing rather than information property enclosure through the Creative Commons license (see www.creativecommons.org). This is closely related to the open software movement and other similar developments grounded in the notion of knowledge commons (Hess and Ostrom 2007). The tragic commons hypothesis would appear to suggest that such positive efforts must fail, but the practical experience is otherwise often enough to reinforce the view that tragedy can be averted.

The commons-theory perspective is also applicable to certain forms of nonprofit organization and voluntary action whenever conditions of voluntary participation, shared mission or purpose, and pooled resources occur (Lohmann 1992a, 1992b, 2005; Lohmann and Lohmann, 2002). Voluntary association, it has been suggested, is key to understanding the limits of the commons tragedy, and having communications transcend the limits of isolated individuality is essential to association. Rational commoners whose interest in survival is not threatened can easily look beyond pursuit of their individual self-interest and will, in most instances, discover a rational basis for enlightened self-interest grounded in cooperation. In terms of the metaphor, hundreds of years of agricultural history teach us that under most circumstances five dairymen whose unfettered self-interest leads them to graze 100 cows each in a common pasture with a carrying capacity of 350 cows will not, ordinarily overgraze the pasture once they realize the physical limits they face. Real farmers the world over are far too pragmatic to allow this to happen. Rather than standing idly by as the carrying capacity of their common fields fail, they are more likely to engage one another in dialogue and form an association to handle self-assigned allotments of a safe, fairly conservative, figure divisible by five (e.g., 60 cows each, for a total of 300). If they are "scientific" farmers, they are also likely to agree to experimentally increase their individual allotments one cow at a time until they observe the effects on their common pasture of some optimal carrying capacity. In the same vein, discussants in a deliberation or dialogue do not typically stand by, even in the face of leadership failures, and allow the discussion to be permanently hijacked or scuttled by free riders.

In other words, whatever kind of commons is under discussion, the commoners are not likely to remain tragically trapped by their own narrow self-interest but to reconceptualize their self-interest to include a group interest and the establishment of agreed-upon rules to guide their new understandings; they are also likely to continue to associate voluntarily in order to deal with their collective problem. Dialogue, for purposes of understanding, and deliberation, to formulate rules to guide collective behavior, will be essential parts of this process in all such circumstances. Agricultural history, anthropology and social science, and common law are filled with thousands of examples of precisely this commonsense problem solving across thousands of years. Agricultural irrigation, for example, in has been virtually impossible without such collaboration.

In this way, association or the associative commons is a distinct institutional ideal type comparable in many respects to the state, the market, or the family (or, more broadly, the intimate sphere of private life). Examples of commons associations range widely, from irrigation systems to contemporary mutual-aid and self-help groups (Borkman 1999), common-fields agriculture (Maine 1876), ancient Japanese neighborhood associations and Buddhist fund-raising practices (Lohmann 1995a), Latin American fiestas, contemporary nonprofit fundraising campaigns (Lohmann 1992), and all contemporary forms of deliberation and dialogue.

Commons theory projects that in groups where three initial conditions (open and unrestrained participation, shared resources, and shared purposes) are present, two additional conditions are likely to emerge to avert a commons tragedy: *social capital* formation, grounded in trust and a sense of mutuality, or *philia*, among participants, will extend the capabilities of participants over and beyond what they can do alone, and *a shared moral order* or normative structure to regulate participants' behavior in the group will limit the potentially tragic effects of unconstrained self-interest. "We agree to limit the number of cows we graze" is an example of such a moral order, which may be expressed in diverse forms such as legally binding contracts, "gentlemen's agreements," or any of a number of others.

The two emergent conditions of social capital formation and a shared moral order are critically important to the perspective of "the tragedy of the commons." Where they occur, a tragedy is likely to be averted (whether in the form of overgrazing, as in Hardin's famous example; overfishing, as in some of Ostrom's examples; or social disorganization and conflict in the case of deliberation and dialogue), provided only that the commoners have estimated correctly. Such processes are not perfect and are subject to trial and error. In reality, calculation errors do occur even in cooperation: A cooperative agreement to graze eighty cows each in the example given earlier would exceed the carrying capacity of the pasture in the same manner as unfettered individual self-interest. Once this was evident, however, further negotiations and redefined rules would be highly likely.

From this, a strong connection begins to emerge between commons theory and deliberation and dialogue. I wish to propose two major points: First, deliberation and dialogue generally takes place within group settings that approximate the first three conditions of the commons ideal type; that is, participation is voluntary, different people attend with their own agendas because common purposes have been identified or are at least suspected, and resources (notably personal knowledge and insights) are shared. Second, the emergence of social capital, initially in the form of trust and a sense of mutuality, and construction of a new or reconstituted normative outlook typically result from successful efforts at deliberation and dialogue.[1]

The pracademic implication of the first point is that the insights of voluntary action—notably, the form known in social work, sociology, and other fields as community organization—can be used to facilitate deliberation and dialogue (Milofsky 1987). This offers, among other things, an important explanation for why so much of deliberation and dialogue activity takes place in nonprofit settings. The pracademic implication is that recent work on social capital formation and the social construction of moral outlooks can be harnessed to further the aims and objectives of deliberation and dialogue (see my chapter 17 in this book for further development of this point).

BACKGROUND

Theoretical work in this area has gradually converged with practical insights from my teaching. Like several of the other authors in this volume, I teach in a public university in central Appalachia where many of the students come from rural and small-town settings.[2] In the wake of the bombing of the Meir Federal Building in Oklahoma City in 1995, on top of threats to the welfare-state paradigm and the longer-term but nonetheless dramatic rise of incivility in American life, it became increasingly clear to me that the time had come to reposition my graduate social policy seminar away from presentation of the "received truths" of the social work/social policy tradition. (These developments were summarized in Lohmann [1992b].) I was concerned that the conventional curricular approach was merely reinforcing the silence of Appalachian students who are, even under the best of circumstances, not socialized to speak out publicly on social policy issues and questions. The problem is especially acute for those students who bring into the classroom their desire for a career in social work combined with assorted "nonstandard" viewpoints that are at variance with the received truths of the social work profession. Such students may be personally in favor of school prayer, for example, or opposed on moral grounds to a woman's right to choose or may hold other, similar opinions that diverge from national social work norms. Silence, in this case, becomes a tactical posture that has the effect of further undermining already weak norms of public participation.

After nearly forty years of teaching in Appalachia (at the University of Tennessee and West Virginia University), I could hardly be unaware of the lack of political efficacy and the sense of powerlessness or "quiescence" that students from the region bring into the classroom (see Gaventa 1980 for an acute analysis of the reasons for this). The larger (and largely unseen) forces that continue to govern the politics of Appalachia are taken so much for granted that conventional arguments for policy advocacy and civic engagement that make sense nationally either fall largely on deaf ears or take on the character of revolutionary acts, and conventional "empowerment" approaches often fail to connect. Many students learn from the time they are small children that the ubiquitous other ("they") control everything and that there is little more to be said; why bother trying what you know must fail? These are hardly ideal conditions for the growth of active, engaged forms of citizenship and often make for an overwhelming sense of futility in the policy classroom.

In recent years, I have sought in different ways to move toward a more dialogical and deliberative approach to teaching social policy in which students focus on exploring their own views about current issues and explaining and justifying them to others who may disagree.[3] Sad to say, long-sought reconciliation of differences between supporters and opponents on issues such as abortion, welfare-as-anyone-knows-it, or real social security are still elusive. Even so, students regularly report leaving the course with a new and greater sense of their own efficacy as citizen-professionals and a stronger sense that their opinions matter. Based on the experience of this course, I have recently joined with others who have their own, similar insights into the region (including the other authors in this book) in efforts to promote a stronger sense of active citizenship in the state and region.

COMMONS THEORY

In *The Commons: New Perspectives on Nonprofit Organization, Voluntary Action, and Philanthropy* (Lohmann 1992b), the ideal type of a commons is contrasted with incentive-driven firms and rule-directed public bureaus to reach beyond narrowly culture-bound conceptions of "nonprofit organizations." The commons model of association also identifies an important role for strategic conversation—deliberation and dialogue—in the formulation and continuation of all forms of nonprofit practice.

Community practitioners in social work and deliberation and dialogue sometimes inquire what the "practical" implications of this bit of high-blown theorizing might be. Most recently, this question has arisen within the context of the mission of the Nova Institute at West Virginia University.[4] Implicit in this question is another: What connection is there between nonprofit social services organizations and deliberation and dialogue? While there are several possible implications, the most intriguing involves voluntary-action commons as the matrix out of which the formation of new institutions of democratic practice might arise. Quite literally, in a familiar formula we all recognize, engaged talk stimulates action, some portion of which will be of enduring value and become institutionalized over time.

To further clarify this assertion, the perspective of the commons is the central point of this chapter, which seeks, first, to step apart from the assumptions and viewpoints of incentive- and rule-based interpretations of practice and policy in the public arena and nonprofit worlds *and* the customary discursive and conversational assumptions of deliberation and dialogue and, second, to redirect a line of discussion and research on practice and policy questions affecting the nonprofit sector within the broad perspective variously identified as dialogical, interactive, interpretive, or pragmatic. For ease of understanding, I shall refer to variations in this broad view in what follows as a pragmatic or dialogical perspective. For a fuller philosophical basis of this point of view see Bernstein (1971, 1976, 1981, 2010), Habermas (1984), and Heath (2001).

PRAGMATIC PERSPECTIVES

Pragmatic (also sometimes called problem-solving) perspectives are part of a longstanding tradition of actual practice in nonprofit social services, voluntary action, and philanthropy studies.[5] The essentials of pragmatism, from a policy and practice (pracademic) standpoint, include emphasis upon learning processes; evaluating actions in terms of their consequences; emphasis on certain parallels between scientific and democratic decision processes; explicit rejection of dualism, particularly as it supports different approaches to resolving factual and value problems (reflected linguistically in the dualistic either/or merged by the term pracademic); nonserial selection of means and ends in light of one another; consequentialism, or emphasis on evaluation by results or outcomes; and a strong interactional (as opposed to structural) approach to organizations.

At least from the time of John Dewey, pragmatic problem-solving models have been important approaches to practice issues in groups and voluntary action. While much of this activity in social work has been framed as community organization, social planning, or social development, it is important to remember that in the community forms of deliberation and dialogue are almost constantly a part of such efforts. This same perspective figures importantly in a number of organizational, management, planning, and policy models. The emphasis in the work of the pragmatists Dewey, Mead, James, and Peirce is on democratic action, science, and face-to-face interaction; the more recent work from interactional, constructivist, negotiated order, strengths, and other perspectives shares that emphasis and developed out of the earlier work.

The commons theory of association enables a shift of attention away from large, wealthy, powerful, and bureaucratic institutions and quasi-commercial nonprofit firms engaged solely in service delivery. Instead, the theory emphasizes participatory, collective, mutual, and expressive endeavors, which are often also smaller in scale and scope, in control of fewer and more limited resources, capable of wielding less social influence, and dialogical in nature. That is, the commons theory of association seeks to locate the "heart and soul" of the third sector in self-defining, conversationally constructed commons whose "raw materials" are deliberation and dialogue. So how do participation and collective and expressive action take place?

The incorporation statutes, tax policies, and service-contracting strategies of the welfare state provide the skeletal structure of the contemporary commons. Further, the clearest expressions of the pursuit of common goods are to be found in the past and present conversations of settlement houses, community centers, community churches, self-help and mutual-aid groups, volunteer fire departments, hobby clubs, scientific societies, and similar groups, clubs, associations, and societies. These social institutions are capable of determining for themselves (through discussion) their own rules of participation and engagement, and they carry out their own agendas, largely unaided by outsiders, using their own resources and building a satisfactory sense of social capital (which the ancient Greeks called *philia*) and moral order.

It is a principal thesis of this chapter that the ultimate advance of public deliberation and sustained dialogue is not to be found in the promotion of these forms of public talk as abstract principles or ends in themselves, nor in the advocacy of specific methodologies of talking. The real promise of these approaches will come only through the building of new forms of discursive democratic institutions—groups, associations, organizations, and movements—in which talk designed to advance principles of self-efficacy, self-control, and self-governance plays a central role. This was the approach taken by early pioneers of deliberative democracy like Jane Addams and Mary Parker Follett, and the same approach remains workable today.

Uncoerced, cooperative, mutual, shared fair play in pursuit of self-identified goals or ends, as known in the theory as common goods, is (or should be) as fundamental to social work as service delivery. It is this model of common action that nonprofit law recognizes and tax policy encourages. It is this model of joint action that civics texts and politicians (in their better moments) extol. It is such action that is often referred to as "grassroots" and "community-based." And it is this model that is encoded in the "civic republicanism" (to use an arcane and misleading label) of the historic social work ideal of personal growth and development within a developing social environment.

Regrettably, this message is all too often blurred, blunted, and maligned by wealthy and powerful institutional interests seeking to use the cover of the commons to serve their own interests. The important role of defining the third, community, or social sector has been to an important degree co-opted by the large foundations, national-association oligarchies, and quasi-commercial nonprofit firms that so effectively position themselves to speak in the name of the third sector today even as they seek to transform its fundamental character.

SO WHAT?

Several seemingly unrelated intellectual and practical trends have been converging in recent decades and form the backdrop for this current effort. These include the adoption by the Obama campaign of a more deliberative approach to national politics; the growth of deliberation and dialogue in communities across the country; and, theoretically, the resurgence of interest in pragmatism among philosophers and, in particular, the selective embrace of pragmatism and interactional social science by Jürgen Habermas, the heir apparent of European critical theory (Geuss 1981). Unfortunately, the pracademic importance of this resurgence has been dampened somewhat by the general din over "postmodernism" and the reaction against "relativism."

Through the work of philosophers like Richard Bernstein and Joseph Heath, the continuing American dialogues over the meaning of Habermas's dialogical theories have the potential of reopening broader interest in the potentials of democratic organization and participation, which since early in the twentieth century energized discussions of citizen and client participation, volunteerism, collaboration, social democracy, community, and a range of related philosophical works by John Dewey, Charles H. Cooley, Mary Parker Follett, and others (Bernstein 1971, 1978, 1981, 2010; Habermas 1984; Heath 2001).

Guided by such traditional and contemporary theoretical concerns, the objectives of a suitable project to explore the policy and practice implications of the commons theory of association for deliberation and dialogue can be summarized as follows:

- Recapture the radical democratic practice and policy implications of Charles S. Peirce's pragmatic model of scientific community and John Dewey's model of democratic community.

For the first time in human history modern societies are increasingly positioning themselves against any systematically silenced portions of the population and toward giving voice to all citizens. Expressed freedoms of speech, religion, and association once largely implicit or unenforced (in First Amendment court rulings like *NAACP v. Alabama* [1958] and in the U.N. Declaration of Human Rights) have been universalized and embraced by most nations. However, the institutional challenges of actually realizing these ideals and enabling meaningful and fruitful conversations for all remain daunting.

- Operationalize the convergence of instrumental, objectivist, and relativist perspectives that Richard Bernstein and others see in the critical theory of Jürgen Habermas, with its central focus on the ideal speech act (Bernstein 1981).

- Establish more vigorous, pragmatic critical theory as the basis for fundamental social criticism and social reconstruction; inherent in such a model are the "moments" of public deliberation as a mode of social criticism and the processes of sustained dialogue, which build social capital (relationship and trust).

■ Ultimately, discover and embrace more vigorous models of civil society consisting of an integrated community of emancipated and enlightened citizens realizing their collective life through the medium of unconstrained interaction and dialogue. It is a key thesis of the commons model that non-profit organizations offer the "principia media" for genuine movement in that direction.

Focusing on this convergence of voluntary action and deliberation and dialogue also points toward the need for a "third way" in public life (Giddens 2000, 2001; Loyal 2003) Essentially, Hardin's dualistic (1968) posing of the issue of collective choice between the tragedy of unrestrained individual self-interest and the promise of collective public interest exposes this need for the third sector. And the idea of common goods spelled out in the commons theory of association (Lohmann 1992b) may be seen as opening up that third possibility. Pragmatic approaches to policy concerned with addressing the broad middle ground between private market and political state will likely offer alternatives to both the discredited doctrines of state socialism and the highly fashionable but equally dubious doctrines of antistatist individualism, social Darwinism, and laissez-faire market economics. These latter positions erupted back into political fashion in the 1980s after nearly a century of well-deserved neglect and still have the potential to permanently damage the future of democracy (Phillips 2006).

CONCLUSION

The metaphor of the commons poses two quite different lessons for the practice of deliberation and dialogue: For neoclassical economists and practicing lawyers and accountants, as well as certain philosophers, behavioral psychologists, and others of a rationalist mind, the message should be one of relief and hope: There is more to life than the unfettered display of naked self-interest. Self-interested individuals can find ways to talk together and form a common front, and they do so regularly. You may continue to hold to the tragic position that the quest for common meaning is a futile one, if you choose. Meanwhile, if you will look around you, you may see that there are many of us who believe it doesn't have to be that way.

Collective action—in this case, the collective talk of deliberation and dialogue—does not have to be seen in fundamentally tragic terms. This is as true for the husband and wife locked in the desperate combat of a marital dispute as it is of diplomatic representatives of two nations. Neighbors do find ways to build shared fences, and conflicting groups can also find common ground. And the key ingredient in all cases is the element of meaningful conversation—a key form of which is what is here termed deliberation and dialogue.

The message of commons theory to true believers in deliberation and dialogue may be the flip side of the same point: The process of finding common ground is not a given. People do not always automatically solve all problems in this way. Deliberation and dialogue do not automatically lead to reconciliation in all circumstances, and even when they will, getting there can be sweaty, exhausting hard work.

The underlying policy and practice imperative of the commons theory of association should be seen as nothing less than a renaissance of the objective articulated early in the twentieth century by Jane Addams, John Dewey, Mary Parker Follett, and others: recreating the endangered democratic public sphere by revitalizing neighborhood and community life. What clearer rationale could there be for deliberation and dialogue? Isn't this what "citizen participation" and "community development" and "coproduction" are (or should be) all about?

The challenge of practice in the commons continues to be not simply one of how to make myself understood and how best to serve my own interests and achieve my own ends but also one of rediscovering the "we." In what is often termed "interest-group politics," of course, this is a relatively simple process of finding likeminded people and coalescing with them to prevail over others who want something else. The challenges of practice at the present, however, arise from the voiceless, who lack (or have lost) the capacity to speak their minds, and even more from the challenges of cacophony: How, in a world of many voices, with many views, can we not only speak but also listen and genuinely understand what others may be saying? And, reaching that understanding, how can we then learn to act together in democratic community? Deliberation and dialogue programs organized by nonprofit organizations on the principles of the commons offer an important place to start.

Notes

1. Other aspects of the emergence of social capital, in the form of trust and relationships, are explored in other chapters in this volume, by David Robinson (chap. 4) and the author (chap. 17).

2. In the lexicon of the Appalachian Regional Commission, West Virginia *is* (or is the predominant part of) Central Appalachia.

3. In 2005, for example, on the tenth anniversary of the Oklahoma City bombing, students in the seven sections of the policy course were asked by their instructors to conduct public deliberation sessions throughout the state in the first-ever statewide celebration of Deliberation Day. We even sought (unsuccessfully) to enlist the governor to proclaim the day West Virginia Deliberation Day. We held nearly 150 deliberation events in all parts of the state that day and received television coverage on the local news. As anticipated, the governor's office did not respond.

4. The Nova Institute is an outgrowth of the classroom initiative I discuss earlier, together with the appointment of Jon Van Til, my coeditor and the institute's cofounder, as Carlson Distinguished Professor of Social Work.

5. This is quite distinct from most contemporary conceptual perspectives that, apart from those held by Van Til, Milofsky, myself, and others working in the voluntary-action tradition, seek largely to formulate the problem of nonprofit organization in bureaucratic terms as a problem of transmitting incentives rather than developing understanding and formulating rules rather than formulating community. From this perspective, it may appear to border on complete incoherence to suggest a connection between deliberation and dialogue and nonprofit organization.

15

QUESTION MAPPING: A METHOD FOR ORGANIZING AND SUSTAINING DIALOGUE

Richard F. Ludeman and Erna Gelles

The quality of our lives is determined by the quality of our thinking. The quality of our thinking, in turn, is determined by the quality of our questions, for questions are the engine, the driving force behind thinking.

—L. ELDER AND R. PAUL, *THE FOUNDATION FOR CRITICAL THINKING*

COMMUNITY DIALOGUE and deliberation can be structured in a variety of ways, but regardless of form, all such efforts seek to increase understanding about issues of mutual concern. Issues worthy of this level of citizen investment invariably involve multiple layers and stakeholders. Those who are engaged often struggle to sort out the central issue, the relationships among related issues, and competing priorities. Making progress in communal inquiry requires methods for making sense of this complexity.

Peter Senge (1990) popularized the concepts of systems thinking in the workplace. He advocated "seeing wholes" rather than parts and relationships instead of linear cause-effect chains. The models and tools of systems thinking do not eliminate complexity but they do enable practitioners to articulate connections, gain new insights, and ultimately improve their effectiveness. This same spirit guides question mapping (Ludeman 2003), a tool for framing issues that seeks to both deepen understanding and provide a blueprint for moving forward.

Question mapping is a process for defining the central issue while identifying related issues and their relationships to the central issue. The outcome of a session is a graphical representation, or map, of the results. In this chapter we describe how question mapping works in two different scenarios. The first outlines the process for small-group facilitation while the second offers a case study based on interpreting the transcripts from a nonprofit leadership summit. The specific results of this summit illustrate how question mapping can serve as a catalyst for progress by eliciting the collective intelligence of the community.

KEY CONCEPTS

Question mapping begins with the simple premise that a clear and shared definition of an issue is essential to collective efforts to address it. While this is not a controversial assertion, our experience has been that in practice a lack of clarity is far more common than is generally acknowledged. In fact, we believe that many disagreements about solutions are, unbeknownst to the participants, actually disagreements regarding what question should be addressed.

The second premise inherent in question mapping is that any reasonably complex issue exists not in isolation but within a web of related issues each of which contributes to framing the central issue. Like the first premise, this idea may have intuitive appeal, but it is rarely reflected in practice because of the complications it brings. Instead the tendency is to narrow the dialogue in the interest of focus or broaden it in the spirit of exploration, thereby running the risk of either impoverishing or overwhelming the inquiry. Question mapping is an attempt to resolve this dilemma.

Finally, Question mapping is rooted in the generative power of questions. Questions stimulate thinking, promote conversation, and provide direction for further inquiry. Compared to statements, questions are intrinsically better suited to public deliberation and dialogue. Statements imply conclusions, prompt win/lose debates, and can lead groups into intellectual cul-de-sacs, thereby inhibiting the pursuit of learning and clarity, which are key motivations for engaging with others to address common concerns.

To illustrate this point, imagine community leaders agreeing that their primary concern is that local schools have deteriorated. As a statement it rests at the point that initial—and potentially superficial—consensus is reached. Turning it into a question, however, gives it life again. There are many ways the central issue could be articulated. For example:

- Why have local schools deteriorated?
- How can we rebuild our schools?
- What impact does the quality of our schools have on our community?

The dialogue generated in search of agreement about the central issue concerning these schools would illuminate important values, motivations, and assumptions behind the initial consensus. The clarity provided by this discourse would open up new possibilities for framing, understanding, and ultimately addressing the issue. Furthermore, as we explained later, all initial formulations of the central question can potentially become a part of the final question map but with the added value of another level of specificity and a fuller context.

SMALL-GROUP FACILITATION

The departure point for question mapping is a working version of the central issue in the form of a question, e.g., "Why have our schools deteriorated?" Precision is not required at this point, nor is consensus—just a reasonable formulation of the opportunity or problem.

STEP 1: ARTICULATING THE CENTRAL ISSUE

To begin, each participant writes his or her own version of the central question on a Post-it note. A volunteer initiates the next phase by placing his or her note the middle of the question mapping grid (see figure 15.1), briefly explaining the rationale of the particular framing inherent in the question. Participants then take turns placing their questions on the grid relative to those already posted, offering the reasoning behind their questions and placement decisions. Note that relative to the center square, the top row captures broader questions, the bottom row more detailed or specific questions. The left column collects questions related to background issues, and the right column questions pertaining to future or follow-up considerations.

Note that the "presenting participant" may rearrange any or all other notes during her turn. For example, she may displace the question in the middle with her own and move the former central question to another position on the grid. During this time it is important that group members focus on seeking clarification rather than evaluating the merits of a particular question or placement decision.

STEP 2: ACHIEVING CONSENSUS ON THE CENTRAL ISSUE

After everyone's version of the central question has been shared and placed on the grid, the session leader facilitates dialogue and discussion, rearranging,

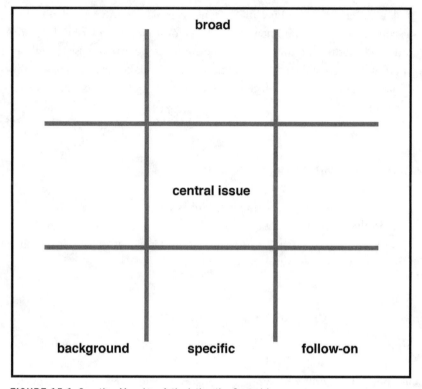

FIGURE 15.1 Question Mapping: Articulating the Central Issue

For reference it may be useful to label the cells as if the central issue were the center of a compass, i.e., top row is north, bottom row is south, left-hand column is west, and right-hand column is east. Using this system each cell has a direction, e.g., the top, right-hand cell is the NE cell.

rewriting, and adding new questions to the map as the group deems appropriate. The group continues until it is satisfied it has reached consensus and clarity in terms of articulating the central issue. The final version could be one of the original notes, a synthesis of several, or something entirely new. At this point the central issue will be in the center of the grid surrounded the other suggested questions that were not selected as the final version (see figure 15.2).

STEP 3: DEVELOPING THE FULL CONTEXT

The central issue becomes a reference point and anchor for identifying and organizing related issues in order to develop a full context. Given the central

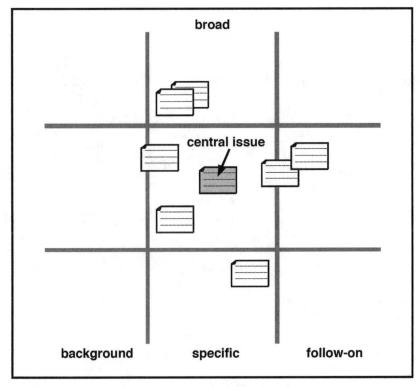

FIGURE 15.2 Question Mapping: Preserving Ideas from Step 2

The ideas and suggestions "left over" from the process of identifying the central question should be left on the grid since they provide an excellent transition to step 3 as potential candidates for inclusion as related questions.

issue, participants generate as many other relevant issues as they feel need to be considered, again phrased as questions. For example, if the central question is, "Why have our schools deteriorated?" related questions might include, "What evidence do we have of this deterioration?" or "What do we mean by deterioration?"

The process of recording and posting questions outlined in step 1 is repeated, this time for the related questions. The facilitator then guides the group through the process of finalizing the map, including the relative relationships of the related issues.

As a final check of the process the group should audit the results both vertically and horizontally within the logic of the question mapping grid. In other words, when reading horizontally across each row, do the items actually seem to progress from background through follow-up questions?

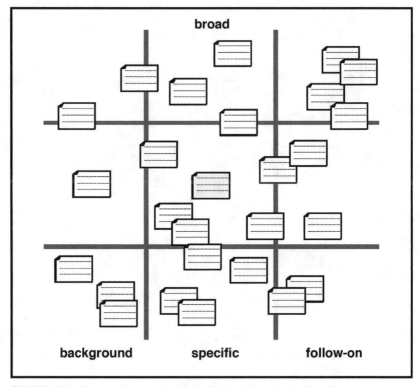

FIGURE 15.3 Question Mapping: Prompting Related Questions in Step 3

To prompt a thorough exploration of related issues the major modes of thinking can be used as catalysts.

Critical thinking asks, Why? It analyzes assumptions and logic, e.g., How do you know? From what point of view is this true?

Systems thinking asks, How? It considers the whole and is concerned with linkages, relationships, and patterns, e.g., Where does this come from? What happens next? What else is affected?

Creative thinking asks, What if? It brings forth fresh perspectives and alternative interpretations, e.g., What could be different? What if you could start from scratch?

Likewise, when reading vertically down each column, do the entries seem to progress from a more general level to more specific questions? After any needed adjustments the question map at the end of this step presents a mosaic of the full issue. What once might have remained isolated fragments of inquiry now constitute a whole with the potential to inform integrated efforts to address the issue (see figure 15.3).

STEP 4: DETERMINING NEXT STEPS

The full dimensions of an issue, whether an opportunity or a problem, will often both exceed available resources and transcend organizational boundaries. Therefore, determining priorities and scope are essential in order to

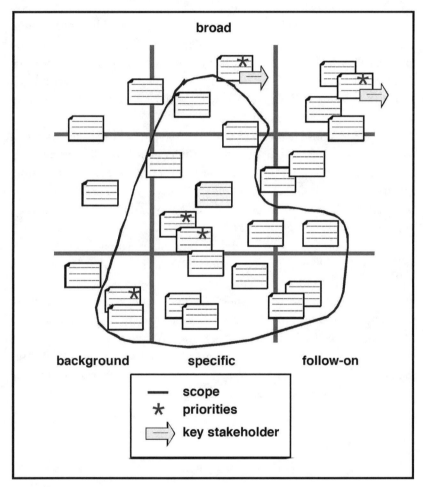

FIGURE 15.4 Iterations and Question Maps

A question map captures the thinking of a particular group at a specific point in time. Over time there will be shifts in the external environment, new learning and insights, and changes in group membership. Therefore, it is valuable to revisit a given question map when there has been significant movement in one or more of these contextual factors.

transform the thinking and insights captured in a question map into a blue-print for action.

Each section of the map offers its own value. The top row represents the broader picture and is useful for testing alignment, i.e., do the questions in this row resonate with larger community or organizational goals? The bottom row elaborates more detailed planning and research needs. The left column calls attention to important background information, possible upstream connections, and potential root causes. The right column anticipates implications, identifies possible downstream connections, and provides direction for the future. Within this framework each cell can be interpreted for additional meaning. For example, the top, right-hand cell (NE) articulates broad, future-oriented questions, thereby providing material for strategic-planning initiatives.

Within the constellation of questions a handful will tend to emerge as priorities given their potential to affect the central issue. If the group has difficulty choosing priorities it may be helpful to consider questions from an "if/then" standpoint, i.e., if we answered this question, then what will be we able to do? Or, alternatively, if we didn't answer this question right away, then what would be impeded?

The scope or boundary of what the group will take on is defined by those questions they choose to address directly. Note also that it is possible to identify priorities outside the group's scope. These are either key questions the group needs answered by others in order to pursue the central issue or questions the group wants to share based on the perceived value to other stakeholders (see figure 15.4).

The completion of this final step provides a holistic picture of the issue. It is an explicit representation of the shared response to the two fundamental questions underlying all group efforts: What, exactly, is the issue, and where do we go from here?

POSTEVENT ANALYSIS: A CASE STUDY

BACKGROUND

In late 2003 an urban, university-based nonprofit-management institute convened a summit of third-sector leaders. The purpose of the summit was to generate conversations and capture ideas around community and statewide issues. Attendance was close to 300, reflecting a sense of urgency about an environment wherein diminishing resources and increasing demands for services were having profound effects on the ability of organizations to accomplish their missions.

The day was divided into two sessions. The morning session was entitled "Philanthropy at the Crossroads: Changing Relationships Between Funders and Organizations." The afternoon session was designated "Facing the Perfect Storm: Just Coping or Real Leadership?" Each session began with a facilitated central conversation (fishbowl) with eight preselected community leaders. Attendees listened from twenty-eight round tables that surrounded a raised central podium. After fifty minutes the conversation moved from the central podium to the tables, where trained volunteer facilitators guided and note takers recorded the dialogue inspired by the fishbowl conversations.

APPLYING QUESTION MAPPING

To analyze the outcomes of the leadership summit, question mapping was applied retrospectively to the transcripts from the fifty-six breakout table conversations (twenty-eight from each session). Although analogous to the small-group facilitation process outlined above, a postevent analysis is different in that the question map is interpreted after the fact as an implied result rather that created "live" as an explicit result. Nevertheless, a postevent analysis can provide similar benefits in terms of clarity and direction.

The specific implementation of question mapping in a postevent context can take a variety of forms. In this case a reviewer carefully analyzed a sample of six transcripts from each session and annotated them for key ideas, concepts, and themes. Along the way this content was translated into a master list of questions. In some cases the questions were essentially quotations of participants' commentary. However, most questions were based on the reviewer's interpretation of the underlying or implied questions. This list of questions was further refined by grouping them into topic areas, an iterative process that included some consolidation as well as reformulation of several questions to better reflect their full implications.

The results of this first stage were used to refine the initial framing of each session as described in the summit brochure. This is analogous to steps 1 and 2 in the small-group facilitation process, "Articulating the Central Issue" and "Achieving Consensus on the Central Issue" (see table 15.1).

Next, the remaining questions were arranged on the question mapping grid based on their relationships to the central issue (see tables 15.2 and 15.3). This, too, was an iterative process that began with an initial placement of

TABLE 15.1 Reframing the Central Issue

SESSION	INITIAL FRAMING FROM PROGRAM	CENTRAL ISSUE— QUESTION MAP
Philanthropy at the Crossroads	Discussion will explore the changing role of many foundations and donors in proactively shaping and affecting the work of nonprofit organizations. Initial framing questions include: • Is the new wave of "venture capital" a more strategic approach to philanthropy that defines a stronger partnership between funder and nonprofit leaders? • When does this more direct approach "cross the line" into micro-management and heavy-handed funder direction? • How should nonprofit groups respond to a greater degree of involvement and direction from their funding sources in how to implement their plan?	What role should funders play in shaping an organization and its programs?
Facing the Perfect Storm	The forum will explore the impact of federal, state and local funding cuts that have resulted in fiscal crises for our organizations, our clients, and our communities. Initial framing questions include: • What is happening to our community as we struggle? • Is competition replacing collaboration? • What are the implications for our organizations and the communities they serve? • How is the face of the third sector changing under these constraints? • What is or should be the role of leadership in this process?	What can nonprofits learn from these difficult times in order to emerge stronger?

all the items that was then checked and rechecked for fit both horizontally and vertically. This is analogous to step 3 in the small-group facilitation process, "Developing the Full Context." In addition, a second reviewer read the sample transcripts and critiqued the initial question maps. The draft versions of both question maps were then shared with over a dozen attendees, including members of the organizing committee.

TABLE 15.2 Question Map of Philanthropy at the Crossroads

	Context and Alignment: Higher-Level Questions	
• What trends are influencing the funder/organization relationship? Is there a paradigm shift and if so how can we describe it? • To what extent are funders strategic and attentive to systemic relationships (e.g., adult literacy is integral to children's literacy. • How do we reconcile long-term impact and short-term funding?	• What is the framework that describes the overall funder/organization relationship, and how does this aspect fit? • What are the elements of this relationship and how do they vary by type of funder? How do they vary by type of organization?	• What are the implications of different levels and types of funder involvement? • *How do we map community needs and NPOs to identify gaps and opportunities as well as facilitate the matching of funders and organizations? Who is in the best position to do this?* • How do we encourage social entrepreneurship without creating potentially problematic fragmentation?
• How do changes in government programs, priorities, and spending directly and indirectly affect NPOs? (5) How can we influence this process? *• When is collaboration productive; when is it counterproductive and how can funders help organizations to determine this?* *• What form does competition take in the nonprofit sector? When is it healthy, when is it detrimental?*	Central Question What role should funders play in shaping an organization and its programs?	*• How do we get government to acknowledge NPOs' public service work so that they engage us and cushion funding transitions?* • By what process and criteria should NPOs evaluate and respond to different levels and types of funder involvement? • What can we do to increase mutual understanding and satisfaction between funders and organizations? *• How can NPOs intelligently evaluate options for working with other organizations?*
• What does collaboration really mean? • How do we develop measures/metrics that are meaningful and practical? Are all outcomes measurable? *• Does it make sense to tie money to outcome-based projects and not provide administrative support?*	• What is the range of current approaches/practices? What's working, what's not? • What are the opinions/positions of funders and organizations regarding this role? What do they have in common, what are the differences?	• When mission, planning, or process is at odds with funder or strings are attached, how can the relationship be preserved, or should it? • How does an organization determine the right mix of funding sources?
	Research and Plans: More Specific Questions	

Left vertical heading: Root Cause and Context: Background Questions

Right vertical heading: Direction and Plans: Follow-Up Questions

Italics = Common to both sessions.

TABLE 15.3 Question Map of the Perfect Storm

	Context and Alignment: Higher-Level Questions	
• What are the sources of the discrepancy between the importance of the nonprofit sector and its reputation and influence?	• As a sector how do we increase our influence, especially in the realm of policymaking? Are there core issues that would unite people? • Where is the leadership? What is the relationship among ego, passion, and partnership in the context of leadership? Where are our visionaries and activists?	• How do we move from reactive to active? How do we find our collective voice and the means to advocate? • How do we develop a systems approach in order to work together on root causes rather than separately on the symptoms? • How can we focus on increasing the size of the pie rather than the process of how it's allocated?
• How do changes in government programs, priorities, and spending directly and indirectly affect NPOs? How can we influence this process? • What does collaboration really mean? When does it work, when is it counterproductive? What forms can it take? • What form does competition take in the nonprofit sector? When is it healthy, when is it detrimental?	Central Question What can nonprofits learn from these difficult times in order to emerge stronger?	• How can we mitigate the downward spiral created by a troubled economy—higher demand for services and fewer available resources? • How do we map community needs and NPOs to find gaps and opportunities as well as facilitate the matching of funders and organizations? Who is in the best position to do this? • What can we do to increase understanding, integration, and synergy among the business, government, and nonprofit sectors? What can each sector learn from the others?
• To what extent do we need to educate ourselves about the broad community issues—"vision of betterment" for the entire community? • To what extent do nonprofit leaders—executive directors and board members—need to put more emphasis on their role as community change agents?	• How can NPOs intelligently evaluate options for working with other organizations within and between sectors? • Is organizing collectively, e.g., "chamber idea," a good idea and feasible? How would it be funded? How would we find common ground while effectively representing our diversity and passions?	• How do we educate the public about our longstanding and instrumental role in serving society, e.g., hospitals and education? • Would magnifying the pain of inadequate resources help awaken the general public or alienate them? How do we tap hidden and newly established wealth in the community?

Left vertical axis label: Root Cause and Context: Background Questions

Right vertical axis label: Direction and Plans: Follow-Up Questions

TABLE 15.3 (*Continued*)

• What is the source of the impression that NPOs do not require administrative costs to do their work? Are board members aware of this funder perception as well as their fiduciary role?	• How do we engage youth in the sector's critical work, harnessing their passion and vitality? • What can we learn from our growing diverse population about how to engage communities in service? • How do we turn the Summit's conclusions into action and policy? What is within our direct power to change?

Research and Plans: More
Specific Questions

Italics = Common to both sessions.

TABLE 15.4 Revisions to Initial Question Maps

ITEMS BY MAP	A.M. SESSION	P.M. SESSION
Initial number of items	18	14
Added to original grid	4	8
New placement	4	2
Reworded	2	2

Note that a postevent question mapping analysis does not require that reviewers attend the event. In this case, only the second reviewer attended the summit.

Although the feedback on the initial question maps was positive, another round of analysis was undertaken by the second reviewer, who read all fifty-six transcripts in order to identify elements not captured in the sample analysis. While the central questions remained the same, there were a number of edits to the initial question maps based on this more comprehensive process. (See table 15.4 for a summary of revisions by type).

A number of alternative approaches could have been taken in this post-event analysis. For example, a group of reviewers could have read all the transcripts and then engaged in a facilitated small-group session to create the question maps collaboratively. Or several individuals could create their own question maps and then reconcile them through follow-up dialogue.

REFLECTING ON THE RESULTS

The fourth and final step of the small-group facilitation process presented earlier is "Determining Next Steps." Although this aspect was not formally part of the follow-up for this summit, the resulting question maps nevertheless offer guidance in a variety of forms. The most immediate use was a presentation that provided context and validation to a group of nonprofit leaders considering the formation of a statewide nonprofit association, an opportunity captured in the question map of the afternoon session. Additionally, the nonprofit institute that sponsored the summit views the collection of questions as a useful source of potential research topics as well as possible themes for future summits or seminars.

More broadly, the results of this summit suggest the presence of core issues that are likely to show up in a range of question maps. These issues would be of particular interest to those seeking to increase the sector's overall effectiveness. In this case five issues were common to both sessions:

- How do we map community needs and NPOs to identify gaps and opportunities as well as facilitate the matching of funders and organizations? Who is in the best position to do this?
- How do changes in government programs, priorities, and spending directly and indirectly affect NPOs? How can we influence this process?
- When is collaboration productive, when is it counterproductive, and how can funders help organizations to determine this?
- What form does competition take in the nonprofit sector? When is it healthy, when is it detrimental?
- How can NPOs intelligently evaluate options for working with other organizations?

The sentiments reflected in these questions capture participants' frustration with systemic issues in the nonprofit environment, including fragmentation, a lack of information, and limited communication channels. Perhaps it would be productive to convene a question mapping session to consider a question such as the following: How can we build better connections in order to better serve the greater community?

CONCLUSION

Question mapping is a step back but not backward. It illuminates broad themes and incorporates specific questions, enabling those engaged in collective efforts to make sense of the full context of an issue. The iterative process of framing and exploring invites new insights, ideas, and possibilities. The resulting question maps offer multiple avenues for action, increasing the probability of success as well as expanding opportunities for participation.

As a method question mapping both contributes to and is dependent upon the quality of the related dialogue. Ultimately, the measure of its value is the extent to which it enhances both the process and outcomes of group inquiry. As with all such efforts, realizing the full benefit requires the collective will and individual courage to confront issues too complicated for easy answers yet too important to defer.

16

APPLYING FAMILY THERAPY PRINCIPLES TO THE BODY POLITIC THROUGH SUSTAINED DIALOGUE

Neal Newfield and Susan Newfield

IN MANY CITIES ACROSS THE United States, Muslim Americans talk across the dinner table about Jews and their military aggression in the Middle East and the latest civilian death tolls. In these same cities Jewish Americans discuss the current jihad movement in the Middle East and wonder when Muslim terrorism will stop. Now imagine a dialogue between these two groups. Their history of conflict and knotted relationships would result in recrimination on both sides.

Across town, a couple sits on a couch furious with each other as they endlessly debate whether the curtains in their apartment should be beige or sand colored. Despite the fact that one of these conflicts is geopolitical in scope and the other is strictly between partners, there is a similarity in process between the two. Both have a history of conflict, both are fighting over territory, and both are attempting to define themselves through the argument.

For over thirty years Harold Saunders worked in government as a diplomat. Most notable was his participation in the shuttle diplomacy of Henry Kissinger and his participation as assistant secretary of state in the Camp David accords. His sustained dialogue model is inductive and developed from the process he saw unfolding before him. His model is pragmatic and relationship oriented. He describes the peace process as "a human or political, as well as a diplomatic and negotiating, process that works simultaneously on multiple levels" (Saunders 1999, xix).

Sustained dialogue combines the emotional aspects of conflict with an attempt to cognitively understand and map the dimensions of that conflict, pinpointing problems and developing an action plan. Ignoring either the emotional or the analytic dimension seldom leads to a lasting peace. Sustained dialogue is a wedding of the two dimensions (Katnani and Parker 2003, 11). As Saunders points out, conflicts that are deeply rooted in human relationships may not be ready for negation or mediation. Negotiating the surface symptoms of a conflict frequently results in only a temporary cessation of violence (Saunders 1999, 32). The same may be said concerning custody disputes in hotly contested divorces. The judge may hand down a decision that has the force of law. People, however, can not be forced to uphold the spirit of the law, and court decisions are often contested or circumvented, leading to fractious lawsuits, countersuits, and more fighting.

The theories and interventions that contribute to peace in families may also be applied to larger systems, and they may account for the change that is seen to occur through sustained dialogue.

FIVE-STAGE MODEL

What distinguishes family therapy from simple talk within families is that conversation is shaped toward a purpose. The purpose is to change patterns of interaction and relationships so that problem solving can occur and conflicts can be resolved. The same can also be said for sustained dialogue. The sustained dialogue model is presented as a five-stage process. These stages are well discussed (Nemeroff and Tukey this volume; Katnani and Parker 2003; Saunders 1999). Our focus will be on the first two stages of sustained dialogue. It is in these stages that relationship issues are center-stage and the human dimension is of foremost concern. Participants develop a comfort zone and inform others of experiences that shape their decisions and points of view. Disclosing their experiences to others helps make sense of previous decisions and posturing. Without this context orientation, the decisions may appear unreasonable. As people narrate their personal experiences, it humanizes the other side and increases the possibility of empathy.

Sharing food and conversation during breaks from the work also increases the probability of people interacting just as people and not as combatants. Neal, in helping to facilitate a dialogue between the Muslim and Jewish communities, has found that the formal meeting frequently flows into conversations in the parking lot. These chats introduce novelty through interaction among individuals who may not have had the opportunity to have such conversations previously. These friendly conversations hold the seeds of friendship and may facilitate the higher purposes of the committee and their community dialogues.

A general principle of family therapy is that in conflicted relationships it is necessary to metacommunicate. That is to say, one must communicate about how one communicates. There is a necessary focus on not just what is said but how it is said and how this reflects the nature of the way people define relationships between themselves and the parties with whom they are in conflict. As relationships become less combative over time, one has less need to focus on maintaining a positive working relationship and avoiding being baited into fights. Conversations can focus on discussion of solutions and choices.

Saunders's choice of the word "deliberation" (Saunders 1999, 62) to characterize the search for common ground is an interesting one since it intersects with the work of David Matthews in *Politics for People* (1999). Matthews outlines a deliberative process for helping communities identify common ground in order to move forward politically. This process has its roots in the town meeting, where people might have differences in values and conflicting interests but generally are not blood enemies. The focus of the model is on structuring public dialogue in a way that eschews debate and identifies common interests. Participants can use shared interests to develop common goals. Sustained dialogue without the concept of relationship is quite similar to the Matthews's public deliberation model.

STAGE ONE

Stage one of the Saunders model, "Deciding to Engage," includes:

1. Identifying and gathering resources to support the dialogue
2. Initiating a dialogue
3. Selecting someone who can execute the responsibilities of a moderator
4. Recruiting participants
5. Building and sustaining commitment among the participants
6. Building trust

In family therapy this stage is described by strategic therapists as the struggle for structure and initiative. While the struggle begins in stage 1, it is continuous throughout the change process. It is imperative that the therapist maintain control of structural issues while the clients take the initiative in therapy, the second struggle, in order for the enterprise to be a success. We maintain that this is also true for sustained dialogue groups.

Structural issues for both sustained dialogue and family therapy include gathering resources, identifying who should be included in the sessions and where the meeting should occur, and the moderator or therapist's asserting his or her authority to stop, start, and direct conversation. We will discuss those areas where family therapy has the most to contribute.

RESOURCES AND RECRUITING PARTICIPANTS

An important principle of family therapy is recruiting people for the therapy who can get the job of change done. You need the necessary resources for change in the room, or you are doomed to failure before you begin. Here we are not just talking about a changing a problem but changing relationships that will sustain the resolved problem.

A network of organizations that calls for a dialogue has the advantage of recruiting diverse and strong participants while maintaining a net of communication and influence that can be used later when the sustained dialogue moves to the implementation of solutions. However, the organizations that help initiate the dialogue and perhaps even provide a space for the dialogue and food for the participants must not participate in the dialogue itself. If the intent is to change relationships then the relationships brought into the dialogue room must be accessible to change. If individuals come as organizational representatives, they are obligated to follow the planks in their organization's platform. This hinders individual flexibility and impairs the dialogue. A participant's relationship with a sponsoring organization would confuse whether he represents the organization or himself. Personal beliefs can be hidden behind organizational assertions. When people represent themselves, they cannot hide behind their organization's position. Later, when relationships between the parties in the dialogue have been modified, organizational ties can be used to leverage change.

To relate this to family therapy: adolescents who skip school are frequently told by their parents that the school will not allow this behavior. Such a stance disaffiliates the parents from the need to take action. Furthermore, giving the organization the responsibility for change disempowers the relationship between the parents and adolescent. When the parents assert that school should not be skipped and then take action, true change occurs. The change is not just a surface solution to missed school but an alteration of the relationship between the parents and between the parents and the adolescent. This is no less true concerning the relationships among people, the body politic, and organizations.

Each sustained dialogue group will have its own process. By process, we mean how people attempt to define relationships within the group. In order for the group to foment new ways of relating it must be a place safe for expression, experimentation, and defining relationships. Ground rules, for example, those detailed by Katnani and Parker (2003, 106), such as "I statements," listening, avoiding interruptions, and confidentiality, help facilitate a redefining of relationships. The "Covenant" that Saunders recommends (1999, 271) can also be a useful compact among dialogue group members. Excluding friends and close associates from the same dialogue group is also wise. Such individuals tend to reinforce established patterns of relating while becoming a voice for stability rather than for change.

In order for people to change, novelty must be introduced into how they define relationships. In therapy with families who already have a defined membership the burden of introducing novelty falls on the therapist, who must encourage people to view old behavior in new ways. This invites a different behavioral response. For instance, if the behavior of a child is no longer viewed as the result of mental illness but a result of misbehaving, the response of the parents may change. Being bad invites a different behavior from parents than being ill. The behavior is the same, but the consequences change as the frame changes. Conversely, changing behaviors will often change perceptions. Hadassah Hospital in Israel, for example, treats all victims of violence with equal care and respect whether Muslim or Jewish. Consequently, many patients dramatically change their perceptions of would-be adversaries.

In sustained dialogue the moderator does not have to be the introducer of novelty. Since invitees to the dialogue are in conflict they are in all likelihood self-segregating in order to minimize uncomfortable and possibly threatening behavior. To engage in a dialogue civilly invites storytelling. As people listen to the stories in stage 2, links are made to their own stories outside of their conscious awareness. Additionally, simple acts such as sharing a meal remind people indirectly that even our enemies are human.

INITIATING A DIALOGUE

Sustained dialogue requires the organizers of the dialogue to "identify those who want to change the dynamics of the relationship, to end the conflict and to build a future in which parties to the conflict can work together from defined common ground" (Saunders 1999, 89). People will frequently enter family therapy as visitors. They are sent by others to be fixed and assert that they don't have a problem and so are "just visiting." Since the participants in a sustained dialogue have self-identified as wanting change, they will not be "visitors" to the dialogue. They may, however, be "complainants" (de Shazer 1988a, 87–89). These people will define themselves as wanting change, but the change that they are looking for is only from the other party to the conflict. They will punctuate the conflict situation in a manner that makes them the hero or victim while casting the other parties to the conflict as villains. This is nicely illustrated in this poem by Ogden Nash:

> He drinks because she scolds, he thinks;
> She thinks she scolds because he drinks;
> And neither will admit what's true,
> That he's a sot and she's a shrew.

Complaining about each other's behavior in a linear fashion, each sees the other as the cause. People put arbitrary endings on events that simplify human interaction and tend to put their own actions in the best light. Their friends or the organized groups of which they are a part may then support these points of view.

We realize that there are one-sided relationships and true victims in the world. When a woman is raped, for instance, it would be wrong to imply that she contributed to the assault. Sustained conflict, however, is often complicated, and it is useful to broaden the stories and allow them to be interconnected in order for the disputants to apprehend how they organize one another's behavior in unpleasant ways.

The Catholic militia groups of Northern Ireland saw the assassinations they carried out and their bombing of pubs and government buildings as caused by the actions of the Protestants on the other side. What they were blind to was how their actions, in turn, invited the response of the other. The Protestants, for their part, have trouble seeing how their historic subjugation of the Catholics in the name of nationalism also contributes to the conflict. This interactional dance, or circularity as it is called in the family therapy literature, is frequently invisible to participants.

BUILDING COMMITMENT AND TRUST

Nemeroff and Tukey identify structural issues that build commitment or at least do not increase participant inconvenience and erode commitment (this volume). Time is precious, so meetings should be scheduled for the convenience of the group members. Starting and stopping times should be strictly adhered to. Nice surroundings for the meetings create an environment conducive to talking. We would also note that a well-appointed room and other markers of status such as a nice view from the window and spaciousness indirectly communicate the worth of the group to others. Serving beverages and food is also a statement that the participants are valued.

Some groups, because of the level of conflict, must remain anonymous. One of the authors of this chapter, who is a photographer, recalls a meeting where he was expressly asked not to take photographs of the participants. The participants' talking with one another may have been considered by some a traitorous act. In less contentious dialogues, such as race relations on university campuses, acknowledging the dialogues and the service they provide to the university community may raise their perceived worth in the eyes of potential participants. Publishing awards and any recognition the group receives also serves a similar purpose.

Beyond structural consideration, a good moderator can do other things to facilitate the group. Quickly learning the names and personal interests of all participants expedites the building of personal relationships. The moderator should also try to make personal contact with each person in the group. Harold Saunders in A *Public Peace Process* (1999, xvii) recounts his first meeting with Golda Meir after the war broke out. Saunders's wife had just passed away, and Meir said, "I am terribly sorry about your loss. I lost a lot of people too; I guess we feel somewhat the same way." A history of hundreds of such personal exchanges within a dialogue group builds commitment, disrupts the pattern of the participants see their antagonists, and opens up the possibility of new perceptions.

In the beginning phase for all groups there is a tendency for the participants to look to the leader for guidance. There are few people who do not respond well to honest praise. In praising people it is best to be specific and be prepared to back your comment up with documentation. Avoid global praise, for instance, "I can tell you are a caring person." Consider the evidence that led you to the global statement: "In telling Pho that his judgment of Westerners was harsh you appeared to struggle with how to make your criticism so he could hear you. I appreciate that." Since moderators will seldom be able to respond to all praiseworthy behavior, postsession comments and e-mails are appropriate ways to appreciate people. E-mails are best considered to be a nonsecure way of communicating. Dialogues that must remain secret should not be done in e-mail.

Participants in a dialogue, as in family therapy, will have different styles. Some wade in and take the floor; others sit back and assess the lay of the land before participating. While participant guidelines suggest that they listen and not interrupt, issues of balance are important for the moderator to consider. If one of the sides to a conflict is perceived to monopolize the time, participants may waiver in their commitment to the group. Time in each meeting does not have to be equally apportioned, but disputing parties should perceive that they were given an equal opportunity to express themselves over time. During the first few meeting of a dialogue, the moderator should be particularly attentive to this issue and attempt a balanced participation within each meeting. As people develop relationships with the moderator and the participants, they will be more forgiving and this will be less critical.

The moderator should look for natural pauses in the conversation. These pauses can be used to solicit other points of view. If time balance appears to be an issue for the group the moderator may go as far as to say, "We have been talking about one particular point of view for a while. Can we hear another point of view?" If a meeting has been particularly one-sided in use of time, this can be balanced by starting the next meeting by soliciting other points of view. If the moderator judges that there are people who want to talk but are not, she can gently prompt them to do so. When people remain cautious about talking, a good strategy is to approach them in private. Listen to what the obstacles to talking are and help identify solutions. It is important that people know that every effort will be made to create a space that is safe for dialogue but that they will not be pressured to talk.

Many dialogue groups, particularly on university campuses, have moderators who are also participants. In such instances, for the sake of balance, comoderators should represent different constituencies within the group. Practice wisdom among family therapists and therapists in general is that cotherapy is more difficult than having just one therapist. The point extends easily to group moderators. If comoderation is arranged, the moderators should anticipate that they will spend a great deal of time outside of the dialogue, examining the process and how they define the relationships among themselves. To ignore processing how the dialogue group ran and their reactions to one another as moderators can be an invitation to another layer of tensions and struggles, which will inevitably spread to the dialogue group as participants take sides. We believe a single moderator, who is not a participant, best serves most groups. The moderator should be someone whom those participating in the dialogue view as reputable, with a history that illustrates his interest in the topic and an ability to see many sides of an issue.

Sustained dialogue groups need to have trust in their moderators, but trust is a slippery word. Initial trust of the moderator is based on the endorsement from the people who helped select her and their reputation among the dialogue participants. The moderator would be well served by the organizing group strongly touting her skills when introducing her to the participants for the first time. We have little reason to trust someone until she has proven herself.

The trust that is most essential is participants' confidence that the moderator can help them alter their relationships and in so doing open up possibilities for conflict resolution. Alexander et al. (1976) and Barton and Alexander (1981), where functional family therapy was first developed, identify two skill sets that, when combined, result in the ability to influence relationships and are the best predictors of successful change: relationship skills and structuring skills.

Relationship skills keep people in therapy. Good family therapists tend to have strong relationship skills. Relationship skills will also serve sustained dialogue moderators and foster trust in the dialogue process as well as commitment to the process. Relationship skills include interpersonal warmth, responding to participants in a nonblaming manner, the ability to diffuse tension through humor, judiciously using self-disclosure to provide information to participants, and being able to integrate the affective and behavioral realms of people's experience (Barton and Alexander 1981, 430). These last two characteristics may be less obvious to the reader and will therefore be discussed.

In most cases, moderators will have had their own experiences with acrimonious disputes, prejudice, discrimination, and xenophobia. Personal struggles can become indirect teaching stories and provide useful information. In using such stories the moderator should avoid being heroic in all the stories lest he be considered a braggart. On occasion, when we do groups together, we have told the following story: Neal, because of his experiences with violence, seldom sits in front of windows at restaurants, always sits facing the door, has an exit strategy, and has some awareness of who is entering and leaving. Susan, because of her experiences, tends to see what is beautiful in the environment. Neither perception is right or wrong, but both are certainly skewed. This bifurcation usually gets a good laugh when we conduct groups together and talk about our "guns and roses" experiences. This story, among other things, informs participants as to the fluidity and personal nature of perception.

Many statements that people make are incomplete. Either they ignore the affective or the behavioral, or they accent one more than the other. It is important to listen to what is unsaid or unaccented, which is often communicated nonverbally and may be contrary to the verbal message or give that message a different twist. A dialogue participant may say the following, for instance: "Illegal immigrants should just leave. They don't belong here." Such a statement is behavioral in its scope; there is no affective component. The moderator notes that the participant looks troubled and slightly fearful and responds with the following: "The presence of illegal immigrants troubles and scares you somewhat." The participant then goes on to say how his father is a janitor at a plant and may be losing his job because illegal immigrants will work for a cheaper wage. This new information frames the issue in a more complex way and will provide material for the problem solving that occurs later. The unsaid also frames the participant in a more human way and invites empathy for his statement, which may have been viewed as judgmental.

STAGE TWO

Stage two of the Saunders model, "Mapping and Naming Problems and Relationships," includes:

1. Establishing the character or tone of the group
2. Initiating discussion
3. Storytelling
4. Generating a sense of linked relationships

5. Managing emotions

6. Mapping the problems that prompted the dialogue

7. Prioritizing problems for attention

8. Overcoming resistance to acknowledging the legitimacy of opponents

ESTABLISHING THE CHARACTER OR TONE

In order for the dialogue group or family therapy to be effective, it must result in a different form of relating to the conflict than the participants have experienced in the past. People tend to stick to fixed patterns or processes of relating. If you do not believe we are patterning animals, conduct the following experiment: Raise your hands above your head, interlace your fingers, and bring your hands down. If your right thumb is on top, you are right-thumbed, and if your left is on top you are left-thumbed. There is no relationship between being right- and left-thumbed and right- and left-handedness. Interlace your fingers in the opposite way and see how awkward it feels. Before this experiment, you probably did not even know you were right- or left-thumbed. You have no emotional commitment to the way you interlace your fingers, yet to change this pattern would be challenging. Now imagine changing a pattern of behavior that your relationships support and to which you are emotionally and intellectually committed.

Beginning family therapists are often concerned that they will miss critical times of intervention. Supervisors will frequently tell them, "Just wait. If you could not muster what to say, the pattern will occur again." Generally the more conflicted a relationship, the more fixed and immutable the patterns of relating. In fact, one way of characterizing problem relationships is that they have inflexible patterns. This is no less true of conflicting groups in a sustained dialogue.

The moderator of a sustained dialogue, in an attempt to structure the conversation, will have participants affirm covenant statements such as the one detailed by Saunders (1999, 271) and encourage participants to use ground rules (Katnani and Parker 2003, 106). While these are worthwhile interventions and may retard unproductive patterns of interacting, such negative patterns are more enduring. It will take time and an alteration in relationship before they will change.

Preachers on the pulpit have a style of patterned speech with which they deliver their sermon. Most people can make at least an attempt at recreating the speech patterns, word choices, and cadence of such speech. Individuals experienced in arguing one side of a conflict also have a method of delivering their message that is dependent on a selective review of history, careful positioning on the argument, the use of polemics, and an established speech pattern. As Saunders points out (1999, 112), sustained dialogue requires new habits. The emphasis is on talking analytically and civilly as opposed to talking polemically or positionally, which will not lead to change.

Covenants, civility, and analytical talk slow down negative exchanges and open up the possibility of different patterns of interaction. They give the participants an opportunity to think before responding. Sustained dialogue moderators slow the interactional process down for the sake of thinking. Developing what Saunders calls whole relationships is primary to changing interactional patterns, and we will be discuss it in the section on storytelling and generating a sense of linked relationships.

INITIATING DISCUSSION

Moderators structure dialogues so that a new pattern of relationship can occur. It is the burden of participants to take the initiative and talk in a new way. Our experiences with conflictual relationships in family therapy tell us that it is not difficult to get people to talk. What is difficult is to structure the conversation in a manner that is different from their familiar ways of talking. Still, occasionally, you may have groups that are hesitant to talk. In the event that this occurs, it is best to reassess safety issues. The most common reason for people not talking is that they do not feel safe. Issues of confidentiality, which are part of the convent, should be reviewed. If there are legal proceedings that involve people in the group and the issues being considered, this could be an impediment to discussion. Participants may be concerned that group members could be subpoenaed.

In "Diving In: A Handbook for Improving Race Relations on College Campuses Through the Process of Stained Dialogue" (this volume), Nemeroff and Tukey recommend a process of careful documentation and a rotating note taker. There may, however, be situations where it is not appropriate to take notes in the group. Divorce mediators, as a matter of course, take notes to be used during the mediation and shred them in front of the parties at the end of each meeting.

When people begin a sustained dialogue they have no real reason to trust one another. They are strangers in conflict. Trust begins when people find they have not been harmed after taking small risks. There are several strategies that moderators can use to facilitate this. The moderator can pose a question and let each party respond or assign reflective tasks that people can complete outside of the group and report on within the group (Nemeroff and Tukey, this volume). Saunders suggests that in groups where silence is an issue, people write a statement outside of the group detailing why the do not feel comfortable opening up (1999, 119). A variation on this, when there are enough members and diversity to ensure anonymity, is to have participants anonymously write their concerns about participating on index cards. The responses are then read by the moderator and discussed by the group

We usually begin addressing conflicts in families by telling participants that we would like to give each person a few minutes to talk uninterrupted about what they would like to see change for the family and for him- or herself. Beginning with the favored outcome, an approach suggested in strategic family therapy, starts discussion on a positive note and emphasizes that we are there for the purpose of change, which may encourage the participants to begin. After each person has spoken, the moderator can summarize the commonalities among their desires and comments.

Another approach, suggested by solution-focused therapy (Berg 1994, 91–97, 133; de Shazer 1988b, 131–51), is to identify exceptions or times when antagonistic couples and families have gotten along. This approach can be applied to individuals from conflicting groups. When was there a momentary reduction in tension or peace between your groups? What was it that you were doing that was helping this happen and what were they doing as well? Such questions help begin developing relationship linkages.

STORYTELLING AND GENERATING LINKED RELATIONSHIPS

Sustained dialogue is about changing relationships and in doing so establishing the bedrock of lasting conflict resolution between groups. Change is related to developing modifications in stories and begins with the processing of people's experiences. In stage 2 people are invited to tell their stories. The couple in the Ogden Nash poem illustrates that it is human nature to punctuate stories in a linear manner: her nagging makes me drink. Such a story does not link relationships. To link relationships would mean examining how he invites his wife to be a nag. Richer relationship linking would also go on to examine how his behavior contributes to her nagging. The story would then be circular in its view and in its causal explanations of how each keeps the cycle going.

People will begin their storytelling with unlinked accounts or linear stories. The family therapist Donald Johnson used to say, "Why should we not believe that people are always doing the best that they can?" The task of a dialogue facilitator is to assist people in linking linear patterns into circular ones. It is only when the connections between others' behavior and one's own are made that linear patterns are recognized. Once circularity is perceived, the solution becomes a joint responsibility, and the previous patterns become open to change. This is well illustrated by the playwright Jean-Paul Sartre in *No Exit*. Garcin is escorted to hell, where he expects to be tortured by red-hot pincers. Instead, he is in a room with two women for all of eternity. Each is destined to be the others' torturer in an economy of power. Garcin, in talking to one of the women, Inez, states: "They've laid their snare damned cunningly—like a cobweb. If you make any movement, if you raise your hand to fan yourself, Estelle and I feel a little tug. Alone, none of us can save himself or herself; we're linked together inextricably." This is the state of conflict with which sustained dialogue facilitators deal.

Family therapy has taught us that few individuals see themselves as the villains or devils in relationships. More likely they see themselves as reasonable people who have been victims of the other's behavior and occasionally act in heroic ways. This difference in perceptions is at least in part caused by how events are punctuated. People place artificial endings and beginnings on events that shape their point of view.

Imagine that during a sustained dialogue a man tells the group that a member of his family was brutally killed as part of an ongoing conflict. The natural inclination is to think of him as a victim of a brutal assault. Further on in the conversation, you find out that the family member was killed after a raid, in which he was involved, that resulted in the deaths of several members of the other group. If we stopped here, whom would your sympathies be aligned with? Adding to this history, you learn his participation in the conflict began after a daughter was killed in a bombing incident. Perceptions are fluid. Endings and beginnings are accepted illusions that are more or less useful for people.

In marital therapy it is diagnostic when the members of a couple present their story. Each member of a couple in conflict has stories that so poorly match the other's that it is sometimes difficult to believe that they are married. Good relationships, in contrast, have commonly held storylines. As people move through a sustained dialogue and become less conflictual the threads of their stories will have greater congruence. This is not to say that the stories are more reality based than previous stories, just that they are more useful to a sustained working relationship.

History is frequently used by participants in a conflict in a manner similar to a Rorschach inkblot test. The perceiver organizes the blots based on his view of the world and confuses his view with "reality." "Reality" is always filtered through our perceptions and so is not knowable. One need look no further than women's studies and black studies programs for fresh views of U.S. history that challenge past perceptions of reality. In altering personal histories, three tools are available to the dialogue moderator: punctuation, changing histories, and generating a sense of linked relationships. The cause and effect of a series of events can be altered by moving the punctuation. One may move the beginning of a series of events further back in time, thus adding additional elements to a sequence. The same thing can be done to endings. A question concerning what happens before or what happened after lead to the rewriting of a sequence and may change the meaning associated with events.

According to Cloé Madanes, a cofounder of strategic therapy, people usually have five to seven events that they organize as a history to justify who they are and what they are doing (personal communication, 1991). There is a tendency to overlook other events that do not support this perception of self. Add to these events and you change who the person is. These events are overlooked because of what we jokingly call the VW phenomena. When you are thinking about buying a car there is a tendency to see cars of the type you may be interested in while previously you did not notice them. Add to a person's perceptions and you increase the likelihood of a change in behavior.

Similarly, according to solution-focused therapy, people with a particular problem are often so focused on that problem that they do not notice when it is not there. On the other hand, they may discount those times when the problem did not happen as unimportant because they did not last long enough or were not intense enough. A depressed individual may not notice times she was not depressed because they were of short duration and so were dismissed as unimportant. Alternatively, she may be less depressed and dismiss this because she did not feel ecstatic. Identifying times when a problem does not happen locates solutions that are already in place but have been overlooked. Such solutions need to be identified and expanded.

Generating linkages in problems is essential to creating cooperation between parties to a conflict. If I believe there is a problem and that the problem is entirely of your making, all I can do is complain. It is not my problem to solve. Often in family therapy, a parent will complain about a child or partner while not seeing any connection between his own behavior and the problem. From this vantage point, the parent has no sense of responsibility for change. If one sees a child, for example, as a pathological liar, then there is only a one-party solution—the child must change. If the child lies because she is judged and punished too harshly it becomes a linked-relationship problem: Wherever you find a liar you will find a judge, and judges would not exist if there were not people who commit offenses.

Asking circular questions creates linking between the action/response patterns of the dialogue partners. Two sample circular questions are presented here. When there was a time of peace, what were you doing, what was their response, and how did that effect you? How did it feel to have the antagonism diminished, what did you do because of that, and how did they respond to what you did?

MANAGING EMOTIONS

People who enter into sustained dialogue begin with conflictual patterns of relating that are both typical and predictable. While conflict may be uncomfortable, it does offer the security of predictability. The changed talk of sustained dialogue, on the other hand, is scary for that reason. Additionally, dyads in conflict are inherently unstable. When two people argue a third person is located who will take sides. Think of two friends who are breaking up; typically one or both of them will come to you for commiseration. You are, as a friend, expected to side with that one against the "outrageous behavior" of the former partner. To do otherwise is considered traitorous.

People will desire to form coalitions within sustained dialogues based on points of view. As points of view change, so will these coalitions, and this change can provoke anxiety. Restrictions on not being in the same dialogue group as an established friend and not being able to represent an organization subvert already established coalitions. If the moderators are not identified with a particular side they should expect that participants will attempt to coalesce with them. It is important that they remain neutral. The easiest way not to take sides is to avoid supporting any particular position. A difficult and more sophisticated way of remaining neutral is to take sides with portions of each person's position. This is done through reframing undesirable responses in a way that emphasizes the unsaid positive aspects. If one person were to scream at another, for instance, his response might be framed as a desperate attempt to be heard, although this may not be the best way to get attention.

Honest and frank dialogue requires that participants be aware of one another's sense of hurt, slights, anger, and even outrage. A good dialogue moderator will slow down the process of discussion when meetings become heated so that individuals may pick their words carefully and maintain civility. The moderator should uphold her prerogative of taking a brief recess to allow participants to cool down if she believes that such a time out is to the benefit of the dialogue process. Such an agreement can become part of the covenant for the group.

MAPPING THE PROBLEMS THAT
PROMPT DIALOGUE AND PRIORITIZING

Parties to a sustained dialogue have a deeply rooted history of conflict. They may be hurt, angry, sad, outraged, and indignant. In all likelihood they will believe themselves to be justified in their behavior and looking for change from the other side. Stories will be told that justify their position. In short, as mentioned previously, they are complainants. They will perceive that they have a problem but feel it is the responsibility of the other party to change. In a frank mapping of the situation that has precipitated the dialogue, members will be able to identify sources of conflict and how the conflict has influenced their relationship. A fuller picture of the conflict is created when the linearity of positions is replaced with the double description of how each side's behavior helps sustain the conflict. It is difficult to accept the legitimacy of an antagonist's position and one's own responsibility in sustaining conflict.

Acceptance of double descriptions for problems or the formulation of circular causal explanations signals the ending of stage 2. If stage 2 has been successful the emphasis of the sustained dialogue can shift and begin to take relationship more for granted while placing greater emphasis on sequencing problems so that an effective plan of correction can be formulated. When the relationships within the sustained dialogue group are healthier, the group can be more task focused.

OVERCOMING RESISTANCE TO ACKNOWLEDGING
THE LEGITIMACY OF OPPONENTS

The acceptance of linked relationships or circular description of problems requires acknowledging one's own contributions to a problem while also acknowledging that one's opponent has a legitimate point of view. In family therapy it is axiomatic that participants will see their own positions as being reasonable. Furthermore, since we normally see ourselves as reasonable it may feel traitorous or disloyal for our loved ones to be unsupportive. In a sustained dialogue, similarly close relationships with the antagonists may not be present. Thus there is no sense of disloyalty if they do not agree with our perception. It is still a challenge, however, to see their position as reasonable. More challenging is acknowledging their position as legitimate and acting in a supportive manner toward their point of view. To honestly look at the other side's position as legitimate and to take action accordingly may feel like the act of a traitor even when there is cognitive understanding of the reasons. The heart has its own logic.

Saunders (1999) identifies two means of moving past this resistance. First is a walk through history. Participants identify key historical events, acknowledge traumatic events, and go through a process of contrition and forgiveness. This is similar to historically oriented therapy. Such matters can also be addressed through a more here-and-now orientation where resistances are dealt with as they become obstacles to solving present problems. The bias in contemporary therapy is toward a more efficient focus on the here and now. The past is addressed as it surfaces in the present relationships.

A BRIEF COMMENT ON STAGES THREE THROUGH FIVE

Stage models are a great pedagogical device but are at best a soft tool that only somewhat approximates the real world. In a sustained dialogue group, there will be participants in various stages. Who is in which stage will depend on the issues discussed and the characteristics of each individual's life. Moderators would be wise to monitor relationship issues and be prepared to digress into previous stage issues many times in the life of the group. Often, running groups consists of taking two steps forward and one step back.

A CLOSING WORD ON PROCESS

Key to understanding human interaction from a family-therapy orientation is the ability to read interpersonal process. Most models of family therapy tell you what to view and what to do when it comes to interpersonal process.

Process is how people use both their verbal and nonverbal interactions to define their relationships with others. On a date, for instance, there are rules of exclusivity. It would be bad form for your date to get up from the table and go sit with someone else. Boundaries are drawn around the candidate couple for the night, and their behavior serves to support the relationship rules. A good "mantra" for attempting to understand process in sustained dialogue is a question: "How is this behavior an attempt to define relationships?" Everything that participants do should be examined in terms of how it is an attempt to define their relationships to others in the group.

SECTION IV

BUILDING PRACTICE AND RESEARCH

Introduction

THE THEORETICAL LITERATURE on deliberative democracy has grown substantially in recent years, and a great many academic and theoretical propositions have been advanced for expanding the role of deliberation and dialogue in public life and problem solving. At the same time, a large and growing community of practitioners in communities across the country is working every day to deal with real issues and solve problems by talking them out. Yet the actual interface between theory and practice in this arena has been extremely limited, and considerable resistance is encountered from both theorists and practitioners to the "pracademic" ideal that theory should be informed by practice and vice versa. Throughout this volume, we have sought to bring together considerations of theory and practice.

In this final section, two additional chapters are offered that bear on this issue. In the first, coeditor Roger A. Lohmann, founding director of the Nova Institute, takes on the question of locating and marshalling the resources necessary to mount effective public deliberation or sustained dialogue efforts. While it would be premature to call this a bona fide "economics of deliberation and dialogue," this chapter points in that direction. (Were we attempting to reach a different, more theoretical audience, in fact, this chapter would probably have the word "prolegomena" in the title; even so, it represents a very preliminary beginning.)

Finally, Jon Van Til and Dolly Ford look toward the future and offer a position of cautious optimism regarding the futures of both public deliberation and sustained dialogue.

17

SOCIAL ENTREPRENEURSHIP IN THE PRACTICE
OF DELIBERATION AND DIALOGUE

Roger A. Lohmann

EARLIER IN THIS VOLUME, JON Van Til reviews the major foundational activities in the emergence of public deliberation and sustained dialogue as distinctive approaches to public talk. His focus is on the efforts of a number of social-change agents using a variety of distinct approaches. In important respects, public deliberation and sustained dialogue are just two components of a much larger ensemble of approaches collaborating, competing, and sometimes conflicting with one another for public attention and the scarce resources necessary to make public talk and peaceful coexistence among groups more real. John Van Til and Lisa Bedinger review the pros and cons of several of these approaches in earlier chapters in this volume. Over recent decades since peacemaking and citizen participation arrived on the scene, philosophers, notably Jürgen Habermas (1984) have detailed more deeply than ever before the pragmatic, communicative, or conversational basis of democratic political institutions—something Harold Saunders (2005) adeptly terms "politics as relationship."

At the same time, guided typically by their own insights into and intuitions of these systematic scholarly soundings and their own sometimes profound pracademic understandings, several generations of community practitioners in social work and elsewhere have in their own noisy, boisterous, bumptious ways gone about establishing a diverse web of claims, calls for action, coalitions, organizations, networks, and programs. Some of these represent genuine breakthroughs and innovations; others are merely clever twists on wording and effective marketing.

Regardless, the underlying insight is solid and profound: genuine public conversation is not spontaneous, random, or well supported in an era of deep and abiding institutional commitments to "democracy" as a name for politics controlled by huge, well-heeled corporate interest groups.[1] Hence, most individuals, groups, or communities acting upon their interest in advancing public talk face a relatively daunting range of limited and narrow options. But many face the challenges of making public talk happen with enthusiasm, drive, and ingenuity that can be truly awe-inspiring.

In the practice of public talk, just as in social service, community development, and numerous other fields, the quest for resources and public support has generally come to be known as "grantsmanship."[2] It was called this for the very good, practical reason that in the period from 1965 through 1980, "the age of grants" (Lohmann and Lohmann 2002), support for deliberation and dialogue most typically took the form of government or foundation grants. Whereas in the distant European or colonial American past, these social entrepreneurs might have sought out individual wealthy or aristocratic patrons for support, in contemporary society institutional grants most often do the trick.

One tempting notion can be dismissed. Talk is not, in this case, cheap. It is unlikely that greater collective commitment to deliberation and dialogue or deliberative democracy in most communities will come about without significant infusions of additional resources. It is also unlikely that deliberation and dialogue will come into widespread use simply because they are good ideas. If they are to be more widely adopted, strategies and practices need to be planned, organized, staged, conducted, and taught by skilled and knowledgeable practitioners, organizers, and teachers and guided by informed and targeted research. All of these things are costly in both money and time. Citizen-to-citizen deliberations and dialogue to address long-term public conflicts will never be cost-free endeavors. Public and strategic conversations unfold through time and take up time in people's lives, time they cannot spend in other pursuits as a result.

In the pracademic domain outlined in this book, where scholarly and practice interests truly meet and converge, grantsmanship—the pursuit of grant funding for programs and services—is but one important way of supporting public talk, one type of change agency or, as it is increasingly known in our commercial civilization, social enterprise. The change agents who write grants and in myriad other ways stimulate public support for deliberation and dialogue are, truly, social entrepreneurs. Likewise, the committees, organizations (mostly nonprofit), networks, and communities they foster and sustain represent important contemporary forms of social enterprise. "Social enterprise," "entrepreneurship," and "entrepreneurs" are popular terms at the moment and mean many different things to different users. So what do we mean by them?

> An entrepreneur has been defined . . . as the catalytic agent who sets into motion new enterprises with new combinations of production and exchange. . . . Although the concept of 'entrepreneurship' is closely linked with the for-profit sector and may seem out of place in the nonprofit world, it is not. Both kinds of enterprises are the result of the entrepreneur's innovation, leadership, imagination, effort, and ability. . . . [W]e define entrepreneurs in either sector as self-directed, innovative leaders who start an enterprise, with new combinations of production and exchange to either promote goods and services for private profit or to promote a social cause.
>
> (HANDY, RANADE, AND KASSAM 2007, 384)

Such terms seldom appear in discussions of deliberation and dialogue and probably don't occur together elsewhere in this book, in part because most authors are focused on the main event—the conversations themselves—and not the backstage logistics that made those conversations possible.[3] At least one other chapter in this book, Bedinger's, deals with some of the backstage logistics or the social technology of deliberation and dialogue, though not with the resources and costs involved. Thus, some clarification may be necessary before the relevance of this chapter to the enterprise of this book may be clear.

The Ashoka Foundation, an international nonprofit/nongovernmental organization (or INGO) devoted to developing the practice of social entrepreneurship, for example, says, "The job of a social entrepreneur is to recognize when a part of society is stuck and to provide new ways to get it unstuck" (http://www.ashoka.org/fellows/social_entrepreneur.cfm). "Stuck" is a term that characterizes very nicely many conflict situations where sustained dialogue can apply. "Stuck" is also a term that Mansbridge (1990), Barber (1998c), and others might be comfortable with to describe their critiques of democracy in contemporary society. In its current interest-group and representational forms, democracy does indeed appear at times to be stuck.

But how are we to get a divided community or democracy unstuck? Bill Drayton, the CEO, chair, and founder of Ashoka, and thus a social entrepreneur in our sense, offers this rather fulsome metaphor: "Social entrepreneurs are not content just to give a fish or teach how to fish. They will

not rest until they have revolutionized the fishing industry" (http://www
.skollfoundation.org/aboutsocialentrepreneurship/index.asp).

Is such talk of social entrepreneurship something completely and entirely new? Certainly not. Social workers and others have been talking about
similar matters for decades. However, lack of novelty shouldn't be seen as a
particularly damning criticism: social change theory and practice have an
extensive history of periodically putting old wine into new bottles, a history
that probably can be traced most of the way back to ancient Greek philosophers for those who wish to do so. What is most noteworthy about the
social-entrepreneurial model today is the remarkable number of potential
entrepreneurs/change agents/reformers who are energized by this notion.
Also of interest is that many of them and their organizations are new to the
social-change game. At a time when other competing models of gradual or
incremental change (e.g., many planned-change and development models)
appear to have largely run their course, advancing democracy through social
enterprises devoted to "selling democracy" may be one of the most viable
options available.

The twin concepts of social entrepreneurs (people) and social enterprises
(organizations) thus offer a fairly neat and tidy way to begin to get at certain
important but largely neglected aspects of the rapidly growing institutional
framework of organizations and networks of people devoting substantial
amounts of time, energy, and resources to advancing the cause of more
deliberative forms of democracy.

In general terms I wish to suggest first that advancing the practice of
deliberation and dialogue in the contemporary United States is a social-
entrepreneurial challenge for individuals, groups, organizations, and communities.[4] At any given point, delivering even a brief program of deliberation
on a widespread basis or a program of sustained dialogue over an extended
period requires acquiring and using significant resources: human, social,
financial, and intellectual capital. As David Robinson's chapter in this book
shows, the success of deliberation and dialogue is deeply embedded in notions of social capital: networks of trust and relationships that form the matrix within which meaningful economic relations can be established.

In the new global democratic order, interest in deliberation and dialogue
as a manifestation of civil society is genuinely international, as the example
of "shuttle diplomacy" in which Harold Saunders played a critical role first
revealed so clearly. The authors of this book have been involved as social entrepreneurs in religious, ethnic, gender, class, and other "cross-difference"

deliberation and dialogue efforts in more than a dozen countries on four continents. Such efforts are usually carried out by social entrepreneurs who share a similar profile; studies of nonprofit entrepreneurs have identified several characteristics: willingness to take risks, self-directedness, leadership, innovation, and a focus on what can be done for and with others (Pilz 1995, quoted in Handy, Ranade, and Kassam 2007). And these, in general, are the same resource expectations felt by the leaders of deliberation and dialogue efforts, as this edited e-mail message, sent over the NCDD discussion list in 2006, suggests: "We started an annual deliberative and dialogue forum on [insert your favorite topic here] *and need funding support/collaboration in implementing this program across the* [insert your community here], on an ongoing basis."

Practitioners and academics alike typically see the essence of deliberation and dialogue in terms of enhanced communication and expression of views. Some may also see this in idealistic terms as reflecting the eventual triumph of reason and noble ideals over ignorance, error, and falsehoods. Some—guided by a profound insight of recent feminist political theory—might see this as a triumph of voice over silence. Yet sooner or later, the underlying economic reality of resource limits must be reckoned with; greater measures of deliberative democracy and more widespread recognition of the importance of relationships in resolving conflict require the strategic deployment of substantial resources in contemporary postindustrial society. And it isn't always clear where those resources are to come from.

Even with an abundance of volunteers, the ideals of deliberation and dialogue can make relatively little headway in the general polity or advance beyond the status of noble but impractical ideas without significant investments of time, energy, and other resources. Thus, a fundamental concern for anyone working in these efforts must be where these resources are to be found. As Handy, Ranade, and Kassam (2007) notes: "Entrepreneurs, whether producing goods and services under the aegis of for-profit institutions or nonprofit organizations face similar challenges: identifying opportunities, promoting innovative ideas, implementing ideas into viable enterprises, mobilizing resources, and undertaking risks inherent in starting a new project."

A pracademic union of attention to the theoretical concerns that have interested many legal and political theorists over recent decades with the urgency of organizing a particular set of conversations in a particular place at a particular time is likely to involve an approach to social change much like that described by contemporary social-entrepreneurial thinkers. Advancing deliberation and dialogue becomes a matter of "selling" the recognition that there is a problem with interest-group democracy or with community violence to potential sponsors and then selling distinct, identifiable branded efforts at deliberation and dialogue as legitimate approaches to this problem.

The problem of sustained dialogue currently involves a particularly challenging sales and marketing task: even in the best of circumstances, there is the challenge of convincing the emotionally wrought parties to a conflict that talk is better than fighting. In a post-9/11 world with major segments of our national community fervently committed to imperialism, the notion of conflict resolution by any means other than armed intervention, aggression, and violence seems to many to be an anachronism: Why talk with your enemies? Isn't it better, safer, or more secure to brand them as terrorist and to imprison, torture, and kill them? In this, as in other cases, the entrepreneurial challenges of resources is remarkably recursive. Even talking about whether to talk about such matters requires time and access to other resources!

In economic terms, the current supply of willing sellers for the concept of more widespread deliberation and dialogue appears larger than the supply of available buyers willing to invest resources. There may be a market for deliberation and dialogue, but it has some distinctive characteristics. It is, for example, largely a third-party market in which those who consume the services are not the same as those asked to pay the bills. While huge numbers of our contemporaries would readily pay fifty dollars or more for a concert, sporting event, or article of clothing, we suspect that few, if any, would pay a comparable amount to participate in any type of citizenship process.[5] Thus, the market for deliberation and dialogue seems peculiarly skewed; social entrepreneurs/producers willing to organize and conduct deliberation and dialogue events are currently more numerous than either third-party buyers of such services or the citizen-participants who are the ultimate consumers of such services. It is also possible, however, that the skew runs along an entirely different diagonal, a kind of idealism gap or philanthropic deficit: that merely seeing the need for deliberation and dialogue does not result in personal willingness to make the necessary resource commitments in any of the usual forms—personal expenditures, willingness to pay higher taxes, or voluntary, philanthropic donations. Grant or donated funds are believed to be so essential (including for legitimation purposes) that more self-sustaining entrepreneurial approaches are seldom tested.

This might suggest that the heart of the resource problem for support of deliberation and dialogue is what in economics is recognized as a problem of cost allocation: why should people, groups, organizations, foundations, government agencies, and others commit their time and the other scarce resources at their disposal to public deliberation or sustained dialogue when there are so many other legitimate, worthwhile activities for them to invest in?[6]

In this vein, opportunity cost may be the most important resource issue facing both public deliberation and sustained dialogue today. This is the heart of the entrepreneurial challenge facing those change agents seeking to promote deliberative democracy. While the problem is usually addressed from a narrowly limited "commonsense" perspective (where can we get a grant to do this activity? would people pay to attend this event?), this chapter suggests that there are few simple answers to be found in that direction. Large numbers of grant makers and donors are not likely to forgo their current interests and shift their priorities to support deliberation and dialogue any time soon. Thus, the problem of securing resources for deliberation and dialogue activities needs to be recognized for what it is using concepts like social entrepreneurship and social capital: an issue of human-, political-, and social-capital acquisition and market formation. This involves several related questions that together outline an approach to what it is that can be gained and given up:

- Who are the potential "stakeholders" with something important to gain or lose from deliberation or dialogue (including such important gains as a deeper sense of citizenship or peace for participants in a conflict and losses of power, face, or wealth)?
- Can any of the anticipated losers be redefined as winners?
- What are the actual costs of participation for participants (not just dollar outlays but opportunity costs and so on)?
- What are the opportunity costs for funders? (Why, in particular, should a donor or foundation faced with many different requests fund a deliberation or dialogue effort?)
- What are the products/packages (services or benefits) offered by deliberation or dialogue?
- Are those products distinctive, and do they possess clear brand identity (as, for example, Head Start, Habitat for Humanity, the Red Cross, and United Way do)?

- Are those products, services, and benefits being packaged in ways that genuinely appeal to potential participants?

An important research agenda resides in questions of where, how, and why such choices will be made. The direction of resources to this set of concerns, whether in the form of grants, donations, fees and user payments, volunteer time, or some other medium will depend on the answers to those questions.

The opportunity cost of sustained dialogue can be measured fairly precisely—and, in some cases, quite dramatically—in terms of the cost of conflict averted and accompanying violence deferred as a consequence of dialogue.[7] This leads to a familiar cost-benefit formulation: the effectiveness of dialogue and deliberation can be measured in terms of the reduced likelihood of communities incurring losses from property destruction, death, work and business disrupted, and expenditures for police, fire, and military services. (This is the background of much of the research reported in this volume, especially the work of Nolan et al.) These and other, quite real consequences will be higher in some instances and at some times than at others. In general, the cost of sustained dialogue in any given community will be variable while the costs of putting on the program will remain relatively more constant. Thus, the anticipated benefit will rise and fall accordingly.

Of particular note is the likelihood that the cost-benefit ratio of sustained dialogue will be greatest—that is, the benefits will be proportionately greatest relative to the costs incurred—in the period when conflict is high but before the outbreak of violence. It probably costs no more to initiate a sustained dialogue when the likelihood of violence is high than at other times, but the payoffs will almost certainly be more immediate, obvious, and significant. Focusing on such a cost-benefit model allows us to see more clearly the dilemma this poses: if one point of the term "sustained" in the Saunders model of sustained dialogue is that there are advantages to conducting dialogue in noncrisis periods—indeed, to preventing whenever possible the rise of such crises—why do we so often wait until a crisis arises before acting? There is another research agenda in answering that question.

The opportunity cost of public deliberation is somewhat more complex to conceptualize in entrepreneurial terms. There are additional factors to consider, such as the opportunity cost of leadership. Sustained dialogue most often occurs in fairly dramatic conditions of conflict and violence and is typically a matter of loss of public goods where everyone is affected and action by leaders is required, even demanded. Public deliberation efforts often arise under much less urgent conditions. Why would a community leader enter into a difficult and costly sustained dialogue effort, for example, when it could potentially raise difficult or embarrassing questions and when doing nothing is a viable alternative? A public relations campaign to spin the issue will almost certainly be less costly. Such logic can easily lead to a high probability that public officials will oppose (tacitly and quietly, at least) many such efforts. What is the alternative against which the deliberation of citizens is to be measured or compared? Silence? Is this an issue of voice? Of public representation of differing points of view? Of simple enactment of rites of citizenship? A great deal of current thinking appears to center principally around two related themes: declines in civic participation and associated losses of social capital, in the form of diminished public trust and the reduced effectiveness of social networks.

For significant numbers of potentially active citizens and community leaders, the opportunity cost of participation in deliberation and dialogue must currently appear to be too high, as reflected by relatively widespread indifference and unwillingness to participate in civic life. Addressing this issue as a matter of opportunity cost offers a way to bring resource concerns directly up against the issues of declining civic participation and the unwillingness to confront racial, cultural, and other conflicts. How bad, for example, must a community conflict become before large numbers of people will see engaging it as less costly than continuing to ignore it? At what point does the cost of inaction begin to exceed the cost of doing something?

Treating issues of participation in deliberation and dialogue as issues of social enterprise in this sense has not been at all common. Yet doing so allows an important connection between the vital ends of such efforts and the means to realize those ends. It also provides a fundamental and far-reaching framework for direct comparisons of the resources required for various models of deliberation and dialogue. What are the costs (including opportunity costs) and benefits of each? Comparing the costs and benefits of these models in even roughly comparable circumstances would be one way to make useful observations on the relative contributions of each in public life. The challenge, however, is that enthusiasts for any community project seldom wish to have their enthusiasm dampened by asking this kind of question. In most instances, we all would prefer to ask the familiar rhetorical questions: Why don't "they" (nonparticipants and potential supporters) understand what "we" are trying to do? Why don't they get it? Why can't we reach them and get them involved? The general hypothetical answer to all of these questions offered by of the cost perspective is: because the costs they see of participating, or even getting informed, outweigh any benefits they perceive.

The challenge of practice in this area, then, becomes one of how to meet or, better yet lower, those opportunity costs for potential supporters or participants. In deliberation and dialogue this typically involves comparing incomparables (e.g., dollar outlays with the advantages of citizenship or conflict prevented or deferred), and it must be said that we really aren't very good at that. One challenge for social entrepreneurs in this area that is directly linked to the prospect of future success of these efforts is to find better ways of making such comparisons.

Fitting a social entrepreneurial model to deliberation and dialogue is no idle conjecture: The contemporary practice of deliberation and dialogue is already evolving within a social-entrepreneurial environment. Each of the authors in this volume, along with thousands of others around the world, is, has been, or will be an entrepreneur in this area. The dominant forms of contemporary deliberation and dialogue practice frequently unfold within nonprofit grassroots and community organizations, using processes and actors in widely recognized modern forms of social change induced through voluntary action. Most often, they must at some point "pay for themselves" through soliciting donations, grant writing, or some other resource stream. The incidental evidence gathered by several years of participation in the NCDD discussion list suggests that a substantial portion of current activity takes place in these nonprofit community venues and with the community, state, national, and regional consultants who service them.

Typically, community-level social entrepreneurs in this area seek to package, promote, and disseminate programs or products in a marketplace of ideas dominated largely by nonprofit organizations. For at least the past century, the dominant motif of such efforts has been a problem-focused one. In efforts to advance these and other good ideas, the problems of encouraging greater civic involvement and addressing major social conflicts are being packaged, marketed, and "sold" by numerous local, regional, national, and international nonprofit social entrepreneurs. Much like Professor Harold Hill, practitioners in this area frequently promote the notion that there is "trouble, my friends, right here in River City." Declining or inadequate civic participation and the threat of violence, it should be noted, generally offer general-purpose, problem-focused approaches. Relatively few post-problematic designs, such as assorted "wellness" and "strengths" perspectives, are in evidence. Yet it is worth weighing the advantages that might arise from adopting more positive outlooks, such as the wellness approach to prevention in health care or the emerging strengths perspective in social work. The problem of prospective violence and threat, for example, is indeed a daunting one in many communities. But it is also frequently a powerful fundraising tool; the entire history of military, police, and security budgets shows this. On the other hand, as Saunders's model ably attests, we (individuals, groups, and communities) have within us the strengths (human and social capital, as it were) to confront those prospects and build the necessary relationships—if we can find the resources necessary to do so. David Bornstein uses the strengths perspective to note: "Social entrepreneurs identify resources where people only see problems" (quoted at http://www.pbs.org/opb/thenewheroes/whatis/). This same theme is woven into the entrepreneurial model of the Skoll Foundation, which defines a social entrepreneur as "society's change agent; [a] pioneer of innovations that benefit humanity" (http://www.skollfoundation.org/aboutsocialentrepreneurship/index.asp).

There is some evidence to suggest that things are shifting somewhat away from problem-focused approaches and toward "less-negative" empowerment, wellness, and strengths models. To the extent this is the case, it is reflected in the changing nature of entrepreneurial actions. It remains to be seen how, whether, and under what circumstances, deliberation and dialogue campaigns can be sold on strengths rather than problems. Even so, public policy discussion and conflict resolution are currently not recognized marketable consumer goods for which people would be willing to purchase admission as they might tickets to an athletic event, museum exhibition, medical appointment, concert, movie, or day at a theme park. Thus, financing deliberation or dialogue activities through participant sales seems only remotely possible at present. There are, in other words, no existing product markets for deliberation and dialogue.

Nonprofit social enterprise of this sort conforms to a characteristic form of the "dual dyad" of voluntary action (see figure 17.1), which involves two distinct but related sales campaigns for deliberation and dialogue efforts. Letts and Ryan (1999) refers to this as managing "upstream" (donors) and "downstream" (clients and services). Rather than the conventional interaction of buyers and sellers found in markets, grant- and donor-supported situations generally involve two separate initiatives by nonprofits (or trustees), with two distinct groups: donors, able to commit the necessary resources,

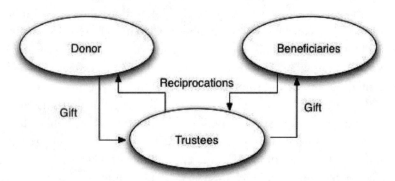

Ordinary Gift Reciprocity

Dual-Dyad Reciprocity in Benefactory

FIGURE 17.1

and beneficiaries, interested in gaining from the deliberation or dialogue experience. First, there is the challenge of selling the concepts of deliberation and dialogue to patrons—foundations, government agencies, and other financial agents—to gain the necessary resources.[8] The second initiative involves using the resources acquired in this way to market participation in the deliberative or dialogical experience to assorted bodies of citizens or parties to a conflict. In the nonprofit form of such entrepreneurship, foundations, government agencies, donors, and other resource providers must first be sold on the need for a set of conversations and be willing to put up the enabling resources. Only then are the various idea brokers of deliberation and dialogue positioned for the second sale—encouraging widespread "free" (or subsidized, low-cost) participation in actual deliberation and dialogue sessions.

Focusing on the entrepreneurial aspects of deliberation and dialogue also raises the possibility of direct, market activities: product development and testing, direct sales to willing consumers, and the like. A number of regional and national consultants have already discovered this. We see, for example, the distinct "brand identity" of the products of the National Issues Forum and the PCP "brand" of the Public Conversations Project. The Jefferson Center has even gone to the trouble of trademarking the term "Citizen Jury" (see "Citizen Jury Process" at http://www.jefferson-center.org).

For many community advocates in nonprofit settings, however, direct marketing and trademarking of deliberation and dialogue "products" may appear to be too daunting a challenge, involving substantial risks and only limited prospects of returns on investment. All in all, the dual dyad of nonprofit action within the traditional nonprofit sector regime of "upstream" funding and "downstream" pro bono service is widely seen as the most feasible available alternative, as well as one that is well understood in social work.

The field of deliberation and dialogue may currently be in a stage where nonprofit activity is a necessary form of research and development: How could anyone be an intelligent consumer of deliberation and dialogue products (that is, be willing to invest an amount equal to the full cost of participation), when none of us is really sure, yet, what those products and those costs are? Who knew fifty years ago what day-care centers and intermediate-care facilities for the elderly were? Today, one can approach purchases of such services with some semblance of knowledge, information on quality, and the like. This is not yet true with deliberation and dialogue, and there is, of course, no assurance it ever will be.

The issues involved here are complex: If the residents of Belfast, Northern Ireland, could, for the price of 5 pounds sterling each (or 500 or 5,000 each), engage in sustained dialogue that would guarantee a permanent end of the troubles, would they be willing to do so? If Americans could, for the price of $200 each, purchase a share in a more directly deliberative democracy would they? Both questions are moot because no one can realistically make any such assurances at present.

In the case of public deliberation, of course, there are additional reasons the immersion experience of citizenship should not be packaged and sold like a day at Disneyland; to do so undermines the reality and immediacy of the actual experience in subtle but profound ways. By contrast, limited markets have already emerged for some types of private and even public conflict resolution (such as family therapy, marriage counseling, and generic forms of mediation services), in which consumers are willing to pay for the costs of the intervention effort. However, the application of sustained dialogue on a broader societal scale to such problems as ethnic, religious, or racial conflict is not something easily reducible to a marketable commodity. The public-goods nature of peace and the numerous "externalities" of the issue are simply too overwhelming to make that very likely.

Thus, as a practical matter social entrepreneurship in deliberation and dialogue typically involves pursuit of strategies like grant writing; fundraising and development; promotion and sale of assorted guidebooks, pamphlets, and other promotional materials; fee-based consulting; conference presentations and workshops; creation of nonprofit organizations or networks; and other tactics to promote particular ideas, "models," programs, or other packaged approaches to solving particular social problems. Such activities may not be entrepreneurial in the ordinary business sense; profit maximization should almost certainly take a back seat to service. Indeed, the devices and tactics of entrepreneurial activity are usually seen as necessary evils; what must be done to advance agendas that are largely civic, humanitarian, and professional in nature. But whether or not we see them as evil, social entrepreneurial activities are certainly a necessary part of contemporary deliberation and dialogue.

Entrepreneurial activity has also been working to fashion a secondary marketplace of ideas in which the large and growing number of social entrepreneurs interested in selling their ideas about deliberation and dialogue through various means are also in pursuit of the limited range of financial and institutional support in hopes of attracting the attention of much larger audiences of idea consumers. Apparently, one cannot yet make a living selling public deliberation directly to the public, but one can make a living at developing models of conflict resolution and all of the assorted training and support activities designed to enable others to do so. (As I wrote this, a discussion was ongoing on the NCDD list on this very question: How can one make a living doing D&D?)

The dual-dyad situation faced by nonprofit deliberation and dialogue entrepreneurs—the need to find resources in order to provide services— also conforms in several respects and is related to a dual-dyad model of public-opinion formation, with entrepreneurs in the role of "opinion leaders."[9] Much contemporary deliberation and dialogue entrepreneurship is directed at forming, capturing, or converting foundations, public agencies, professional associations, publishers, and other potential opinion makers.[10] These assorted platforms and programs can then serve as "bully pulpits" for reaching out to large audiences of citizens with messages of participation and active citizenship. Perhaps the strongest reason for such entrepreneurial thinking is to be found in the temporary nature of this strategy: Foundations, in particular, are well known for the gossamer nature of their support. Prior experience predicts that those that can be convinced to fund deliberation and dialogue projects will inevitably see their support as short-term underwriting of "innovation," "demonstration," and "change" efforts and not capital formation or institution building; the expectation will be that long-term operational funds must come from elsewhere. (Where, exactly, is seldom a concern.) At the same time, based on experiences with "community action" in the late 1960s, politicians and government agencies are unlikely to provide much support: Active, participating citizens, particularly those with grievances, are notoriously rambunctious and unruly and inclined to all manner of unpredictable behavior.

However, the key danger in this entrepreneurial model is not its anti-establishmentarianism. It is the risk of commodifying civic action and problem solving into vendible products and the associated goal and mission displacements. While "bread and circuses" approaches to deliberation and dialogue as political entertainment may hold short-term advantages for politicians and bureaucrats, they offer little in the way of genuine deliberative democracy. When the point is reached that any particular sponsor becomes more interested in sales of its handbooks or the "gate proceeds" of attendance at its events than in their impact upon community governance, commodification has set in.

To some extent, the dilemma of potential commodification is inherent in current models of deliberation and dialogue. The risk inherent in necessary resource seeking is of allowing the legitimate need for resources to turn active citizenship and social problem solving into packaged experiences, after the manner, perhaps, of some forms of ecotourism. The challenge is how to generate the resources necessary to carry out programs encouraging more active citizenship and yet prevent the inversion of means and ends so that maintenance of deliberation and dialogue enterprises and the production and sale of D&D products do not become ends in themselves? How do we retain the vitality of something like the "silver-haired legislature" experience, where senior citizens can have a day filled with all of the thrills but none of the risks and dangers of being an elected official, gaining a "new insight into state government" (http://www.shls.org/index.html), yet go home largely unchanged by the experience?

To their credit, most deliberation and dialogue entrepreneurs appear aware, to varying degrees, of these dangers and seem willing to confront them. The concept of social entrepreneurship has been approached in many different ways by its various advocates and in the process has attracted many subtleties of meaning. For some, the term connotes little more than a fashionable cliché of the present age, roughly comparable to similarly vacuous labels of the recent past like "social change" and "change agent" (which, in turn, largely replaced nineteenth-century terms like "revolution," "revolutionary," "reform," and "reformer"). In skilled hands, the entrepreneurial model has been used to bring together images of social innovation and resultant changes with connotations of organizational leadership, the use of sophisticated management tools, and the kind of resource acquisition or "capital formation" necessary to make meaningful changes in a culture as self-aware and ironic and a society as organizationally complex as ours.

CONCLUSION

Focusing on deliberation and dialogue as problems of social entrepreneurship calls attention to an inherent challenge for international, national, regional, and community leaders of deliberation and dialogue efforts: where to obtain the necessary resources to carry out—to capitalize—organized programs of deliberation and dialogue. The problem is inherently complex, in part, because there is currently nothing resembling an economics of conversation, even strategic conversation, or the cost of discussion. The challenge of the social entrepreneur, in brief, is to sell that which is not for sale, to cover the costs of civic and conflict-resolution activities, which have no price.

This is additionally complex because of the difficulties of drawing any hard and fast connections between these conversations and events that are prevented as a result. According to the theory, when dialogue occurs, conflict is resolved and violence is prevented or minimized; when deliberation among citizens takes place, engagement happens and democracy works better. Yet this is exactly where formulating the resource issue as a problem of opportunity cost and cost-benefit consideration becomes valuable: Can we say what the cost of not engaging in sustained dialogue or public deliberation is? As a matter of fact, we can. Using an opportunity-cost approach, these costs can be measured in terms of the increased risks of violence, citizen apathy, and nonparticipation. And as these risks are clarified and estimated, the rationale for committing resources to deliberation and dialogue is strengthened accordingly.

Two conclusions follow from this: First, in the short run, with the absence of hard and fast evidence establishing the costs and benefits of deliberation and dialogue, one of the tasks for leaders in the deliberation and dialogue movement will continue to be to rhetorically make such connections. This is a major subtext running, for example, through the published work of David Matthews and Harold Saunders and through several of the chapters in this book. In the longer run, the focus on social entrepreneurship must be a major part of the case for greater research emphasis and scholarly attention to deliberation and dialogue, particularly from the vantage point of the costs of not engaging and the benefits of doing so.

Notes

1. Ostrander (2007) is a case study that documents the decisions by three major national foundations to cease funding community civic-engagement programs.
2. The term "grantsmanship" entered the language in the anonymous manner of most new words, but one of the early adopters, Norman Kiritz, was also one of the pioneering social entrepreneurs when he founded the Grantsmanship Center in 1972. He deserves to be remembered by all for this.
3. One main theoretical fault line that this discussion seeks to bridge is between the "rationalist/materialist" economic perspective and the "communicative interactionism" of the softer social sciences. Another major theoretical fault line emerges ultimately from the Scottish moralists' "commonsense" perspective and the continental reaction against Adam Smith and the "materialistic" classical economists. These differences are built deeply into the current disciplinary and professional structure. Social work is one of the few disciplines that has tried, often unsuccessfully, to bridge such fault lines.
4. The basic topic of this chapter emerged in conversations with Harold Saunders and others over the challenge of locating resources to carry out programs of sustained dialogue.
5. This may, in fact, be shown to be a false assumption, but there have been few attempts to test it.

6. It may not be clear to the reader, but "cost" in this sense is focused on the future and planned or projected events, as opposed to the conventional accounting usage, which adopts a historical perspective on past events. Sources often use the term "opportunity cost" to refer to this usage and the term "cost outlay" to refer to the other.

7. In several previous publications, I have explored this theme of the opportunity cost of problem solving under the heading of the "problem-free interval."

8. The basic design of the dual dyad is laid out in part in Lohmann and Lohmann (2002). In brief, the point is the necessary yoking of two separate and distinct sets of transactions: one to raise funds, the other to deliver the goods, in this case, deliberation or dialogue sessions.

9. In important respects, this process was first identified in the "two-step flow of communication" (Lazarsfeld, Berelson, and Gaudet 1948; Berelson, Lazarsfeld, and McPhee 1986), in which public opinion is formed as various "opinion makers" receive and interpret news and information and pass their opinions on to others who in turn adopt the views they hear from the opinion makers.

10. Most notable in this regard, perhaps, is the Kettering Foundation's ongoing commitment to brands (one might even call them related product lines), including the National Issues Forum, Public Choice, and products like public deliberation, and the Jefferson Center's trademarked Citizen Juries. Community design teams, question mapping, appreciative inquiry, and many other emerging brands are also of note.

18

THE FUTURE OF DELIBERATION AND DIALOGUE STUDIES

Jon Van Til and Dolly Ford

THE CHAPTERS OF THIS BOOK describe the contemporary movement to develop sustained dialogue and public deliberation as means of deepening and enriching the participation of individuals and groups in society. The case our authors have made is both theoretical and practical—"pracademic," in our terminology. Dialogue and deliberation are at the heart of the concept of democratic participation in solving entrenched problems, and such public conversations can work in a variety of settings to enhance the role of citizens as active members of a democratic society.

Sustained dialogue and democratic deliberation may be seen as part of an ongoing intellectual movement that finds a basic test of democracy in the quantity and quality of public dialogue that it engenders. We share with many, many others the intuition that democracy has come nowhere near exhausting its potentials and that much more is possible in our governments, communities, and public institutions. One of us has recently suggested that three criteria be included when we seek to comprehend and extend the reach of democracy in the institutions of our time (Van Til 2008). Citizen action, he argues, is most appropriate and effective when it is:

1. Conducted through the practice of sustained dialogue and democratic deliberation
2. Directed toward tasks that reconstruct society's commons
3. Aimed toward constructing politics of relationship

To elaborate:

1. Sustained dialogue and public deliberation, as we have seen in this volume, are forms of structured human interaction that address, name, and

frame issues of mutual concern. These approaches involve processes of public deliberation or public talk wherein citizen participants engage in designed and moderated discussions with the goal of increasing understanding and reducing conflict among themselves and the solidary groups to which they may belong. The argument here is that if democratic participation is to mean more than adding one more data point to national opinion polls, participatory networks will need to social-capitalize—to provide and facilitate methods by which opinion is cultivated and assured and not simply mobilized.

2. Reconstructing the commons is an approach that draws upon the pioneering work of one of our editors, Roger Lohmann (1992b), and Elinor Ostrom (1990) and, most recently, Yochim Benkler (2006). Lohmann has argued that public life is formed and structured in and through the institutions, resources, and common goods of voluntary action and that communication is the primary vehicle for this. As such, the third sector is a social space within which caring, sharing, and communal action may be advanced. "What really counts is the informed, voluntary, and self-actualizing activity of individuals, joined with others in a search to build a better, fairer, and more productive society." The worth of a society "should be judged by the content of the actions and outcomes these structures generate and assure" (Van Til 2000, 214).

3. Building a genuine politics of relationship has been highlighted as a central criterion in the recent work of Robert Putnam (2000), Michael Gecan (2004), and Harold Saunders (2005). What makes a difference here are "connections among people who know one another" (Putnam, Feldstein, and Cohen 2003, 9). Saunders elaborates the dimensions of such relationships as "giving hands and voice to the process of continuous interaction in political, social, and economic life. It is both a framework for analysis and an instrument of change" (Saunders 2005, 60).

Sustained dialogue is not only important theoretically as a component of active democratic participation, but it is also a tool to advance the quality of individual and community life. At West Virginia University, we have been striving through the Nova Institute to promote the use of dialogue and deliberation to enhance citizen-to-citizen exchange; to rebuild the commons and the sense of community and shared enterprise that goes along with it; and to advance understanding of the ways in which human social relationships figure importantly in this process. This book is an important step in that direction.

CONTRIBUTORS

NICK ACHESON is a lecturer in social policy and member of the Social and Policy Research Institute at the University of Ulster. His research interests focus on voluntary action and social movements in regions of ethnic conflict and the reshaping of voluntary action in contemporary reforms of the welfare state.

RONALD ALTHOUSE is a professor of sociology and formerly chair of the Division of Sociology and Anthropology at West Virginia University. He has a long record of involvement in community sociology and survey research in the Appalachian Region.

LISA BEDINGER is a dialogue and deliberation practitioner with a focus in organizing, convening and moderating diversity deliberations on college and university campuses.

COREY COLYER is an associate professor and director of graduate studies in the Division of Sociology and Anthropology at West Virginia University. His research focuses on people processing institutions and the interaction between agencies of social control.

NORMAN CONTI is an associate professor in the Department of Sociology and the Graduate Center for Social and Public Policy at Duquesne University. He has published ethnographies of recruitment, socialization, ethics training, and masculinity in policing as well as an analysis of the social networks that develop within recruit cohorts.

DOLLY FORD is a social worker at the WVU Children's Hospital. She was formerly a senior lecturer and program director of the Nova Institute at West Virginia University. She is interested in organizing and moderating campus and community deliberations.

ERNA GELLES is an associate professor of public administration in the Hatfield School of Government at Portland State University. Her research and teaching interests are largely in nonprofit theory and management. Her community-based research and practice is integrally linked with organizations serving diverse populations.

JERI KIRBY is a Ph.D. candidate in political science and lecturer in the Division of Sociology and Anthropology, West Virginia University, where she teaches courses in deviance and social control.

ROGER A. LOHMANN is a professor emeritus of social work and chairman of the board of the Nova Institute at West Virginia University. He is editor emeritus of *Nonprofit Management* *and Leadership*, author of *Breaking Even* (1980) and *The Commons* (1992), coauthor of *Social Administration* (2002), and coeditor of *Rural Social Work Practice*. He developed and taught a deliberation-based advanced social policy course in the MSW program at West Virginia.

RICHARD F. LUDEMAN is founder and principal of Carta Nova Consulting, in Portland, Oregon.

JENNIFER MCINTOSH is executive officer for social justice and director, AA/EEO at West Virginia University.

CARL MILOFSKY is professor of sociology at Bucknell University in Lewisburg, Pennsylvania. He is author of *Smallville: Institutionalizing Community in Small Town America*; coauthor with Albert Hunter of *Pragmatic Liberalism: Constructing a Civil Society*; and coeditor with Ram Cnaan of *The Handbook of Community Movements and Local Organizations*.

CHARLES MORRIS is associate director of the Office of Social Justice at West Virginia University.

TEDDY NEMEROFF was a cofounder of the first campus sustained dialogue initiative at Princeton University. After a stint in management consulting, he founded a sustained dialogue program to address political and economic conflict at an NGO in South Africa. Teddy graduated from Columbia Law School in 2009.

NEAL NEWFIELD is an associate professor of social work at West Virginia University and a documentary photographer. He has taught a travel course on peace and reconciliation in Ireland/Northern Ireland and for the past five years has been helping to develop social work as a discipline in Vietnam and Cambodia.

SUSAN NEWFIELD is an associate professor of nursing at West Virginia University with interests in community mental health and human system relationships. For a decade she has run a high school clinic for troubled teens. Susan works in Vietnam and Cambodia furthering women's health and mental health nursing.

JIM NOLAN is an associate professor in the Division of Sociology and Anthropology at West Virginia University where he teaches courses in the area of crime and social control. His research currently focuses on neighborhood dynamics and public safety, police procedures, crime measurement, and hate crimes.

PRIYA PARKER was cofounder of Sustained Dialogue at the University of Virginia and second program director of the Sustained Dialogue Campus Network. She has worked for the Dalai Lama's peace foundation and as a policy analyst for PRS Legislative Research in New Delhi. Priya is pursuing her MPA from the Harvard Kennedy School and MBA from MIT Sloan.

DAVID ROBINSON is a partner in Robinson Driver Partnership, director of the New Zealand Social and Civic Policy Institute, and a senior research associate at the Institute of Policy Studies, Victoria University of Wellington.

DAVID M. RYFE is associate professor and senior scholar in the Reynolds School of Journalism, University of Nevada, Reno. He has written extensively on the practice of public deliberation, political communication, and American news media.

HAROLD H. SAUNDERS is president of the International Institute for Sustained Dialogue and director of international affairs at the Kettering Foundation. As assistant secretary of state, he was a principal drafter of the Camp David accords. He is author of *A Public Peace Process: Sustained Dialogue to Transform Racial and Ethnic Conflicts* and *Politics Is About Relationship*.

DAVID TUKEY, cofounder at Princeton University of the first sustained dialogue organization on campus, holds a Ph.D. in neuroscience and is a neurobiologist at NYU Medical Center. He serves on boards of the International Institute for Sustained Dialogue and Princeton Prize in Race Relations and chairs the board of the Sustained Dialogue Campus Network. He was a deputy regional campaign manager for McCain-Palin.

JON VAN TIL is professor emeritus of urban studies and community planning at Rutgers University, Camden. His ten books include *Breaching Derry's Walls* (2008), *Growing Civil Society* (2000, 2008), and *Mapping the Third Sector* (1988). He is a Fulbright Specialist in Hungary.

DAVID WILLIAMS is professor emeritus and former assistant dean for the School of Applied Social Sciences and chair of the Department of Public Administration at West Virginia University.

APPENDIX

CORE PRINCIPLES FOR PUBLIC ENGAGEMENT
Developed collaboratively by members of leading public engagement organizations (Draft 04-06-09, www.thataway.org/2009/pep_project)

THERE ARE MANY WAYS THAT people can come together to deal with issues that affect their lives. We believe that public engagement involves convening diverse yet representative groups of people to wrestle with information from a variety of viewpoints, in conversations that are well facilitated, providing direction for their own community activities or public judgments that will be seriously considered by policymakers and their fellow citizens. It is our stance that quality public engagement must take into consideration seven core principles if it is to effectively build mutual understanding, meaningfully affect policy development, and inspire collaborative action among citizens and institutions.

The following seven principles overlap and reinforce one another in practice. They serve as ideals to pursue and as criteria for judging quality. Rather than promoting partisan agendas, the implementation of these principles generates authentic stakeholder engagement around public issues.

THE SEVEN CORE PRINCIPLES

1. *Planning and Preparation*: Plan, design, and convene the engagement specifically to serve both the purpose of the effort and the needs of participants.
2. *Inclusion and Diversity*: Incorporate diverse voices, ideas, and information to lay the groundwork for quality outcomes and democratic legitimacy.
3. *Collaboration and Shared Purpose*: Support organizers, participants, and those engaged in follow-up to work well together for the common good.
4. *Listening and Learning*: Help participants listen, explore and learn without predetermined outcomes—and evaluate public engagement efforts for lessons.

5. *Transparency and Trust*: Promote openness and provide a public record of the people, resources, forums, and outcomes involved.

6. *Impact and Action*: Ensure each participatory effort has real potential to make a difference.

7. *Sustained Participation and Democratic Culture*: Promote a culture of participation with programs and institutions that support ongoing quality public engagement.

This list represents a consensus in the field of dialogue and deliberation, but most practices tend to emphasize or apply these principles differently or to reach beyond this basic consensus in one way or another. To learn more about such diverse understandings and applications, consult the online version of these guidelines at www.thataway.org/2009/pep_project.

Finally, we believe the use of technology should be generally encouraged whenever appropriate to enhance and not impede these seven values—and also that these seven principles apply to both online and offline efforts. However, there is not yet consensus in our field on standards for the use of technology that would warrant the inclusion of specific online or electronic guidelines in this document.

The National Coalition for Dialogue and Deliberation, the International Association of Public Participation, and the Co-Intelligence Institute are leading this collaborative effort to develop a standard set of principles that, we hope, organizations in the field of public engagement can agree on. With new attention and emphasis on collaboration, participation, and transparency thanks to the leadership and vision of the Obama administration, we feel it is more important than ever to provide clarity about what we consider to be quality public engagement.

REFERENCES

Acheson, N., and C. Milofsky. 2004. Peace building and participation in Northern Ireland: Marginal social movements and the policy process since the 'Good Friday' agreement. Paper presented at the fifth Biennial Conference of the International Society for Third Sector Research, Toronto, Canada.

Acheson, N., B. Harvey, and A. Williamson. 2005. State welfare and the development of voluntary action: The case of Ireland, north and south." *Voluntas* 16 (2): 181–202.

Alexander, J. F., C. Barton, R. S. Schiavo, and B. V. Parsons. 1976. Systems-behavioral intervention with families of delinquents: Therapist characteristics, family behavior, and outcome. *Journal of Consulting and Clinical Psychology* 44:656–64.

Alimo, C., R. Kelly, and C. Clark. 2002. Diversity initiatives in higher education: Intergroup dialogue program student outcomes and implications for campus radical climate: A case study. *Mulitcultural Education* 10 (1): 49–53.

Andersen, T. 1991. *The reflecting team: Dialogues and dialogues about the dialogues.* New York: Norton.

Aristotle. 1991. *The art of rhetoric.* Trans. H. C. Lawson-Tancred. London: Penguin.

Bachrach, P., and M. S. Baratz. 1962. Two faces of power. *The American Political Science Review* 56 (4): 947–52.

Barber, B. R. 1984. *Strong democracy: Participatory politics for a new age.* Berkeley: University of California Press.

——. 1988. *The conquest of politics: Liberal philosophy in democratic times.* Princeton, N.J.: Princeton University Press.

——. 1998a. *A passion for democracy: American essays.* Princeton, N.J.: Princeton University Press.

——. 1998b. *A place for us: How to make society civil and democracy strong.* New York: Hill and Wang.

———. 1998c. Mary Parker Follett as democratic hero. Foreword to M. P. Follett, *The new state; Group organization, the solution to popular government*, x–xix. University Park: Pennsylvania State University Press.

Barton, C., and J. F. Alexander. 1981. Functional family therapy. In *Handbook of family therapy*, ed. A. S. Gurman and D. P. Kniskern, 403–43. New York: Brunner/Mazel.

Bateson, G., and Bateson, M.C. [1987] 2005. *Angels fear: Towards an epistemology of the sacred*. Cresskill, N.J.: Hampton Press.

Benkler, Y. 2006. *The wealth of networks: How social production transforms markets and freedom*. New Haven, Conn.: Yale University Press.

Berelson, B., P. F. Lazarsfeld, and W. N. McPhee. 1986. *Voting: A study of opinion formation in a presidential campaign*. Chicago: University of Chicago Press.

Berg, I. K. 1994. *Family based services*. New York: Norton.

Berger, B. 2009. Political theory, political science, and the end of civic engagement. *Perspectives on Politics* 7 (2): 335–50.

Bernstein, R. 1971. *Praxis and action*. Philadelphia: University of Pennsylvania Press.

———. 1976. *The restructuring of social and political theory*. Philadelphia: University of Pennsylvania Press.

———. 1981. *Beyond objectivism and relativism*. Philadelphia: University of Pennsylvania Press.

———. 2010. *The pragmatic turn*. New York: Polity.

Bingham, L. B., T. Nabatchi, and R. O'Leary. 2005. The new governance: Practices and processes for stakeholder and citizen participation in the work of government. *Public Administration Review* 65 (September/October 2005): 547–58.

Bion, W. R. 1959. *Experiences in groups*. New York: Basic Books.

Block, P. 1996. *Stewardship: Choosing service over self-interest*. San Francisco: Berrett-Koehler.

Bohm, D., D. Factor, and P. Garrett. 1991. Dialogue: A proposal. http://www.cgl.org/Dialogue.html. Retrieved March 21, 2006.

Bohte, J. 2007. Governmental efficiency in our time: Is the "what" really more important than the "how"? *Public Administration Review* 67 (5): 811–15.

Borkman, T. J. 1999. *Understanding self-help/mutual aid: Experiential learning in the commons*. New Brunswick, N.J.: Rutgers University Press.

Bourdieu, P. 1986. The forms of capital. In *Handbook of theory and research for the sociology of education*, ed. J. Richardson. Westport, Conn.: Greenwood Press.

Boyte, H. C. 2005. Reframing democracy: Governance, civic agency, and politics. *Public Administration Review* 65 (September/October 2005): 536–46.

Brooks, D. 2000. *Bobos in paradise*. New York: Simon and Schuster.

Brown, C. R., and G. L. Mazza. 1997. *Healing into action: A leadership guide for creating diverse communities*. Washington, D.C.: National Coalition Building Initiative.

Burkhalter, S., J. Gastil, and T. Kelshaw. 2002. A conceptual definition and theoretical model of public deliberation in small face-to-face groups. *Communication Theory* 12:398–422.

Burtt, S. 1993. The politics of virtue today: A critique and a proposal. *American Political Science Review* 87 (2): 360–68.

Button, M., and K. Mattson. 1999. Deliberative democracy in practice: Challenges and prospects for civic deliberation. *Polity* 31:609–37.

Button, M., and D. Ryfe. 2004. What can we learn from the practice of deliberative democracy? In *The deliberative democracy handbook: Strategies for effective civic engagement in the twenty-first century*, ed. J. Gastil and P. Levine, 2–34. San Francisco: Jossey-Bass.

Chambers, S. 2003. Deliberative democratic theory. *Annual Review of Political Science* 6:307–26.

Citizen Choicework. 2010. http://www.publicagenda.org/public-engagement -materials/citizen-choicework-technical-assistance. Retrieved October 12, 2010.

Clark, C. 2002. Diversity issues in higher education: Intergroup dialogue on campus. *Mulitcultural Education* 9 (4): 30–32.

Cody, J. 2002. Conceptualising social capital—frameworks. In *Building social capital*, ed. D. Robinson. Wellington: Institute of Policy Studies.

Cohen, J. L., and A. Arato. 1992. *Civil society and political theory*. Cambridge, Mass.: MIT Press.

Coleman, J. 1988. Social capital in the creation of human capital. *American Journal of Sociology* 94, Supplement: S95–S120.

Conti, N., and J. J. Nolan. 2005. Policing the Platonic cave: Ethics and efficacy in police training. *Policing and Society* 15 (2): 166–86.

Cote, S., and T. Healy. 2001. *The well-being of nations: The role of social and human capital*. Paris: OECD.

Croly, H. D. [1909] 2005. *The promise of American life*. New York: Cosimo Classics.

Crosby, N., J. Kelly, and P. Schaefer. 1986. Citizen panels: A new approach to citizen participation. *Public Administration Review* 46 (2): 170–78.

Cunningham, W. J. 1998. *Theoretical framework for conflict resolution*. Auckland: University of Auckland.

Dahl, R. A. 1963. *Modern political analysis*. Englewood Cliffs, N.J.: Prentice-Hall.

Daubon, R., and H. Saunders. 2002. Operationalizing social capital: A strategy to enhance communities' "capacity to concert." *International Studies Perspectives* 3:179.

Deegan, M. J. 1984. The sociology—not social work—of Jane Addams. Paper presented at the Association of Humanist Sociologists, October, Chicago, Ill.

———. 1988. *Jane Addams and the men of the Chicago School, 1892–1918*. New Brunswick, N.J.: Transaction Press.

Delli Carpini, M., F. L. Cook, and L. R. Jacobs. 2004. Public deliberation, discursive participation, and citizen engagement: A review of the literature. *Annual Review of Political Science* 7:315–44.

Delli Carpini, M., and S. Keeter. 1996. *What Americans know about politics and why it matters*. New Haven, Conn.: Yale University Press.

De Shazer, S. 1988a. *Clues: Investigating solutions in brief therapy*. New York: Norton.

———. 1988b. Utilization: The foundation of solutions. In *Developing Ericksonian therapy: State of the art*, ed. J. K. Zeig and S. R. Lankton, 112–24. Bristol, Penn.: Brunner/Mazel.

Dewey, J. 1910. *How we think*. Boston: D.C. Heath.

———. 1993. *The political writings*. Ed. D. Morris and I. Shapiro. Indianapolis: Hackett.

Druckman, J. 2002. The implications of framing effects for citizen competence. *Political Behavior* 23:225–56.

Durkheim, E. [1895] 1982. *The rules of sociological method*. Trans. W. D. Halls. New York: MacMillan.

Eliasoph, N. 1998. *Avoiding politics: How Americans produce apathy in everyday life*. New York: Cambridge University Press.

Elshtain, J. B. 2002. *Jane Addams and the dream of American democracy: A life*. New York: Basic Books.

Elstub, S. 2008. *Towards a deliberative and associational democracy*. Edinburgh: Edinburgh University Press.

Federal Bureau of Investigation. 2001. *Crime in the United States, 2000*. Washington, D.C.: FBI.

Festenstein, M. 2009. Dewey's political philosophy. In *The Stanford encyclopedia of philosophy*. http://plato.stanford.edu/archives/spr2009/entries/dewey-political.

Fiorina, M. 1999. Extreme voices: A dark side of civic engagement. In *Civic engagement in American democracy*, ed. Theda Skocpol and Morris Fiorina, 395–425. Washington, D.C.: Brookings.

Fischer, M., C. Nackenoff, and W. E. Chmielewski. 2009. *Jane Addams and the practice of democracy*. Urbana: University of Illinois Press.

Fishkin, J. 1995. *The voice of the people: Public opinion and democracy*. New Haven, Conn.: Yale University Press.

Fishkin, J. S., and Laslett, P. 2003. *Debating deliberative democracy*. Malden, Mass.: Blackwell.

Flavin-McDonald, C., and M. Holme Barrett. 1999. The Topsfield Foundation: Fostering democratic community building through face to face dialogue. *New Directions for Adult and Continuing Education* (81): 25–36.

Florida, R. 2002. *The rise of the creative class.* New York: Basic Books.

Follett, M. P. 1896. *The Speaker of the House of Representatives.* New York: Longmans, Green.

———. [1896] 1974. *The Speaker of the House of Representatives.* New York: B. Franklin Reprints.

———. 1918. *The new state: Group organization, the solution of popular government.* New York,: Longmans, Green.

———. [1918] 1965. *The new state: Group organization, the solution of popular government.* Gloucester, Mass.,: Peter Smith.

———. [1918] 1998. *The new state: Group organization the solution of popular government.* University Park: Pennsylvania State University Press.

———. 1924. *Creative experience.* New York: Longmans, Green.

———. 1949. *Freedom and co-ordination: Lectures in business organisation.* London: Management Publications Trust.

———. [1949] 1987. *Freedom and co-ordination: Lectures in business organization.* New York: Garland.

——— 1957. *ha-Mihnal ha-dinami.* [n.p.]

Freeman, S. 2000. Deliberative democracy: A sympathetic comment. *Philosophy and Public Affairs* 29:371–419.

Freire, P. [1970] 1973. *Pedagogy of the oppressed.* New York: Continuum.

Gamson, W. 1992. *Talking politics.* Cambridge: Cambridge University Press.

Gamson, W., and A. Modigliani. 1989. Media discourse and public opinion on nuclear power: A constructionist approach. *American Journal of Sociology* 95:1–37.

Garfinkel, H. 1967. *Studies in ethnomethodology.* Englewood Cliffs, N.J.: Prentice-Hall.

Gastil, J. 2000. *By popular demand: Revitalizing representative democracy through deliberative elections.* Berkeley: University of California Press.

Gastil, J., and J. P. Dillard. 1999. Increasing political sophistication through public deliberation. *Political Communication* 16 (1): 3–23.

Gaventa, J. 1980. *Power and powerlessness: Quiescence and rebellion in an Appalachian valley.* Urbana: University of Illinois Press.

Gecan, M. 2004. *Going public: An organizer's guide to citizen action.* New York: Anchor.

Geuss, R. 1981. *The idea of a critical theory: Habermas and the Frankfurt School.* New York: Cambridge University Press.

Giddens, A. 2000. *The third way and its critics.* Cambridge: Polity.

———, ed. 2001. *The global third way debate.* Cambridge: Polity.

Gitterman, A. 2004. The mutual aid model. In *Handbook of social work with groups*, ed. C. Garvin, L. M. Gutiérrez, and M. J. Galinsky, 93–110. New York: Guilford Press.

Glen, J. M. 2006. The Myles Horton reader: Education for social change. *History of Education Quarterly* 46 (1): 128–30.

Goffman, E. 1952. On cooling the mark out: Some aspects of adaptation to failure. *Psychiatry* 15 (4): 451–63.

——. 1974. *Frame analysis: An essay on the organization of experience*. Cambridge, Mass.: Harvard University Press.

——. 1981. *Forms of talk*. Philadelphia: University of Pennsylvania Press.

Goodin, R. E. 2003. *Reflective democracy*. Oxford: Oxford University Press.

Gutmann, A. 2004. *Why deliberative democracy?* Princeton, N.J.: Princeton University Press.

Gutmann, A., and D. Thompson. 2002. Deliberative democracy beyond process. *Journal of Political Philosophy* 10 (2): 153–74.

Habermas, J. 1984. *The theory of communicative action*. Boston: Beacon Press.

Handy, F., B. Ranade, and M. Kassam. 2007. To profit or not to profit: Women entrepreneurs in India. *Nonprofit Management and Leadership* 17 (4): 383–402.

Hanna, P., and B. Harrison. 2004. *Word and world: Practice and the foundations of language*. Cambridge: Cambridge University Press.

Hanifan, L. J. 1916. The Rural School Community Center. *Annals of the American Academy of Political and Social Science* 67:130–38.

Hardin, G. 1968. The tragedy of the commons. *Science* 162:1243–48.

——. 1998. Essays on science and society: Extensions of "The tragedy of the commons." *Science* 280:682.

Harwood, R. C. 2005. *Hope unraveled: The people's retreat and our way back*. Dayton, Ohio: Kettering Foundation Press.

Heath, J. 2001. *Communicative action and rational choice*. Studies in Contemporary German Social Thought. Cambridge, Mass.: MIT Press.

Hendriks, C. 2002. Institutions of deliberative democratic processes and interest groups: Roles, tensions, and incentives. *Australian Journal of Public Administration* 61:64–75.

Herndon, C., and T. Garcia. 2005. Sustained Dialogue Campus Network. *IISD Research* 2005, 2.

Herzig, M. 2006. Personal dialogue and e-mail communication.

Hess, C., and E. Ostrom. 2007. *Understanding knowledge as a commons: From theory to practice*. Cambridge, Mass.: MIT Press.

Holt, L. 1999. Rationality is hard work: Some further notes on the disruptive effects of deliberation. *Philosophy and Psychology* 12:215–19.

Horton, A. I. 1989. *The Highlander Folk School: A history of its major programs, 1932–1961*. Brooklyn, N.Y.: Carlson.

Hunold, C. 2001. Corporatism, pluralism, and democracy: Toward a deliberative theory of bureaucratic accountability." *Governance* 14 (2): 151–67.

Irvin, R. A., and J. Stansbury. 2004. Citizen participation in decision making: Is it worth the effort? *Public Administration Review* 64 (1): 55–65.

Jeavons, T. H. 1994. *When the bottom line is faithlessness*. Bloomington: Indiana University Press.

Katnani, D., and P. Parker. 2003. Embracing a vision, implementing sustained dialogue on college campuses: A handbook for student leaders. Unpublished.

King, C. S., K. M. Feltey, and B. O. N. Susel. "The question of participation: Toward authentic public participation in public administration." *Public Administration Review* 58, no. 4 (1998): 317–26.

Kirby, J. L. 2006. *Understanding the psychosocial development of neighborhoods: Implications for situational policing*. Morgantown: West Virginia University.

Knight, L. W. 2005. *Citizen: Jane Addams and the struggle for democracy*. Chicago: University of Chicago Press.

Kuklinski, J., and N. Hurley. 1996. It's a matter of interpretation. In *Political persuasion and attitude change*, ed. D. Mutz, P. Sniderman, and R. Brody, 125–44. Ann Arbor: University of Michigan Press.

Kuklinski, J., R. Riggle, V. Ottati, N. Schwarz, and R. Wyer. 1993. Thinking about political tolerance, more or less, with more or less information. In *Reconsidering the democratic public*, ed. G. Marcus and R. Hanson, 225–47. University Park: Pennsylvania State University Press.

Kymlicka, W. 1995. *Multicultural citizenship: A liberal theory of minority rights*. Oxford: Oxford University Press.

Lasch, C. 1986. *The new radicalism in America, 1889–1963: The intellectual as a social type*. New York: Norton.

———. 1995. *The revolt of the elites and the betrayal of democracy*. New York: Norton.

Lave, J., and E. Wenger. 1991. *Situated learning: Legitimate peripheral participation*. Cambridge: Cambridge University Press.

Lazarsfeld, P. F., B. Berelson, and H. Gaudet. 1948. *The people's choice: How the voter makes up his mind in a presidential campaign*. New York: Columbia University Press.

Leighninger, M., and M. McCoy. 1998. Mobilizing citizens: Study circles offer a new approach to citizenship. *National Civic Review* 87 (2): 183–89.

Levin, I., S. Schnieder, and G. Gaeth. 1998. All frames are not created equal: A typology and critical analysis of framing effects. *Organizational Behavior and Human Decision Processes* 76:149–88.

Lewin, K. 1943. Psychology and the process of group living. *Journal of Social Psychology* 17:113–31.

———. 1948. *Resolving social conflicts*. New York: Harper.

Lohmann, R. A. 1992a. The commons: A multidisciplinary approach to nonprofit organizations, voluntary action, and philanthropy. *Nonprofit and Voluntary Sector Quarterly* 21 (3): 309–24.

———. 1992b. *The commons: New perspectives on nonprofit organization, voluntary action, and philanthropy.* San Francisco: Jossey-Bass.

———. 1995a. Buddhist commons in Asia. *Voluntas* 6 (2): 1–19, 140–58.

———. 1995b. Commons: Can this be the name of thirdness? *Nonprofit and Voluntary Sector Quarterly* 25 (1): 7.

———. 1995c. The commons: Nonprofit organizations and the third sector in everyday life. Benedum Distinguished Scholar lecture.

———. 2005. The third sector in rural America. In *Rural Social Work Practice*, ed. N. Lohmann and R. Lohmann, 86–104. New York: Columbia University Press.

———. 2006. *The commons.* Morgantown: West Virginia University Press.

———. 2007. Charity, philanthropy, public service, or enterprise: What are the big questions of nonprofit management today? *Public Administration Review* 67 (3): 437–44.

Lohmann, R., and N. Lohmann. 2002. *Social administration.* Foundations of Social Work Knowledge series. New York: Columbia University Press.

———, eds. 2005. *Rural social work practice.* New York: Columbia University Press.

Loyal, S. 2003. *The sociology of Anthony Giddens.* Sterling, Va.: Pluto Press.

Ludeman, R. F. 2003. *Question mapping.* Portland, Ore.: Carta Nova Consulting.

Maine, H. S. 1876. *Village-communities in the East and West.* New York: H. Holt and Company.

Maloney, E. 2002. *The secret history of the IRA.* London: Allen Lane/Penguin Press.

Manning, P. K. 1977. Rules in organizational context: Narcotics law enforcement in two settings. *Sociological Quarterly* 18 (1): 44–61.

Mansbridge, J. J. 1990. *Beyond self interest.* Chicago: University of Chicago Press.

Mathews, D. F. 1994. *Politics for people: Finding a responsible public voice.* Urbana: University of Illinois Press.

Mathews, D., and N. McAfee. 2003. *Making choices together: The power of public deliberation.* Dayton, Ohio: Kettering Foundation.

Mattson, K. 1998. Reading Follett: An introduction to *The new state.* In *The new state: Group organization, the solution to popular government,* by M. P. Follett, ed. K. Mattson, xxix–lix. University Park: Pennsylvania State University Press.

McCoy, M. L., and P. L. Scully. 2002. Deliberative dialogue to expand civic engagement: What kind of talk does democracy need? *National Civic Review* 91 (2): 117–35.

McGuinness, B. 2002. *Approaches to Wittgenstein.* London: Routledge.

Menand, L. 1997. *Pragmatism: A reader.* New York: Vintage.

Mendelberg, T. 2002. The deliberative citizen: Theory and evidence. *Political Decision Making, Deliberation, and Participation* 6:151–93.

Mendelberg, T., and J. Oleske. 2000. Race and public deliberation. *Political Communication* 17:169–91.

Milofsky, C. 1987. *Community organization.* New York: Oxford University Press.

Mitchell, G. 1999. *Making peace.* Berkeley: University of California.

Nagda, B. A., M. L. Spearmon, L. C. Holley, S. Harding, M. L. Balassone, D. Moise-Swanson, et al. 1999. Intergroup dialogues: An innovative approach to teaching about diversity and justice in social work programs. *Journal of Social Work Education* 35 (3): 433–49.

Narayan, D. 2000. *Voices of the poor: Can anyone hear us?* Oxford: Oxford University Press for the World Bank.

Nemeroff, T. 2004. Chapter II: A square is always a rectangle, but a rectangle is not always a square: knowing the essence of sustained dialogue. Unpublished. International Institute for Sustained Dialogue Research.

——. 2005a. Developing practice areas in sustained dialogue. *IIsD Research* 2005, 2.

——. 2005b. Empowering Zimbabwean youth through sustained dialogue. *IISD Research* 2005, 1, 6.

——. 2005d. Interview with Richard Ratlou. *IISD Research* 2005, 1–3.

——. 2005e. Monitoring and evaluation for sustained dialogue. *IISD Research* 2005, 1.

——. 2005f. Overview of IDASA's sustained dialogue work, 2005: A year of realities. *IISD Research* 2005, 2, 13.

——. 2005g. Reflections on sustained dialogue in rural KwaZulu Natal. *IISD Research* 2005, 2.

Nemeroff, T., and L. Adams. 2005. Piloting sustained dialogue in South Africa: Two case studies. *IISD Research* 2005, 2.

Nemeroff, T., and S. R. Ratlou. 2005. Preface to exploring the civil-economic connection paper I: The catering question: Conflict or cooperation at the Denneboom Interchange? *IISD Research* 2005, 2, introduction.

Nolan, J., N. Conti, and J. McDevitt. 2004. Situational policing: Neighborhood development and crime control. *Policing and Society* 14 (2): 99–117.

——. 2005. *Situational policing.* Washington, D.C.: Federal Bureau of Investigation.

Olson, M. 1965. *The logic of collective action: Public good and the theory of groups.* Harvard Economic Studies 124. Cambridge, Mass.: Harvard University Press.

Olson, R. D. 1996. *Toward a social technology of peace: A sociology of conflict resolution.* Oxford, Ohio: R. Olson.

Ostrander, S. A. 2007. Case Study: Innovation, accountability, and independence at three private foundations funding higher education civic engagement, 1995 to 2005. *Nonprofit Management and Leadership* 18 (2): 237–53.

Ostrom, E. 1990. *Governing the commons: The evolution of institutions for collective action.* The Political Economy of Institutions and Decisions series. Cambridge: Cambridge University Press.

Ostrom, E., R. Gardner, and J. Walker. 1994. *Rules, games, and common-pool resources.* Ann Arbor: University of Michigan Press.

Ostrom, V. 1997. *The meaning of democracy and the vulnerability of democracies: A response to Tocqueville's challenge.* Ann Arbor: University of Michigan Press.

Pan, Z., and G. M. Kosicki. 1993. Framing analysis: An approach to news discourse. *Political Communication* 10:55–75.

Pearce, W. B., and S. W. Littlejohn. 1997. *Moral conflict: When social worlds collide.* Thousand Oaks, Calif.: Sage.

Perlstein, R. 2008. *Nixonland: The rise of a president and the fracturing of America.* New York: Scribner.

Perry, M. 2002. *Population 485.* New York: Harper Collins.

Peter, F. 2009. *Democratic legitimacy.* New York: Routledge.

Phillips, K. P. 2006. *American theocracy: The peril and politics of radical religion, oil, and borrowed money in the twenty-first century.* New York: Viking.

Piven, F. F., and R. A. Cloward. 1993. *Regulating the poor: The functions of public welfare.* Updated ed. New York: Vintage.

Plein, L., K. E. Green, and D. G. Williams. 1998. Organic planning: A new approach to public participation in local governance. *The Social Science Journal* 35 (4): 509–23.

Porter, E. 2000. Creating dialogical spaces in Northern Ireland. *International Feminist Journal of Politics* (2): 163–84.

Porter, N. 2003. *The elusive quest: Reconciliation in Northern Ireland.* Belfast: Blackstaff Press.

Presser, L., and C. A. Hamilton. 2006. The micro-politics of victim-offender mediation. *Sociological Inquiry* 76 (3) 316–42.

Putnam, R. D. 2000. *Bowling alone: The collapse and renewal of American community.* New York: Simon and Schuster.

Putnam, R. D., L. M. Feldstein, and D. Cohen. *Better together: Restoring the American community.* New York: Simon and Schuster, 2003.

Rioch, M. 1975. Group relations: Rationale and technique. In *Group relations reader 1,* ed. A. Colman and D. Braxton. Washington, D.C.: A. K. Rice Institute.

Roberts, N. C. 1997. Public deliberation: An alternative approach to crafting policy and setting direction. *Public Administration Review* 57 (2): 124–32.

———. 2008. *The age of direct citizen participation.* Armonk, N.Y.: M. E. Sharpe.

Robinson, B., and D. Robinson. 2002. Possible aids from physics and engineering to assist understanding social capital. In *Building social capital*, ed. D. Robinson. Wellington: Institute of Policy Studies.

Rodin, J., and S. P. Steinberg. 2003. *Public discourse in America: Conversation and community in the twenty-first century*. Philadelphia: University of Pennsylvania Press.

Rosenberg, S. 2002. *The not so common sense: Differences in how people judge social and political life*. New Haven, Conn.: Yale University Press.

Ryfe, D. 2002. The practice of deliberative democracy: A study of sixteen organizations. *Political Communication* (16): 359–78.

———. 2005. Does deliberative democracy work? *Annual Review of Political Science* 7:49–71.

Ryle, M., and P. G. Richards. 1988. *The commons under scrutiny*. London: Routledge.

Saltmarsh, J. A. 2004. Creating a personal and political culture of engagement in higher education. Retrieved from http://www.publicwork.org/pdf/workbench /saltmarsh_reflections.pdf.

Sampson, R. J., and S. W. Raudenbush. 1999. Systematic social observation of public spaces: A new look at disorder in urban neighborhoods. *American Journal of Sociology* 105 (3): 603–51.

Sampson, R. J., S. W. Raudenbush, and F. Earls. 1997. Neighborhoods and violent crime: A multilevel study of collective efficacy. *Science* 277:918–24.

Saunders, H. H. 1999. *A public peace process: Sustained dialogue to transform racial and ethnic conflicts*. New York: Palgrave.

———. (2005) *Politics is about relationship: A blueprint for the citizens' century*. New York: Palgrave Macmillan.

Schachter, H. L. 1997. *Reinventing government or reinventing ourselves: The role of citizen owners in making a better government*. New York: State University of New York Press.

Scheufele, D. A. 1999. Framing as a theory of media effects. *Journal of communication* 49 (1): 103–22.

Senge, P. 1990. *The fifth discipline*. New York: Currency Doubleday.

Sirianni, C., and L. A. Friedland. 2001. *Civic innovation in America: Community empowerment, public policy, and the movement for civic renewal*. Berkeley: University of California Press, 2001.

Slim, R. 2004a. Paper presented at the Annual Sustained Dialogue Campus Network Conference, University of Virginia, April 12.

———. 2004b. Some reflections on our institutional identity, approach, and patterns of engagement with our partners. *IISD Research 2004*, 3–5.

———. 2005. Lessons learned from our practice with the Arab-American-European Dialogue. *IISD Research 2005*, 6.

Smith, G., and C. Huntsman. 1997. Reframing the metaphor of the citizen-government relationship: A value-centered perspective. *Public Administration Review* 57 (4): 309–18.

Stivers, C. 2009. A civic machinery for democratic expression: Jane Addams on public administration. In *Jane Addams and the practice of democracy*, ed. M. Fischer, C. Nackenoff, and W. E. Chmielewski, 87–97. Urbana: University of Illinois Press.

Sukolski, M. 2002. Effective, inclusive social capital. In *Building social capital*, ed. D. Robinson. Wellington: Institute of Policy Studies.

Surowiecki, J. 2004. *The wisdom of crowds: Why the many are smarter than the few and how collective wisdom shapes business, economies, societies, and nations.* New York: Doubleday.

Taber, C., M, Lodge, and J. Glathar. 2001. The motivated construction of political judgments. In *Citizens and politics: Perspectives from political psychology*, ed. J. Kuklinski, 198–226. Cambridge: Cambridge University Press.

Tannen, D., ed. 1993. *Framing in discourse.* New York: Oxford University Press.

Taylor, R. B. 2001. *Breaking away from broken windows: Baltimore neighborhoods and the nationwide fight against crime, grime, fear, and decline.* Boulder, Colo.: Westview Press.

Tetlock, P. 1983. Accountability and the perseverance of first impressions. *Social Psychology Quarterly* 46:285–92.

——. 1985. Accountability: A social check on the fundamental attribution error. *Social Psychology Quarterly* 48:227–36.

——. 2001. Coping with trade-offs: Psychological constraints and political implications. In *Elements of reason: Cognition, choice, and the bounds of rationality*, ed. A. Lupia, M. McCubbins, and S. Popkin, 239–63. Cambridge: Cambridge University Press.

Thomas, J. C. 1995. *Public participation in public decisions: New skills and strategies for public managers.* San Francisco: Jossey-Bass.

Van Til, J. 2000. *Growing civil society.* Bloomington: Indiana University Press.

——. 2008. *Breaching Derry's walls: The quest for a lasting peace in Northern Ireland.* Lanham, Md.: University Press of America.

Verba, S., K. Lehman Schlozman, H. Brady, and N, Nie. 1993. Citizen activity: Who participates? What do they say? *American Political Science Review* 87 (2): 303–18.

von Bertalanffy, L. 1968. *General system theory: Foundations, development, applications.* New York: George Braziller.

Voorhees, J. 2002. *Dialogue sustained: The multilevel peace process and the Dartmouth conference.* Washington, D.C.: United States Institute of Peace Press; Charles F. Kettering Foundation.

Vroom, V. H., and P. Yetton. 1973. *Leadership and decision making.* Pittsburgh, Penn.: University of Pittsburgh Press.

Warren, M. 2001. *Democracy and association*. Princeton, N.J.: Princeton University Press.

Westbrook, R. B. 1991. *John Dewey and American democracy*. Ithaca, N.Y.: Cornell University Press.

Wheatley, M. 2002. *Turning to one another: Simple conversations to restore hope to the future*. San Francisco: Berrett-Koehler.

Wheelan, S. A. 1994. *Group processes: A developmental perspective*. Boston: Allyn and Bacon.

Wheen, F. 2004. *Idiot proof: Deluded celebrities, irrational power brokers, media morons, and the erosion of common sense*. New York: Public Affairs.

Wiesbord, M., and S. Janoff. 2000. *Future search: An action guide to finding common ground in organizations and communities*. 2nd ed. San Francisco: Berrett Koehler.

Wilensky, H. L., and C. N. Lebeaux. 1965. *Industrial society and social welfare: The impact of industrialization on the supply and organization of social welfare services in the United States*. New York: Free Press.

Williams, D. G. 1992. *Plenary review: A macro-policy approach to improve public policy*. Morgantown, W.V.: Think About Press for the Interactivity Foundation.

Wilson, P. A. 2004. Deep democracy: The inner practice of civic engagement. *Fieldnotes: A Newsletter of the Shambala Institute*, no 3 (February). http://soa.utexas.edu/people/docs/wilson/Fieldnotesarticle.pdf. Accessed October 21, 2010.

Wittgenstein, L. 1953. *Philosophical investigations*. Trans. G. E. M. Anscombe. New York: Macmillan.

Woods, E. H. [1929] 1971. *Robert A. Woods, champion of democracy*. Boston: Houghton Mifflin.

Woolcock, M., and D. Narayan. 2000. Social capital: Implications for development theory, research, and policy. *World Bank Research Observer* 15:225–51. Retrieved from http://www.worldbank.org/research/journals/wbro/obsaug00/pdf/(5)Woolcock%20%20Narayan.pdf.

Yang, K. 2005. Public administrators' trust in citizens: A missing link in citizen involvement efforts. *Public Administration Review* 65 (May/June 2005): 273–85.

Yankelovich, D. 1991. *Coming to public judgement: Making democracy work in a complex world*. Syracuse, N.Y.: Syracuse University Press.

Yukl, G. A. 1981. *Leadership in organizations*. Englewood Cliffs, N.J.: Prentice-Hall.

Zaller, J. 1992. *The nature of origins of mass opinion*. Cambridge: Cambridge University Press.

INDEX